BlackBerry Storm Made Simple

Written for the Storm 9500 and 9530, and the Storm2 9520, 9530, and 9550

**Martin Trautschold
and
Gary Mazo**

Apress®

BlackBerry Storm2 Made Simple

ISBN-13 (pbk): 978-1-4302-3120-2

ISBN-13 (electronic): 978-1-4302-3121-9

Printed and bound in the United States of America 9 8 7 6 5 4 3 2 1

President and Publisher: Paul Manning
Lead Editor: Steve Anglin
Development Editor: James Markham
Editorial Board: Clay Andres, Steve Anglin, Mark Beckner, Ewan Buckingham, Gary Cornell, Jonathan Gennick, Jonathan Hassell, Michelle Lowman, Matthew Moodie, Duncan Parkes, Jeffrey Pepper, Frank Pohlmann, Douglas Pundick, Ben Renow-Clarke, Dominic Shakeshaft, Matt Wade, Tom Welsh
Coordinating Editor: Laurin Becker
Copy Editor: Mary Behr, Mary Ann Fugate, Damon Larson, Patrick Meador
Production Support: Patrick Cunningham
Indexer: BIM Indexing & Proofreading Services
Cover Designer: Anna Ishchenko

Distributed to the book trade worldwide by Springer Science+Business Media, LLC., 233 Spring Street, 6th Floor, New York, NY 10013. Phone 1-800-SPRINGER, fax (201) 348-4505, e-mail orders-ny@springer-sbm.com, or visit www.springeronline.com.

For information on translations, please e-mail rights@apress.com, or visit www.apress.com.

Apress and friends of ED books may be purchased in bulk for academic, corporate, or promotional use. eBook versions and licenses are also available for most titles. For more information, reference our Special Bulk Sales–eBook Licensing web page at www.apress.com/info/bulksales.

This book is dedicated to our families—to our wives, Julie and Gloria, and to our kids, Sophie, Livvie and Cece, and Ari, Dan, Sara, Billy, Elise and Jonah.

Without their love, support, and understanding, we could never take on projects like this one. Now that the book is done, we will gladly share our BlackBerrys with them – for a little while!

Contents

About the Authors

Martin Trautschold is the founder and CEO of Made Simple Learning, a leading provider of Apple iPad, iPhone, iPod touch, BlackBerry, and Palm webOS books and video tutorials. He has been a successful entrepreneur in the mobile device training and software business since 2001. With Made Simple Learning, he helped to train thousands of BlackBerry Smartphone users with short, to-the-point video tutorials. Martin has now co-authored fifteen "Made Simple" guide books. He also co-founded, ran for 3 years, and then sold a mobile device software company. Prior to this, Martin spent 15 years in technology and business consulting in the US and Japan. He holds an engineering degree from Princeton University and an MBA from the Kellogg School at Northwestern University. Martin and his wife, Julia, have three daughters. He enjoys rowing and cycling. Martin can be reached at martin@madesimplelearning.com.

Gary Mazo is Vice President of Made Simple Learning and is a writer, a college professor, a gadget nut, and an ordained rabbi. Gary joined Made Simple Learning in 2007 and has co-authored the last thirteen books in the Made Simple series. Along with Martin, and Kevin Michaluk from CrackBerry.com, Gary co-wrote *CrackBerry: True Tales of BlackBerry Use and Abuse*—a book about BlackBerry addiction and how to get a grip on one's BlackBerry use. This book is being refreshed and reprinted by Apress and will be available this fall. Gary also teaches writing, philosophy, technical writing, and more at the University of Phoenix. He holds a BA in anthropology from Brandeis University. Gary earned his M.A.H.L (Masters in Hebrew Letters) as well as ordination as Rabbi from the Hebrew Union College-Jewish Institute of Religion in Cincinnati, Ohio. He has served congregations in Dayton, Ohio, Cherry Hill, New Jersey and Cape Cod, Massachusetts.

Gary is married to Gloria Schwartz Mazo; they have six children. Gary can be reached at: gary@madesimplelearning.com.

Acknowledgments

A book like this takes many people to put together. We would like to thank Apress for believing in us and our unique style of writing.

We would like to thank our Editors, Jim and Laurin, and the entire editorial team at Apress.

We would like to thank our families for their patience and support in allowing us to pursue projects such as this one.

Part **I**

Quick Start Guide

In your hands is one of the most capable devices to hit the market in quite some time: the BlackBerry Storm. This Quick Start Guide will help get you and your new Storm up and running in a hurry. You'll learn all about the keys, buttons, and ports, and how to use the responsive touch screen to help you get around. Our app reference tables will introduce you to the apps on your Storm and serve as a quick way to find out how to accomplish a task.

Quick Start

This Quick Start is meant to be just that—a tool that can help you jump right in and find information in this book—and learn the basics of how to get around and enjoy your Storm right away.

We start with the nuts and bolts in the "Learning Your Way Around" section—what all the keys, buttons, switches, and symbols mean and do on your Storm. You will learn how to get inside the back of your Storm to remove and replace the battery, SIM card, and media card. You'll also learn how to use the **Green Phone** key, **Red Phone** key, **Menu** key, and **Escape** key.

Then we move on to the "Touch Screen Gestures" section, where we show you all the best tips and tricks for getting around using the touch screen, including how to start apps, get into folders, and perform some time-saving tasks.

In the "Copying, Pasting, and Multitasking" section, we cover the very useful copy-and-paste function and how to jump between apps on your Storm.

You'll want to know how to type on your Storm, so in the "Mastering Your Virtual Keyboards" section, we cover the three keyboards and some useful tips for getting more out of each one.

In "Working with the Wireless Network," we help you understand how the letters, numbers, and symbols at the top of your Storm screen tell you that you can make phone calls, send SMS text messages, send and receive email, or browse the Web. We also show you how to handle your Storm on an airplane, when you might need to turn off the radios.

In "App Reference Tables," we've organized the app icons into general categories so you can quickly browse the icons and jump to a section in the book to learn more about the app a particular icon represents. Here are the tables:

- Getting Set Up
- Staying in Touch
- Staying Organized
- Being Productive
- Being Entertained
- Networking Socially
- Personalizing Your Storm

Learning Your Way Around

To help you get comfortable with your Storm, we start with the basics—what the keys, buttons, ports, and symbols do, and how to open up the back cover to get at your battery, media, and SIM card. Then we move into how you start apps and navigate the menus. We end this section with a number of very useful time-saving tips and tricks for getting around the touch screen.

Overview of Your Storm

Figure 1 shows many of the things you can do with the buttons and ports on your Storm. Go ahead and try out a few things to see what happens. Your phone multitasks (that is it can do multiple tasks at once). Try pressing the **Menu** key for 2 seconds, press and hold the **Green Phone** key (to dial from the address book), press the side **Convenience** keys, press and click an icon, and then press the **Escape** key to see what happens. Have some fun getting acquainted with your device.

Power & Lock Key
Press & Hold to Power On/Off. Tap to lock / unlock the touch screen

 # unopened Messages

Repeat Notification Light

Mute Key
Mute Phone/Ringer or Pause/Play Music or Video playback

Bluetooth®

Wireless Strength
1-5 Bars / OFF / X

Battery Strength

Active Sound Profile
How Phone, Email, Calendar, Task Alarms
more notify You - Ring, Vibrate or Mute
TIP: Change your Ringtone "Set Ringtones/Alerts" > "Phone"

Headphone Jack

Wireless Data Network
3G (logo)* (high speed)
1XEV, EDGE* (mid. speed)
1X, GPRS* (low speed)
GSM*, 1x (Voice & SMS only)
* = Requires SIM Card in phone

Home Screen Wallpaper
Background (Menu Key > Options to change this picture)

Volume Up & Down Keys

Left Convenience Key
May be PTT or Voice Dial
(Set in Options > Screen/Keyboard)

GPS Indicator
E911 only without 3 signal signs

Micro USB Port
Socket to plug in the USB cable or the power charger.

TIP: Press your Home Screen anywhere in the picture to see all your icons.

Your Top Icons
Customize to Top 4, 8, or 12 by pressing Menu key > Options – Homescreen preferences

Right Side Convenience Key
May start Camera
(Set in Options > Screen/Keyboard)

Green Phone Key ("Send")
Start phone call, see call logs, Press & hold to Dial by Name

Menu Key
Click to see all icons or menus. TIP: Press and hold to see multitasking window.

Escape / Back
Press to backup or exit Apps

Red Phone Key ("End")
Press to End a phone call, multitask by jumping to Home Screen

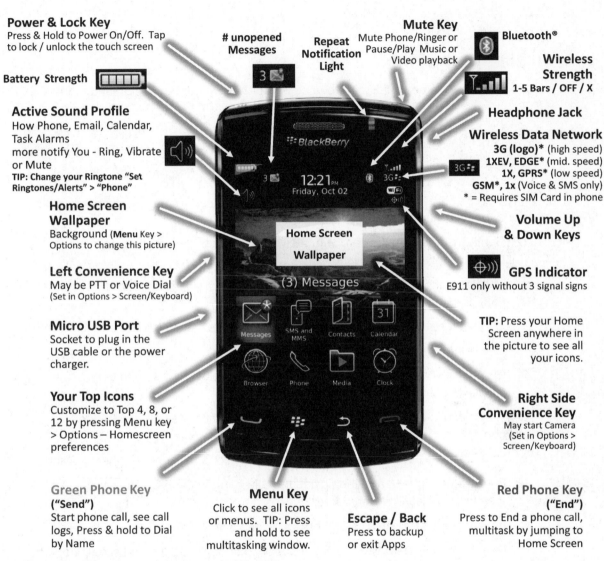

Figure 1. *Keys, buttons, and, ports on the BlackBerry Storm*

Inside Your Storm

You have to get inside your Storm to access your battery, SIM card slot, and media card slot. The following instructions and Figure 2 show you how.

> **TIP:** To remove the back cover, press the notch at the bottom and lift up the battery cover off the back of the BlackBerry.

To insert a memory card (MicroSD format), you do not need to remove the battery. Just perform the following steps:

1. Gently place the media card with the metal contacts facing down and the notch toward the top left.

2. Then slide it completely up into the media card slot near the bottom right of the device.

To remove the memory card, slide it down out of the notch and lift it up.

To remove or replace the battery, do the following:

1. Gently put your fingernail next to the top edges of the battery (the gray semicircles) and pry it up and out.

2. To replace it, insert it from the bottom edge and then press the top edge down.

To insert a SIM card (required to connect to a GSM phone network), do the following:

1. Remove the battery, and then place the SIM card on the left edge with the notch in the upper-left corner.

2. Slide it completely into the SIM card slot (see below).

To replace the back cover, place it on the bottom half of the device and slide it up to the top until it clicks or locks into place.

Camera Lens
Keep clean for highest
quality pictures.

**Replacing the Back
Cover:** Insert the top
of the cover in these
notches at the top
edge. Then push down
the bottom of the
cover until it 'clicks'
into place and locks.

SIM Card Slot
Battery needs to be
removed to insert or
remove the SIM Card.

A SIM Card is required to
access a **GSM network**.
Not required for **CDMA
network** access.

**Removing the
Back Cover:**
Press this battery latch
cover and lift the
cover up off of the
BlackBerry.

Camera Flash
Keep clean for the
brightest flash.

Battery
Remove by prying up at the gray
circles here with your fingernail and
lift out from top edge.

Media Card Slot
MicroSD Format.
Place into this slot with metal
contacts face down and notch of
media card facing toward top left.
Slide card up until it clicks into
place.

Inserting the SIM Card
Remove battery. Hold SIM card so
notch faces down to left. Slide SIM
Card completely down into this
holder.

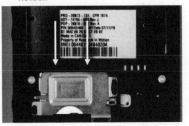

Images courtesy BlackBerry.com

Figure 2. *Inside your Storm—the battery, media card, and SIM card slots*

The Power and Lock Key

At the top left of your BlackBerry is your **Power and Lock** key. Press
and hold it to power on and off your device. Simply tap it to lock the
BlackBerry, and tap again to unlock. If you have enabled password
security (see page 558), then you will need to enter your password to
unlock it.

The Mute Key

On the top-right edge of your BlackBerry is the **Mute and Pause/Play**
key. Tap this key to mute a ringing phone call, mute yourself on a phone
call, and pause any playing media (e.g., a video, song, or audio book).
Tap it again to un-mute or un-pause the media.

The Green Phone Key

Start up your phone by pressing this **Green Phone** key from any location.

TIP: Call Any Underlined Phone Number

Pressing the Green Phone key when you see any underlined phone number (e.g., <u>313-555-1212</u> in an email signature, web site, note, etc.) will start a call to that number. You can learn about your phone screen (dial pad, call logs, and contact dialing) in Chapter 10 "Phone Basics" starting on page 229.

The Menu Key (BlackBerry Button)

The **Menu** key—that key with the BlackBerry logo—is the doorway to all the possibilities of your device. In every application, pressing this key brings up a menu with all of the options for the app. From the basic home screen, pressing this key brings up all the other icons.

TIP: Pressing and clicking in the middle of the home screen (above the icons) will show you all your icons.

From a contact, pressing the **Menu** key allows you to call, email, SMS, or communicate in other ways with that particular contact. Just try pressing it in every program you open to see the myriad of possibilities.

Multitasking with the Menu key

You can multitask using the **Menu** key. Just press and hold it to bring up the multitasking pop-up window, which will allow you to multitask by taking the following steps.

1. Press and hold the **Menu** key
    to see the pop-up window
   of running apps.

2. Swipe left or right to the app you
   want to start and click it.

3. Click the **Home** app if you don't see
   the icon you want to start. Then
   click the icon you want to start from
   the home screen.

4. Repeat the procedure to return to
   the app you started in.

Learn more about multitasking
(also called Application Switching)
on page 368.

The Escape/Back Key

 This key does just what its name suggests—it goes back to where
you were before. It also prompts you to save, delete, or discard things
you might be working on. If you do something wrong or find yourself
wanting to get back to where you were a second ago, just press this
key.

The Red Phone Key

This is equivalent to the "end" key that you may be familiar with from
your old phone. You can end your calls, ignore calls, and perform
other familiar actions with the **Red Phone** key.

You can also multitask using the **Red Phone** key. Just press it (when not on a call) and
you'll jump right to the home screen. For example, if you're writing an email and need to
check the calendar or schedule a new event, you can do the following:

1. Press the **Red Phone** key to jump to the home screen.

2. Start the calendar to check your schedule.

3. Press the **Red Phone** key again to return to the home screen.

4. Press and click the **Messages** icon to return exactly to where you left off composing your email message.

> **TIP:** Knowing when your information is saved
>
> When you use the **Red Phone** key or press and hold the **Menu** key to jump out of an app everything you were doing in the app you are leaving is saved. For example, if you are in the middle of typing an email message and need to check your Calendar. Using the **Red Phone** key or pressing and holding the **Menu** key to jump to the Calendar will leave your email message exactly as it was. This allows you to jump back to the Messages app and finish your email.
>
> You will only lose unsaved information, like an email message half written (and be warned about it) when you use the **Escape** key or press the **Menu** key and select **Exit** or **Close** from the menu.

Touch Screen Gestures

The BlackBerry Storm is the first BlackBerry with a touch screen, and with the Storm2, the screen and overall device responsiveness has been improved. Research in Motion (RIM), the maker of the BlackBerry, has included an innovation that they call SurePress. With this feature, the entire screen can actually be pressed (or clicked), giving you positive feedback that you are clicking the image of a button or key shown on the screen. If you have used an older BlackBerry model, then this touch screen will take a little getting used to, because there is no trackpad, trackball, trackwheel, or physical keyboard. However, with a little patience and practice as you work through this first section of the book, you will soon become comfortable doing things with your Storm.

You can pretty much do anything on your Storm by using a combination of the following:

- Touch screen gestures
- Pressing soft keys on the screen
- Using the four navigation buttons on the bottom of the BlackBerry
- Pressing the **Convenience** keys on the sides (see page 214)

Here is a summary of the basic touch screen gestures:

- **Lightly touch**: To highlight an icon, menu item, or other item on the screen lightly touch with your finger, but don't click down on the screen.

- **Touch and hover**: To see the name of a specific icon or search for email messages lightly touch with your finger and keep it over the icon or email message, but don't click down on the screen.

- **Press and click**: To start an icon, select a menu item, or select an answer press and physically click down on the glass screen.

- **Swipe across**: To move to the next email message or day in your calendar swipe your finger in one direction to drag items on the screen in that direction

- **Scroll up/down**: To see what is above the top or below the bottom of the screen lightly touch and drag your finger up or down but don't press and click.

- **Multi-touch**: To cut or copy text, tap the beginning and end of the text that you want to cut or copy with two fingers simultaneously.

In the sections that follow, we will show you exactly how to master each of these gestures. Read the following pages for a graphical step-by-step description of how to get around and master your BlackBerry Storm.

Basic Touch Screen Gestures

Go ahead and play around with your new Storm as shown in Figure 3. Try touching, then press and physically click the glass down on an icon to start it then press the **Escape** key to back out. Try just hovering your finger over an icon. Press the **Menu** key and then swipe up to see all your icons. Press the **Escape** key to get back to your home screen.

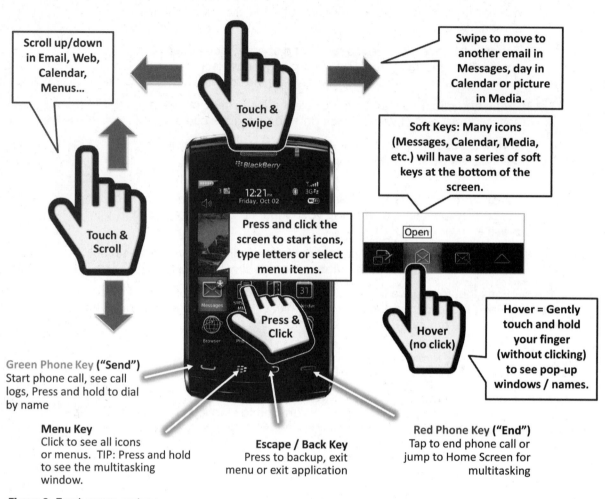

Scroll up/down in Email, Web, Calendar, Menus...

Touch & Swipe

Swipe to move to another email in Messages, day in Calendar or picture in Media.

Soft Keys: Many icons (Messages, Calendar, Media, etc.) will have a series of soft keys at the bottom of the screen.

Touch & Scroll

Press and click the screen to start icons, type letters or select menu items.

Open

Press & Click

Hover (no click)

Hover = Gently touch and hold your finger (without clicking) to see pop-up windows / names.

Green Phone Key ("Send") Start phone call, see call logs, Press and hold to dial by name

Menu Key Click to see all icons or menus. TIP: Press and hold to see the multitasking window.

Escape / Back Key Press to backup, exit menu or exit application

Red Phone Key ("End") Tap to end phone call or jump to Home Screen for multitasking

Figure 3. *Touch screen gestures*

Starting and Exiting an App

You use the touch screen, **Menu** key, and **Escape** key to navigate around, open folders, and select apps (See Figure 4). The **Escape** key will get you back out one step at a time, and the **Red Phone** key will jump you all the way back to the home screen.

NOTE: You can change the background image (also called the wallpaper) and the home screen image. You can also change the look and feel or theme of your Storm by clicking the Options icon and selecting Theme (see page 209). To learn more about how to move icons, see page 195, and to learn about hiding icons, see page 195.

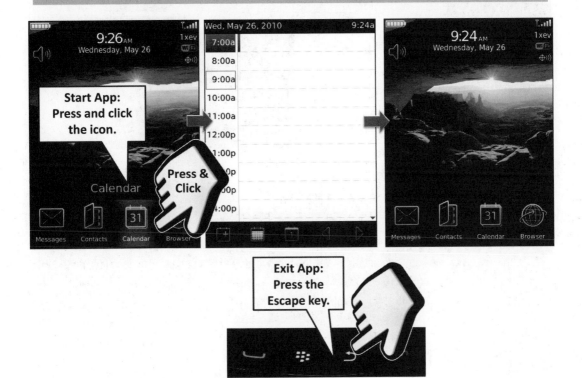

Figure 4. *How to start and exit apps and folders*

Opening Folders

You will notice some icons look like folders . You can use these folders to organize sets of icons into logical groups. There will be a few folders already on your Storm, but you can create more folders, as shown in Chapter 8: As shown in Figure 5, pressing and clicking the **Media** folder will reveal all the media-related icons. Press the **Escape** key to back out one level and close the folder.

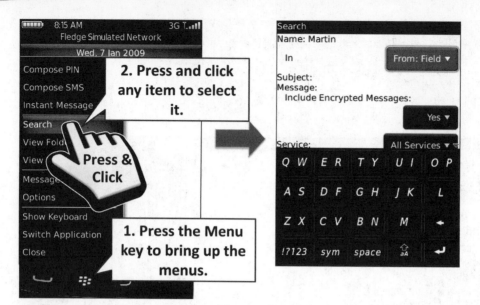

Figure 5. *Opening folders where you store and organize icons*

NOTE: Icon versus App

In this book we use both icon and app. We thought we should clarify here. The icon is simply the picture on the Home screen that starts the app. For example, you click on the Messages icon to start the Messages app.

Two Types of Menus: Full and Short

You will see two types of menus on your Storm. The full menu (Figure 6) appears when you press the **Menu** key and the short menu appears when you tap something on the screen.

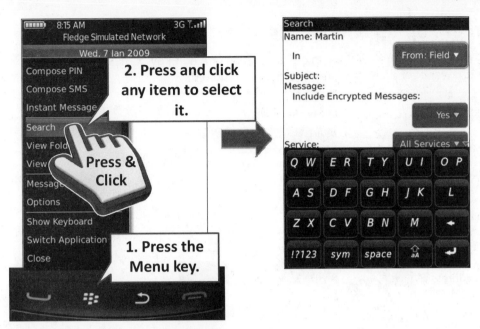

Figure 6. *Press the Menu key to see the full menu.*

There are many things you can press (e.g., an email address) that will pop up a context-sensitive short menu (see Figure 7).

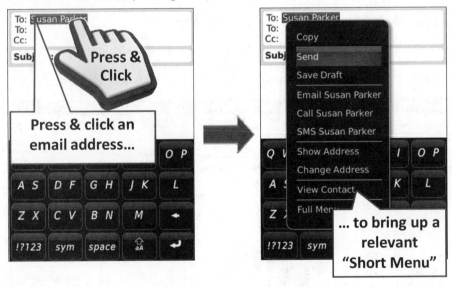

Figure 7. *Press an item on the screen to see the relevant short menu.*

Hover for Pop-Up Information

You can see information (such as an email address or a soft key name) if you gently touch and hover over an item on the screen (see Figure 8).

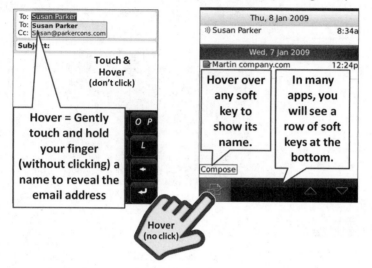

Figure 8. *Hover to see pop-up information such as email addresses and soft key names.*

Swipe Gesture: Move to Next Day, Picture, Email

The Storm gives you the ability to swipe through items such as days in your calendar or pictures in your photo directory. To swipe, as shown in Figure 9, gently touch and slide your finger, and the app will move to the next/previous screen (calendar day, email, etc.).

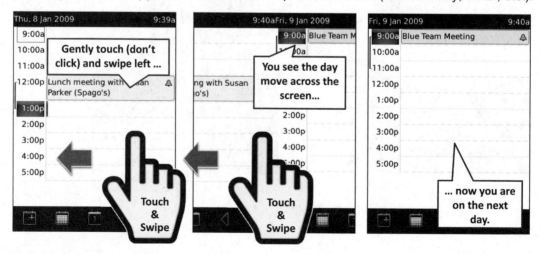

Figure 9. *Swipe to move through calendar days.*

Scrolling Up or Down

If you want to scroll, simply place your finger on the screen and drag it up or down on the screen. You can swipe it up or down quickly to move faster (see Figure 10).

Scrolling Up: Start at bottom, tap and slide up

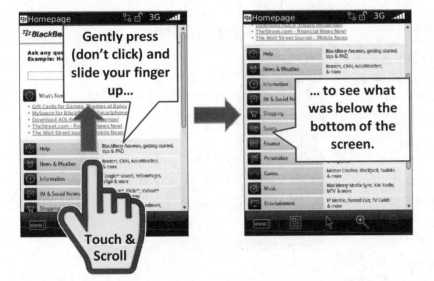

Scrolling Down: Start at top, tap and slide down

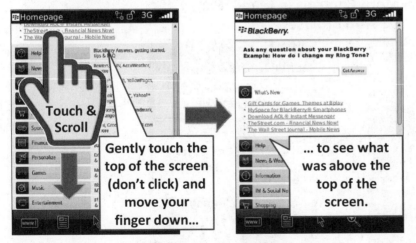

Figure 10. *Touch and slide your finger to scroll up and down the screen.*

Scrolling Menus and Showing Soft Keys

You can use the same touch-and-scroll movement to view more menu items. Also, when listening to music or watching a video, the controls will disappear. To bring them back, simply tap the screen (see Figure 11).

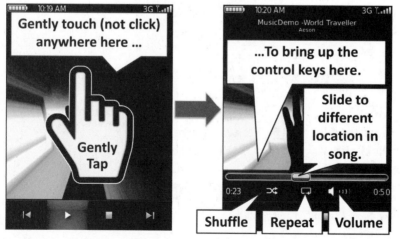

Figure 11. *Menu scrolling (top) and tapping to show or hide soft keys in the media player (bottom).*

Save Time with the Space Key

You can use the **space** key to save time when you are typing email addresses, web addresses, and typing the ends of sentences. As you can see in Figure 12, you can use the **space** key to simplify typing in an email address. For instance, typing:

susan space company space com generates susan@company.com

Similarly, to get the "dots" in a web address, typing:

www space google space com yields www.google.com

In addition, pressing the **space** key twice will enter an automatic period and make the next letter you type uppercase.

- Use the **Space** key when typing:

    Email Addresses
    - Type:
        - susan **Space** company **Space** com

    Web Addresses
    - Get the dot "." in the address:
    - Type:
        - www **Space** google **Space** com

TIP: Save time typing emails by pressing the space key twice at the end of each sentence. You will get an automatic period and the next letter will be uppercase.

Figure 12. *Using the space key to save time typing email addresses, web site addresses, and more.*

Copying, Pasting, and Multitasking

A few very useful tricks on your Storm are copying, pasting, and multitasking (i.e., jumping between applications—also referred to as application switching).

Copy and Paste

You may find times when you want to cut/copy and paste text from one app into another. One example might be copying directions for a trip from an email message into a calendar event so that you have them available when you need them (see Figure 13).

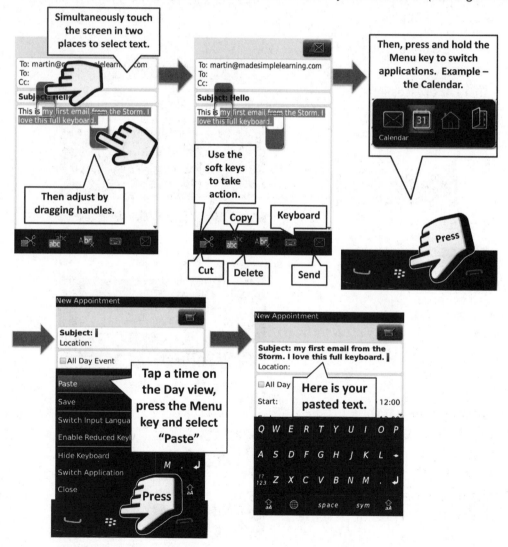

Figure 13. *Copying and pasting from an email message to a calendar event.*

Multitasking (Application Switching)

There may be times when you want to leave one app running, quickly jump to another, and then jump back. For example, if you are in the calendar and want to jump to **Messages** to check the requested time for a meeting, and then jump back, you would use what is called multitasking (application switching) on your Storm (see Figure 14).

1. Press and hold the **Menu** key until you see the pop-up window.

2. Swipe back and forth to find the icon you want to start, and then press and click it.

3. If you don't see it, press and click **Home**, and then start the app.

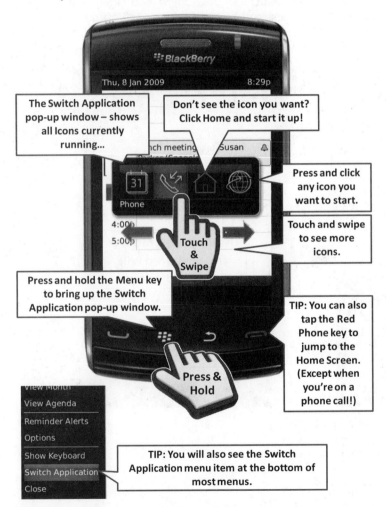

Figure 14. *How to multitask, or switch applications, on your Storm*

Mastering Your Virtual Keyboards

Typing on your Storm is quite flexible. You will need to press and click to type a letter, but you have three keyboard options from which to choose to type. In the following sections, we give you some basics to help you get started with each of the three types. You can even customize your Storm to show you your favorite keyboard when you are holding your Storm in vertical (portrait) orientation.

Hiding and Showing the Virtual Keyboards

Swipe your finger down to hide the virtual keyboard. Sometimes, when you hide the keyboard, you will see the soft keys at the bottom of the screen (see Figure 15). To display the keyboard again, tap the keyboard soft key in the lower-left corner of the screen.

TIP: You can assign one of your two side **Convenience** keys to show and hide the virtual keyboard—this can be quite useful. See page 214 to learn how to do this.

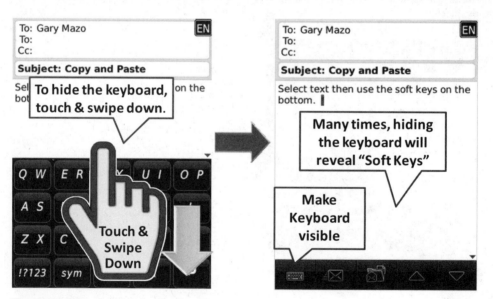

Figure 15. *Hiding and showing the virtual keyboard*

Choose from Three Keyboards

You have three types of keyboards from which to choose on your Storm. You should be able to find one that suits your needs. The full keyboard gives you a single letter per key and is available when you hold your Storm in both vertical and horizontal orientations. The other two keyboards are only available when you are holding your Storm in vertical orientation. The SureType keyboard has larger keys with two letters per key. The Storm does a pretty good job of guessing the words you are typing based on the sequence of keys. The third keyboard is the MultiTap, which looks like an old-fashioned mobile phone keyboard. There are three to four letters on each key, and you press the key one, two, three, or four times for each letter (see Figure 16).

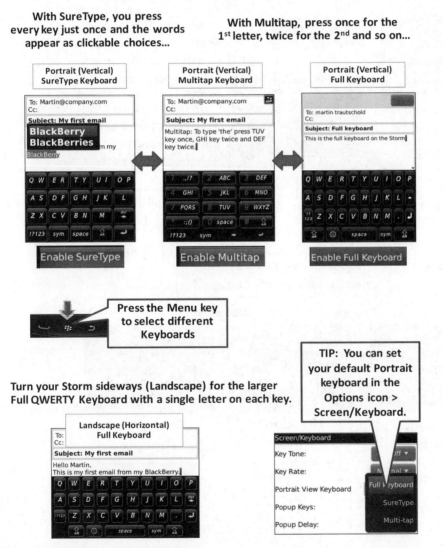

Figure 16. *Three types of keyboards on your storm*

SureType Keyboard Typing (Vertical)

With the SureType keyboard, you press each key only once and the Storm will guess what you are trying to type. It even takes into account the names and addresses from your Contact list when it guesses. When you see the word you want to appear in the pop-up window, press the **space** key to select it (see Figure 17).

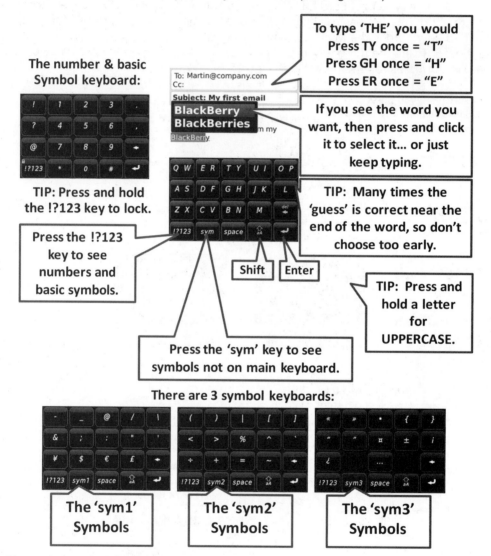

To type 'THE' you would
Press TY once = "T"
Press GH once = "H"
Press ER once = "E"

The number & basic
Symbol keyboard:

TIP: Press and hold
the !?123 key to lock.

Press the !?123
key to see
numbers and
basic symbols.

If you see the word you
want, then press and click
it to select it... or just
keep typing.

TIP: Many times the
'guess' is correct near the
end of the word, so don't
choose too early.

Shift   Enter

TIP: Press and
hold a letter
for
UPPERCASE.

Press the 'sym' key to see
symbols not on main keyboard.

There are 3 symbol keyboards:

The 'sym1'
Symbols

The 'sym2'
Symbols

The 'sym3'
Symbols

Figure 17. *Typing with the SureType keyboard*

MultiTap Keyboard Typing (Vertical)

With the MultiTap keyboard, you press the key one, two, three, or four times to get the desired letter or symbol (see Figure 18).

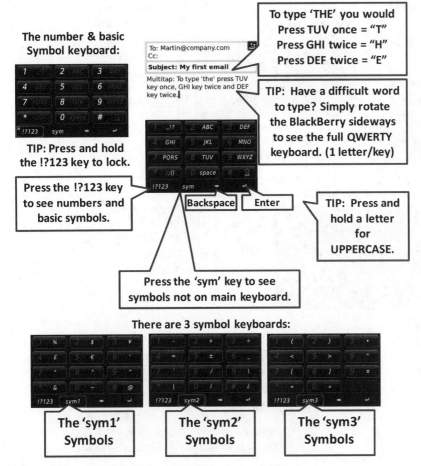

The number & basic Symbol keyboard:

To type 'THE' you would
Press TUV once = "T"
Press GHI twice = "H"
Press DEF twice = "E"

To: Martin@company.com
Cc:
Subject: My first email

Multitap: To type 'the' press TUV key once, GHI key twice and DEF key twice.

TIP: Have a difficult word to type? Simply rotate the BlackBerry sideways to see the full QWERTY keyboard. (1 letter/key)

TIP: Press and hold the !?123 key to lock.

Press the !?123 key to see numbers and basic symbols.

Backspace   Enter

TIP: Press and hold a letter for UPPERCASE.

Press the 'sym' key to see symbols not on main keyboard.

There are 3 symbol keyboards:

The 'sym1' Symbols

The 'sym2' Symbols

The 'sym3' Symbols

Figure 18. *Typing with the MultiTap keyboard*

Full Keyboard (Vertical or Horizontal)

The full keyboard gives you a single letter per key, so it is the easiest keyboard to understand. When you press **A**, you get an **A**. It also is available in both vertical and horizontal orientation.

TIP: You can set your Storm vertical keyboard to default to the full, SureType, or MultiTap format with the **Options** app's **Screen and Keyboard** setting.

The Full Keyboard has a single letter on each key.
A great way to increase speed and accuracy.

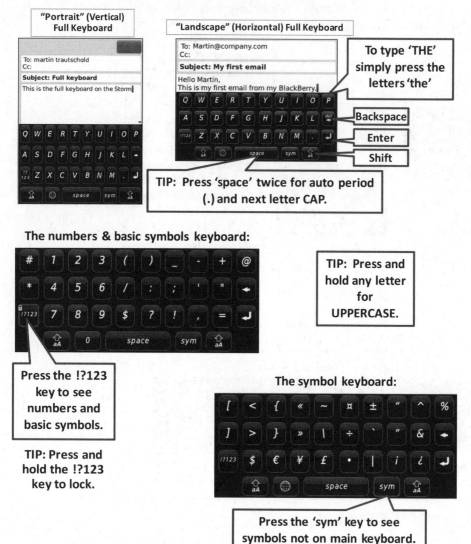

Figure 19. *The full keyboard is available in both vertical and horizontal orientations.*

Working with the Wireless Network

Since most of the functions on your Storm work only when you are connected to the internet (email, web, App World, Facebook, etc.), you need to know when you're connected. Understanding how to read the status bar can save you time and frustration.

You will also want to know how to quickly turn off your wireless radio or other radios when you get on an airplane.

Reading Your Wireless Network Status

In Table 1, we show you how to read the status icons at the top of your Storm screen so you can save time and stay connected. Check marks indicate that a connection is active and an X indicates an inactive connection. Check out our "Fixing Problems" chapter on page 563 for help with getting this working.

Table 1. *Reading Your Wireless Network Status*

In the Upper-Right Corner, If You See Letters and Symbols	Email and Web	Phone Calls	SMS Text	Speed of Data Connection
3G : (3G with logo)	✓	✓	✓	High
1XEV or EDGE	✓	✓	✓	Medium
1X or GPRS	✓	✓	✓	Slow
WiFi (with any letters shown)	✓	✓	✓	High
WiFi (without letters)	✓	X	X	High
1X, EDGE, GPRS, GSM, or 3G	X	✓	✓	None
⊤ OFF ⊤ X	X	X	X	None

Wireless Network Signal Strength

The following list shows the various wireless signal strength icons that will appear (signal strength varies between one and five bars):

Strong signal:		4-5 bars is a strong signal – fast downloads, web browsing and email should, good voice quality
Weak signal:		1-2 bars is a weak signal – all data functions will be slower and possibly voice calls may be broken up.
No signal:		Your radio is on, but no wireless signal is available.
Radio off:		Your radio is turned off. Click the **Manage Connections** icon to turn it back on.

Traveling with Your Storm: Airplane Mode

When you travel, on most airlines you can simply turn off all your wireless connections (mobile network radio and Bluetooth) and continue using your BlackBerry. Here's how to turn off your wireless connections:

1. Press and click the **Manage Connections** icon.

2. Press and click **Turn All Connections Off** until you see the word **Off** next to your wireless signal strength indicator.

3. When you land and want to turn your connections on again, press and click **Manage Connections** again.

4. Press and click the top option: **Restore Connections**.

> **TIP:** To check/uncheck any option, just press and click it.

5. Some airlines will allow you to keep your Wi-Fi connection turned on while in flight. This allows you to use Wi-Fi connectivity without having your mobile network radio on (which might interfere with the airline's communication systems). Press and click **Wi-Fi** to turn it back on.

App Reference Tables

This section groups the apps on your Storm, as well as other apps you can download, into handy reference tables. Each table gives you a brief description of the app and tells where to find more information in this book.

> **NOTE:** The hotkeys listed in the following tables only work after you turn them on (see page 195 for instruction on this).

Getting Set Up

In Table 2 are some apps and quick links to help you get your email, Bluetooth, contacts, calendar, and more loaded onto your device. You can even boost the memory by adding a memory card, which is important to install if you'd like to have more pictures, videos, and music on your Storm.

Table 2. *Getting Set Up*

To Do This . . .	Use This . . .	Where to Learn More
Find your setup icons	Setup folder	Press and click this icon to see your other setup icons.
Set up email, date/time, fonts, Wi-Fi, and more.	Setup Wizard	Page 47.
Set up or change your internet email	Email Settings	Page 50.
Set up your Bluetooth headset	Set Up Bluetooth	Page 489.
Share addresses, calendar, tasks, and notes with your computer	BlackBerry Desktop Manager (for Windows or Apple Mac)	Windows: Page 84. Mac: Page 143.
Add memory to store your music, videos, and pictures	Media card *Image Courtesy SanDisk Corp.*	Adding it: Page 405. Using it: Page 440.
Load up your music, pictures, and videos	Mass Storage Mode (Windows or Mac)	Page 407.
Fine-tune your internet email signature and more	Your wireless carrier web site	See list of web sites on page 71

Staying in Touch

Getting familiar with the apps in Table 3 will help you stay in touch with your friends and colleagues. Whether you prefer calling, emailing, texting, or using instant messaging, your BlackBerry has many options. Use the browser to stay up to date with the latest happenings on the Web.

Table 3. *Staying in Touch*

To Do This . . .	Use This . . .		Where to Learn More
Read and reply to Email		Messages	Email: Page 289. PIN Messaging: Page 385. Attachments: Page 302.
Send and read SMS text and MMS messages		SMS and MMS	Page 374.
Connect to a Wi-Fi network		Set Up Wi-Fi	Page 456.
Get on the internet/browse the Web		Browser	Page 501.
Call voicemail		The 1 key	Page 241.
Start a call, dial by name, and view call logs		Green Phone key	Phone: Page 229. Call Logs: Page 242.
Dial by voice		Voice Dialing	Page 249.
Send an instant message to another BlackBerry user		BlackBerry Messenger	Page 390.

Use your favorite instant messengers		AOL, Google, Yahoo, Windows Messenger, etc.	Page 401.
Turn off the radio (important when flying on an airplane)		Manage Connections	Page 565.
Maximize your battery life to talk, message, and play more		Use the battery life tips in this book	Page 573.

Staying Organized

From organizing and finding your contacts to managing your calendar, taking written or voice notes, and calculating a tip using your built-in calculator, your BlackBerry can help you do it all. See the apps in Table 4.

Table 4. *Staying Organized*

To Do This . . .	Use This . . .		Where to Learn More
Manage your contact names and numbers		Contacts	Basics: Page 315. Add New: Page 317.
Manage your calendar		Calendar	Page 333. Sync to PC: Page 88. Sync to Mac: Page 143.
Set a wakeup alarm, or use a countdown timer or stopwatch		Clock	Page 544.
Store all your important passwords		Password Keeper	Page 548.

| Find lost names, email, calendar entries, and more | | Search | Page 551. |

Being Productive

Sometimes you need to get work done on your Storm. Use the apps shown in Table 5 to get things done on your BlackBerry.

Table 5. *Being Productive*

To Do This . . .	Use This . . .		Where to Learn More
Manage your to-do list		Tasks	Page 357. Sync to PC: Page 88. Sync to Mac: Page 143.
Find Things, Get Directions, See Traffic		Google Maps	Page 535.
Take notes, store your grocery list, and more		MemoPad	Page 363. Sync to PC: Page 88. Sync to Mac: Page 143.
Leave yourself a voice note		Voice Note Recorder	Page 547.
View and edit Microsoft Office Word, Excel, and PowerPoint		Word to Go, Sheet to Go, Slideshow to Go	Page 304.
Use the built-in text-based help		Help	Page 563
Calculate your MPG (miles per gallon) or meal tips, or convert units		Calculator	Page 543.

Being Entertained

Use the apps in Table 6 to have fun with your BlackBerry Storm.

Table 6. *Being Entertained*

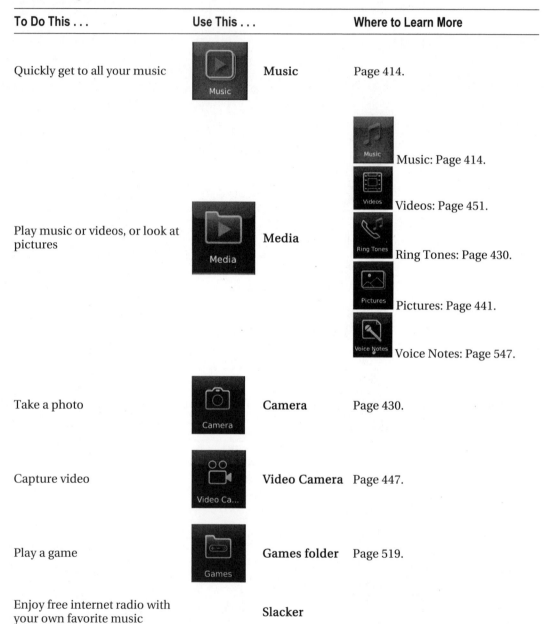

To Do This . . .	Use This . . .		Where to Learn More
Quickly get to all your music		**Music**	Page 414.
Play music or videos, or look at pictures		**Media**	Music: Page 414. Videos: Page 451. Ring Tones: Page 430. Pictures: Page 441. Voice Notes: Page 547.
Take a photo		**Camera**	Page 430.
Capture video		**Video Camera**	Page 447.
Play a game		**Games folder**	Page 519.
Enjoy free internet radio with your own favorite music		**Slacker**	

Enjoy free internet radio with your own favorite music Pandora   Page 424.

Networking Socially

Connect and stay up to date with friends, colleagues, and professional networks using the social networking tools on your Storm (see Table 7).

Table 7. *Networking Socially*

To Do This . . .	Use This (Hotkey) . . .	Where to Learn More
Connect with Facebook friends	Facebook	Page 271.
Follow people and tweet using Twitter	Twitter	Page 277.
Connect with colleagues	LinkedIn	Page 283.

Personalizing Your Storm

Use the apps in Table 8 to personalize the look and feel of your Storm.

Table 8. *Personalizing Your Storm*

To Do This . . .	Use This . . .	Where to Learn More
Change your phone ringer	Sounds	Page 219
Change your background home screen picture	Media folder	Home screen Options: Page 214 Pictures: Page 214 Use Camera: Page 431

Change your font size		Options > Screen/Keyboard	Page 208
Change your programmable **Convenience** keys		Options > Screen/Keyboard	Page 214.
Change your theme (i.e., the device's entire look and feel)	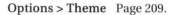	Options > Theme	Page 209.

Adding and Removing Apps

Use the apps shown in Table 9 to add software and capabilities to your BlackBerry.

Table 9. *Adding and Removing Apps*

To Do This	Use This		Where to Learn More
Download apps for your Storm		BlackBerry App World	Page 467.
Add new icons and programs		Browser	Page 515.
Find all the apps you've downloaded		Downloads folder	Page 517.
Remove icons and programs		Options	Advanced Options ➤ Applications Page 521.

Part II

Introduction

Welcome to your new Storm. In this section we will introduce you to how the book is organized and where to find useful information. Inside the front and back cover, check out "Day in the Life" section, where we give you some scenarios to describe how you can use your Storm for work and play. We even show you how to find some great tips and tricks sent right to your Storm.

Introduction

Congratulations on Your Storm!

The BlackBerry Storm2 is the second generation of the first touch screen BlackBerry ever released. The screen sensitivity, processor, and memory have all been upgraded and enhanced for a better and faster experience. With this guide, we hope to help you tap into the power of this great smartphone.

In 2001 the BlackBerry name came into the marketplace. One popular story is that the keys on the very early devices looked like seeds to some of the creators. The creators looked at various seeded fruit and decided that "BlackBerry" would be a friendly and inviting name for the device.

However, the origin of the name is less important than understanding the philosophy. One thing to understand from the outset is that this is not just a phone. The BlackBerry is a computer—a sophisticated messaging device that does a bunch of things at the same time—and a phone.

The BlackBerry takes most of the major needs that we have—information, communication, constant contact, accessibility, and more—and puts them in one device that can do just about everything.

Unique Features on the BlackBerry Storm

Your BlackBerry Storm has many shared features with the BlackBerry family and some unique features as well. Following are some of the key features (some of which are described in greater detail in the following subsections):

- Unique touch screen design
- Built-in social networking

- SurePress keyboard
- Camera (3.2 megapixel) with flash and auto focus
- Media player (for pictures, video, and audio)
- Video recording
- Memory Expansion with MicroSD Media Card
- 3G capability

Touch Screen

Having a touch screen is nothing new these days. What separates the Storm from the rest is that RIM has made a touch screen that supports different types of gestures and touches.

Built-In Social Networking

Use your Storm for accessing your Facebook page, YouTube, Flickr and virtually every IM program. Keep in touch with everyone in the ways you like most.

SurePress Keyboard

The SurePress design allows you to press and click the on-screen keyboard to select anything from a link in your browser to the correct letter when typing.

Media Card: Expansion Memory Card

Your Storm comes bundled with an 8 or 16GB MicroSD card that allows you to store large numbers of pictures, music tracks, and videos.

Always on, Always Connected

Perhaps nothing sums up what a BlackBerry can do better than the fact that it always keeps you connected (which virtually no other device can do). Your BlackBerry will push your email (up to ten different accounts) right into your hand—all the time, day and night. (Now, you can put limitations on that—but the reason it is sometimes called a CrackBerry is that once you experience this, you might not want to limit it at all!)

You may be used to turning your old cell phone on and off and only checking it to see if you missed a call. Your BlackBerry stays on all the time—even when it is in standby mode, it is still on. You will find yourself looking at it not only to see if you missed a call, but to see what emails have come in, who is sending you an instant message, who just posted a note on your Facebook page, what time your next appointment is, what you need to pick up at the store, and so on. In short, your life can be managed from your BlackBerry.

Things This Powerful Are Not Always Easy to Grasp—At First

Your BlackBerry is grouped into the category of things called "smartphones" by many. A BlackBerry, however, is really . . . a BlackBerry—more than a smartphone by any other name, because it does so much so well.

The pros of that are clear—in your hand is probably the most capable and most complicated technology available today.

The cons are that the BlackBerry, especially the first touch screen model, is not always intuitive at first use. For some, this is frustrating—they want their BlackBerry to do what their old phone did—in just the same way.

Like a computer, your BlackBerry has a unique operating system (OS) that is proprietary and only found on other BlackBerry devices. Your Storm takes the OS one step further and adds an innovative new touch technology that takes a little getting used to.

Take your time—this is not a device to pick up for an hour and then throw down in frustration—there is a lot to learn here. Remember when you got your first Windows or Mac computer? When we did, we didn't know what a window was, let alone where to find things or how to type a letter—it took time.

With the BlackBerry—like most other things in our lives—the more we invest in learning, the more we will ultimately get out of it.

Getting the Most out of This Book

You can read this book cover to cover, but you can also peruse it in a modular fashion, by chapter or topic. Maybe you just want to check out BlackBerry App World, try the web browser, and get set up with your email and contacts; or you might just want to load up your music. You can do all this and more with our book.

You will soon realize that your Storm is a very powerful device. There are, however, many secrets locked inside, which we help you unlock throughout this book.

Take your time—this book can help you on your way to learn how to best use, work, and have fun with your new Storm. Use this book to get up to speed and learn all the best tips and tricks more quickly.

But remember that devices this powerful are not always easy to grasp—at first. You will get the most out of your Storm if you can read a section and then try out what you read. For most people, reading about and then doing an activity gives us a much higher retention rate than simply reading alone. So, in order to learn and remember what you learn, we recommend the following: *read a little, try a little on your Storm, and repeat!*

How This Book Is Organized

Knowing how this book is organized will help you more quickly locate things important to you. Here we show you the main organization of this book. Remember to take advantage of our abridged table of contents, detailed table of contents, and comprehensive index to help you quickly pinpoint items of interest.

A Day in the Life of a Storm User

Located inside the front and back cover, this is an excellent piece of information full of easy-to-access cross-reference page numbers. So if you see something you want to learn, simply thumb to that page and learn about it—all in just a few minutes.

Part 1: Quick Start Guide

The Quick Start Guide covers the following topics:

Learning your way around: Learn about the keys, buttons, and ports on your Storm, as well as how to get inside and change the battery, SIM card, and memory card. Then learn many time-saving tips about getting around quickly, as well as how to multitask.

Touch screen gestures: We show you all the best tips and tricks for getting around the touch screen. We cover how to start apps and get into folders, as well as some time-saving techniques.

Copying, pasting, and multitasking: We cover the very useful copy-and-paste function and how to jump between apps on your Storm.

Mastering your virtual keyboards: We explore the three keyboards (full, SureType, and MultiTap) and provide some useful tips about how to get more out of each one.

Working with the wireless network: Learn how to read the letters, numbers, and symbols at the top of your Storm screen so you know when you can make phone calls, send SMS text messages, send and receive email, and browse the Web. Also learn how to handle your Storm on an airplane.

App references: This section includes a series of reference tables that allow you to quickly peruse the icons or apps in particular categories. Get a thumbnail of what all the apps do on your Storm and quick page numbers to jump right to the details of how to get the most out of each app in this book.

Part 2: Introduction

You are here now . . .

Part 3: You and Your Storm

This is the meat of the book, organized in 36 easy-to-understand chapters packed with loads of pictures to guide you every step of the way.

Quickly Locating Notes, Tips, and Cautions

If you flip through this book, you can instantly see these items based on their formatting. For example, if you wanted to find all the calendar tips, you would flip to the Calendar chapter –and quickly find them.

NOTE: Notes, tips, and cautions are all formatted like this, with a gray background, to help you see them more quickly.

Free BlackBerry Email Tips and Free Videos

Check out the authors' web site at www.madesimplelearning.com for a series of very useful BlackBerry tips and tricks. On this site, we have taken a selection of great tips out of this book and even added a few new ones. Click the Free Tips section and register for your tips in order to receive a tip right in your Storm inbox about once a week. Learning in small chunks is a great way to master your Storm.

The authors also offer some free videos on their web site to show you how to use Desktop Manager for Windows. In addition, there are over 100 video tutorials to show you how to use your Storm that you can watch on your computer and your BlackBerry.

Part III

You and Your Storm

This part is the heart of the book. In this section, you'll find chapters explaining each key features of your Storm. You'll see that most chapters focus on an individual app or a specific type of application. Many of the chapters discuss applications that come with your Storm, but we also include some fun and useful apps you can download from BlackBerry App World. Sure, the Storm is for fun, but it's for a whole lot more as well, so you'll learn how to be productive with Word to Go, Sheet to Go, and Slideshow to Go in this part, too. We finish with some handy troubleshooting tips that can help if your Storm isn't working quite right.

Chapter 1

Email Setup

This chapter is about setting up your BlackBerry. If someone has not set it up for you, you are going to need to do it yourself or, after reading this, you might get someone else to do it for you. Actually, its not that hard. If you want to add an email account, then you will need to refer to this chapter as well.

Your BlackBerry supports a wide array of email accounts including (Google, Comcast, Yahoo, MSN, or more generic POP3/IMAP accounts as well as Microsoft Exchange and Lotus Domino corporate accounts). The various types of accounts will have different wireless sync capapbilites for contacts, calendars in addition to email. We show you all the differences and help you get each type set up in this chapter.

Currently, the two types of email accounts that provide for syncing of your contacts are Gmail (Google Mail) and Microsoft Exchange/Lotus Domino accounts connected to a BlackBerry Enterprise Server (BES).

Sometimes email setup can cause problems; we show you how to fix some common errors and make sure you receive all your email on both your computer and your BlackBerry. While you can adjust email setup from your BlackBerry, you may also want to adjust your email settings from your computer, we cover that in this chapter.

If your BlackBerry is tied to a BES, we show you how to get connected or 'activated' on the server. And, more recently, RIM, BlackBerry's maker, announced a free version of the BES software. This is a fantasic value if your organization uses Microsoft Exchange and would like to take advantage of the BES features without additional software licensing and, in most cases, without additional hardware costs.

CAUTION: Before you read any further, or use the Setup Wizard or anything else, please take a few minutes to check out the Quick Start Guide earlier in this book, if you haven't already. It is meant to help you find lots of useful things in this book, as well as give you some great beginning and advanced time-saving tips and tricks so you can get up and running quickly.

The Setup Wizard

When you first turn on your Storm, you will likely be presented with the Setup Wizard. If you ignored or closed it, you can get back to it by locating the **Setup Wizard** icon, and pressing and clicking it. You may need to press and click the **Setup** folder in order to find the **Setup Wizard** icon:

You will be presented with screens similar to the ones that follow.

NOTE: These screens will vary based on your carrier and are updated quite often by BlackBerry, so you might see them in a different order or see some different screens altogether.

Follow the steps suggested; they will give you a good jump start on getting your BlackBerry set up and learning some of the basics.

Just press and click any field (e.g., date, time, or time zone) to make an adjustment, and then scroll down to press and click **Next**.

You will see a couple of screens covering the basics of navigation (see Figure 1-1).

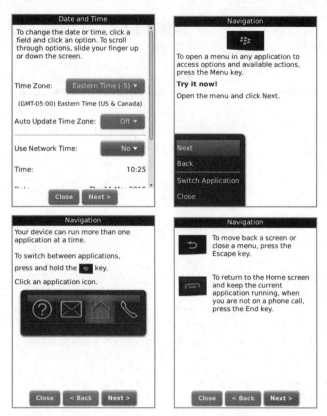

Figure 1-1. *Setup Wizard initial screens*

You'll also see some screens about SureType, MultiTap, and full keyboard typing. (See Chapter 6 for typing tips). You can even select your default portrait keyboard (vertical orientation). If you like to have a single letter on each key, go for the full keyboard, as shown in Figure 1-2.

Figure 1-2. *Setup Wizard typing tips screens*

Finally, you will see a screen similar to the one to the right. (You may see a few different items listed.)

Date and Time: See page 206.

Navigation and Typing Tutorials – See pages 3 and 167.

Email Setup: See page 50.

Setting up Bluetooth: See page 489.

Setup Wi-Fi: See page 455.

Font: See page 208.

Help: See page 184.

Setup Wizard
Date and Time
Navigation and Typing Tutorials
Email Setup
Set up Wi-Fi®
Font
Language and Text Input
Learn about the touch screen
Help

Setting Up Email the First Time

Your BlackBerry is designed to retrieve your email from up to ten different email accounts and, if you are connected to a BES, one corporate email account. When your BlackBerry receives your email, all your messages will be displayed in your **Messages** box.

You can set up and adjust your email right from your BlackBerry, including adjusting your email signature which might say something like:

Hello from my BlackBerry Storm

Sent from my Verizon Wireless BlackBerry.

You can also set up and make adjustments to email accounts from your carrier's web site (see page 71).

> **NOTE:** If you want to set up your BlackBerry to work with email coming from a BES, skip to the "Setting Up Your Corporate Email" section on page 53.

Personal or Internet Email Setup

In order to setup your personal or internet email accounts, you need to use one of two apps. You can set up your personal or internet email from the Setup Wizard or the **Email Settings** icon:

1. Press and click the **Email Settings** icon.

2. Accept all user agreements. To continue, press and Click **I Agree**.

3. You may need to create an email settings account for your BlackBerry if this is the first time you are logging in.

> **NOTE:** If you are logging into your email settings account, be sure to click the check box next to **Remember me on this device**, and you won't have to keep entering your username/password every time.

4. Now you will be taken to the Email Setup web site, as if you had just pressed and clicked the **Email Settings** icon.

5. Choose **Add** to set up your BlackBerry to send and receive email from an email account you already own.

> **CAUTION:** Usually you will choose **Add**. Only choose **Create** if you wish to create a brand new email account that is tied exclusively to this BlackBerry.

6. Now select from the various types of email accounts. In this case, we'll choose **Gmail**.

7. If you have another type of account (e.g., Yahoo, AOL, etc.), click that entry.

8. If you don't see your email account type, then click **Other**.

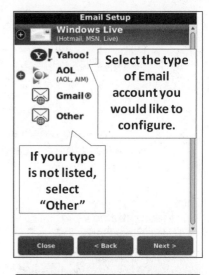

9. Next, type your full email address (name@gmail.com) and password, and then click **Next** to attempt the login.

> **TIP:** Click the **Show Password** check box to see the letters in your password—this can be helpful to prevent mistyping it.

10. If everything is correct, then you will see a screen similar to this one:

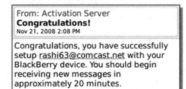

If you're having trouble entering your email address or password, you can press the **Menu** key and select **Full Keyboard**, or turn the BlackBerry 90 degrees to horizontal (landscape) mode to get a full keyboard that allows you type more accurately.

Once each email account is set up correctly, you will see an activation email message in your **Messages** box (Figure 1-3), and within 15 to 20 minutes, email should start flowing in to your BlackBerry.

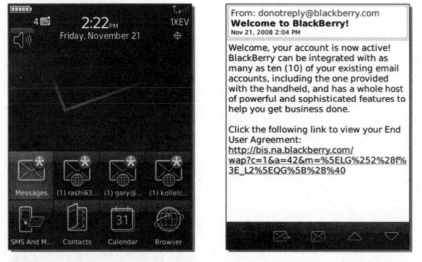

Figure 1-3. *Successful email account setup showing new icons and an email message*

Setting Up Your Corporate Email

Your help desk or information technology department will typically set up your corporate email (i.e., enterprise activation). If not, all you need is your activation password and you can set this up on your own—right from the BlackBerry, using the Setup Wizard.

NOTE: If you have not received your activation password, then you need to ask your help desk or technology support department for that password before you can complete this process.

Setting Up Corporate Email Using the Setup Wizard

The following exercise shows you how to set up your corporate email with the Setup Wizard:

1. Start the Setup Wizard and select Email Setup, and then choose **I want to use a work email account with a BlackBerry Enterprise Server** from the menu.

2. Make sure that you have received your enterprise activation password.

3. Type in the email address along with the activation password you received from your help desk or system administrator.

4. Press the Menu key and select Activate.

5. You will then see many messages on the screen, such as **Establishing Secure Connection, Downloading Contacts, Downloading Calendar, Downloading Tasks,** and so on. The entire process may take 15 minutes or more depending on how much data is being sent, as well as the strength of your wireless connection.

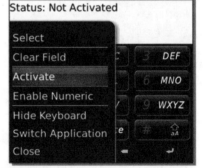

6. If you see an error message, then verify your password, that your wireless radio is turned on, and that you are in a strong coverage area. If you still have problems, then please contact your technology support group.

7. Once you have seen all the enterprise activation messages go by, and you see a completion message, then try your email and check your address book and calendar to see if it looks like everything was loaded correctly. If not, then contact your help desk for support.

TIP: You can also get to the **Enterprise Activation** screen by going to your **Options** icon, selecting **Advanced Options**, and then selecting **Enterprise Activation** from the list.

> Advanced Options
> Accessibility
> Applications
> Browser
> Browser Push
> Cell Broadcast Settings
> Default Services
> Enterprise Activation
> GPS

How Can I Tell If I Am Activated on the BlackBerry Server?

A simple rule of thumb is that if you can send and receive email and you have names in your BlackBerry address book (which you can access through the **Contacts** icon), then it has been successfully set up (enterprise activation is complete).

To verify that your BlackBerry is successfully configured with your server, do the following:

1. Start your BlackBerry contact list/address book.

2. Click the **Menu** key.

3. Swipe up or down on the menu to find a menu item called **Lookup**. If you see **Lookup**, then you are connected. (The **Lookup** command allows you to do a Global Address List (GAL) lookup from your BES to find anyone in your organization—and then add them to your personal address book on your BlackBerry.)

Maintaining Your Email Accounts

You may need to add, edit, or delete email accounts. You also might want to fine-tune your email signature (by default, it's "Sent from my [carrier name] BlackBerry"), which gets attached to the bottom of each email you send from your Storm.

Adding More Personal Email Addresses

You can add up to ten email addresses to your Storm. Only one can be an enterprise or corporate email address, but the rest can all be personal addresses, such as POP3 or IMAP addresses.

1. Press and click the **Personal Email Setup** icon (it may be in your **Setup** folder).

2. Enter your username and password if requested, and click **Log In**.

3. Scroll down to the bottom of the list of email addresses and click the **Add** button.

4. Follow the steps to add the new account as described previously.

Hiding Extra Email Account Icons

As you set up each email account, a new icon will appear on your home screen tied to that particular account. If you like having individual icons, you can leave them alone. However, since all your email goes into your main **Messages** box, you can hide these icons to clean up your home screen. Follow these steps to hide these extra icons:

1. Highlight the icon you want to hide by gently touching it.

2. Press the **Menu** key.

3. Select **Hide**.

If you want to get the icon back, then
follow the steps to shown in the "Hiding
and Showing Icons" section of Chapter 8,
on page 199.

Editing and Deleting an Email Account (Signature and Advanced Settings)

To change your email account name, password, signature, advanced settings, or
synchronization options, you need to edit your email account settings. If you don't use a
certain email account anymore, you may want to delete that particular address.

1. Press and click the **Email
    Settings** icon, which may be in
    your **Setup** folder.

2. Log in if requested.

3. Press and click the particular
    email account you want to edit
    or delete.

4. To delete the account, select
    Delete from the short menu
    and confirm your selection. If
    you are done, then press the
    Escape key to exit to your
    home screen.

5. To edit the account, select **Edit**
    from the short menu.

6. Now you can adjust the following items in the **General Options** section:

   ■ Email account name: The name for the email account icon.

   ■ **Your name**: The name that appears instead of the email address when you send messages; also known as the friendly name.

   ■ **Signature**: The signature attached to each email you send from your BlackBerry. Usually, you will want to change this from **Sent from my [carrier name] BlackBerry** to something more personal, like your name and phone number, or your company name.

7. Scroll down to click **Login Information** to be able to change your password for this account.

8. Click **Delivery Options** to be able to add an email account to send auto-blind carbon copies of every email you send from your BlackBerry.

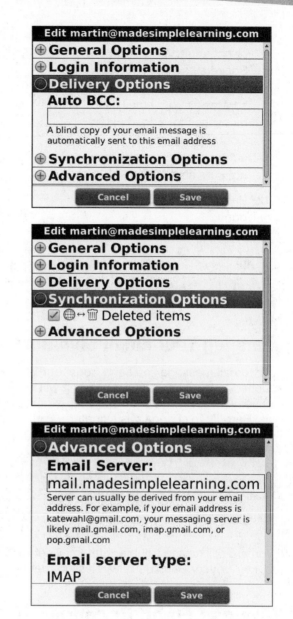

9. Click **Synchronization Options** to adjust whether or not email messages you delete on your BlackBerry are synced wirelessly to also be deleted on your main email inbox. To check or uncheck the box, highlight it and press the **Space** key.

10. Scroll down to **Advanced Options** to adjust the **Email Server** name. Contact your email administrator for help if you are not sure about the **Email Server** name.

11. Scroll down to select whether or not you use SSL (Secure Sockets Layer). This is a security protocol that scrambles your email messages for added safety. Contact your email administrator for help if you are not sure about SSL.

12. Press and click **Save** when done.

Edit martin@madesimplelearning.com
Email server type: IMAP **Port:** 993 ☑Use SSL **Timeout:** 120 seconds
Cancel   Save

> **TIP:** Press the **space** key to get the @ (at) and . (dot) symbols whenever typing an email. For example, for sara@company.com, type, Sara *space* company *space* com.

Changing Your Email Signature

Every email message you send from your BlackBerry will have an auto-signature attached to the bottom of it. Usually it will have your carrier name on it. For example, if you use AT&T, then your default auto-signature may say "Sent from my Verizon Wireless BlackBerry." To change this signature, you need to follow step 6 above.

> **NOTE:** If you are not sure of your advanced email settings, open up your mail client on your computer. If using Microsoft Outlook or similar, and click **Accounts** or **Email Accounts** from the menu. Then review the advanced settings for that account. If you use web mail exclusively, then contact your service provider to ask for assistance with getting your BlackBerry set up.

If you are still having trouble with email setup, then please contact your email service provider or your BlackBerry wireless carrier (phone company) technical support.

Wireless Email Reconciliation

The BlackBerry allows you to turn on or off wireless reconciliation, which is the feature that synchronizes deletion of email between your regular mailbox and your BlackBerry. In other words, you can set it up so that if you delete an email on your BlackBerry, the same email message is also automatically deleted from your regular email account.

Disable Wireless Email Reconciliation

Usually, this is turned on by default, but you can disable it.

NOTE: If you work at an organization that supplied your BlackBerry to you, this feature may be controlled centrally by your administrator and may not be adjustable.

Some wireless carriers (phone companies) do not support this feature (or don't support it fully) unless your BlackBerry is tied to a BES.

1. Click the **Messages** icon.

2. Press the **Menu** key and select **Options** (or press the letter **O** to jump down to **Options**).

3. Then select Email Reconciliation.

4. Set Delete On to Handheld.

5. Set Wireless Reconcile to **Off**.

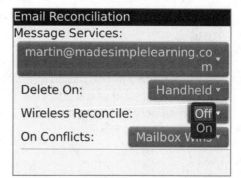

Enable Wireless Reconciliation

To re-enable email reconciliation, set **Delete On to Mailbox & Handheld**, and set **Wireless Reconcile** to On.

Purge Deleted Items

If you have turned on **Wireless Reconcile** and want to get rid of old email that you deleted from either your main email inbox or your BlackBerry, then press the **Menu** key and select **Purge Deleted Items**, and then select the email address.

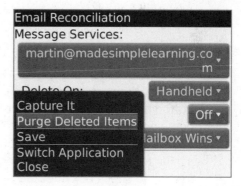

Syncing Google Contacts Using Email Setup

If you use Google for email and to manage your contacts, then you can set up a wireless sync for your Google contacts when you set up your email. This is a great feature because you no longer need to connect your Storm with a sync cable to your computer to update contacts between your Storm and Google. The contact updates, like email, all happen automatically and wirelessly.

Setting Up Google Wireless Contacts Syncing

With BlackBerry 5.0 system software and BlackBerry Internet Service software (assuming your carrier has upgraded), you now can use wireless contact syncing for Google. To do so, follow these steps.

> **CAUTION:** You can also sync your Google contacts using the Google Sync app (see page 351). Do not try to sync Google contacts with both methods—if you do you are asking for trouble. Instead, if you choose to use this method for contact syncing, then use Google Sync for only your Google calendar.

1. Press and click the **Personal Email Setup** icon.

2. Log in if requested.

3. If you have already set up your Gmail account, then press and click that email account and select **Edit** from the short menu. Skip to step 5.

4. If you have not yet set up your Gmail account, then press and click the **Add** button and enter your Gmail account name and password. After the login is successful, you should see a screen similar to the one shown on the right. Leave the check box checked as shown, and click **Next** to finish the setup process. Skip to step 7.

5. When you are editing your Gmail account, scroll down to press and click **Synchronization Options** as shown, and check/uncheck your boxes. Make sure the check box next to **Contacts** is checked.

6. Click the **Save** button.

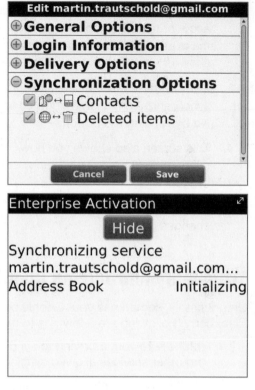

7. The first time you enable this contact sync feature, you will see a screen telling you the progress of the initial sync. If you have many contacts (e.g., 1,000 or more), the first sync could require over 10 minutes to finish.

You may also have to try it a few times if it fails the first time.

At the time of writing, this wireless sync only works with Google/Gmail accounts.

Turning Wireless Contact Syncing On and Off

If you have enabled wireless contact syncing with Google or another service, you can adjust the sync from the Contacts Options screen, as follows.

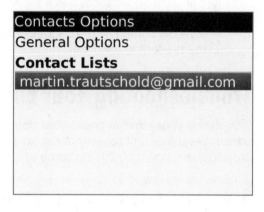

1. Press and click the **Contacts** icon, press the **Menu** key, and select **Options** to see this screen.

2. Now scroll down and click the email account under the contact list to make adjustments using the screen shown.

3. If you want to disable wireless synchronization, change the **Yes** to a **No** by clicking the button.

4. This screen also shows you how many contact entries are being synced.

5. Press the **Menu** key and save your changes.

Contact List Properties
martin.trautschold@gmail.com
Wireless Synchronization: Yes ▾
Number of Entries: 2242

Trouble Synchronizing Google Contacts?

Unfortunately, sometimes your Google contacts do not sync correctly with your BlackBerry. Following are a few tips to try and help you get up and running:

- Make sure you are trying to sync a Gmail account, at publishing time no other services allowed syncing of contacts.

- At the time of writing, you cannot sync Gmail contact groups.

- Make sure you have enabled wireless synchronization on your BlackBerry smartphone. To verify this, on your BlackBerry, start the Contacts application, press the **Menu** key, and select **Options**. Scroll down to your Gmail address under **Contact Lists** and click it. Make sure the setting next to **Wireless Synchronization** is set to **Yes** (see the preceding exercise).

Troubleshooting Your Email Accounts

Sometimes your email accounts just don't work quite right, and unfortunately, sometimes email isn't as easy to set up as just shown. The following subsections provide a few tips for handling some of the more common errors.

Verifying Usernames and Passwords

Your first action, which usually handles about 80 percent of the problems, should be to simply retype your email address and password. The reason for the problem could be as simple as a wrong character typed in your email address or password. Watch how you type the password very carefully, especially if you have numbers or other characters. Always try retyping them a few times before doing anything else.

Verifying That Your Email Server Is POP3 or IMAP

Some email servers cannot be accessed by BlackBerry Internet Service, so you cannot use these types of email accounts on your Storm. Contact your email service provider, tell them you are trying to access your email from a BlackBerry smartphone, and verify that the server is of a type called POP3 or IMAP.

Verifying Your Email Server Settings (Advanced Settings)

Another setup issue might be that your server uses SSL security or has a nonstandard email server name. Contact your service provider to find out about these settings. To change these settings on your Storm, you need to follow the steps shown in the "Edit or Delete Email Account" section on page 57.

Solving a Gmail Enabled IMAP Error Message

If you receive an error message in your email inbox telling you to turn on IMAP settings in Gmail, you need to log into your Gmail account from your computer and follow these steps:

1. Click the **Settings** link (usually in the top-right corner).

2. Click the **Forwarding and POP/IMAP** tab.

3. Make sure that **IMAP Access** is set to **Enable IMAP**, as shown in Figure 1-4.

4. Then click the **Save Changes** button.

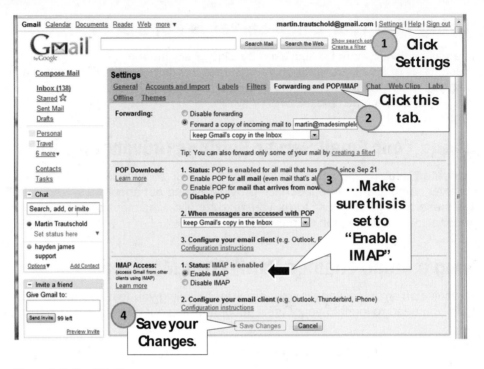

Figure 1-4. *Gmail Settings screen*

5.   After you make this change, you will need to go back into your BlackBerry personal Email setup.

6.   Highlight the invalid account (in this case Gmail), press and click it, and select **Validate** from the short menu.

7.   Type the password for your invalid email account and click **OK**.

8. If everything is correct, then you will see a pop-up saying **Your password has been successfully validated.**

9. Press **OK** to continue.

Validation Required

Validate your email account:

ma⬛⬛⬛⬛⬛⬛⬛⬛⬛⬛⬛⬛co
m

Typ⬛

****

☐ S⬛

> ⓘ Your password has been successfully validated.
>
> OK

Cancel   Next >

Why Is Some Email Missing?

If you download your email messages to your computer using an email program such as Microsoft Outlook, Outlook Express, or similar, and you use BlackBerry Internet Service on your BlackBerry for email, then you need to turn on a specific setting in your computer's email program. If you do not leave a copy of your messages on the server from your computer's email, you may end up receiving all email on your computer, but only a limited set of email on your BlackBerry.

Why Does This Happen?

By default, most email programs pull down or retrieve email from the server every 1 to 5 minutes, and then erase the retrieved messages from the server. By default, BlackBerry Internet Service usually pulls down email every 15 minutes or so. So, if your computer has pulled down the email every 5 minutes and erased it from the server, your BlackBerry will only receive a very limited set of messages (those that haven't yet been pulled down by your computer).

How to Fix This

The answer is to set your computer's email program to keep your messages on the server. This way, the BlackBerry will always receive every email message. Here's how:

1. In your computer email program (e.g., Microsoft Outlook), find the location where you can configure or change your email accounts. For example, Tools, Configure Accounts, Account Settings, or something similar (Figure 1-5).

2. Select or change the appropriate email account. (Sometimes you just double-click the account to edit it.)

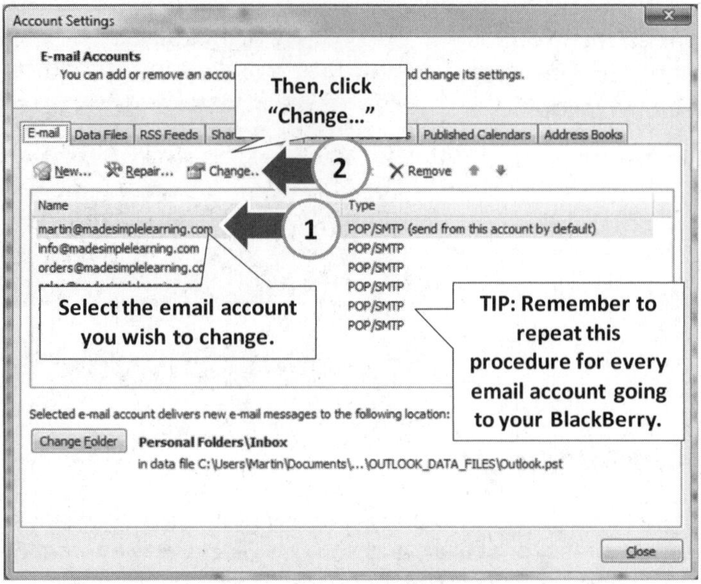

Figure 1-5. *Account Settings screen in Microsoft Outlook*

3. You will then usually go to an Advanced Settings area to make changes to **Leave a copy of the message on the server**. In Microsoft Outlook, click the **More Settings** tab and then the **Advanced** tab (Figure 1-6).

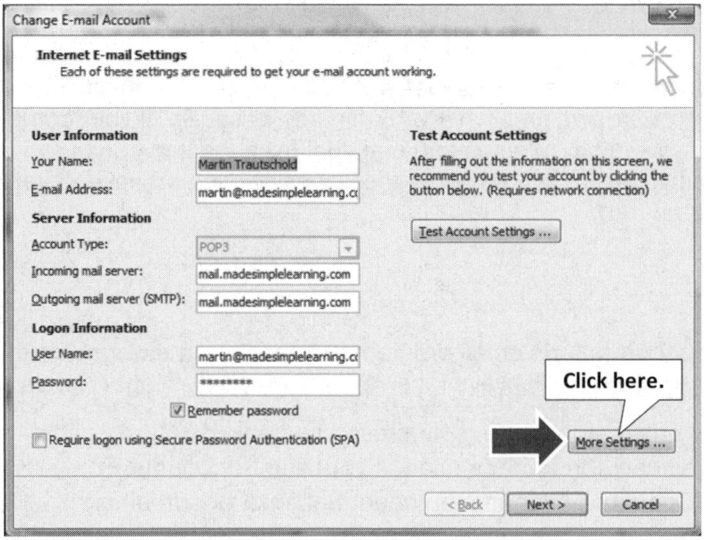

Figure 1-6. *Internet email settings in Microsoft Outlook*

4. At the bottom of the screen, under Delivery, check the Leave a copy of the message on the server box.

5. Then check the Remove from server after [X] days box. We suggest changing the number to about 10. This allows you time to make sure that the message reaches both your BlackBerry and your PC, but doesn't clutter the server for too many days. If you make the number of days too high, you may end up with a "Mail Box Full" error and have your incoming email messages bounced back to the senders.

Internet E-mail Settings

General | Outgoing Server | Connection | Advanced

Server Port Numbers
Incoming server (POP3): 110   Use Defaults
☐ This server requires an encrypted connection (SSL)
Outgoing server (SMTP): 25
Use the following type of encrypted connection: None

Server Timeouts
Short ─ Long 1 minute

Set this to about 10 days.

Delivery
☑ Leave a copy of messages on the server
☑ Remove from server after 10 days
☐ Remove from server when deleted from 'Deleted Items'

Check both of these boxes

OK   Cancel

NOTE: Remember to repeat the preceding process for every email account that you have going to both your computer and your BlackBerry.

Correcting the "Invalid Account. Please Validate" Message

From time to time, you may see an invalid email account message, such as the one shown in Figure 1-6, either on the BlackBerry Email Setup screen or when you log into your wireless carrier's web site. This may happen if you have changed your email account password, or if the system encounters an unforeseen error—through no fault of your own! The following sections provide the steps to correct the problem.

Using Your Computer

You can log into the BlackBerry Internet Service site from your computer to correct the invalid account (see Figure 1-7).

1. Log into your BlackBerry wireless carrier's web client (see page 71 for a list of sites).

Email Accounts

Manage the accounts you are using with your BlackBerry device.

Valid	Email Account	Edit	Filters	Delete
⊗	info@blackberrymadesimple.com	↘	▼	🗑
⊗	martin@blackberrymadesimple.com	↘	▼	🗑

Note: Email accounts marked with ⊗ are invalid. Please click on the ⊗ beside the email account to try to validate it.

Figure 1-7. *BlackBerry Internet Service showing invalid email accounts*

2. Click the **Edit** icon [Edit ↘] next to the invalid account.

3. Enter your information including your password.

4. Save your changes.

5. You will then see a message that says "Your email account has been successfully validated." A check mark will now appear in the **Valid** column, as shown in Figure 1-8.

Email Accounts

Manage the accounts you are using with your BlackBerry device.

Valid	Email Account	Edit	Filters	Delete
✔	info@blackberrymadesimple.com	↘	▼	🗑

Figure 1-8. *Email account successfully validated in BlackBerry Internet Service*

Using Your BlackBerry

1. Click the **Email Settings** icon (usually in the **Setup** folder).

2. After logging in, you will see a screen similar to this one.

3. To correct the invalid account errors, highlight and click on the account, then select **Validate** from the short menu

4. Now retype your password and click **Next** to validate the account.

5. You will see a message similar to the one shown in the image for each validated account.

6. Repeat the process for any other accounts shown as invalid.

Setting Up and Adjusting Email Accounts from Your Computer

Your personal email accounts can also be set up from your computer using your carrier's web site. You also might notice that when you send an email from the BlackBerry, the signature is something very basic, like "Sent from BlackBerry Device via T-Mobile," or "Sent from AT&T Wireless," depending on your carrier. You can easily change your email signature and perform other tasks from your carrier's web site, but you'll first need to create an account. If your account was already set up when you activated your phone, just log in with your username and password and skip ahead to the "Changing Your Email Auto Signature" section on page 75.

Setting Up BlackBerry Email from Your Computer

Using your computer, not your BlackBerry, find your way to your carrier's web site in Internet Explorer, Firefox, or Opera (a partial list of sites is listed following). Once there, log into your personal account page.

> **NOTE:** These web sites change frequently! Some carriers imbed or include the BlackBerry email setup pages within the main carrier web site. Please check with your wireless carrier if the following link is incorrect or you don't see your carrier listed. You may also want to check for updated sites at the bottom of this web page: http://na.blackberry.com/eng/support/blackberry101/setup.jsp#tab_tab_email.

Alltel (USA): www.alltel.blackberry.com

AT&T/Cingular (USA): www.att.blackberry.com

Bell/Solo Mobile (Canada): https://bis.na.blackberry.com/html?brand=bell

Cellular South (USA): https://bis.na.blackberry.com/html?brand=csouth1

Rogers Wireless (Canada): https://bis.na.blackberry.com/html?brand=rogers

Sprint/Nextel (USA): https://bis.na.blackberry.com/html?brand=sprint

T-Mobile (USA): www.t-mobile.com/bis (log into main site)

T-Mobile (Germany): www.instantemail.t-mobile.de

Telus Mobility (Canada): https://bis.na.blackberry.com/html?brand=telus

Verizon Wireless (USA): https://bis.na.blackberry.com/html?brand=vzw

Virgin Mobile (Canada): https://bis.na.blackberry.com/html?brand=virginmobile

Vodafone (UK): https://bis.eu.blackberry.com/html?brand=vodauk

If you cannot find a link directly to your phone company's BlackBerry Internet Service site from this list or from

http://na.blackberry.com/eng/support/blackberry101/setup.jsp#tab_tab_email,

then you should log into your own phone company web site, and look for a button or a tab that says something like **Phone & Accessories**, **Device**, **Handheld** or **Support**, and then **Setup BlackBerry Email** or **Setup Handset Email**. (Each wireless carrier website is different, so we cannot say of these will be buttons, tabs or even if the text will be identical, just do your best to search for something similar.) If you still cannot get to your BlackBerry internet email setup, then please contact your phone company.

On many of the preceding sites, you will first need to create your BlackBerry Internet Service account on a screen similar to this one.

> **Welcome to BlackBerry!**
>
> **New Users**
> You need to create an account to begin sending and receiving email on your BlackBerry device. Please turn on your device and ensure that it is connected to the wireless network. Then click "Create New Account" below to begin.
>
> **Create New Account**
>
> **Existing Users**
> To log in, please provide your user name and password below.
>
> User name: `myusername`   Require Assistance?
>
> Password: `••••••••••`   Forgot Password?
>
> **Log In**

Creating a New Account

To create a new account, follow these steps:

1. Click the **Create New Account** button on your provider's site.

2. You will then see a Legal Agreement. In order to continue, check the **I have read this agreement** box and click the **I Agree** button. After accepting the legal agreement, you should now see a screen like that shown in Figure 1-9.

Account Setup

To begin creating your BlackBerry Service account, type your device details below.

Device PIN: [   ]

Device IMEI: [   ]

[Cancel] [Continue]

To find your PIN perform one of the following actions:
- In the BlackBerry device options or settings, click **Status**.
- Look for the PIN and IMEI information on the outside of the box that your BlackBerry device or BlackBerry-enabled device came in.
- Turn the BlackBerry device off and remove the battery. Look for the sticker on the BlackBerry device with the PIN information where the battery is usually located.

Copyright 2006-2009 Research In Motion Limited. All rights reserved. Legal Information.

Figure 1-9. *Setting up your BlackBerry Internet Service account: Requesting the PIN and IMEI*

3. Both of the numbers you need are located in your **Options** app on your BlackBerry, so refer back to that. Click the **Options** icon.

4. Press the **S** on your keyboard a few times until you get to the **Status** item, and click it.

5. Once in **Status**, look at the lines marked **PIN** and **IMEI**, as shown in Figure 1-10.

Options
Language
Memory
MMS
Mobile Network
Owner
Password
Screen/Keyboard
Security Options
SMS Text
Spell Check
Status
Theme
Voice Dialing

Status

Signal:	−79 dBm
Battery:	40 %
File Free:	41768703 Bytes
PIN:	30488893
IMEI:	359483.02.045299.6

MEID (dec):
     26843 54573 00005 7500

MEID (hex):
          A0000000D 00E09C

Figure 1-10. *Locating your PIN and IMEI on your BlackBerry in the Options app*

6. Type the PIN and IMEI into the web site screen, but remove any spaces or dots. You should then come to a series of screens on the main BlackBerry Internet Service web page (Figures 1-11 through 1-13).

7. Log in or click the link from your carrier's web site to access a screen similar to the one in Figure 1-11.

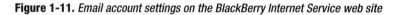

Email Help | Log Out

Email Accounts

Manage the accounts you are using with your BlackBerry device.

Email Accounts	Edit	Filters	Delete
✔ affiliates@madesimplelearning.com			
✔ info@madesimplelearning.com			
✔ martin.trautschold@gmail.com			
✔ martin@madesimplelearning.com			
✔ martintrautschold@yahoo.com			
✔ support@madesimplelearning.com			

Add An Existing Email Account
Set up an existing work or personal email account for BlackBerry device.
ex. Yahoo!®, Gmail™, Microsoft Outlook®

Set Up Account

Click here to setup one of your email accounts to start going to your BlackBerry

BlackBerry Device Email Address ⓘ
Create a new email address for your BlackBerry devi

Create Address

NOTE: Use this only to create a new "BlackBerry only" email address.

Figure 1-11. *Email account settings on the BlackBerry Internet Service web site*

8. Click the **Setup Account** button to input your email address and password (Figure 1-12).

9. Then click **Next** and your account will be set up.

Set Up An Existing Email Account

Set up the BlackBerry Internet Service to deliver email messages from your personal or work email account to your BlackBerry device. Type your email address and the password you use to access the account. Open help to determine which password to type.

Email address: martintrautschold@yahoo.cor

Password: ••••••••••••

Confirm password: ••••••••••••

Cancel   Next

10 Research In Motion Limited. All rights reserved. End User Agreement. Legal Information.

Figure 1-12. *Adding an existing email account to BlackBerry Internet Service*

After the email account is successfully set up, you will receive confirmation email on your BlackBerry, usually titled "Activation."

Shortly thereafter, your first email will come in on the BlackBerry.

Repeat steps 8 and 9 above for each of your email accounts.

Once you have all your email accounts configured, you will see them listed as shown following. You can then customize (**Edit**), filter email (**Filter**), or remove them (**Delete**) by selecting the icons on the right side, as shown in Figure 1-13.

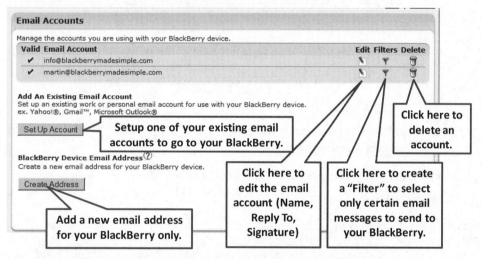

Figure 1-13. *Editing or adding email accounts in the BlackBerry Internet Service*

Changing Your Email Auto-Signature from Your Computer

On your email accounts page you should see an icon for editing each of your accounts that you have set up. You can then add a unique signature for every email account that you have set up.

> **TIP:** You can also change this signature directly from your BlackBerry—see page 57.

1. Select the **Edit** icon next to the email account you wish to work with (Figure 1-13).

2. Make any changes in the fields provided to you (Figure 1-14).

3. In the **Signature** box, simply type in the new signature you wish to appear at the bottom of that particular email account.

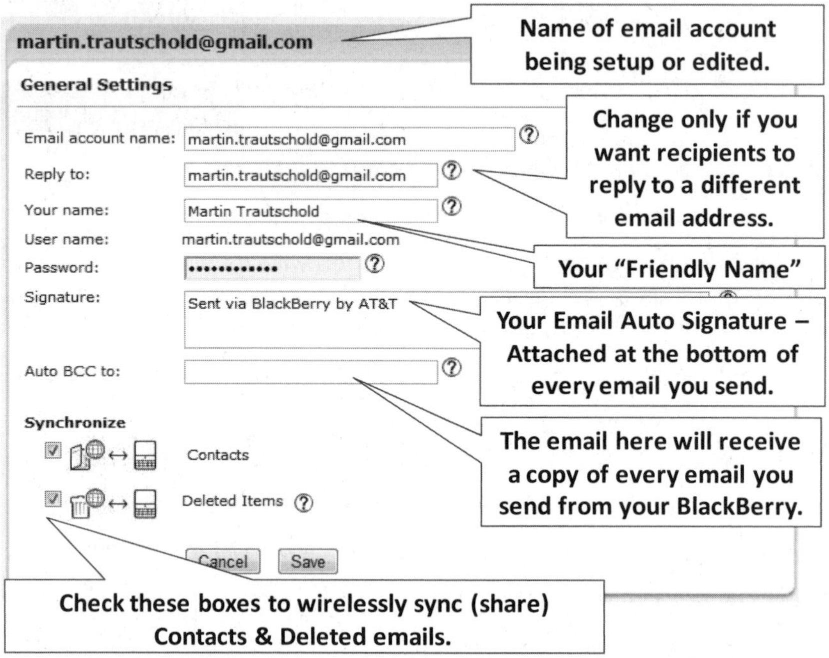

Figure 1-14. *Adjusting settings including auto-signature and sync from BlackBerry Internet Service*

4. Click the **Save** button.

> **NOTE:** At the time of writing, only Gmail has the ability to wirelessly sync or share contacts. We expect more services to be added in the future (e.g., Yahoo, etc.).

We recommend that you test your new settings by sending an email from your BlackBerry to yourself or another email account and verify that the new signature is included.

You can also add signatures that can be selected on the fly from your BlackBerry while typing emails, using the AutoText feature (see page **184**).

Advanced Email Settings from Your Computer

Another thing you can do from your computer is to change advanced settings for your email accounts. In order to do this, you need to click the **Advanced Settings** link (sometimes it does not look clickable) at the top of the email editing screen will show you a screen similar to Figure 1-15. This will allow you to configure settings, such as your specific email server, the port number, and whether or not an encrypted connection is required.

---

martin@madesimplelearning.com

General Settings | **Advanced Settings**

Email server: `mail.madesimplelearning.com`
Email server type: IMAP
Port: `993`
Timeout: 120 seconds
SSL: ☑

[Cancel] [Save]

10 Research In Motion Limited. All rights reserved. End User Agreement, Legal Information.

Figure 1-15. *Advanced Settings screen on the BlackBerry Internet Service web siteBlackBerry Enterprise Server Express*

If you work at an organization that uses a Microsoft Exchange or Microsoft Windows Small Business Server, then you can now acquire the BES Express software for free.

A BES is a server that typically sits behind your organization's firewall and securely connects your BlackBerry to corporate email and data, as well as wirelessly synchronizes (shares) contacts, calendar, tasks, and memo items between your corporate computer and your BlackBerry.

BES allows your organization to gain all the benefits of a BlackBerry Server with no additional software costs. This saves thousands of dollars over the old pricing model by RIM. You might want to let your IT group know about this great new deal if you use BlackBerry devices at your workplace.

Image courtesy of RIM

You should be able to support up to 75 BlackBerry users on the same box as your email server. You can support up to 2,000 users by putting the BES Express software on a separate server.

How to Get the BES Express Software

To acquire BES Express, go to www.blackberry.com and follow these steps:

1. Click the **Software** link at the top.

2. Click **BlackBerry Enterprise Server Express** under **Business Software** in the left column, and you'll see a screen similar to the one shown in Figure 1-16. (You might be able to get straight to the page by typing this link:
http://na.blackberry.com/eng/services/business/server/express.)

3. Then follow the onscreen steps to start the free download.

Figure 1-16. *BES Express Software web site*

4. Once the software is downloaded, the administrator uses a web-based console to set up and administer all the users. The full setup instructions for BES Express are beyond the scope of this book, but please follow the onscreen help and tutorials found at www.blackberry.com (see Figure 1-17).

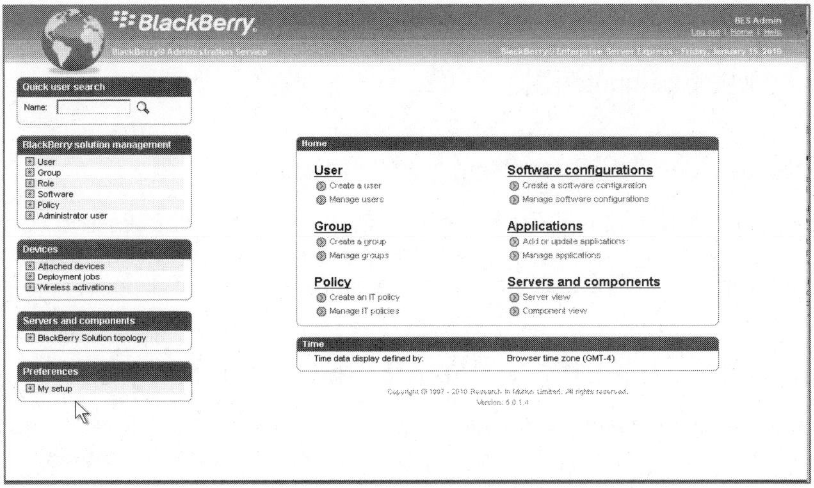

Figure 1-17. *Setting up the BES Express software*

Benefits of Being Connected to a BlackBerry Server

Individuals and small office BlackBerry users can get easy access to a BES. Just perform a web search for "Hosted BES" or "Hosted BlackBerry enterprise server" to locate a number of providers.

TIP: See the "BES Express" section for free BES software.

Connecting your BlackBerry to a BES (version 4.0 and higher) will give you all of the following benefits.

Strong Encryption of Email within Your Organization

All email sent from your BlackBerry to other users in your organization will be fully encrypted with military-grade triple-DES encryption provided by the server.

Full Two-Way Wireless Synchronization

You can set up full two-way wireless updates between your BlackBerry and corporate desktop account for the following:

- Address book
- Calendar
- Task lists
- MemoPad (notes)

This means you will be able to add new information or make changes to anything in your address book, calendar, task list, or MemoPad on your BlackBerry, and in minutes it will appear on your desktop computer.

Securely Connecting to Your Corporate Data

The BES server provides a highly secure connection to corporate data behind your firewall. This can provide productivity benefits to your organization by providing the ability to view and update important information while away from your desk.

Pushing Applications Wirelessly to All Your BlackBerry Users

The BES administrator can create software configurations for groups of users and push them out wirelessly to any or all BlackBerry users. This saves on IT support costs.

Global Address List Lookup

Using Global Address List (GAL) lookup (Lookup for short), you can immediately look up anyone in your organization from your BlackBerry, even if there thousands of people at your organization.

Out of Office Auto Reply and Email Signature

Your out-of-office reply and email signatures are things you can adjust right from your BlackBerry if you are connected to a BlackBerry Server. Go to **Messages** (email), press the **Menu** key, and select **Email Settings** to adjust these items.

Meeting Invitations

Just like on your desktop computer, you may check people's availability; invite attendees to meetings you schedule right on your BlackBerry. And, just like on your desktop, you may accept, decline, or tentatively accept meeting invitations you receive on your BlackBerry. Learn more on page 350.

NOTE: Sending and responding to meeting invitations is a feature available even without having your BlackBerry tied to BES.

NOTE: If you have not received your activation password, then you need to ask your help desk or technology support department for that password before you can complete this process.

Windows PC Setup

This chapter shows you how to install Desktop Manager Software on your Windows computer. Then it shows you how to synchronize your contacts, calendar, tasks and memos, backup and restore, and more.

If you want to transfer files and media, then check out Chapter 3 "Windows PC Media and File Transfer" found on page 123. (You may need some of the instructions in this chapter on how to install Desktop Manager if you want to use it as your method to transfer files.)

Have an Apple Mac computer? Please go to Chapter 4 "Apple Mac Setup" on page 143.

Unless you work at an organization that provides you access to a BES, if you are a Windows user, you will need to use BlackBerry Desktop Manager to do a number of things:

■ Transfer or synchronize your personal information (addresses, calendar, tasks, and notes) between your computer and your BlackBerry.

■ Back up and restore your BlackBerry data.

■ Install or remove an application.

■ Transfer or sync your media (songs, videos, and pictures) to your BlackBerry (see Chapter 3 on page 123)

CAUTION: Do not sync your BlackBerry with several computers .You could corrupt your BlackBerry and/or other databases, and end up with duplicates, or worse yet, deleted items.

Downloading Desktop Manager for Windows

Each new version of RIM's Desktop Manager program has come with more functionality and more versatility than the previous versions. So, it is always a good idea to keep up to date with the latest version of the Desktop Manager software.

The Disk from the BlackBerry Box

It is fairly likely that the disk that arrived with your brand new BlackBerry has a version of Desktop Manager that is already out of date. This is because many times, the CD was produced months ago, and in the meantime a new version has been released. So we recommend grabbing the latest version from the internet directly from www.blackberry.com.

Checking Your Current Version

If you have already installed Desktop Manager, you should check which version you currently have. The easiest was to do that is start up your Desktop Manager program, go to **Help**, and then to **About Desktop Manager**. The version number of your particular version will be shown here. If you don't have version 5.0.1 or higher, it is time to upgrade. Version 6.0 has just been released and is available at www.blackberry.com.

Getting the Latest Version of Desktop Manager

Try typing (or clicking—if you are reading this in e-book format) this link: http://na.blackberry.com/eng/services/desktop/. Otherwise, perform a web search for "BlackBerry Desktop Software download," pick the search result that looks correct, and go to the BlackBerry web site. Then follow the links to get to the download screen shown in Figure 2-1. Click the **Download** button at the bottom to get started.

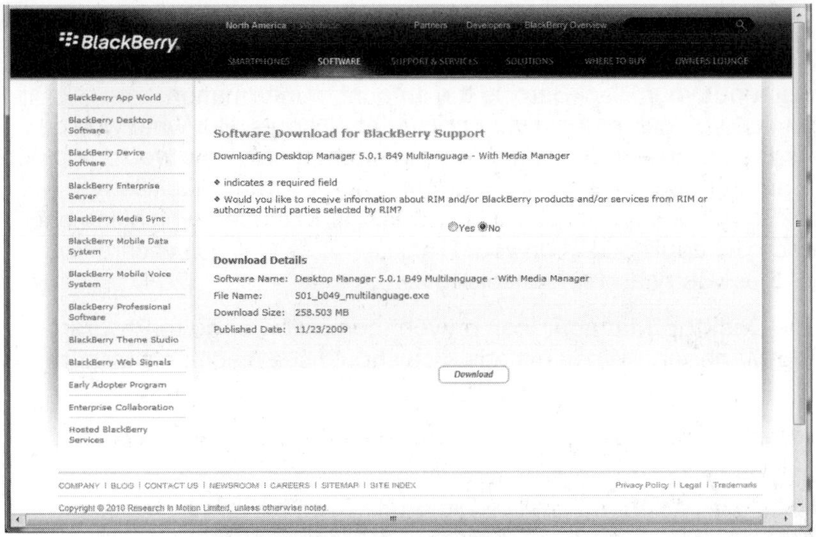

Figure 2-1. *BlackBerry Desktop Manager download page*

Save the file to a place where you will remember it. This is a large file so it may take some time to download.

Installing BlackBerry Desktop Manager

Locate and double-click the installation file that you downloaded. It will usually be in your **Downloads** folder unless you changed the default and will probably look something like Figure 2-2.

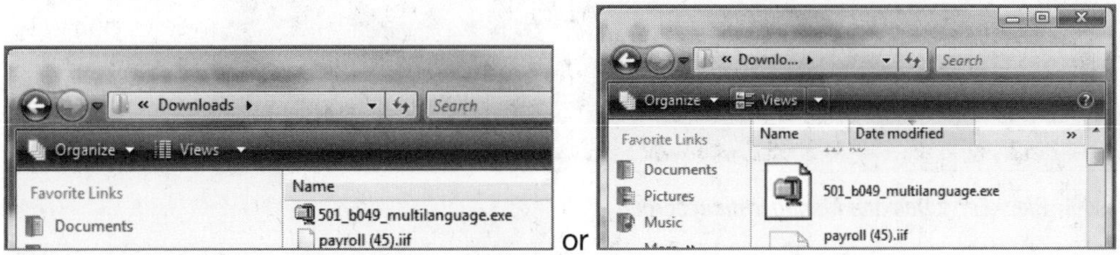

Figure 2-2. *Locating the downloaded installation file on your computer*

What the file looks like will depend on your view in Windows Explorer (e.g., Small Icons, Large Icons, List, or Details). The first few numbers in the file name correspond to the version of Desktop Manager; in Figure 2-2 it is 501 for version 5.0.1.

After you double-click the install file, then follow the directions to complete the installation. Choose **Integrate with a personal email account** unless your BlackBerry is tied to a BES.

Overview of BlackBerry Desktop Manager

One of the great things about your BlackBerry is the amount of information, entertainment, and fun that you can carry in your pocket at all times. But what would happen if you lost your BlackBerry or lost some of your information? How would you get it back? What if you wanted to put music from your computer on your BlackBerry? Fortunately, your BlackBerry comes with BlackBerry Desktop Manager, which can back up information and load new applications on your BlackBerry, as well as synchronize your computer to your BlackBerry and add media to it.

To get started, click the **Desktop Manager** icon on your computer, or go to **Programs ➤ BlackBerry ➤ Desktop Manager.** When it starts, you should see a screen similar to Figure 2-3.

Make sure your BlackBerry is attached to your computer via the USB cable provided.

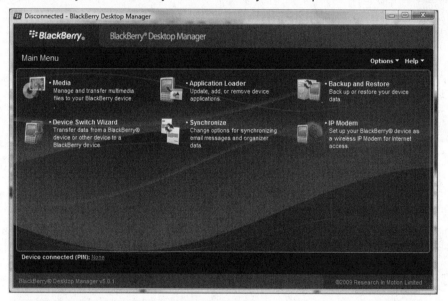

Figure 2-3. *BlackBerry Desktop Manager main screen*

> **NOTE:** Version 5.0.1 is shown in Figure 2-3; your version may be higher.

You will see the following five or six icons (the **IP Modem** icon may not show up for you, we tell you why below) in **Desktop Manager**:

The **Media** icon is for transferring media (songs, videos, pictures, and ringtones) between your computer and your BlackBerry. We discuss the **Media** icon (**Media Manager** and **Media Sync** on page 123).

The **Application Loader** is for installing or removing BlackBerry icons and upgrading your BlackBerry System Software version.

The **Backup and Restore** icon is for making a full backup of all your data on your BlackBerry and restoring (or selected databases) at a later time.

Along the second row is the **Device Switch Wizard.** This **Wizard** can be very helpful for moving your data from an old device (BlackBerry or non-BlackBerry) to a new BlackBerry.

Next is the **Synchronize** icon that controls the settings for synchronizing your data including your **address book**, calendar, tasks, memos and more to keep your computer and your BlackBerry up-to-date with one another.

The **IP Modem** icon allows you to connect your Laptop computer to the internet using your BlackBerry. You may not see the **IP Modem** icon. Some wireless carriers disable this feature within Desktop Manager causing the icon to disappear once you connect your BlackBerry to your computer. Learn more about this **IP Modem** feature in Chapter 26 "Connect as Tethered Modem" on page 477.

TIP: Instead of using Application Loader, you can install new software icons wirelessly right on your BlackBerry; see Chapter 25 "BlackBerry App World" on page 467.

NOTE: Most wireless carriers require you purchase a separate "BlackBerry as a Modem" or "Tethering" data plan in order to use this feature.

Entering Your Device Password

If you have enabled password security on your BlackBerry, you will have to enter your password on your computer right after you connect your BlackBerry to your computer, as shown in Figure 2-4.

Figure 2-4. *BlackBerry Desktop Manager device password screen*

Device Switch Wizard

If you are upgrading from another BlackBerry, Palm, or Windows Mobile device, you will want to use the Device Switch Wizard in Desktop Manager.

- **Device Switch Wizard**
  Transfer data from a BlackBerry® device or other device to a BlackBerry device.

After clicking the Device Switch Wizard, you will see that you have two options depending on the type of device you were using before your BlackBerry Storm, as shown in Figure 2-5.

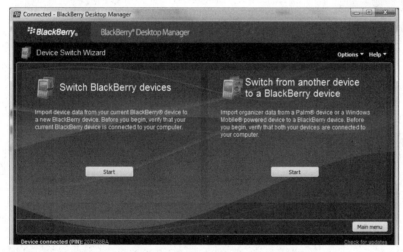

Figure 2-5. *Device Switch Wizard main screen in Desktop Manager*

Moving from another BlackBerry

You'll first need to connect the old (called "current") BlackBerry to your computer in order to get started. Then click the **Start** button and follow the onscreen instructions. Your current BlackBerry data will be backed up to your computer. Then you connect your new Storm to the computer so all data (including email setup and other settings) can be restored.

> **NOTE:** Not all third-party applications on your old BlackBerry will be able to be copied to your new BlackBerry. The Storm will have a newer OS, and may have a different screen size, so some third-party applications that worked fine on your old BlackBerry will not work on the Storm.

Moving from a Palm or Windows Mobile Device

You will need to connect both your Palm/Windows Mobile handheld and your new BlackBerry to your computer at the same time. Then click the **Start** button, and you'll see the screen shown in Figure 2-6. Follow the onscreen directions.

> **NOTE:** Because the devices use different operating systems, not all the information from the Palm or Windows Mobile device will be copied to your BlackBerry.

Welcome to the Migration Wizard

This tool enables you to import desktop organizer data from a Palm®/Treo™ device or a Windows® Mobile™-based device to your BlackBerry® device. You can import contacts, calendar entries, tasks, and memos.

Note: To import desktop organizer data, your computer must be running Microsoft® Windows 2000 or later.

Verify that both the Palm/Treo device or Windows Mobile device and your BlackBerry device are connected to your computer.

Click **Next** to begin.

[Next >]   [Cancel]

Figure 2-6. *BlackBerry Desktop Manager Migration Wizard*

> **NOTE:** You will not be able to copy any icons or software from your Palm/Windows Mobile device to your BlackBerry. If you have a favorite application from Palm/Windows Mobile, then check out BlackBerry App World (see page 467) or the software vendor's web site to see if they have a version compatible with your BlackBerry Storm.

Synchronizing your BlackBerry

You will probably come to rely on your BlackBerry more and more as you get comfortable using it. Think about how much information you have stored in there.

> **TIP:** If you use Google for your contacts, you may already have set up synchronization when you set up your Gmail account (see the "Sync Google Contacts" section of Chapter 1 on page 61).

Now ask yourself, "Is all my information safely stored in my computer?" Then ask, "Is all of my BlackBerry information synchronized or shared with the information in my computer software?" Synchronizing your BlackBerry with Desktop Manager is very important. Your data will be safe and backed up or shared with the correct program on your computer—making things like your calendar, address book, and tasks more useful.

Setting Up the Sync

The first thing to do is to open Desktop Manager as you usually do by clicking the **Desktop Manager** icon on your home screen.

1. Connect your BlackBerry to your computer using the USB cable and make sure you see your BlackBerry PIN number in the lower-left corner, instead of the word **None**.

2. Then click the **Synchronize** icon.

3. Before you sync for the first time, click the **Synchronization** link—right under **Configure** on the left side of the screen.

4. Click the **Synchronization** button on the right side, next to **Configure synchronization settings for my desktop program**.

NOTE: If the **Synchronization** button is grayed out and not clickable, please make sure your BlackBerry is connected to your computer. If you see **None** instead of your PIN number in the lower-left corner, your BlackBerry is not connected to your computer.

Device connected (PIN): None

BlackBerry® Desktop Manager v5.0

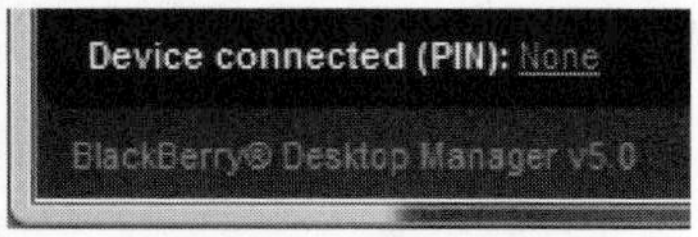

5. Now you will see the main IntelliSync program window shown in Figure 2-7.

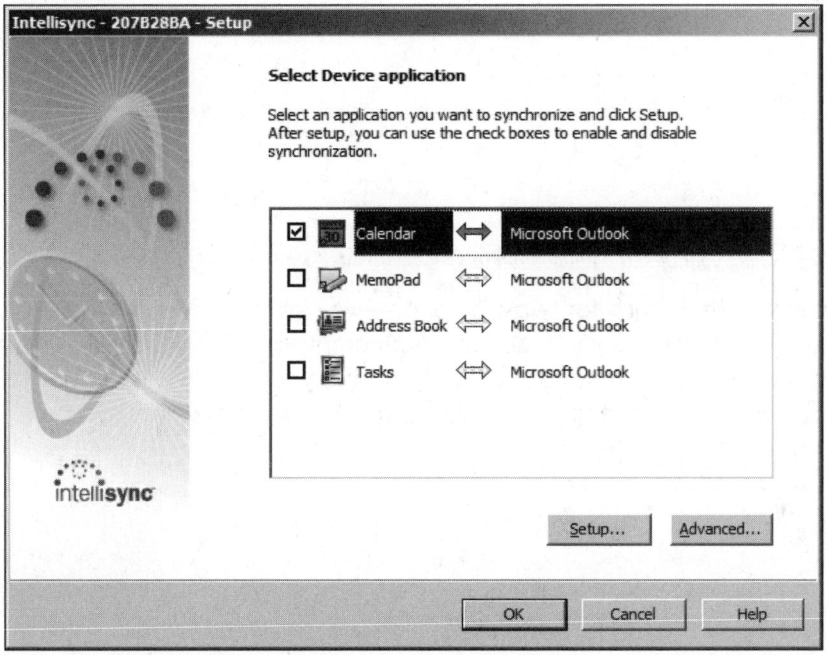

Figure 2-7. *IntelliSync main setup screen in Desktop Manager*

6. To get started, just check the box next to the icon you want to sync (or click the name of the icon, or click the check box and then click the **Setup** button at the bottom). For example, clicking **Calendar** and **Setup** will bring you to screens with details on how to sync your computer's calendar to your BlackBerry.

7. Select your desktop application from the list in Figure 2-8 and click **Next**.

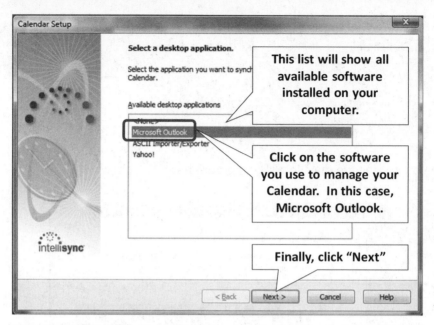

Figure 2-8. *Select your desktop application to sync using IntelliSync in Desktop Manager.*

8. Now you will see options for two-way or one-way sync. Two-way sync means that any changes you make on your computer or BlackBerry will be synchronized to the other device. This is what you usually will want. Under special circumstances, you might require or want one-way sync (see Figure 2-9).

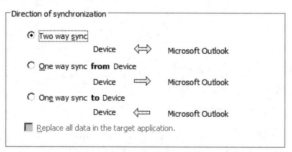

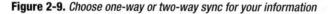

Figure 2-9. *Choose one-way or two-way sync for your information*

9. Click **Next** to see an advanced screen with more options. This screen shows options for the calendar. The screens for the address book, tasks, and MemoPad may have different options. We recommend the settings shown in Figure 2-10 to help make sure you never miss out on any data you enter on your BlackBerry if you forget to sync every day. These settings will sync calendar events up to 30 days old from your BlackBerry and 180 days into the future.

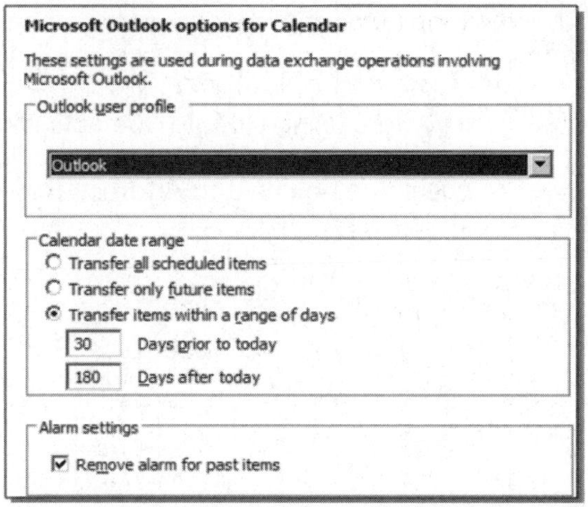

Microsoft Outlook options for Calendar

These settings are used during data exchange operations involving Microsoft Outlook.

Outlook user profile

> Outlook

Calendar date range
- ○ Transfer all scheduled items
- ○ Transfer only future items
- ● Transfer items within a range of days
  - 30   Days prior to today
  - 180   Days after today

Alarm settings
- ☑ Remove alarm for past items

Figure 2-10. *Select additional options for your calendar sync.*

10. Repeat the procedure for all the applications you want synced. Click **Next** then click **Finish** on the next screen. You'll see similar screens for all four applications, with some minor variations (see Figure 2-11).

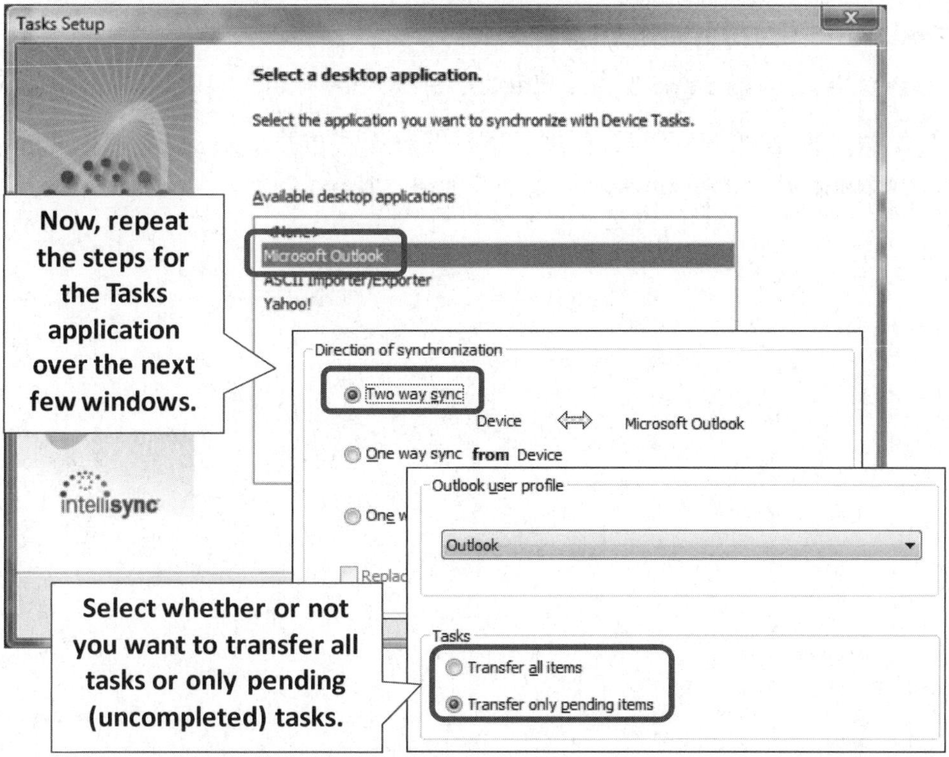

Tasks Setup

Select a desktop application.

Select the application you want to synchronize with Device Tasks.

Available desktop applications

> None?
> Microsoft Outlook
> ASCII Importer/Exporter
> Yahoo!

Now, repeat the steps for the Tasks application over the next few windows.

Direction of synchronization
- ● Two way sync   Device ⟺ Microsoft Outlook
- ○ One way sync **from** Device
- ○ One ...

☐ Replac...

intellisync

Outlook user profile

> Outlook

Select whether or not you want to transfer all tasks or only pending (uncompleted) tasks.

Tasks
- ○ Transfer all items
- ● Transfer only pending items

Figure 2-11. *Task sync options in Desktop Manager*

Once the setup is complete for two-way sync for all four applications, your screen should look similar to the following image.

If you are syncing all four applications, it will look like this:

If you are using Google Contacts wireless sync (see page 351), then you should not check the box next to **Address Book**, as shown here:

After the configuration is set, go back to the main synchronization screen and check the **Synchronize Automatically** box if you want Desktop Manager to automatically synchronize as soon as you connect your BlackBerry to your computer.

Finally, close out all the sync setup windows to save your changes.

Advanced Sync Configuration Screens

In order to see the advanced sync setup screens, follow these steps:

1. Go to the main synchronization screen, as shown previously.

2. Click **Advanced** on the screen shown in Figure 2-12.

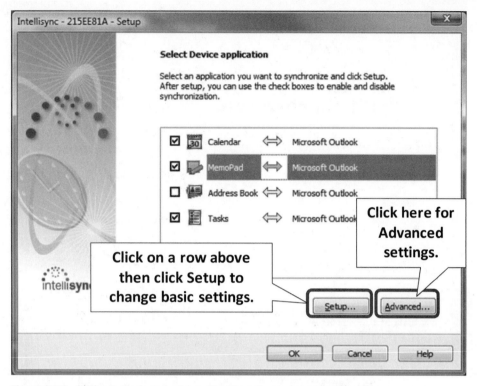

Figure 2-12. *Getting to basic and advanced settings for your sync configuration*

3. After clicking **Advanced**, you will see a screen similar to the one in Figure 2-13.

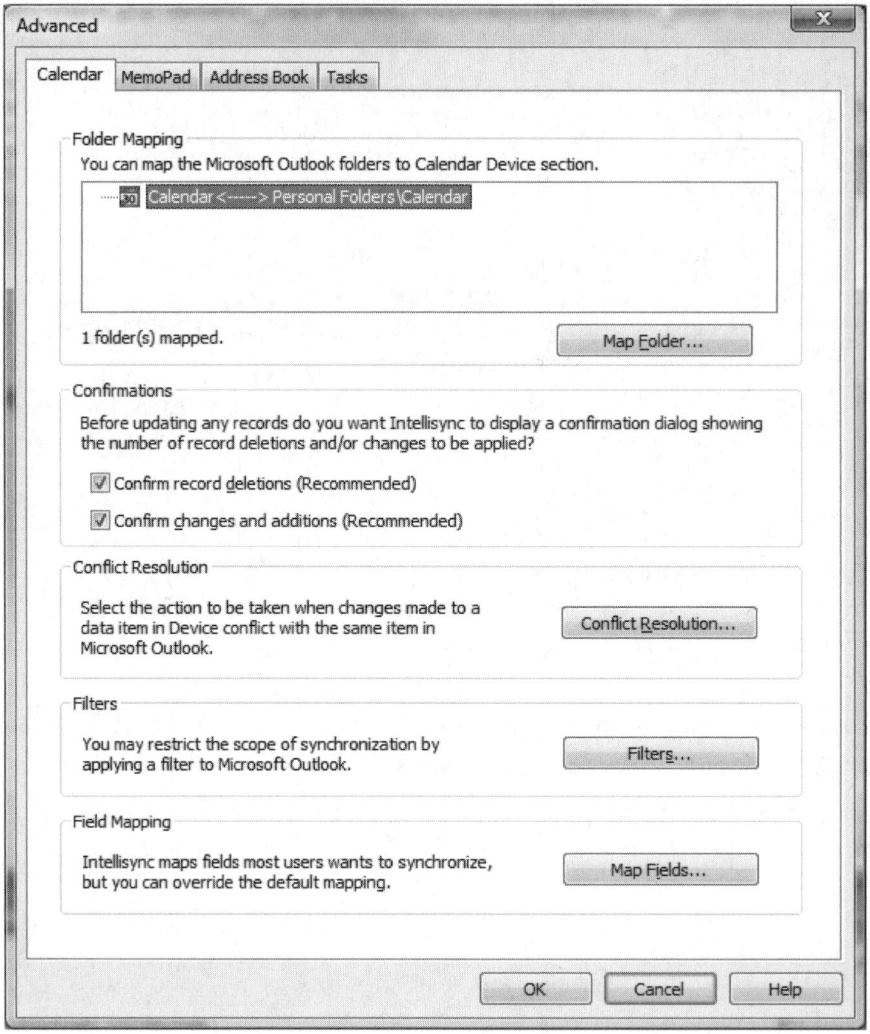

Figure 2-13. *Advanced settings screen for your sync configuration*

From this advanced settings screen, you can perform any of the following actions:

- Mapping folders
- Conflict resolution
- Creating filters
- Field mapping

Mapping Folders

The folder-mapping function allows you to select one or several folders to map from your desktop application to sync to your BlackBerry. In Figure 2-14, there are several Outlook folders from which to choose to map to sync the calendar to the BlackBerry.

1. Use the +/- signs in the left column to expand or collapse the views (see Figure 2-14).

2. Select individual items (such as **Calendar**) from the left by clicking them.

3. Click the **Add** button in the middle to add this item to the sync.

4. To remove a selected item from the sync, click it in the right column, and then click the **Remove** button in the middle.

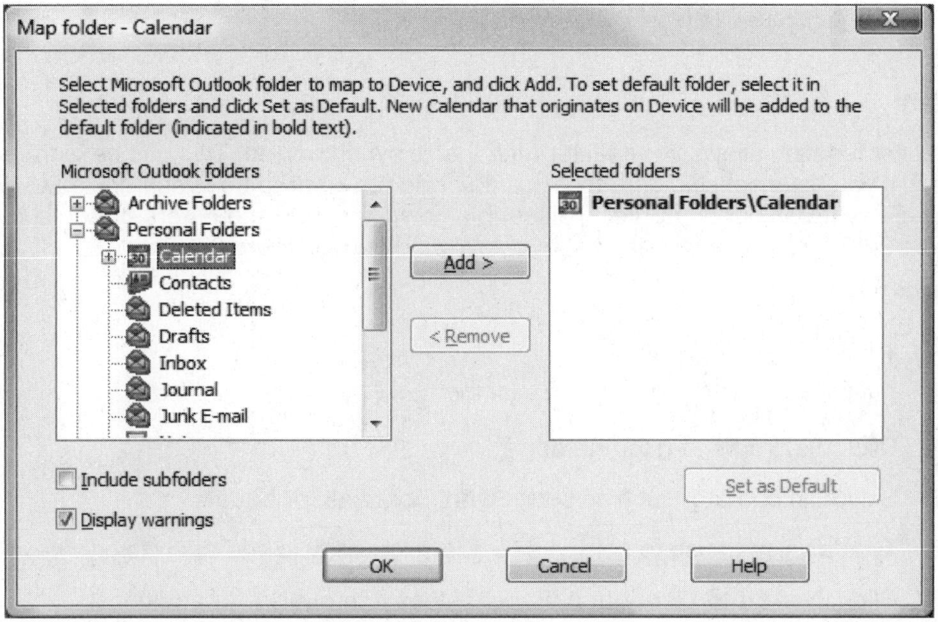

Figure 2-14. *Mapping folders to sync to your BlackBerry*

Conflict Resolution

Most syncs that run you will not see the conflict resolution window. Only when the software determines that information for the same record (same contact, calendar, task or memopad item) has been changed on your BlackBerry and on your computer between a single sync will it ask you to resolve conflicts. The conflict resolution function allows you to determine if you want to review each sync change and determine whether the handheld or your computer will "win" in conflicts (or whether you should be asked each time). Being asked each time is the default and recommended setting. See Figure 2-15.

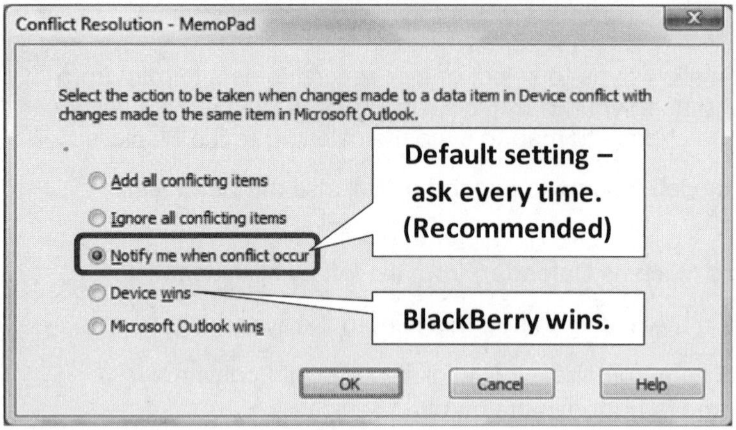

Figure 2-15. *Conflict Resolution window (for MemoPad)*

Filters

The filter function allows you to filter data that is synchronized. This can be extremely useful if you have specific data that you do or do not want to be synchronized to your BlackBerry from your computer. To set up a new filter, click the **Filters** button shown in Figure 2-13 and follow the steps shown following and in Figure 2-16.

1. Click **New**.

2. Enter a name for your filter.

3. Click **OK**.

4. Click the drop-down for **Field.**

5. Select an operator such as **starts with**, **contains**, or **equals**.

6. Type a value to use to compare for the selected field and operator.

7. Click the **Add to List** button. Repeat steps 4 through 7 for additional fields, if desired.

8. Click the **Rules** tab at the top.

9. Select one of the two conditions: **All Conditions** or **One or more**.

10. Click **OK** to return to the screen shown in the upper-right corner of Figure 2-16.

11. Check or uncheck the box that says **Delete from device any data that does not match the filter** as desired. Then click **OK** again to save your changes. .

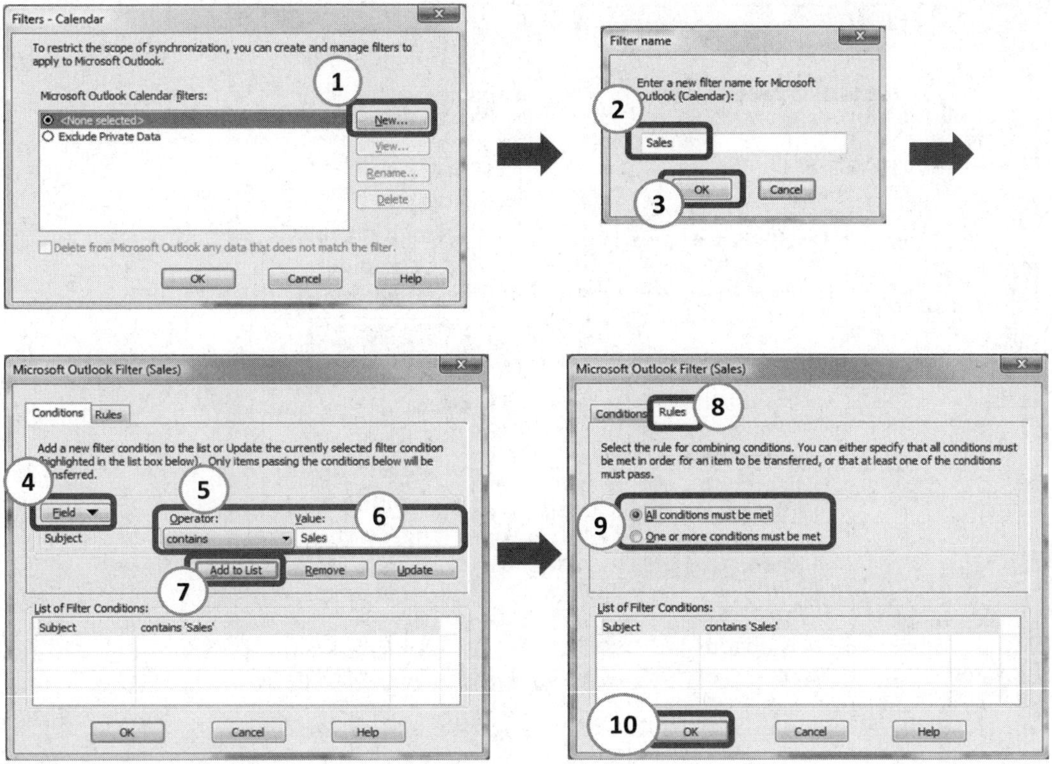

Figure 2-16. *Creating a new sync filter in Desktop Manager*

Field Mapping

The field mapping function allows you to map individual fields from your computer application into your BlackBerry. This can be useful if you need to fine-tune the information that is put onto your BlackBerry (see Figure 2-17). You can perform the following actions:

- To map a field, click between the left and right columns until you see the double arrow.

- To unmap a field, click between the left and right columns until it is blank (the double arrow goes away).

- To change which field is mapped on the right column, drag it up or down and drop it.

You may need to scroll down the list to see all the possible fields to be mapped.

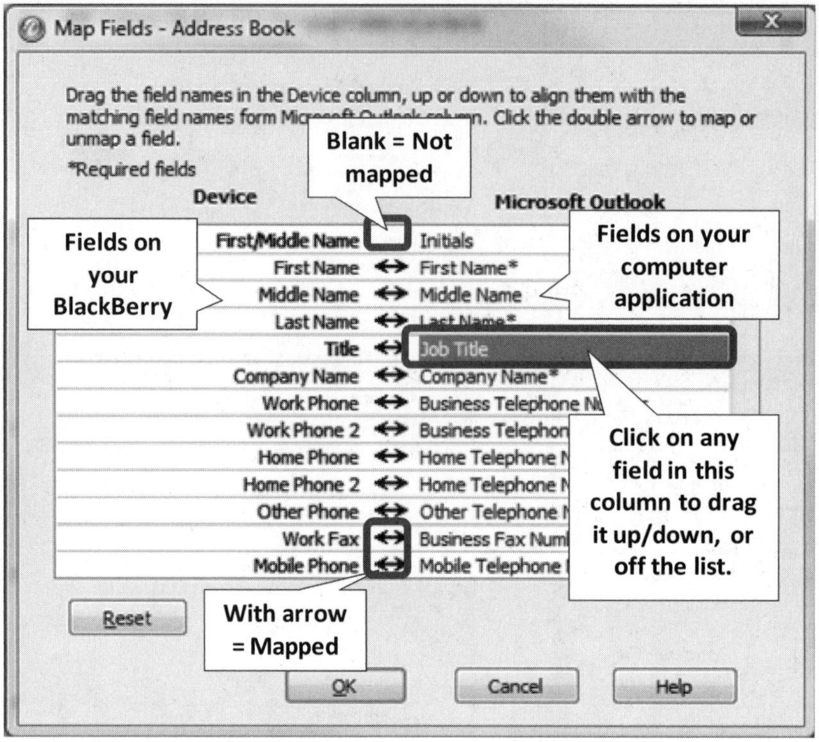

Figure 2-17. *Adjusting field mapping for the sync*

To return to the main Synchronize screen, click **OK** or **Save**.

Running the Sync

To get the sync started the first time, you need to take the following steps. You can automate the sync so you don't have to perform these steps every time. We show you how to automate the sync in the next section.

1. Click the **Synchronize** link in the left-hand column (see Figure 2-18).

2. Make sure the box next to **Synchronize organizer data** is checked.

3. Click the **Synchronize** button in the middle of the window to start your sync.

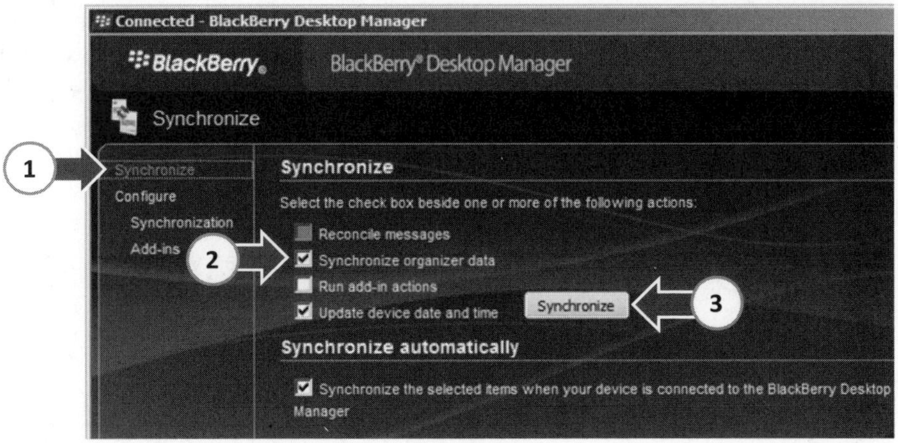

Figure 2-18. *Steps to start the sync in Desktop Manager*

After starting the sync, you will see a small window pop up showing you status of the current sync.

Automating the Sync

If you click the check box at the bottom of the Synchronize screen shown in 2-18, your BlackBerry will automatically sync every time you connect it to your computer.

Accepting or Rejecting Sync Changes

During the sync, if there are additions or deletions found in either the BlackBerry or the computer application, a dialog box will appear giving you the option to accept or reject the changes (see Figure 2-19). Click **Details** if you want to see more about the specific changes found.

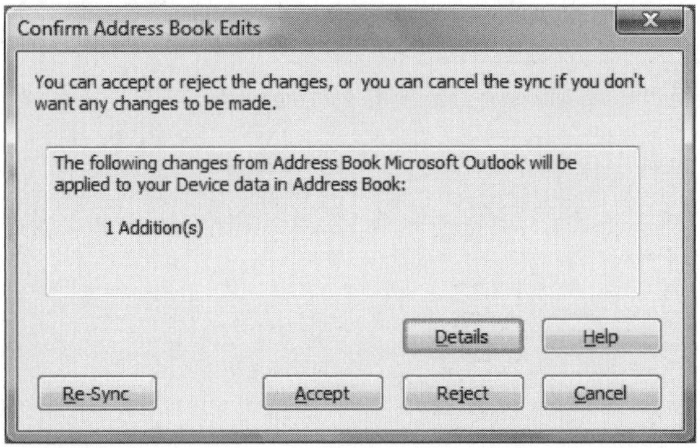

Figure 2-19. *Accepting or rejecting changes found during the sync*

Usually, we recommend accepting the changes unless something looks strange. Finally, the synchronization process will come to an end and your data will be transferred to both your BlackBerry and your computer. If you want more details on what has changed on your BlackBerry and computer, click the **Details** button.

Troubleshooting Your Sync

Sometimes you will encounter errors or warning messages when you try to sync. In this section we try help you through some of the more common issues.

Message that Default Calendar Service Has Changed

Sometimes you may see a message similar to the one shown in Figure 2-20. What usually happens when you add a new email address is that it takes precedence as the default email address or service for all new calendar entries you add on your BlackBerry.

Click **Cancel** on the screen shown in Figure 2-20 and follow the steps following to verify everything is OK before you sync again.

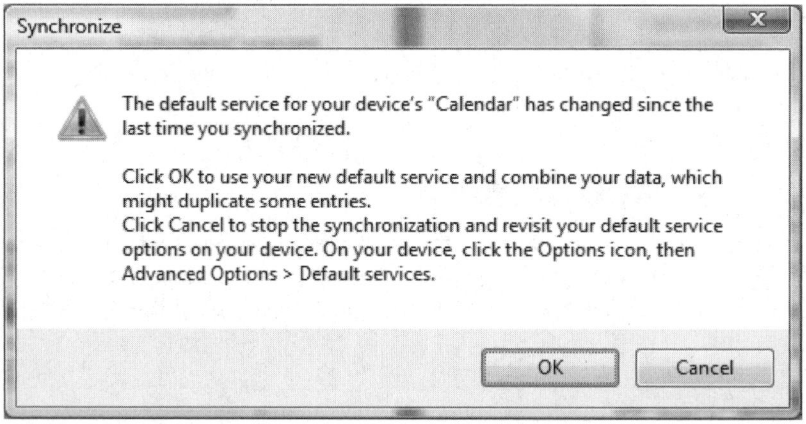

Figure 2-20. *Message informing you that the default calendar service message has changed*

After pressing the **Cancel** button, follow these steps:

1. Click the **Options** icon on your Storm.

2. Click **Advanced Options**.

3. Click **Default Services**.

4. You will see a screen similar to the one shown. Verify that the email address under the **Calendar** item at the top is set correctly. If not, click and adjust it.

5. Press the **Menu** key and select **Save**.

6. Resync using Desktop Manager, and if you see the same error—ignore it by clicking **OK**.

Closing and Restarting Desktop Manager

Try closing down Desktop Manager and restarting it; sometimes this can help with whatever issues you may be having.

Removing and Reconnecting your BlackBerry

Sometimes a simple disconnect and reconnect can also help. Give it a try.

Fixing Specific Errors with Calendar, Address Book, MemoPad, or Task Sync

Try the sync again after it fails and watch it closely, Note where it fails—on the calendar, address book, MemoPad, or tasks—by watching the status screen. Once you figure out where the sync fails, then you can try one thing to get it running again: clearing out the problem database or deleting it from your BlackBerry and starting the sync again.

> **CAUTION:** Performing this process will force you to lose any changes you have made on your BlackBerry since your last successful sync.

1. From the main Desktop Manager screen, click **Backup and Restore**.

2. Click **Backup**. Make a note of the file name and location—you may need to use it later to restore data if this troubleshooting does not work. In Figure 2-21, the backup file name is **Backup-(2008-12-12)-1.ipd** (Figure 2-21).

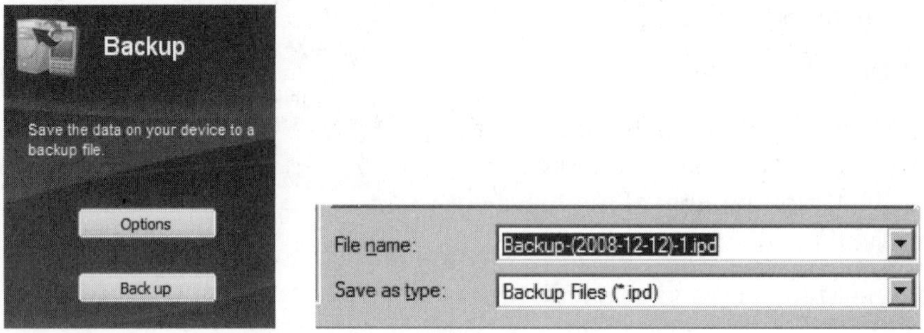

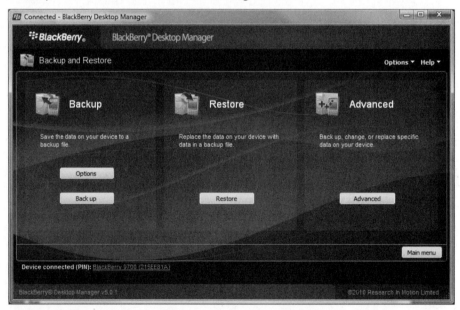

Figure 2-21. *Perform a full backup and note the file name.*

3. Once your full backup is completed, press and click the **Advanced** button from the Backup and Restore screen shown in Figure 2-22.

Figure 2-22. *Main Backup and Restore screen in Desktop Manager*

4. Now you will be on the screen shown in Figure 2-23. Locate the problem database in the right-hand window (BlackBerry). We want to clear out both the **Address Book** and **Address Book - All** databases from the BlackBerry. (Press the **Ctrl** key to click and select more than one database.)

5. Once both are selected in the right-hand window (Device databases), press and click the **Clear** button.

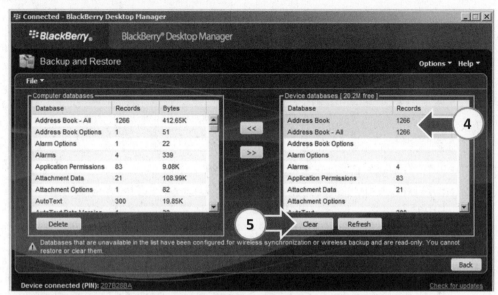

Figure 2-23. *Clear or erase a specific database from the BlackBerry.*

6. Once the databases have been cleared out, press and click the **Back** button.

7. Now try to sync again. Hopefully, this will correct the sync problem.

    If the problem has not been corrected, then you can restore the address book by taking the following steps:

8. Return to the Advanced Backup and Restore window as shown previously.

9. In the upper-right corner, click **File**, and then open the full backup file you just created, as shown in Figure 2-24.

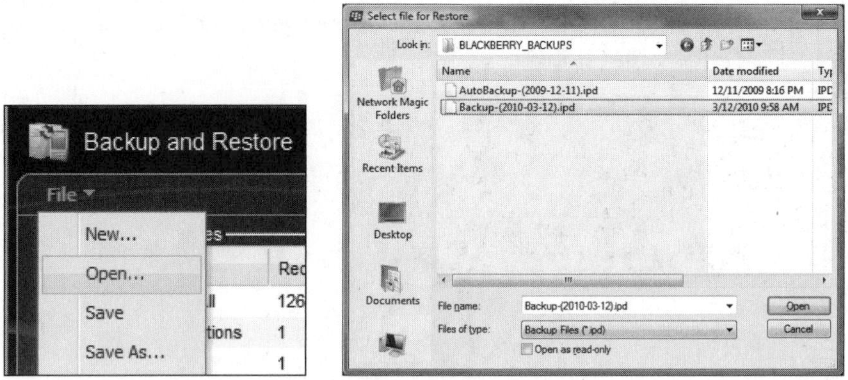

Figure 2-24. *Opening a previous backup file to restore*

10. Now you can highlight the correct databases from the full backup in the left-hand window (**Computer databases**). In this example we have clicked the **Address Book - All** database (see Figure 2-25).

11. To restore the selected database to your BlackBerry, click the ⟫ button in the middle of the screen.

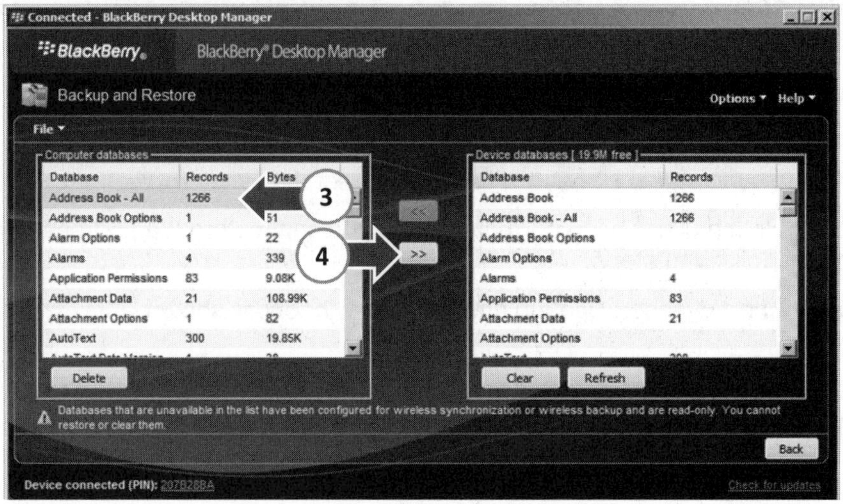

Figure 2-25. *Restoring a particular database to your BlackBerry*

Getting More Help for Desktop Manager Issues

Some of the Desktop Manager sync issues can be particularly tricky. Before you pull out too much hair, you should go try the BlackBerry technical knowledgebase. You should also try some of the more popular BlackBerry online discussion forums to see if others have experienced and solved similar issues.

To use the BlackBerry Knowledgebase, from your computer's web browser, go to
`http://na.blackberry.com/eng/support`. Then click the **BlackBerry Technical Solution
Center** link (or similar) in the left column.

Alternatively, you can pull up your favorite web browser and try a web search for the
particular issue you are facing.

The following are some of the BlackBerry forums that could be helpful with a variety of
issues:

- `www.crackberry.com`
- `www.blackberryforums.com`
- `www.pinstack.com`
- `www.blackberrycool.com`

Application Loader

• Application Loader
Update, add, or remove device
applications.

Use this icon to add or remove software from your
BlackBerry. This is also used to update your BlackBerry
OS or system software. There are easier ways to load or
remove software from your device—see Chapter 25
"BlackBerry App World" on page 467 and Chapter 29
"Adding or Removing Apps" on page 515.

First, make sure your BlackBerry is connected to your computer and showing in the
lower-left corner of the Desktop Manager screen next to **Device connected (PIN)**. If you
see **none**, then you will need to try to get it connected. Some of the easier things to do
are unplugging the USB cable and plugging it in again, plugging the cable into another
USB port, shutting down and restarting Desktop Manager, or restarting your computer.

Now click the **Application Loader** icon to see the screen shown in Figure 2-26.

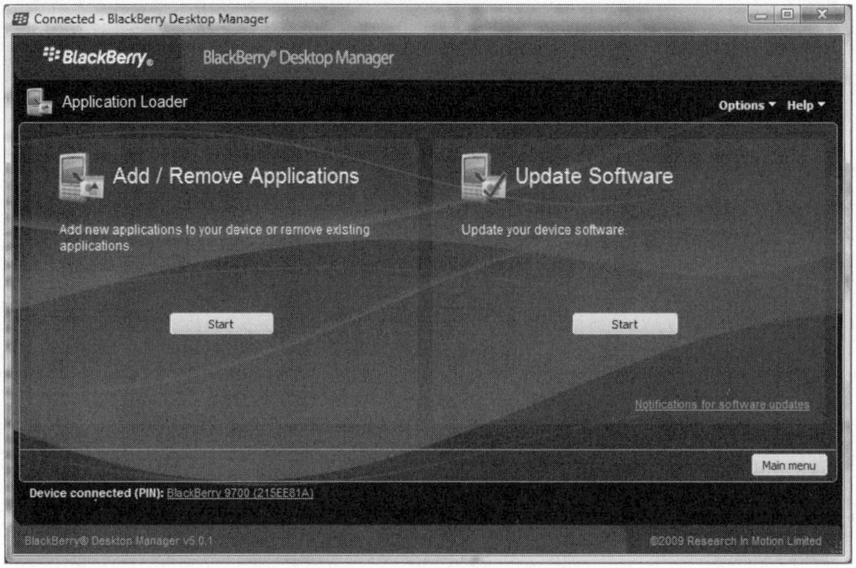

Figure 2-26. *Application Loader main window in Desktop Manager*

Adding and Removing Applications

To add or remove applications, which could be third party or portions of the main system software and core applications (such as language files), follow these steps:

1. Click the **Start** button under **Add/Remove Applications** on the screen in Figure 2-26.

   NOTE: You will first see a task-in-progress window showing you that the software is reading your current BlackBerry configuration and installed software.

   Listed at the top of the screen shown in Figure 2-27 is your current BlackBerry system software (the device in this example is running 5.0.0; your device may show a different version).

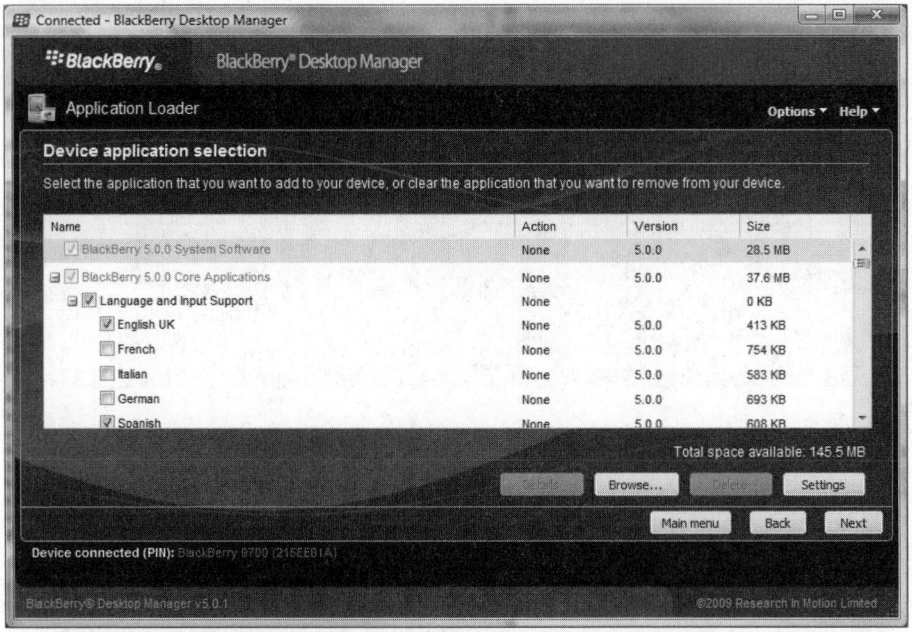

Figure 2-27. *Add/remove software screen in the Application Loader of Desktop Manager*

2. You can add or remove languages using the Application Loader software. To add an item, check the box next to it. To remove an item, uncheck the box next to it.

3. Scroll down using the scroll bar on the right edge to see more language options. Part of the way down you will notice **Supplemental SureType(TM) Wordlists**, as shown in Figure 2-28.

4. If you work in the finance, legal, or medical professions, then you may want to add some of these customized dictionaries. These will help when you use SureType or the spell checker to guess what you are trying to type. In the Figure 2-28, we want to add English financial and medical terms so we checked both of the corresponding boxes. Notice the **Action** column shows **Install** as a status.

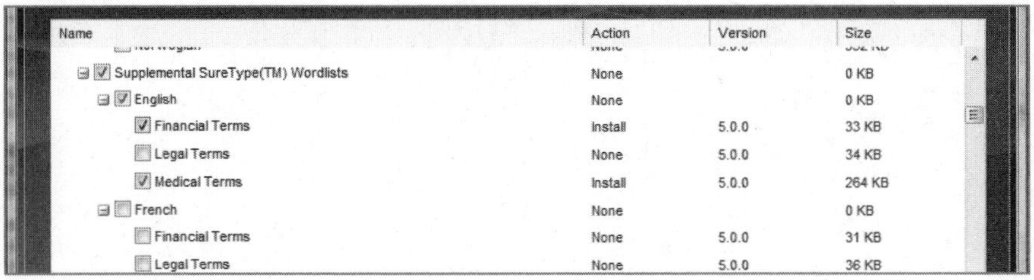

Figure 2-28. *Supplemental word lists for financial, legal, and medical terms*

5. To see all your installed third-party applications, scroll down to the bottom of the list, as shown in Figure 2-29. We have a number of apps installed, and we have decided to remove or uncheck the boxes for two of them: **U2 Mobile Album** and **BlackBerry Developer Conference Mobile Guide**.

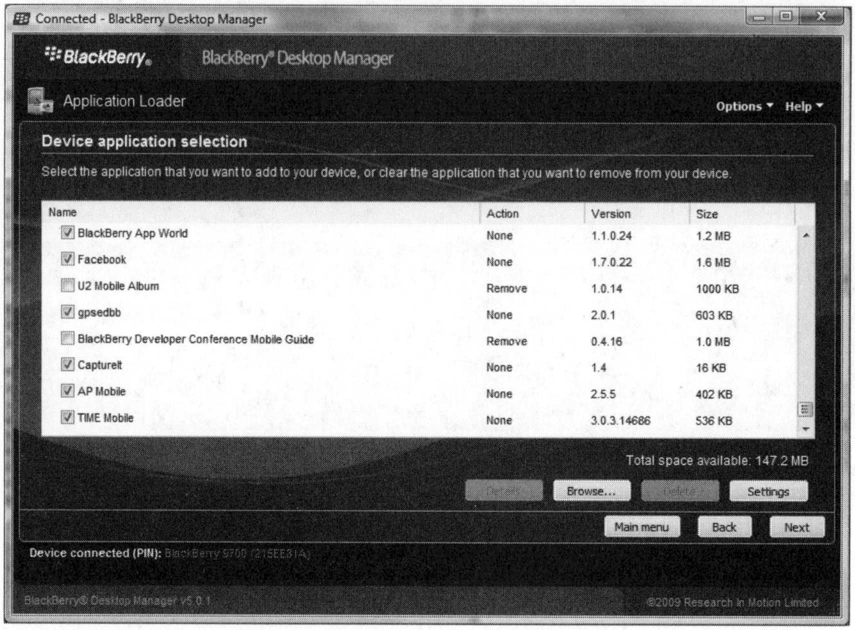

Figure 2-29. *Third-party applications are shown at the bottom of the list.*

6. Finally, to complete the adding or removing of applications, click the **Next** button in the lower-right corner to see the Summary screen shown in Figure 2-30.

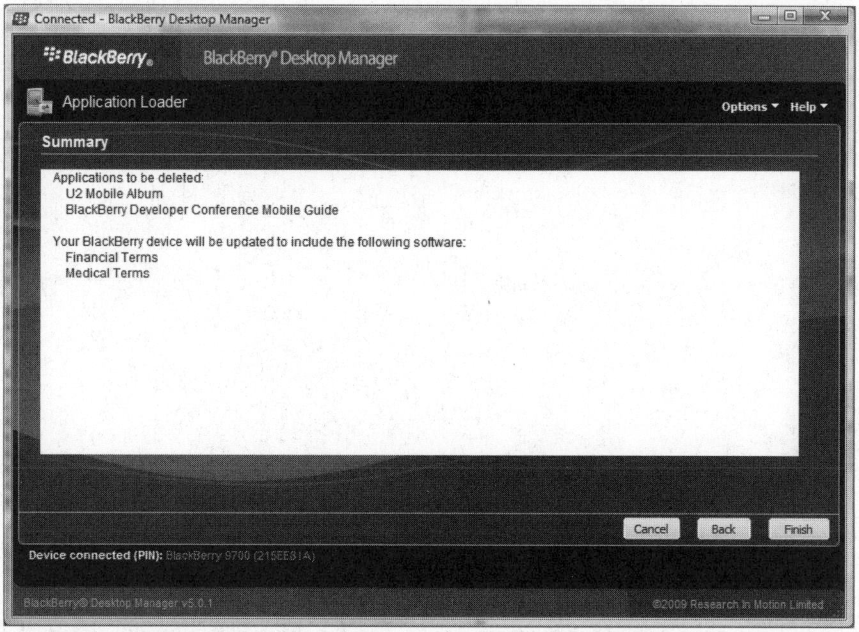

Figure 2-30. *Application Loader summary screen showing your selections*

7. If you see that you have made a mistake, then click **Back** to return to the previous screen; otherwise, click the **Finish** button to execute the listed actions. While the software is working you will see a status window similar Figure 2-31.

In some cases, this process is very fast, taking just a minute or so. However, in other cases, especially if you are updating the system software or any part of it (like adding or removing core dictionaries as we did in this example), you will see a message that says, "This task might take up to 30 minutes to complete."

In our testing, the process took only about 6 minutes (but it felt like 30 minutes!).

Task In Progress (3 of 3)

⚠ **Do not disconnect your device.** Your device or its data might become unusable if you disconnect the device before this process completes.

Task	Status
Download device software	Completed
Loading applications	Completed
Wait for device initialization	●○○○○

Connecting to device (This task might take up to 30 minutes to complete.)

☑ Show details   Cancel

Figure 2-31. *Application Loader status screen*

Have patience while this is happening, because if you disconnect your BlackBerry from your computer during this process, your BlackBerry might become unusable.

Finally, when the process is finished, you should see a small status message in the upper-right corner, as shown in Figure 2-32.

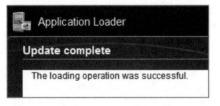

Application Loader

Update complete

The loading operation was successful.

Figure 2-32. *Application Loader successful completion message*

Updating Device Software

Also in the Application Loader, you can update the device software, which is the system software running on your BlackBerry smartphone. You can actually upgrade and downgrade using this feature.

1. Click the **Start** button under the Update Software section of the Application Loader main screen (refer back to Figure 2-26).

2. The software will then check your BlackBerry and the internet to see if there are updates available.

3. Finally, you will see a screen similar to the one shown in Figure 2-33.

4. Depending on what version you have installed on your BlackBerry and what is available, you may see one or more rows with **(Current)**, **(Upgrade)**, or **(Downgrade)** next to them.

a. To upgrade your software, check the box next to the **(Upgrade)** item and click the **Next** button.

b. To downgrade your software, check the box next to the **(Downgrade)** item and click the **Next** button.

c. To make no changes, just click the **Main Menu** button.

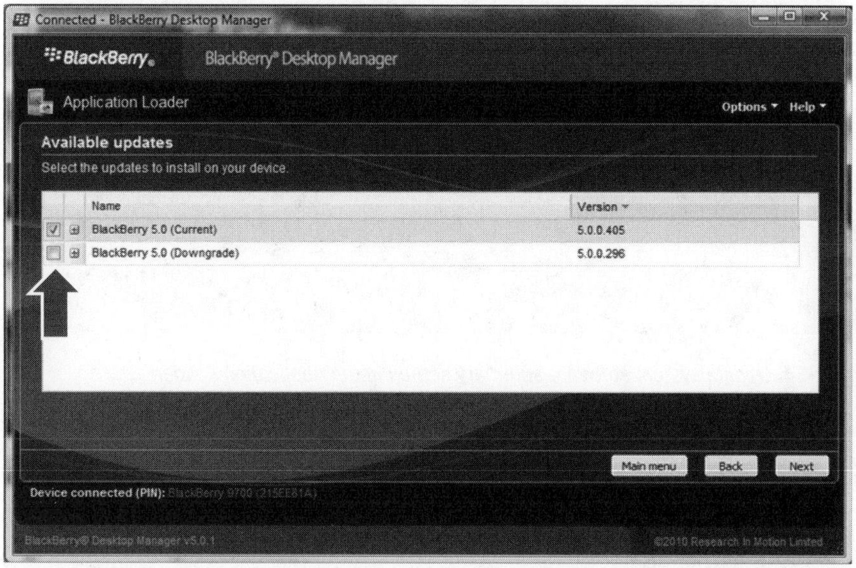

Figure 2-33. *Update system software screen in the Application Loader*

5. If you are upgrading or downgrading software, then you will see some screens telling you that the Desktop Manager software is backing up your BlackBerry, then erasing it and reinstalling software, and then restoring your data. This process could take more than 10 minutes.

6. Finally, you will see a summary screen similar to Figure 2-34.

7. Click the **Main Menu** button to finish the process and return to the main Desktop Manager window.

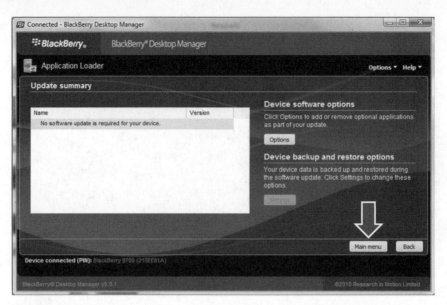

Figure 2-34. *Update system software summary screen in the Application Loader*

Backup and Restore

Use this feature to protect the important data on your BlackBerry. You can also use some of the advanced features to help with troubleshooting your Desktop Manager sync (see page 101.)

Click the **Backup and Restore** icon to see the screen shown in Figure 2-35.

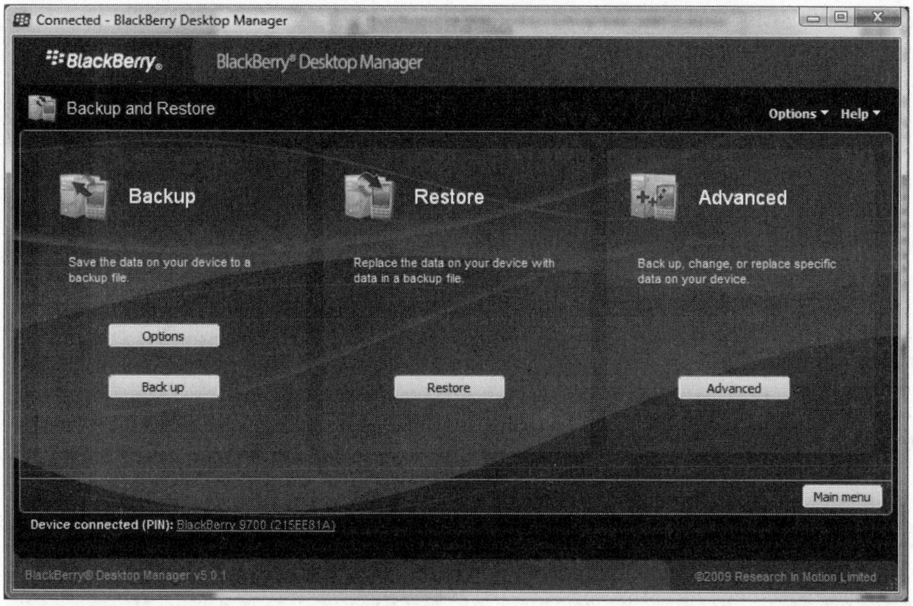

Figure 2-35. *Backup and Restore main window*

Click the Options button under the Backup heading on the left side of the page to see the Backup Options screen, as shown in Figure 2-36.

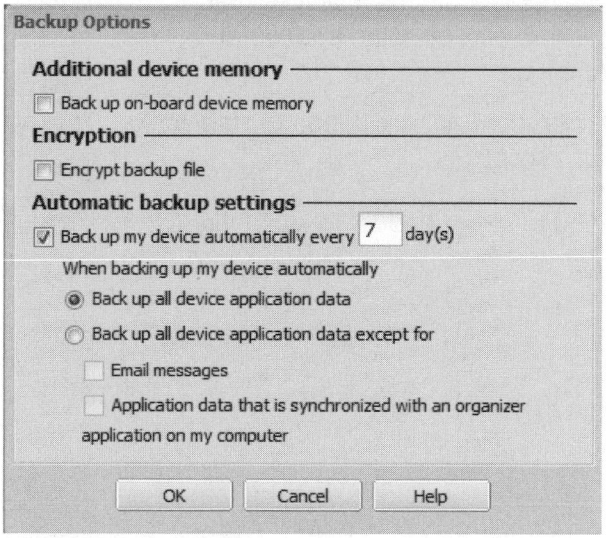

Figure 2-36. *Backup Options screen*

If you want to back up data stored in your main BlackBerry memory (e.g., pictures, video recordings, voice notes, or other information), then you should check the box next to **Back up on-board device memory**.

If you have especially confidential information and want to encrypt your backup file for added security, then check the box next to **Encrypt backup file**.

By default, all your device data is backed up once every seven days. You can adjust this to be any number of days; try fewer days if you are more worried about your data being lost.

The backup can take several minutes or more depending on how much information you have stored on your device. The easiest way to speed up the backup is to back up less information. Since your email is on your computer or email server anyway, you might want to check the **Email Messages** box on this screen, which will skip backing up email. If you sync regularly with your computer, then you could check the box next to **Application data that is synchronized with an organizer application on my computer**.

When you're done, click **OK** to save your settings.

Backing Up Your BlackBerry

In order to backup your BlackBerry, follow these steps:

1. Connect your BlackBerry to your computer.

2. If you are not already in the Backup and Restore menu, from the main Desktop Manager screen, click the **Backup and Restore** icon.

3. Next, click the **Back up** button to start your backup process.

4. A dialog box will pop up asking you to select a folder to store your full backup file (see Figure 2-37).

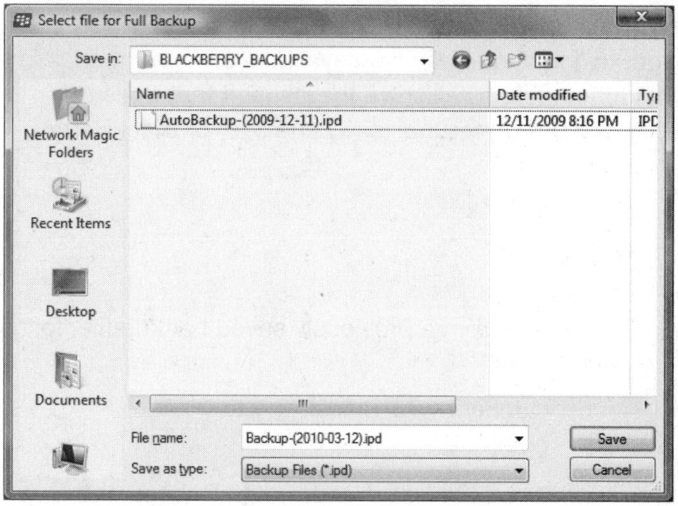

Figure 2-37. *Choose a folder to store the backup file.*

5. Use the drop-down list at the top or one of the icons to the left to select your backup file location.

6. Notice that the file name **Backup-(2010-03-12).ipd** is in year-month-date format so you can easily see the date of your backup.

> **CAUTION:** The authors have both experienced computer hard disk failures. We highly recommend storing the backup on at least one external location. This could be a USB thumb drive, an external USB drive, another computer in your network or any location off of your hard disk.

7. Once you have selected the location of your backup file, click the **Save** button to start the backup. You will then see a status window similar to Figure 2-38.

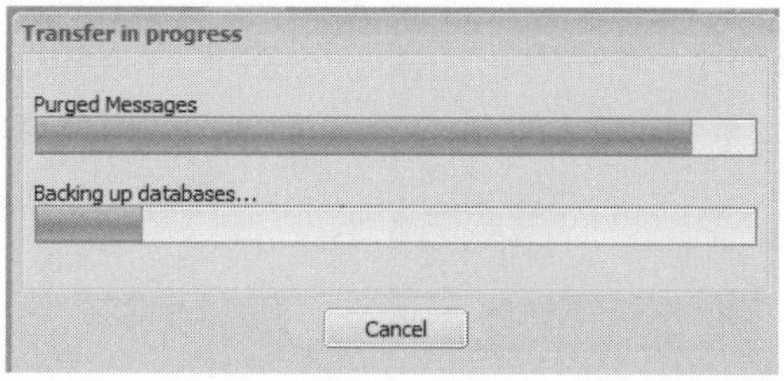

Figure 2-38. *Backup status window*

8. Finally, you will see a "Backup Successfully Created" message. If you see any error message, try looking at any help available on the screen. Sometimes just redoing the backup will solve the issue. If that does not help, try the BlackBerry discussion forums (see page 579) or BlackBerry technical knowledgebase for help.

Restoring Your BlackBerry

To restore from a previously saved backup file, follow these steps:

1. Connect your BlackBerry to your computer.

2. If you are not already in the Backup and Restore menu, from the main Desktop Manager screen, click the **Backup and Restore** icon.

3. Next, click the **Restore** button.

4. A dialog box will pop up asking you to select a folder to store your full backup file (see Figure 2-39).

Figure 2-39. *Select the folder and backup file to use for the restore.*

5. Use the drop-down list at the top or one of the icons to the left to locate your backup file to restore from.

6. Once you have located the file to use to restore data to your BlackBerry, click the **Open** button.

7. Next you will see a list of details of the information contained in the file you just opened. This allows you to confirm you want to use this restore file. Scroll down to see things like total records which is the same as the number of contacts in your (address book) and number of calendar entries: make sure they seem reasonable.

8. Click **Yes** to start the restore process (see Figure 2-40).

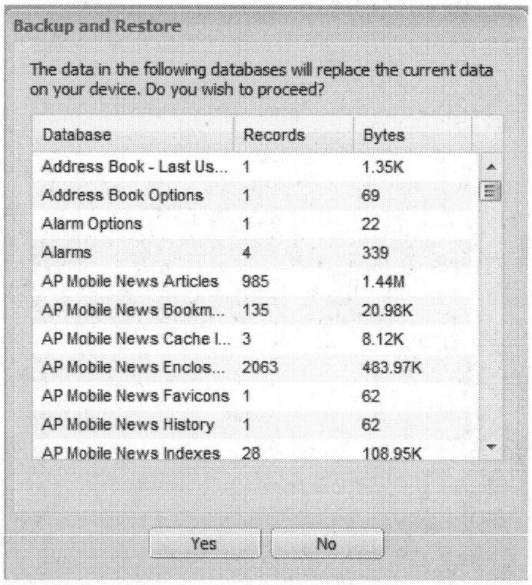

Backup and Restore

The data in the following databases will replace the current data on your device. Do you wish to proceed?

Database	Records	Bytes
Address Book - Last Us...	1	1.35K
Address Book Options	1	69
Alarm Options	1	22
Alarms	4	339
AP Mobile News Articles	985	1.44M
AP Mobile News Bookm...	135	20.98K
AP Mobile News Cache I...	3	8.12K
AP Mobile News Enclos...	2063	483.97K
AP Mobile News Favicons	1	62
AP Mobile News History	1	62
AP Mobile News Indexes	28	108.95K

Yes   No

Figure 2-40. *Confirm restore screen*

NOTE: The screen shown in 2-40 doesn't list a number of address book entries—only **Address Book Options** and **Address Book - Last Used**. This is because we happen to be using a wireless sync with Google Contacts. With any wireless sync, those databases (Addresses, Calendar, etc.) are not able to be backed up or restored using Desktop Manager. All these items are essentially backed up all day long with the wireless sync process.

Advanced Backup and Restore

You can use the Advanced feature in Backup and Restore in order to selectively back up, restore, or erase individual databases (addresses, calendar, MemoPad, etc.) on your BlackBerry.

NOTE: We showed how to erase only your address book and restore it to help with troubleshooting the Desktop Manager sync in the "Fixing Specific Errors" section on page 101.

1. Connect your BlackBerry to your computer.

2. If you are not already in the Backup and Restore menu, from the main Desktop Manager screen, click the **Backup and Restore** icon.

3. Next, click the **Advanced** button in the right portion of the screen to see the screen shown in Figure 2-41.

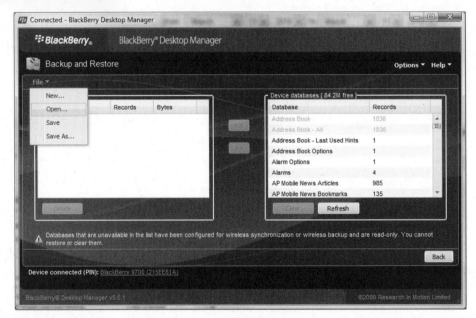

Figure 2-41. *Opening a backup file on the Advanced Backup and Restore screen*

4. The left side of the screen shows a backup file from your computer. If the left side is blank, then you will need to open up a backup file to use. Select **File   Open...**, as shown in Figure 2-41.

5. Navigate to a specific folder and backup file to open and click **Open**.

6. When the file is open, you will see the left-hand window fill up with the contents of that backup file (see Figure 2-42).

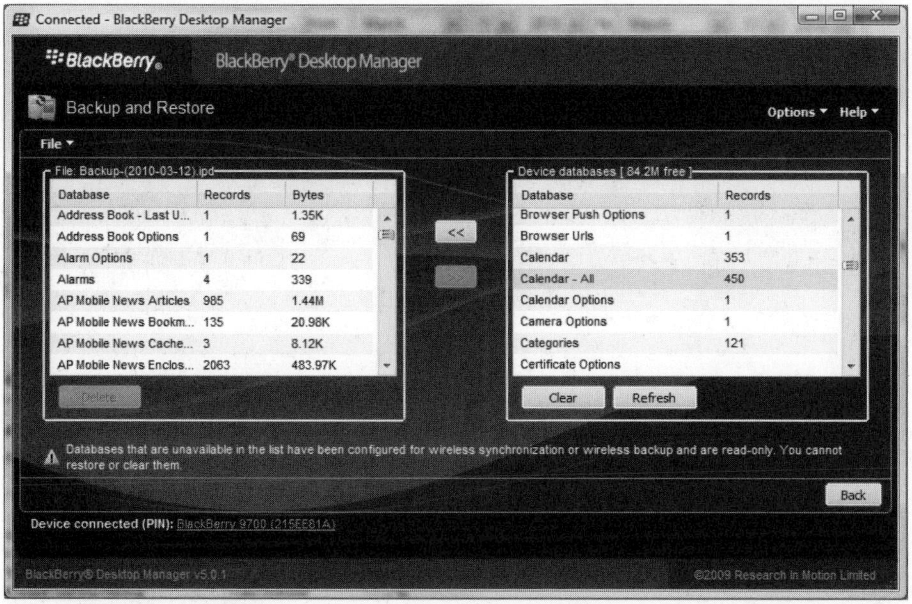

Figure 2-42. *Advanced Backup and Restore screen with backup file open in left window*

Now you can selectively back up, erase, or restore individual databases on your BlackBerry by following the steps outlined next.

Backing Up Specific Databases

In order to selectively back up a single databases or selected databases—for example, the Calendar, Address Book, or NotePad databases—follow these steps and refer to Figure 2-41.

1. Click in the right-hand window (Device databases) to highlight and select a database, or hold the **Ctrl** key on your keyboard to select several databases.

2. Click the << button in the middle to copy that information to the backup file on the left.

Erasing or Clearing Specific Databases

In order to selectively erase or clear a single database or several databases from your BlackBerry, follow these steps and refer to Figure 2-42.

1. Click in the right-hand window (Device databases) to highlight and select a database, or hold the **Ctrl** key on your keyboard to select several databases.

2. Click the **Clear** button under the right-hand window.

3. You will then see the screen shown in Figure 2-43; click **Yes** to confirm
    and delete the listed databases.

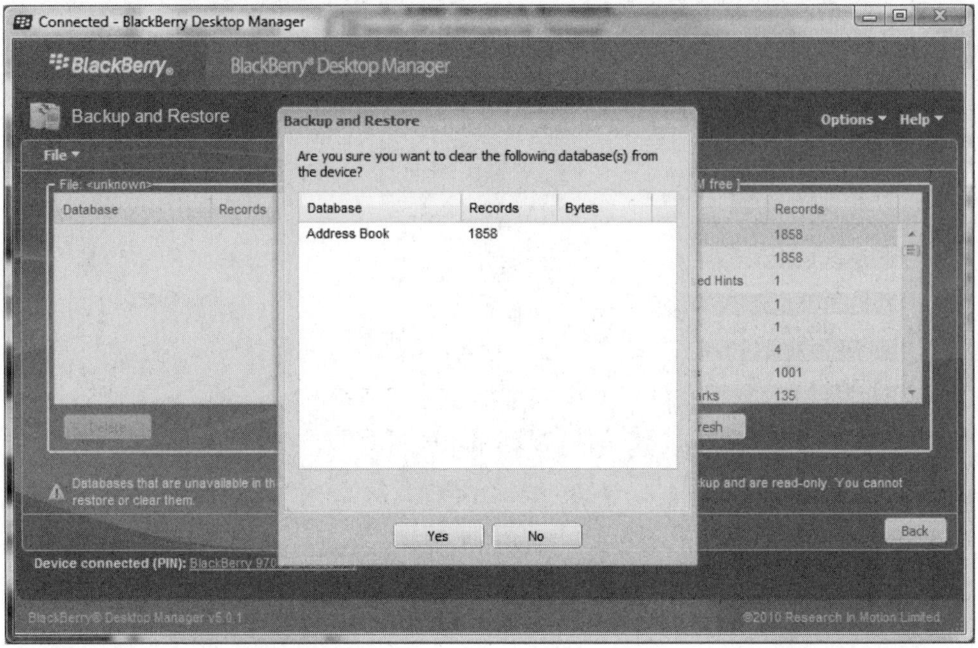

Figure 2-43. *Confirm that you want to clear or erase databases from your BlackBerry.*

How to Restore Specific Databases

In order to restore a file to your BlackBerry, follow these steps and refer to Figure 2-44:

1. You need to have a backup file open in the left window. If the left
    window is blank, click **File** > **Open** in the upper-left corner to open a
    backup file.

2. Click to select one or more database files in the left-hand window under
    File: Backup-(year-month-day).ipd.

3. Click the >> button in the middle to copy that information to your
    BlackBerry on the right side. In Figure 2-43 we have selected the
    Calendar database with 450 entries from the backup, and are getting
    ready to copy it to the BlackBerry.

4. Start the restore process by clicking **Yes** on the next screen which will
    look very similar to Figure 2-43.

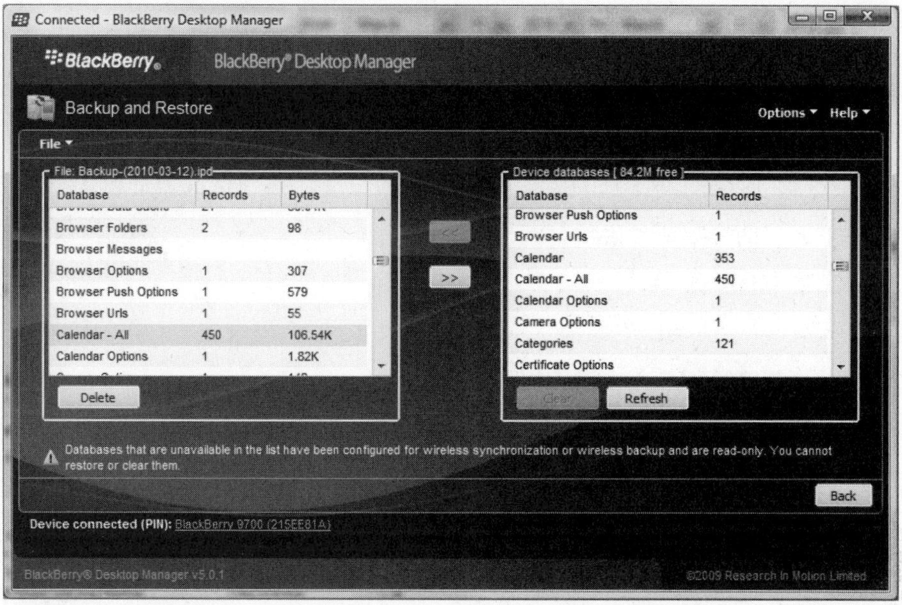

Figure 2-44. *Restoring specific databases from a backup file to your BlackBerry*

IP Modem

You may not see this icon in Desktop Manager because your wireless carrier may have disabled it or may provide separate software.

See Chapter 26 "Connect as Tethered Modem" starting on page 477 to learn how to set up your BlackBerry as an IP modem or dial-up internet connection for your laptop computer.

Windows PC Media and File Transfer

In this chapter we will help you get your important files and media from your Windows computer to your Storm. Your Storm is quite a capable media player on which you can enjoy music, pictures, and videos. Like your computer, your BlackBerry can even edit Microsoft Office documents.

You have a variety of choices about how to transfer documents and media and we explore all the most popular ones in this chapter. You will quickly see that some methods such as Mass Storage Mode transfer work well for large numbers of files, whereas you will want to use the Media Sync program to transfer your music playlists. There are a few ways to load up media (music, videos, pictures) and Microsoft Office documents (for use with Documents to Go) onto your BlackBerry:

- Desktop Manager Media Manager (page 124)
- Desktop Manager BlackBerry Media Sync (page 132)
- Mass Storage Mode Transfer (page 407)
- Email the files to yourself as attachments (*if they are small enough*)

The **Mass Storage Mode** transfer method allows you to directly copy or drag-and-drop any file types to your BlackBerry when it looks like another disk drive to your computer. (you will see a drive C: normally, but when you connect your BlackBerry, you may see a new drive letter such as E:, F:, G:). We recommend this Mass Storage Mode transfer to copy your Microsoft Office documents (for use with Documents to Go) onto your BlackBerry into the **Documents** folder. See page 407.

More options are popping up all the time and will vary depending on who supplied your BlackBerry (for example, Verizon's Rhapsody MediaSync)

Your Storm may already have an 8GB memory card inserted. If you do not have a memory card in your Storm, we highly recommend buying one and getting it inserted. Obviously, the bigger the card, the more media files you can store on your device. See

Chapter 20 "Add Memory and Media" page 405 to learn how to check if you have a card installed and get one installed if you need one.

Using Media Manager (in Desktop Manager)

NOTE: Remember, you should use BlackBerry Media Sync instead of Media Manager if you want to sync iTunes or Windows Media playlists—see page 132.

To use Media Manager, follow these steps.

1. Start Desktop Manager.

2. Plug your BlackBerry device into your computer with the USB cable.

3. Click the **Media** icon.

4. Click the **Launch** button under the **Media Manager** icon.

5. You may see a license agreement that you need to accept before you can continue.

Scanning Your Computer for Media Files

When you start Media Manager for the first time, it may ask if you want it to scan your computer for all music, video, and picture files that could be used on your BlackBerry device. This takes a while to do, but it is worthwhile if you have lots of pictures, music, and videos scattered over your computer, so click **Yes**.

First Time Configuration

To help find media quickly and easily, Media Manager can scan folders on your computer. Any media found will be added to your library. You can choose to have these folders automatically monitored for new media files by enabling the Folder Watching feature. Would you like to scan for media now?

| Yes | No | Remind Me Later |

CAUTION: If you have a lot of media on your computer, this scanning process could take more than 10 minutes to complete.

After you do this, Media Manager will tell you exactly how many of each kind of file it contains. Under the icon for each type of media, you can click **Manage Media** to rename, regroup, or organize your media.

Watched Folder Settings

You may see another window called Watched Folder Settings shown in the figure to the right.). Watched folders are scanned by Media Manager to see if any changes have occurred (new songs, videos, pictures, etc.) that should be synchronized with your BlackBerry.

Once you click **OK**, you will see the software scanning the selected watched folders, and see a status window. You can pause or cancel the process if it takes too long.

Entering Your Password

If you have a device password set on your BlackBerry, you will need to enter it before Media Manager can see the files stored on your BlackBerry.

The Main Media Manager Window

Then once the program loads, you will see a window similar to Figure 3-1.

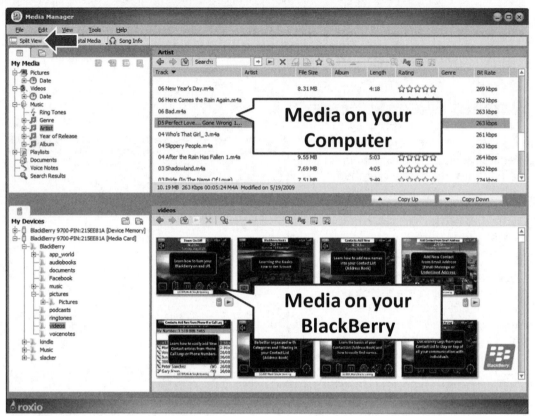

Figure 3-1. *Media Manager main window*

The top half of the Media Manager window shows you the media files that are stored on your computer, and the bottom half shows you the media files stored on your BlackBerry and media card.

Make sure you have clicked **Split View** at the top left in order to see this view of both your computer and your BlackBerry.

You can drag the slider bar above the pictures/media to increase or decrease their size.

Locating Media on Your Computer

Use the top-left portion of the Media Manager window to look for media you want to copy to your computer.

Click the + sign next to any item to expand the view. You can use any of the following methods to help you find media:

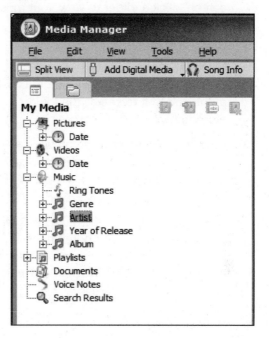

- Click **Music**, and then under that, **Ring Tones, Genre, Artist, Year of Release, Album**.

- Click **Playlists** to view your playlists.

- Click **Pictures** to view pictures and click the **Date** item to narrow views by dates.

- Click **Videos** to view your videos.

- Click **Documents** to view documents compatible with your BlackBerry.

- Click **VoiceNotes** to view voice notes.

- Type a search string in the top row to search for particular media.

Copying Music to Your BlackBerry

The following instructions describe how to copy music to your BlackBerry:

1. In the top half of the Media Manager screen, click a folder to view your music or playlist.

2. In the bottom-left corner of the Media Manager screen, click the + sign next to the BlackBerry entry with **[Media Card]** at the end of it to see all the folders stored on your media card.

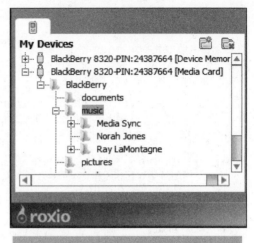

3. Click the folder to which you want to copy your media. In this case, since we are trying to transfer music, we click the **music** folder.

4. Now you should see the music you want to copy from your computer in the top half of the screen and the music folder from your BlackBerry media card in the bottom half of the screen.

NOTE: In Media Manager, you will see your BlackBerry model number instead of the one shown here.

5. Now click to highlight songs, playlists, videos, or any other media in the top window.

6. Click the **Copy Down** button in the middle of the screen.

7. Repeat the procedure for more songs or any other type of media.

8. You may see a window asking you if you want the Media Manager program to copy the song and convert it for optimal playback on the BlackBerry—you can choose to copy with conversion, copy without conversion, or look at advanced conversion options.
We generally recommend letting Media Manager convert your media for optimal playback on your BlackBerry (although this conversion may not work with videos, which are much more challenging to convert than music, and are beyond the scope of this book).

9. Select **OK**, and the song (or songs) will now be copied onto your BlackBerry media card. Verify the copy by looking at the lower window and seeing the song on your media card.

Copying Pictures

Copying pictures is very easy using the **Media Manager** app. In the top window under **My Media,** just select **Pictures** and your pictures will be displayed in the top window. Make sure that down below you collapse the Music menu and open your **Pictures** folder on your media card to ensure that your files will be copied to that folder.

Just select your pictures (if you want more than one, just hold down the **Ctrl** key on your keyboard and then press and click each picture you want—they will all be highlighted). Then click the **Copy Down** button and let them be converted, and they will go right onto your media card (see Figure 3-2).

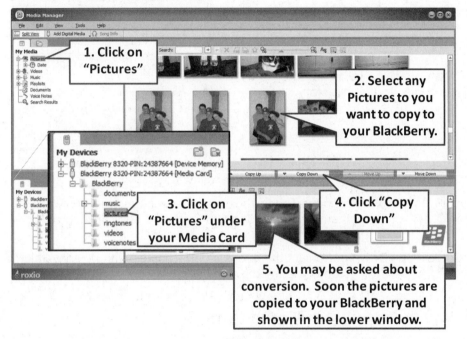

Figure 3-2. *Copying pictures and other items to your BlackBerry using Media Manager*

Copying (Microsoft Office) Documents

Repeat the steps for copying pictures and music, but in the top window under **My Media**, just select **Documents**, and the **Documents** folders on your computer will be displayed in the top window. Navigate to the correct folder for your particular documents.

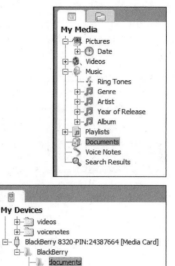

Also, make sure that down below, you open up your **Documents** folder on your media card to ensure that your files will be copied to that directory.

Just select your files in the top window. Then either draw a box around the files, click one and press **Ctrl+A** to select them all, or hold the **Ctrl** key down and click individual files to select them.

Then just click the **Copy Down** button; let the documents be copied with *no* conversion (unlike pictures), and they will go onto your media card.

Deleting Media from Your Media Card

You can use Media Manager to free up space on your media card. We recommend first copying or backing up the items you will delete. Use the drag-and-drop methods described previously to copy items from your media card to your computer (see Figure 3-3).

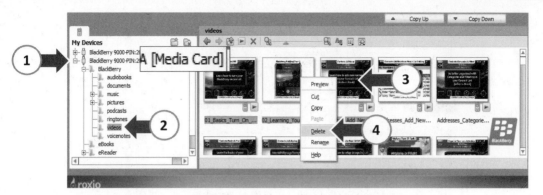

Figure 3-3. *Selecting and deleting media from your BlackBerry with Media Manager*

1. Click the + sign next to BlackBerry nnnn-PIN:xxxxxxx [Media Card] in the lower-left window to see all the folders on the media card.

2. Click a folder from which you wish to delete media on the media card.

3. Select all the items by Ctrl-clicking or Shift-clicking to select a list of items.

4. Once the items to delete are selected, press the Delete key on your keyboard, or right-click and select Delete.

> **TIP:** Videos and songs will usually be the largest items on your BlackBerry—deleting these items will free up more space than deleting individual pictures.

Troubleshooting Media Manager

Sometimes when you are previewing a file or performing some other function, Media Manager will crash and stop responding. If this is the case, you can stop the program by following these steps:

1. On your computer, press **Ctrl+Alt+Delete**.

2. If you are given a choice, then select **Start Task Manager**.

3. From Window Task Manager (Figure 3-4), click the Processes tab.

4. Then scroll down and highlight the image name of **MediaManager**, as shown.

5. Click the **End Process** button at the bottom.

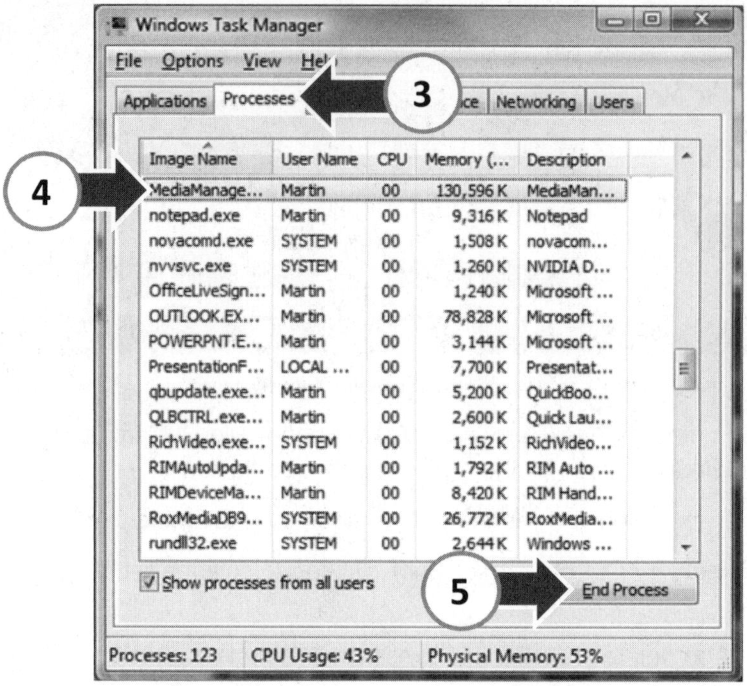

Figure 3-4. *Windows Task Manager*

6. On the screen that says **Do you want to end this process?**, click **End process** to stop the program.

7. Now you can restart the program and try again.

BlackBerry Media Sync

> **NOTE:** You should use BlackBerry Media Manager instead of Media Sync if you want to sync non-iTunes media and you need to convert music and video to be viewable on your BlackBerry (see page 124).

Perhaps the easiest way to get music (and now your album art) into playlists is using the BlackBerry Media Sync program. If you are an iTunes user and you have playlists already in your iTunes program, the Media Sync program allows you to transfer those playlists directly to your BlackBerry.

TIP: Normally, you just launch Media Sync from inside Desktop Manager; however, you can download and run Media Sync separately from BlackBerry Desktop Manager as well. To do this, open up a web browser on your computer, go to www.blackberry.com/mediasync, and click the **Download for PC** link. Once you have the file downloaded, just run the installation program. A window will appear letting you know the application has been installed properly.

To launch the application, just go to Start ➤ All Programs ➤ BlackBerry ➤ Media Sync and click the icon. Make sure that your BlackBerry is connected via the USB cable to your computer—but *don't* have Desktop Manager running when you do this.

Starting Media Sync from Desktop Manager

To use Media Sync from within Desktop Manager, follow these steps.

1. Start BlackBerry Desktop Manager.

2. Plug in your BlackBerry Device with the USB cable.

3. Click the **Media** icon.

4. Click the **Launch** button under the **BlackBerry Media Sync** icon. You may need to accept a license agreement to continue.

5. After clicking **Launch**, you may see a window telling you an update is available. Click the **Download** button and follow the steps to install the updated software.

NOTE: If a song is in iTunes and is DRM protected (see page 140), then it is *not* possible to sync it to your BlackBerry.

Entering Your BlackBerry Password for Media Sync

If you have set a password to protect your BlackBerry, then you will need to enter your password to continue.

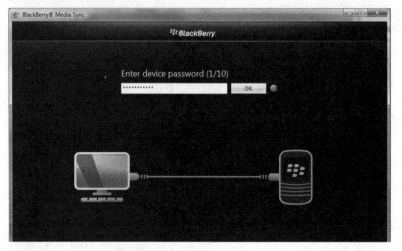

Figure 3-5. *Media Sync password screen*

Media Sync Setup

When you first start Media Sync, it may show you a setup screen similar to Figure 3-6.

1. Change the name of your device if you like.

2. Select where your media should be stored—leave **Store media on** set to **Media Card** as shown in Figure 3-6 (see page 405 to learn about media cards).

3. Use the slider bar to keep more or less space free after the sync. The default is 10 percent, and should be fine.

4. Click **iTunes** or **Windows Media Player** for where you store your music.

5. Click **OK** to continue.

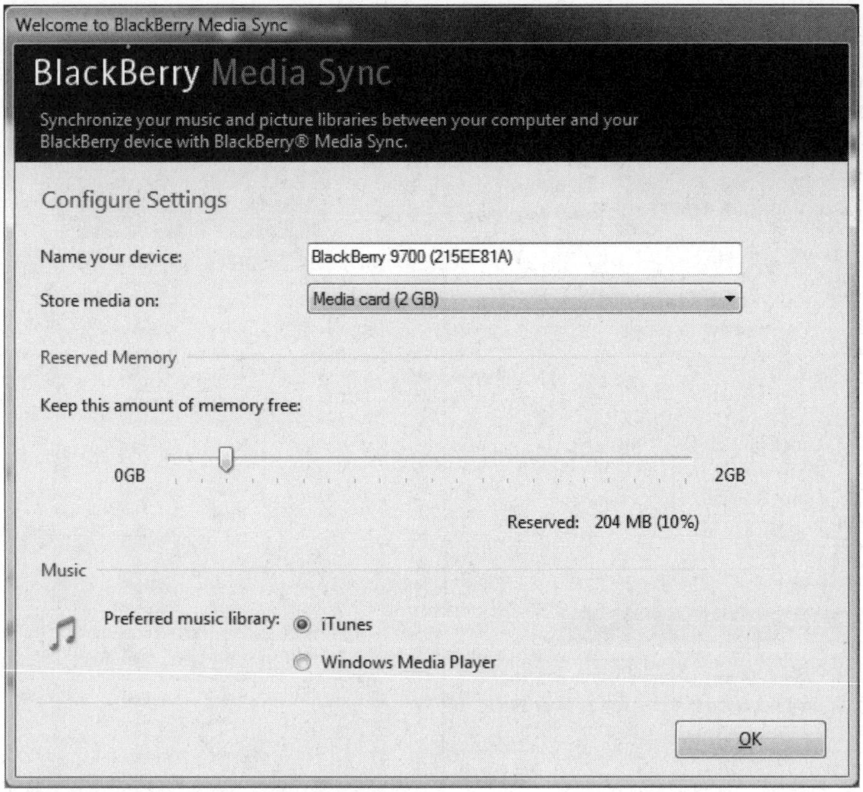

Figure 3-6. *Media Sync options (device)*

After you've completed the initial settings screen, you should then see a screen similar to the one shown in Figure 3-7.

Media Sync: Syncing Music

You are now ready to set up music sync. To do so, take the following steps:

1. Make sure to click the Music tab in the upper-left corner, as shown in Figure 3-7, to configure your music sync.

> **NOTE:** Figure 3-7 shows a BlackBerry 9700 model with a 2GB media card; on your computer you will see the name and model number of your BlackBerry as well as the size of your media card.

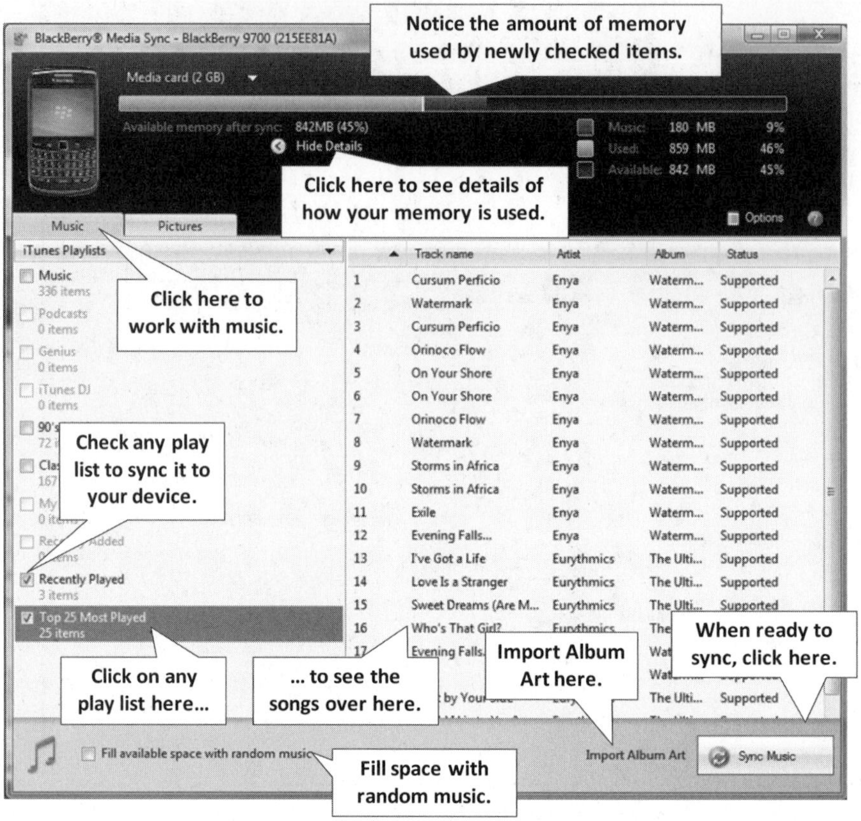

Figure 3-7. *Media Sync screen (Music tab)*

TIP: To get back to the settings screen you just completed, just click the **Options** button in the upper-right corner of Figure 3-7 and click the **Device** tab at the top (see figure 3-5).

2.   To import your album art, just click the **Import Album Art** link next to the **Sync Music** button in the lower-right corner of Figure 3-3. If you are importing from iTunes, iTunes will be automatically started.

NOTE: If iTunes has a dialog box open when it automatically starts, you will have to close out the dialog box and click the **Import Album Art** button again.

Figure 3-8. *Status screen for importing album art in BlackBerry Media Sync*

Once the import is done, you will see a little pop-up window saying it is finished importing album art.

3. To select a playlist to sync to your device, just check the box next to the playlist. When you check it, watch the memory bar at the top to make sure that you have not exceeded available memory with your selections. If you have, just uncheck the playlists until you get back under 100 percent of memory usage.

4. If you want to fill the available space with random music, then place a check next to the box in the lower-left corner that says **Fill available space with random music**.

5. In order to see the details of what is occupying the space on your memory card, click the **Show Details** button underneath the **Available memory after sync** number in the upper-middle part of the window.

6. Once you are done with your selection of playlists, click the **Sync Music** button in the lower-right corner. You will see the sync status in the upper portion of the window.

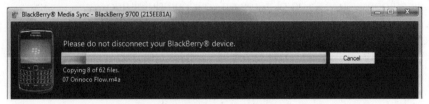

Figure 3-9. *Status screen for syncing files to the BlackBerry*

Media Sync: Syncing Pictures

If you would like to transfer or sync pictures between your BlackBerry and your computer, click the Pictures tab in the upper-left corner, as shown in Figure 3-4.

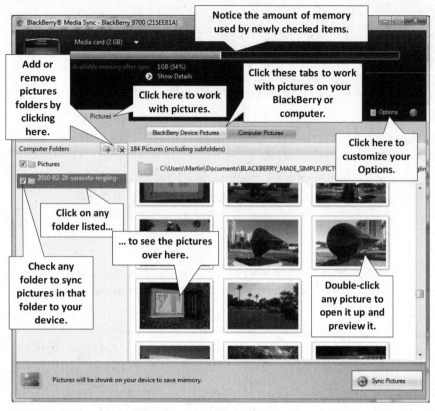

Figure 3-10. *Media Sync screen (Pictures tab)*

1. To switch between viewing pictures on your computer and your BlackBerry, click the buttons in the upper-middle section of the screen (Figure 3-4).

2. To add or remove picture folders on your computer, click the folder + and − icons at the top of the folder column.

3. Once you have folders listed, click a folder to display all pictures in that folder.

4. Check the box next to the folder to sync all the pictures in that folder to your device. If you have previously synced a folder, you can uncheck it to remove those pictures from your device to save space.

When you check each picture folder, watch the memory bar at the top to make sure that you have not exceeded available memory with your selections. If you have, just uncheck the folders until you get back under 100 percent of memory usage.

In the lower-left corner of Figure 3-4, notice the text "Pictures will be shrunk on your device to save memory." That is a setting you can change by clicking the **Options** link in the upper-right corner. See Figure 3-5 and related descriptions for help.

In order to see the details of what is occupying the space on your memory card, click the **Show Details** button underneath the **Available memory after sync** number in the upper-middle part of the window.

Once you are done with your selection of playlists, click the **Sync Pictures** button in the lower-right corner. Your sync status will be shown in the top portion of the window.

Some Songs Could Not Be Synchronized

Look carefully at the **Synchronization complete** message (Figure 3-11). If some songs are protected, then they will not be synced to your BlackBerry. In this example, 35 songs were protected.

Figure 3-11. *Synchronization complete message.*

To see the list, click the **Click to view a list of those songs** link. Then you should see a window similar to Figure 3-12. Click the + sign next to **Protected** to see all the protected songs.

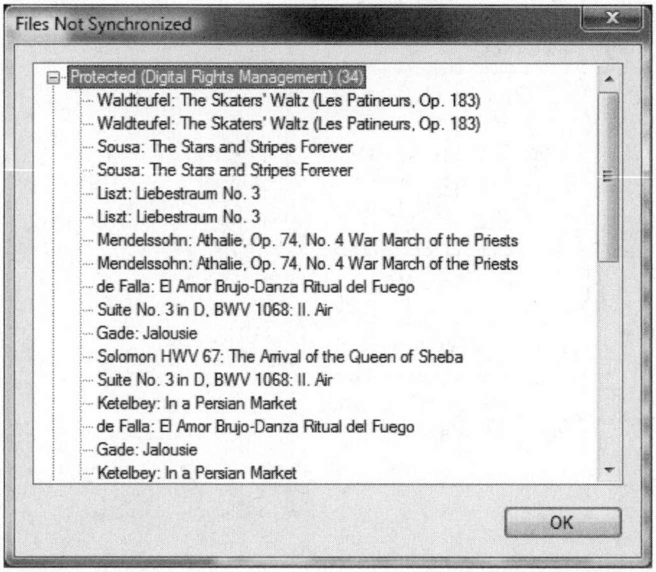

Figure 3-12. *Viewing songs that could not be synced due to DRM protection*

You can learn more about protected songs in the following section.

DRM Protection

Now, it is important to remember that some music that is purchased on iTunes contains DRM restrictions—that means that most iTunes music can only be played on iPods and through iTunes. Most likely these are older songs purchased before the middle of 2009.

Any other music you might have put in your iTunes library—like CDs you loaded into your computer or music that does not have DRM restrictions—will transfer into the appropriate playlist. Make sure that you don't disconnect your BlackBerry while the music is transferring.

Once the sync is done, close out the Media Sync window. (See page 413 to learn how to use music on your BlackBerry.)

Media Sync Options Screen

To see the Options screen (Figure 3-13), you need to click the **Options** button in the upper-right corner of the main Media Sync window (Figure 3-10). Notice there are two tabs at the top: General and Device.

General Tab

Click the General tab at the top of the Options screen to see the screen shown in Figure 3-13.

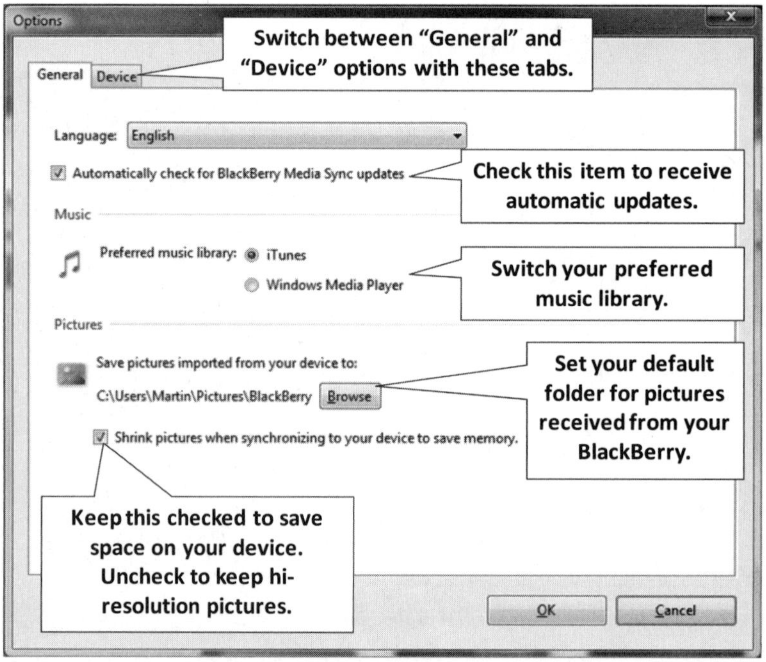

Figure 3-13. *Media Sync options (General tab)*

On the General tab, you can do the following:

- Select your language from the drop-down list.

- Automatically check for Media Sync software updates by checking the corresponding box. (It is checked by default.)

- Select your preferred music library. If you have changed from iTunes to Windows Media Player or vice versa, you can select your preferred music library.

- Select the folder to store pictures that are transferred from your BlackBerry to your computer by clicking the **Browse** button.

- You can also decide how high the resolution should be for pictures you sync to your BlackBerry. The default is to shrink pictures when synchronizing to your device to save memory. Uncheck this box if you want higher resolution pictures and aren't worried about the extra storage space required.

Device Tab

Click the Device tab at the top to see settings related to your device, as shown in Figure 3-14.

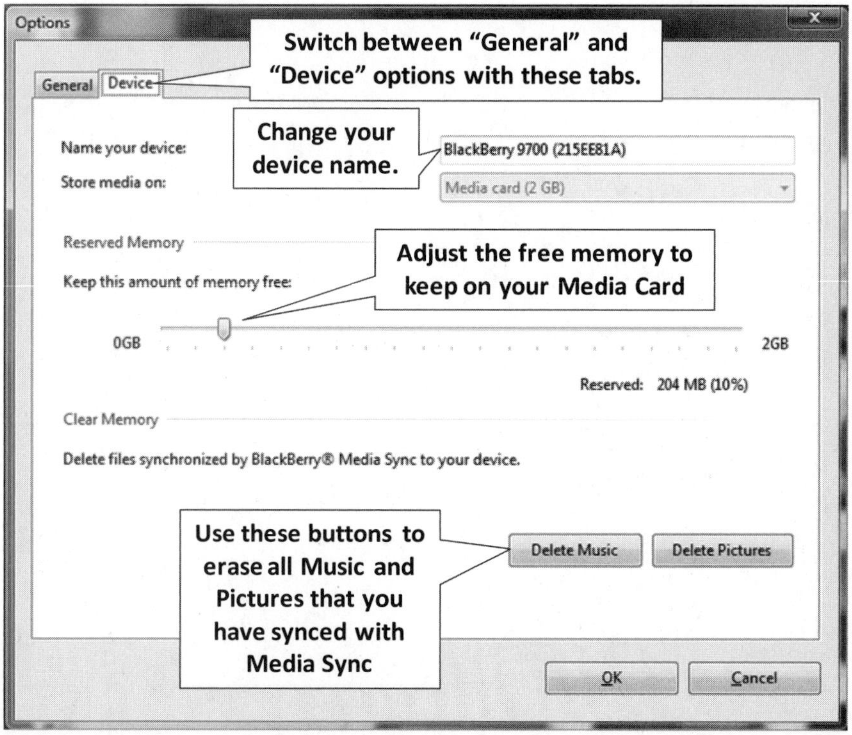

Figure 3-14. *Media Sync options (Device tab)*

On the Device tab, you can do the following:

- Change your device name for your BlackBerry.

- Change the amount of reserved memory on your device after the sync (use the slider bar).

- Erase all the music and pictures synced to your BlackBerry by clicking the **Delete Music** or **Delete Pictures** buttons.

Mass Storage Mode Transfer

In order to transfer files directly to or from your BlackBerry memory card, you will need to use the mass storage mode transfer.   That section happens to be described in the Mac media transfer chapter on page 407.

Apple Mac Setup

This chapter shows you how to install the new BlackBerry Desktop Manager software on your Apple Mac computer and do the basics of synchronizing your contacts, calendar, tasks and memos, backup and restore, and more. If you want to transfer files and media with your Mac, then check out Chapter 5 "Apple Mac Media and File Transfer" on page 159. (You may need some of the instructions in this chapter on how to install Desktop Manager if you want to use it as your method to transfer files.)

Do you have a Microsoft Windows computer? If so please go to page 81.

CAUTION: Do you use more than one computer (e.g., work, home, etc.)? Be sure to check the **with other computers (safer sync)** option on the **Device Options** screen (discussed later) if you plan on syncing your BlackBerry with multiple computers using Desktop Manager. Otherwise, you could end up corrupting your BlackBerry and/or computer databases!

Do you want a wireless, two-way automated sync? Try using Google Contacts, Google Calendar, and Google Sync for your BlackBerry. All these are free applications and give you a full two-way wireless sync.

BlackBerry Desktop Manager for Mac

For years, Windows users have enjoyed seamless synchronization of their contacts, calendar, notes, and tasks with their PC via the BlackBerry Desktop Manager software. Now, for the first time, the peace of mind that comes with knowing your data is fully backed up is available to the Mac user.

If you have never used BlackBerry Desktop Manager, you will now be able to not only synchronize your data, but you will be able to back up, restore, sync your iTunes playlists, and more.

Downloading and Installing Desktop Manager for Mac

Desktop Manager for Mac software is available for free from BlackBerry.com. The following exercise shows you how to install it:

1. Open up your web browser and go to the download page (Figure 4-1): `http://na.blackberry.com/eng/services/desktop/mac.jsp`.

2. Fill out the required information on the download page and then click **Download Now** to download the software.

Figure 4-1. *Locating the download file on the BlackBerry web site*

3. Once the file is downloaded, you will be presented with the screen shown in Figure 4-2.

Figure 4-2. *Starting the installation*

4. Double-click the **BlackBerry Desktop Manager.mpkg** file to begin the installation process.

5. Your Mac will display a warning message similar to the one shown in Figure 4-3.

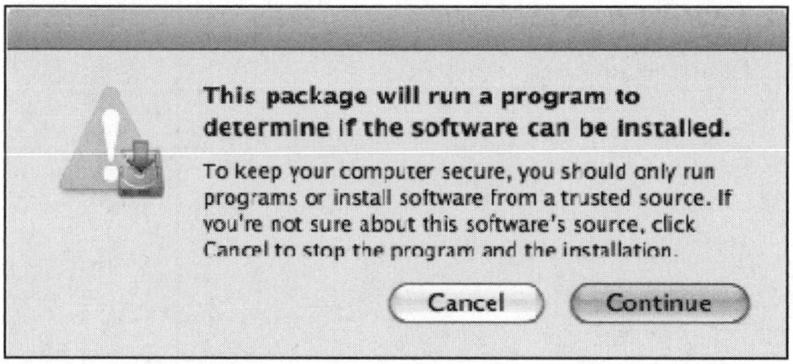

Figure 4-3. *Mac installation warning screen*

6. Select **Continue** to move forward with the installation process.

NOTE: If you have been using either Pocket Mac or the Missing Sync to synchronize your BlackBerry with the Mac, you will receive another warning note letting you know that in order to proceed, the connection between your BlackBerry and the third-party synchronization software will need to be discontinued.

7. If you already have some other software installed, you will see another warning message similar to Figure 4-4. Click **Install Anyway** to move forward with the installation process.

Figure 4-4. *Warning screen about additional BlackBerry software*

8. The installation process will begin. Follow the onscreen prompts as your Mac installs the new Desktop Manager software (see Figure 4-5).

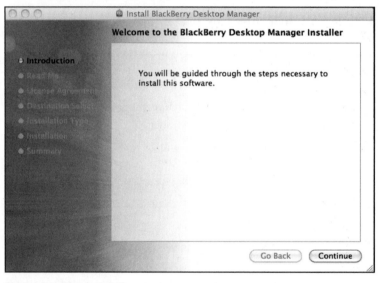

Figure 4-5. *First installation screen*

9. Click **Read License** to read the software license, or click **Agree** to proceed. Figure 4-6.

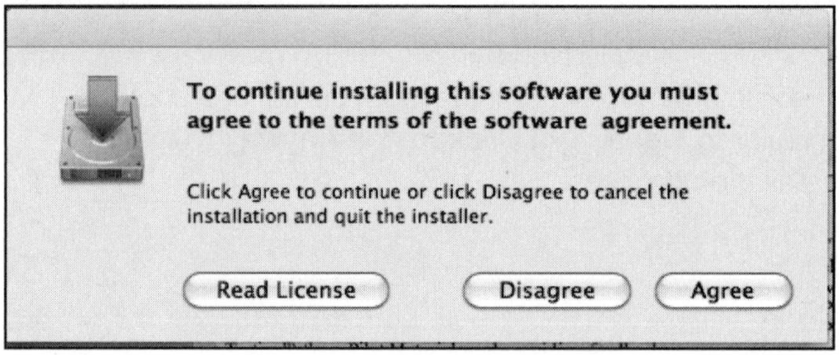

Figure 4-6. *Installation license agreement pop-up window*

10. For most Mac users, only one drive will be shown—but it is possible that you might have more than one possible location for the install. Choose the correct drive and click **Continue** (see Figure 4-7).

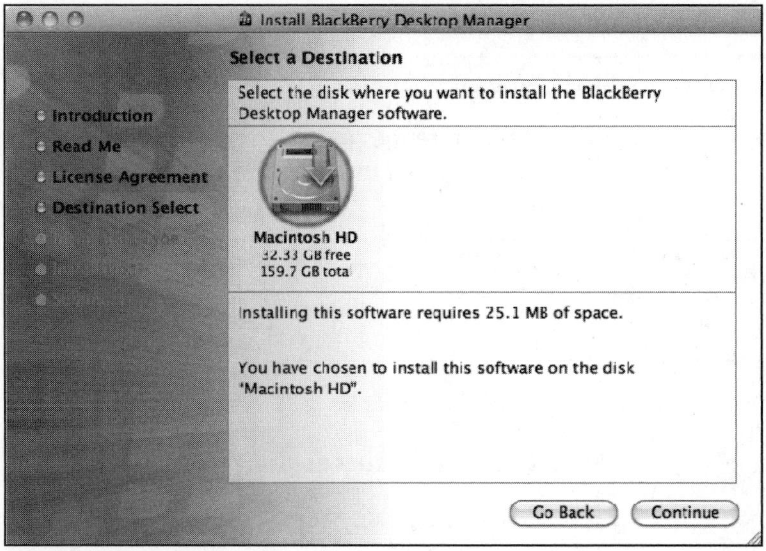

Figure 4-7. *Choose the location of the installation.*

11. If you have a password set on your Mac, you will be prompted to enter it at this time in order to proceed with the installation (Figure 4-8).

Figure 4-8. *A password is required to complete installation.*

12. You will be asked to restart your computer when the installation is complete—just agree to this by clicking **Continue Installation** (Figure 4-9).

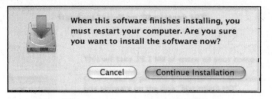

Figure 4-9. *Request to restart after installation*

13. When the installation is complete, before the restart, you should see the screen shown in Figure 4-10 indicating that the software was installed successfully.

Figure 4-10. *Successful software installation screen*

Starting Desktop Manager for the First Time

To locate the Desktop Manager app, click the **Finder** icon and then click your **Applications** icon. The **BlackBerry Desktop Manager** icon will be in your **Applications** directory.

Figure 4-11. *Locating BlackBerry Desktop Manager for Mac*

Double-click the **BlackBerry Desktop Manager** app and the welcome screen will appear, showing you information about your particular BlackBerry (Figure 4-12). On this welcome screen you can adjust your device options.

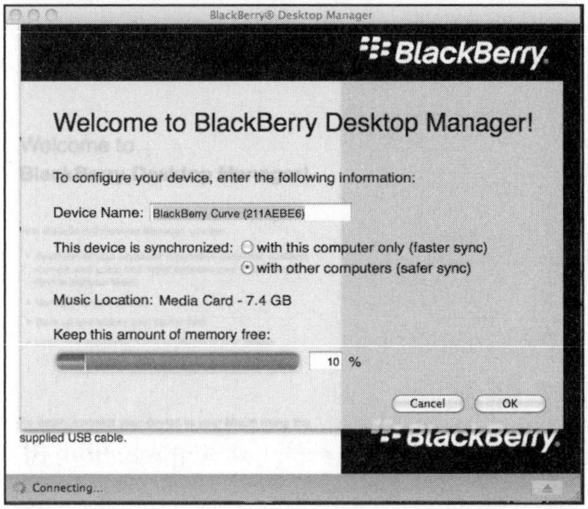

Figure 4-12. *BlackBerry Desktop Manager for Mac welcome screen*

On this screen you should select how to synchronize your BlackBerry in the **This Device is Synchronized** field.

If you synchronize your BlackBerry with other computers, a network server, Google Sync for Calendar, or Google Contacts, select **with other computers (safer sync)**.

If you are only planning on syncing your BlackBerry with this one Mac, you can choose **with this computer only (faster sync)**.

Main View in Desktop Manager

Desktop Manager will show you a picture of your BlackBerry device, a clean interface displaying information along the left-hand bar, and commands along to top bar (Figure 4-13).

NOTE: This figure shows a Storm 8900; your BlackBerry may look slightly different of course.

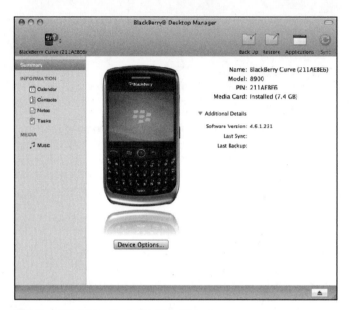

Figure 4-13. *Main view in Desktop Manager*

Using Desktop Manager for Mac

One of the first things you will notice is the **Device Options** button below the picture of your BlackBerry (Figure 4-13).

Clicking this brings you to an options screen (the same screen you saw when you first started Desktop Manager; see Figure 4-14).

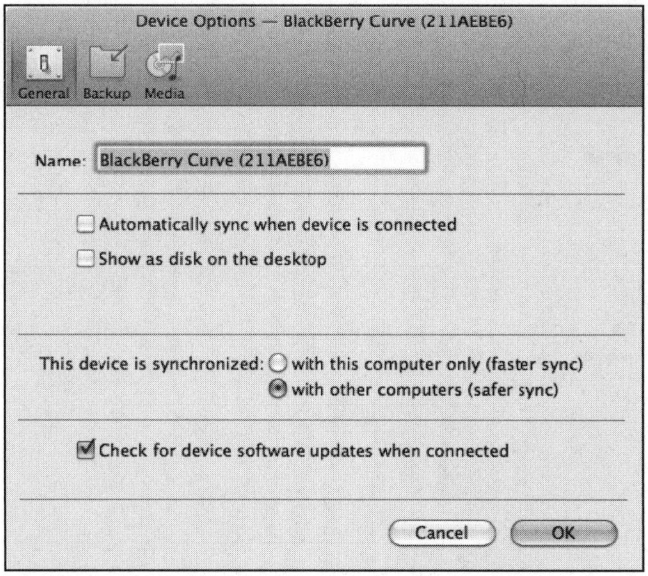

Device Options — BlackBerry Curve (211AEBE6)

General Backup Media

Name: BlackBerry Curve (211AEBE6)

☐ Automatically sync when device is connected
☐ Show as disk on the desktop

This device is synchronized: ○ with this computer only (faster sync)
                             ● with other computers (safer sync)

☑ Check for device software updates when connected

Cancel   OK

Figure 4-14. *Device options in Desktop Manager for Mac*

Device Options

You can rename your device if you like (the default is simply your model and PIN number). If you want to automatically sync your device each time you connect, just check the first check box. If you want to see a desktop icon showing your BlackBerry as an external disk, just check the **Show as disk on the desktop** box. Once you do this, you can easily transfer files between your Mac and your BlackBerry using the drag-and-drop method you use on your Mac to copy between folders and disks.

With the **This device is synchronized** option, you can choose whether you BlackBerry syncs only with this Mac or with other computers. If your BlackBerry syncs with your PC and your Google account, you should select the **with other computers (safer sync)** option selected to avoid duplicating entries in your contacts and calendars.

Backup Options

Click **Backup** icon along the top of the **Device Options** screen.

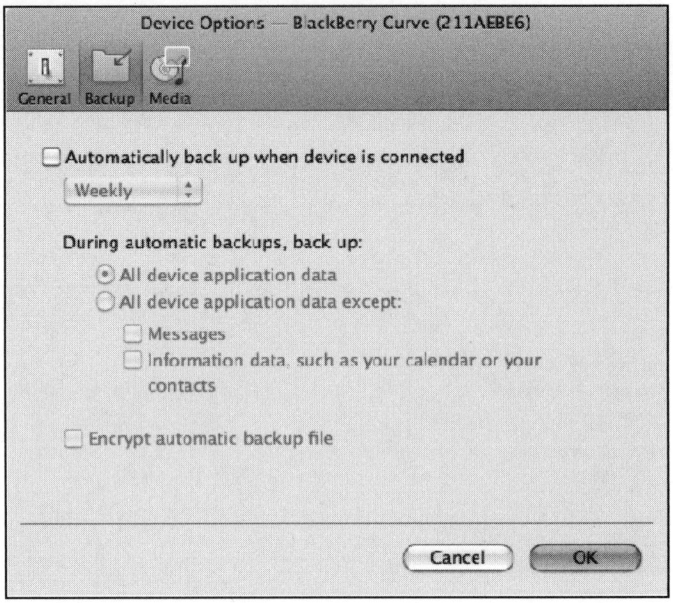

Figure 4-15. *Backup options in Desktop Manager for Mac*

If you want to create a backup each time you connect your device, just check the **Automatically back up when device is connected** box. You can then specify exactly what you wish to be backed up. (We cover the specific backup options in greater detail a little later in the chapter.)

Setting Up Your Sync Options

Click **OK** or **Cancel** to return to the main screen of Desktop Manager (Figure 4-13), and look at the left column under where it says INFORMATION (Figure 4-16).

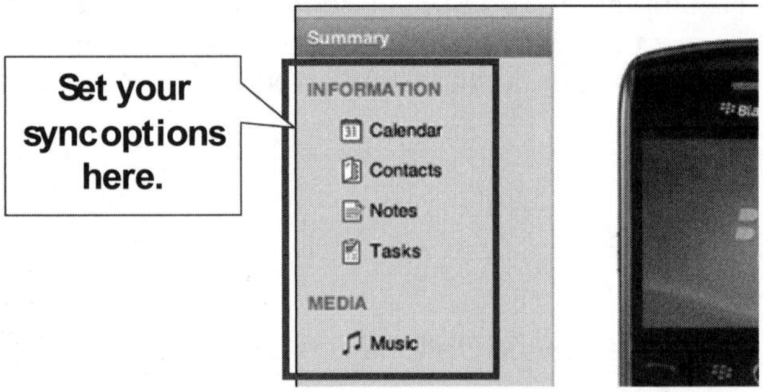

Figure 4-16. *Sync options in Desktop Manager for Mac*

This is where you set the sync options for your calendar, contacts, notes, and tasks.

1. Click any of the items below **INFORMATION**. In this case we will start with the calendar to be taken to the sync setup screen.

2. This screen has a similar look and feel to the calendar sync screen within iTunes, for those who are familiar with syncing an iPhone or iPod touch and a Mac (see Figure 4-17).

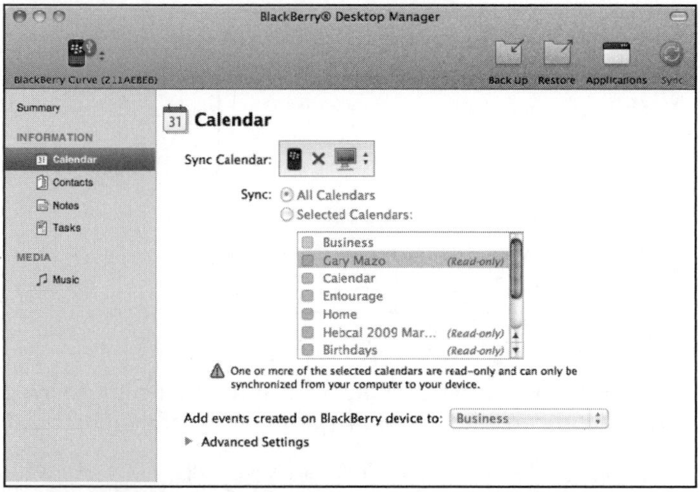

Figure 4-17. *Calendar sync options screen*

3. Desktop Manager will notice all the calendars you have on your BlackBerry. In this example, we use Google Calendar, and have many different calendars, each set to a unique color. You see this in the list of calendars.

4. Click the box with the **Sync Calendar** option. The red X on this icon shows that the BlackBerry calendar will not be synced with the Mac calendars.

5. If you click the box and select the next item in the drop-down, the picture will change to show that now you desire a two-way sync between the Mac calendar and the BlackBerry calendar.

6. You can also select into which calendar you want events to go that you create on your BlackBerry. The default is the Business calendar, but that can be changed to any calendar that you have set up on the device.

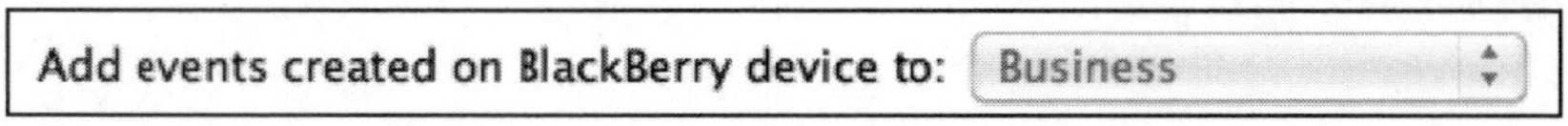

Add events created on BlackBerry device to: Business

Advanced Settings

Click the Advanced Settings tab ▶ Advanced Settings at the bottom, and the options shown in Figure 4-18 will be revealed.

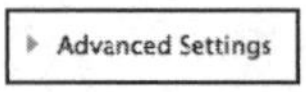

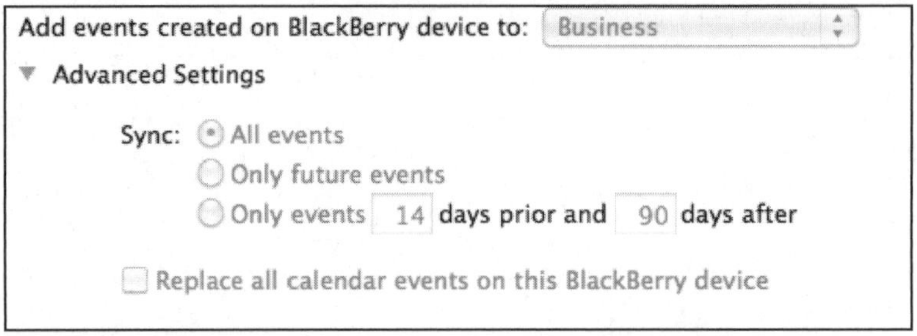

Add events created on BlackBerry device to: [Business   ⬍]

▼ Advanced Settings

      Sync: ⦿ All events
            ⦾ Only future events
            ⦾ Only events [14] days prior and [90] days after

        ☐ Replace all calendar events on this BlackBerry device

Figure 4-18. *Advanced sync settings in Desktop Manager for Mac*

Like Desktop Manager for the PC, you can specify as to whether you want to sync all events or future events only, or you can set individual parameters for synchronization.

> **TIP:** We recommend not selecting **Only future events** unless you have a strong reason to do so. For example, say you made some notes on an event that was held yesterday in the BlackBerry calendar notes field. If you selected **Only future events**, these important notes would not be transferred to your Mac.

To replace all calendar events on the BlackBerry with events from your Mac's calendar, just click the check box at the bottom of the screen.

Syncing Contacts, Calendar, Notes, and Tasks

The procedure for setting the sync options for contacts, tasks, and notes is identical to what was just shown. The only things that change are the groups or events to choose within each category (see Figure 4-19).

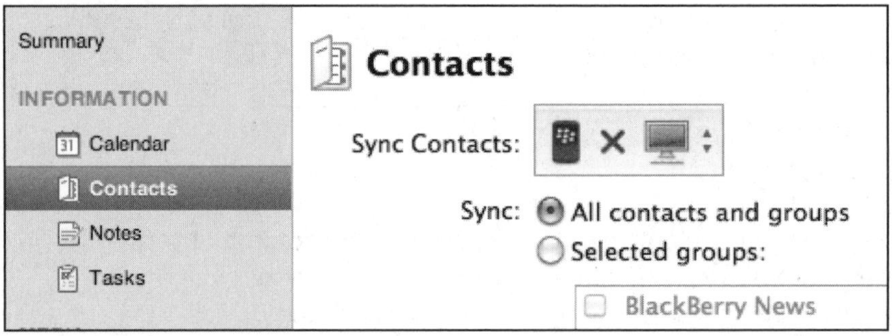

Summary

INFORMATION

  📅 Calendar

  📖 Contacts

  📝 Notes

  📋 Tasks

📖 **Contacts**

Sync Contacts: [📱 ✕ 🖥 ⬍]

    Sync: ⦿ All contacts and groups
          ⦾ Selected groups:

           ☐ BlackBerry News

Figure 4-19. *Sync Contacts setup screen*

On this screen, you can click next to **Sync Contacts**, as discussed previously, and choose either to not sync with the Mac or to perform a two-way sync. You can then choose to sync either all contacts or groups, or only selected groups from your address book.

Backup and Restore

One of the great features now available to Mac users is the ability to backup and restore either you entire BlackBerry contents or just selected information on your Mac. Backup and restore begins with the two icons at the top of the main screen in Desktop Manager.

Using Backup

The following short exercise explains how to use backup:

1. Click the **Back Up** icon [Back Up] and you will be taken to the next screen where you specify exactly which information you wish to be backed up on your Mac (Figure 4-20).

Figure 4-20. *Backup screen in Desktop Manager for Mac*

2. Select either **All data** or **Selected data**, and then choose exactly which items you wish to back up.

3. Let's say that you are only really concerned with backing up your contacts, calendar, and notes—just check off each of those boxes and your backup will complete much faster.

4. You can specify the name of your backup for easy retrieval in the future.

5. Once you have made all your backup selections, click the **Back Up** button and the progress of the backup will be displayed in a dialog box.

Restoring from Backup

We all know that sometimes unexplained things happen and we lose information in our BlackBerry. Maybe we try to update the OS and make a mistake, or maybe we sync with other computers and the information gets corrupted. Now Mac users have a reliable and safe way to restore data on their devices.

1. Click the **Restore** icon along the top row of the main screen in Desktop Manager. You will then be taken to the restore options screen (Figure 4-21).

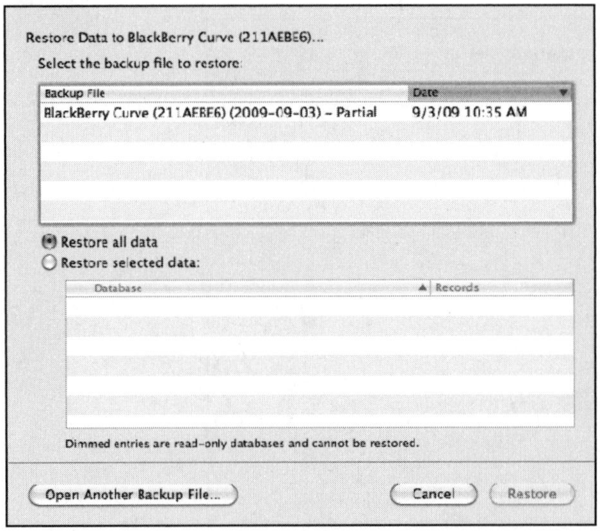

Figure 4-21. *Restore screen in Desktop Manager for Mac*

2. If you have made a backup file on your Mac (which is required so that you'll have a file you can restore), it will be shown in the top box under **Backup File**. If you have multiple backup files, they will all be listed here.

3. Select the file from which you wish to restore information (or, if you did a selective backup, selected data will be displayed in the second screen below.)

4. Click the **Restore** button and your BlackBerry will be restored just as it was when you made the backup file.

Adding and Removing Applications

For the first time, Mac users are now able to add or remove applications on their BlackBerry from the Desktop Manager environment.

1. Click the **Applications** icon (in the upper-right corner of the main screen) and you will be taken to the Install/Remove Applications screen in Desktop Manager (see Figure 4-22).

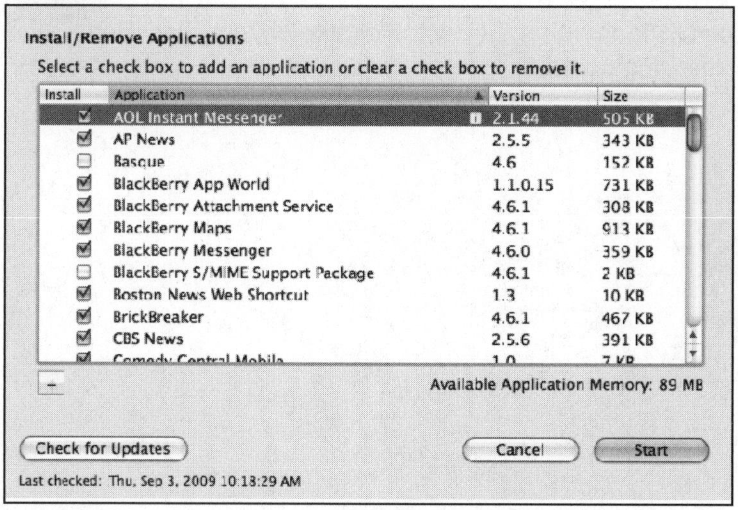

Install/Remove Applications

Select a check box to add an application or clear a check box to remove it.

Install	Application	Version	Size
☑	AOL Instant Messenger	2.1.44	505 KB
☑	AP News	2.5.5	343 KB
☐	Basque	4.6	152 KB
☑	BlackBerry App World	1.1.0.15	731 KB
☑	BlackBerry Attachment Service	4.6.1	308 KB
☑	BlackBerry Maps	4.6.1	913 KB
☑	BlackBerry Messenger	4.6.0	359 KB
☐	BlackBerry S/MIME Support Package	4.6.1	2 KB
☑	Boston News Web Shortcut	1.3	10 KB
☑	BrickBreaker	4.6.1	467 KB
☑	CBS News	2.5.6	391 KB
☑	Comedy Central Mobile	1.0	7 KB

Available Application Memory: 89 MB

Check for Updates — Cancel — Start

Last checked: Thu, Sep 3, 2009 10:18:29 AM

Figure 4-22. *The Install/Remove Applications window in Desktop Manager for Mac*

2. To check for updates, click the **Check for Updates** button in the lower-left corner.

3. Place a check mark in the box for any application that isn't checked already, and it will be installed on your device. Conversely, uncheck any box, and that application will be removed from your BlackBerry.

4. Click the **Start** button, and the selected or deselected applications will be either installed or uninstalled, depending on your selection.

TIP: For peace of mind, it is always a good idea to perform a backup both before and after you add or delete applications from the device.

Setting Up the BlackBerry as a Modem for Your Mac

See our Chapter 26 "Connect with Tethered Modem" page 477 for help with setting up your BlackBerry to connect your Mac to the internet as a dial-up modem.

Automating Synchronization with Desktop Manager for Mac

In order to have your BlackBerry sync every time you connect it to your Mac, you will need change a setting in the Device Options screen.

1. Click the **Device Options** button below the picture of your BlackBerry on the main screen (Figure 4-23).

2. Then check the check box next to **Automatically sync when device is connected**.

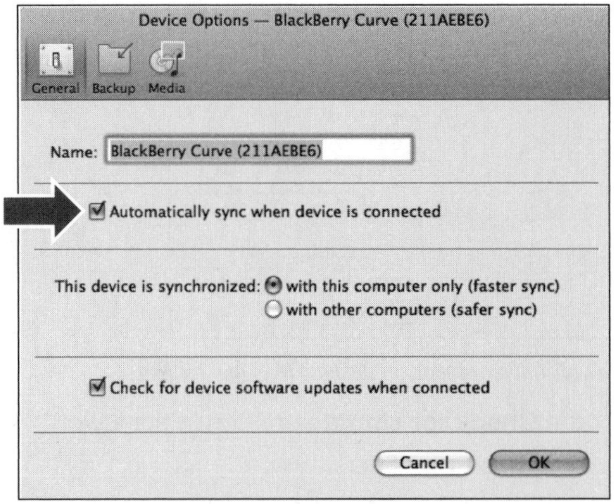

Figure 4-23. *Automate the sync in Desktop Manager for Mac.*

Chapter 5

Apple Mac Media and File Transfer

Your BlackBerry can be a great media player. In order to get all of your songs, videos, and other media onto your BlackBerry, you'll need to learn some of the information in this chapter.

There are a couple of ways to load up media (music, videos, and pictures) and Microsoft Office documents (for use with Documents to Go) onto your BlackBerry:

- Use BlackBerry Desktop Manager for Mac.
- Use Mass Storage Mode transfer.

Syncing Media with Desktop Manager for Mac

Start up Desktop Manager for Mac as shown in the previous chapter and make sure your BlackBerry is connected to your Mac with your USB cable. Click the third icon along the top, called **Media** .

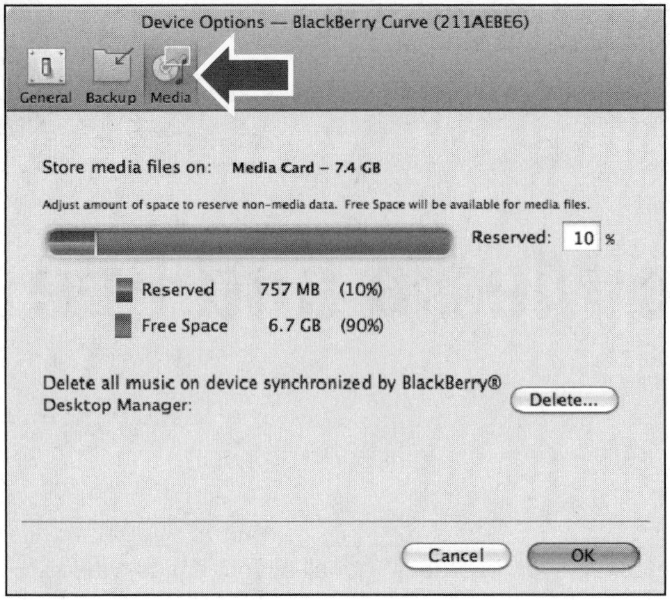

Figure 5-1. *Media Sync in Desktop Manager for Mac*

By default, Desktop Manager will reserve 10 percent of the space on your media card for non-media data. You can adjust this amount in the box. The smaller the number you input, the more space you will have for media files on the media card.

Deleting All Music

Click the **Delete** button under the **Delete all music on device...** statement, and you can remove any or all the music stored on your device.

Why would you want to do that? Let's say that you have been dragging and dropping music onto your BlackBerry (which was one of the only options for Mac users unless you were using Pocket Mac or the Missing Sync.) Or, let's say you were using a program like the Missing Sync (which would sync iTunes playlists, but did not bring in the album art).

You now have the option of syncing your iTunes playlists complete with album art, so you might want to start fresh and get rid of the other music on your BlackBerry.

Syncing Music

BlackBerry Desktop Manager allows you to sync your iTunes playlists right onto the media card of your BlackBerry. Just click the **Music** icon under the **Media** line along the left-hand column of the main screen.

You will then be taken to the **Music Sync** screen. It provides you with some very nice options, as shown in Figure 5-2.

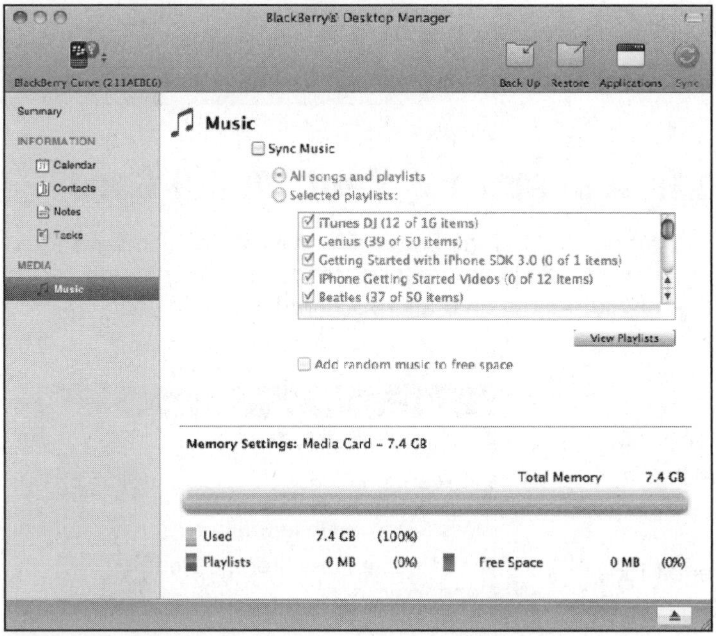

Figure 5-2. *Sync Music screen in Desktop Manager for Mac*

As with iTunes, you can choose to sync all songs and playlists or just selected playlists. Just place a check mark in the **Sync Music** box at the top of the screen, and you can then select which playlists you wish to sync between your Mac and your BlackBerry.

Place a check mark in the **Add random music to free space** box, and additional songs will randomly be placed on to the media card.

On this screen, you can see that I just selected four playlists that I wanted on my BlackBerry—so I placed check marks in the appropriate boxes (see Figure 5-3).

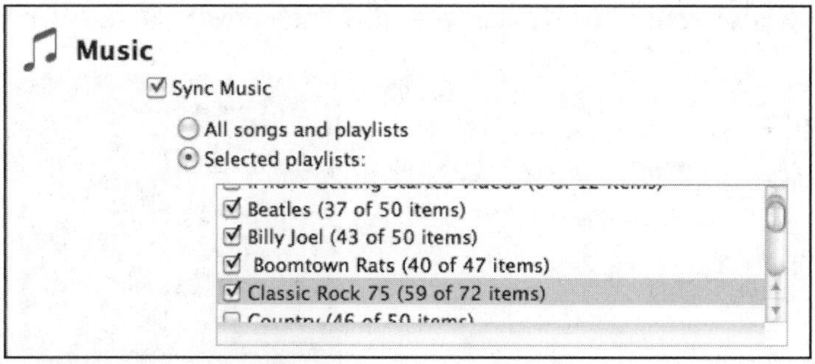

Figure 5-3. *Syncing specific playlists in Desktop Manager for Mac*

Click the **Sync** icon at the top right of the screen to perform the music sync to your BlackBerry.

Back Up   Restore   Applications   Sync

Mass Storage Mode Transfer for Your Media Card

This works whether you have a Windows or a Mac computer. We will show images for the Mac computer process, but it will be fairly similar for a Windows PC. This transfer method assumes you have stored your media on a MicroSD media card in your BlackBerry.

1. To get to this screen, click the **Options** icon, and then scroll down and click **Memory.**

Memory	
Media Card Support:	On ▾
Encryption Mode:	None ▾
Mass Storage Mode Support:	On ▾
Auto Enable Mass Storage Mode Connected:	Yes / No / Prompt ▾
Application Memory Free Space:	51.0 MB

2. Make sure Mass Storage Mode support for your media card is on, and other settings are as shown.

3. Now connect your BlackBerry to your computer with the USB cable. If you selected **Prompt** for **Auto Enable Mass Storage Mode** on the screen just shown, you will see a question similar to this: "Turn on Mass Storage Mode?"

4. Answer yes (you should probably check the box that says "Don't Ask Me Again"). When you answer yes, then your media card will look just like another hard disk to your computer (similar to a USB flash drive).

TIP: If you set the **Auto Enable Mass Storage Mode** setting to **Yes**, then you won't be asked this question; the media card on the BlackBerry will automatically look like a mass storage device (disk drive letter).

Do you want to turn on Mass Storage Mode? You might not be able to access some

?

Yes

Using Your BlackBerry in Mass Storage Mode

NOTE: You will need to install Desktop Manager for Mac in order to be able to use this mass storage option. This is because there are drivers required to connect your BlackBerry to your Mac.

Once connected, your Mac will see your BlackBerry as a mass storage device and mount it as an external drive.

The BlackBerry will also be visible if you click the **Finder** icon in the dock. It will be listed under **Devices**.

Exploring the Drive

Right-click the icon for the BlackBerry and choose **Open**—or double-click on the **Desktop** icon and open the drive (see Figure 5-4).

Now you can explore your BlackBerry as you would any drive. You can copy pictures, music, and video files by just dragging and dropping to the correct folder, or you can delete files from your BlackBerry by clicking the appropriate folder, selecting files, and dragging them to the trash.

NOTE: Your music, video, ring tone, and picture files are located in the folder called BlackBerry.

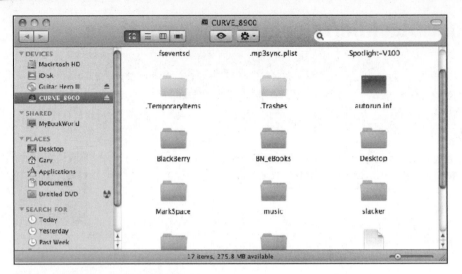

Figure 5-4. *Finding media on the Storm*

Copying Files Using Mass Storage Mode

After your BlackBerry is connected and in Mass Storage Mode, just open up your computer's file management software. On your Mac, start your Finder. Look for another hard disk or BlackBerry model number that has been added. On Windows, open up Windows Explorer.

NOTE: You will see your own BlackBerry model number (e.g., STORM_9550).

When you plug your BlackBerry into your Mac, it will identify the main memory and the contents of the MicroSD card as two separate drives, and place them right on your desktop for easy navigation.

On your Mac, click the **Finder** icon in the lower-left corner of the dock. On Windows, click the disk drive letter that is your BlackBerry media card.

You will see your devices (including both BlackBerry drives) on the top and your places (where you can copy and paste media) on the bottom.

To copy pictures (or other items) from your BlackBerry, follow these steps:

1. Select the pictures from the **BlackBerry/pictures** folder using one of the following methods:

   ■ Draw a box around some pictures to select them.

   ■ Click one picture to select it.

   ■ Press **Command+A** (Mac) **or Ctrl+A** (Windows) to select them all.

   ■ Press the **Cmd** key (Mac) or **Ctrl** key (Windows) and click to select individual pictures.

2. Once selected—Ctrl-click (Mac) or right-click (Windows) one of the selected pictures and select **Cut** (to move) or **Copy** (to copy) (see Figure 5-5).

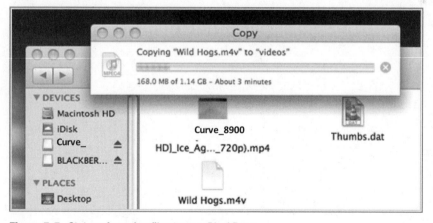

Figure 5-5. *Status of copying files to your BlackBerry*

3. Click any other disk/folder on your computer (e.g., **My Documents**), and navigate to where you want to move/copy the files.

4. Once there, right-click again in the right window where all the files are listed, and select **Paste**.

You can also delete all the pictures/media/songs from your BlackBerry in a similar manner. Navigate to a BlackBerry/(media type) folder such as **BlackBerry/videos**. Press **Ctrl+A** or **Command+A** on your computer keyboard to select all the files, and then press the **Delete** key to delete all the files.

You can also copy files from your computer to your BlackBerry using a similar method. Just go to the files you want to copy and select (highlight them). Then right- click **Copy** and paste them into the correct **BlackBerry/[media type]** folder.

> **NOTE:** Not all videos, images, or songs will be playable or viewable on your BlackBerry. Use Desktop Manager for Mac to transfer the files; most files will be automatically converted for you.

Chapter 6

Typing, Spelling, and Help

In this chapter, we help you get typing as fast and accurately as you can on your Storm keyboards and show you where to get help on your Storm.

If you have not already done so, please check out the **Quick Start Guide** at the beginning of this book for a picture of what every key does on your BlackBerry.

TIP: Multi-Use Buttons—the **Red Phone** key

Many buttons do more than one thing depending on what mode you are in. Try pressing the **Red Phone** key when you're not on a call—it will send you back to your **Home** Screen

TIP: Multitasking (Switch Applications)—Using the **Menu** key and **Red Phone** key

You can multitask using a couple of easy options on your BlackBerry:

Option 1: Press the **Red Phone** key (when not on a call) and you jump right to the Home screen of icons. Then just start your other icon.

Option 2: Press and hold the **Menu** key to see a pop-up window of icons that are running. Select any one or Home to go to your Home screen.

Say you are writing an email and need to check the calendar or want to schedule a new event.

1. Press the **Red Phone** key to jump to the Home screen.
2. Start the calendar to check your schedule.
3. Press the **Red Phone** key again to return to the Home screen.

4. Click on the Messages icon to return exactly to where you left off composing your email message.

Three BlackBerry Keyboards

Your BlackBerry comes with three keyboards that will allow you to type just the way you like. Please see the comprehensive keyboards section in the **Quick Start Guide** on page 3.

Keyboard:	When to use:	More pictures:
SureType keyboard (Portrait Mode)	Short, quick typing tasks, like a quick email or SMS text message.	Page 24
Multitap keyboard (Portrait Mode)	If you are used to quickly typing on another type of phone, this will be familiar for you.	Page 25
Full QWERTY keyboard (Landscape or Portrait Mode)	If you prefer a single letter per key for ease of entry and accuracy, this is the best keyboard for you.	Page 25

Landscape or Portrait - Full Keyboard

Landscape - Full keyboard Mode

When you tilt your BlackBerry Storm sideways into Landscape mode from any program in which you can type, the keyboard will be displayed as a **Full keyboard**.

Portrait - Full keyboard Mode

You can also choose **Enable Full keyboard**

after pressing the **Menu** key in Portrait Mode:

Enable Full Keyboard

See page 25 for more on symbols, caps, and typing numbers.

Portrait - Multitap Keyboard

Portrait - Multitap Mode

This is the more standard cell phone typing technology, where you press the key once for the first letter on the key and twice for the second letter. For example, with the 3/DEF key, you would press it once for "D" and twice to get the "E" and three times to get the "F" in Multitap mode.

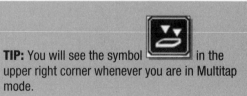

TIP: You will see the symbol in the upper right corner whenever you are in Multitap mode.

See page 25 for more for more on symbols, caps, and typing numbers.

Portrait - SureType Keyboard

Portrait - SureType Mode

This is an innovative technology from BlackBerry that predicts what you are typing from the keys pressed, even though most keys have two letters on them. You only press each key once and the BlackBerry guesses which letter you meant to type based on the context (what you have typed before it) and/or what is in your Address Book. It even learns from you!

When typing with SureType, you will see the pop-up window below (or above) what you are typing. The highlighted word is the one currently being guessed.

If the highlighted word is correct, then press the **space** bar to instantly select it.

If you need to correct it, scroll, tap to highlight, or select a different word or group of letters.

See page 24 for more for more on symbols, caps, and typing numbers.

Wait to Select Corrections in SureType Mode

An important tip when using SureType: wait until the end of the word to select a correction. Many times the SureType system will show you the correct word at the second-to-last or last letter of the word. If you keep adjusting what it guesses after each letter, it will take you all day to type.

Here's an example of faster and slower ways to type with the SureType keyboard.

Faster way to type the word **easy** (4 steps)

1. Press **ER**

2. Press **AS**

3. Press **AS**

4. Press and click on **easy** from the pop-up list (or you could have pressed **TY** and **space**)

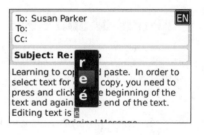

Slower way to type the word **easy** (7 steps)

1. Press **ER**

2. Select **e** from correction list

3. Press **AS**

4. Scroll the correction list once (place your finger on the list and drag up or down) to get to **a**

5. Scroll the correction list again

6. Scroll the correction list again

7. Press and click on the word **easy**. Alternatively, just highlight the correct word and then press the **space** key.

This scrolling up/down the list of SureType options can be quite time consuming.

So we recommend that you continue typing letters until you see your word on the list shown on the screen.

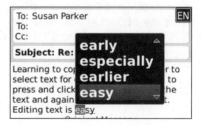

Pop-Ups of Pressed Keys

One nice feature of the virtual keyboard (which may be familiar if you have typed on an iPhone, iPad, or iPod touch) is that little pop-up window that appears above the key you are about to press. This allows you to confirm your finger is on the correct key before you press it.

Pop-Ups of Soft Keys or Buttons

Sometimes you will see buttons or soft keys on the screen and you are not sure what they do.

You can see a little pop-up window showing the name of the soft key or button. This should help you understand what that button does.

In the image to the right, you can see that hovering over the button in the upper right corner reveals that it is the **Save** command for the calendar event.

Show the Keyboard

Sometimes, you will want a keyboard when one isn't on the screen. Simply press the **Menu** key and select **Show Keyboard**.

> **TIP:** Assign the keyboard to one of your convenience keys so you can bring the Virtual keyboard up instantly with a single key click (See page 214). Start your **Options** app, then select **Screen/Keyboard**. Scroll down and change the settings for **Convenience Keys Opens**.

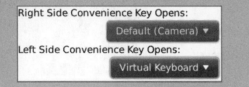

Hide the Keyboard and View Soft Keys

The easiest way to hide the keyboard is to tap the screen and swipe down from the top of the keyboard. In many apps, once the keyboard is hidden, you will see a set of **Soft Keys** along the bottom of the screen (see Figure 6-1). These are great shortcuts for getting common things done.

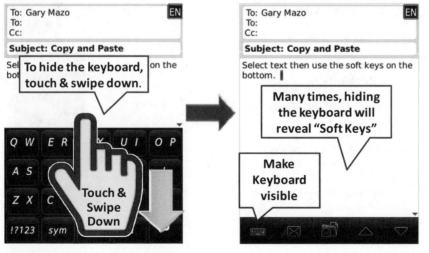

Figure 6-1. *Show or Hide Keyboards*

Switching Between Various Keyboards

You can switch back and forth between various keyboards by pressing the **Menu** key and selecting one of the following:

- Enable Reduced Keyboard
- Enable SureType
- Enable Multitap
- Enable Full Keyboard

> **NOTE:** If you left the keyboard in SureType mode, the BlackBerry will switch to **Multitap** mode when you are in a password field. However, it will stay in **Full Keyboard** mode if you left it there before locking your device.

Setting Your Default Portrait (Vertical) Keyboard

If you prefer to have a particular keyboard appear when your Storm is in the portrait (vertical) orientation, you can set it using these steps:

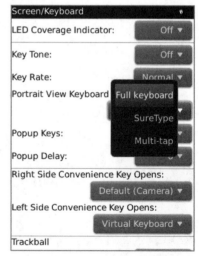

1. From your Home screen, click the **Options** icon.

2. Press and click on **Screen/Keyboard**.

3. Press the button under **Portrait View Keyboard**

4. Change to **Suretype**, **Multitap**, or **Full keyboard**.

5. Press the **Menu** key and **Save** your changes.

Tips for Typing and Editing Text

Typing and making changes to your text on the Storm can be easy using the tips below.

Deleting Characters with the Backspace Key

When a cursor is visible, press the **Backspace** key

to erase letters to the **left** of the cursor. In the image to the right, the letter erased would be the last **r** in **error**.

> **TIP:** Press and hold the **Backspace** key to erase a number of characters.

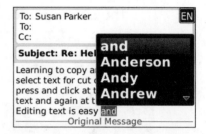

In this image, where there is no cursor, but just a

highlighted word, pressing the **Backspace** key would erase the last highlighted character - the **d** in **and**.

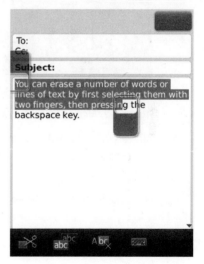

If you want to delete a number of words, an entire sentence, or a paragraph, the fastest way is to follow these steps:

1. Touch the screen simultaneously at the beginning and end of the text you wish to delete to highlight it.

2. Press and click the delete soft key

    at the bottom to delete the highlighted text.

Positioning the Cursor

If you need to edit text in the middle of something you just typed, you can move the cursor by following these steps:

1. Just press and click the screen to put the cursor anywhere in the text.

2. Fine-tune the location of the cursor by using the handles to drag it around. Simply tap and drag the box handles to move the cursor (see Figure 6-2).

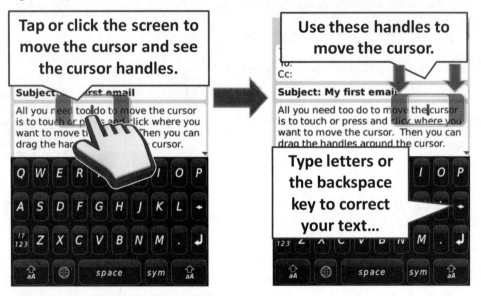

Figure 6-2. *Moving the cursor with the handles*

3. Make your corrections by using the **Backspace** key and type in more text.

4. When you're done, press and click at the end of the text where you were last typing to finish typing your message (see Figure 6-3).

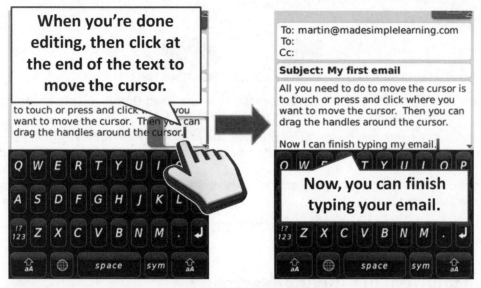

Figure 6-3. *Reposition the cursor at the end of text to finish typing*

TIP: Switch to **Full Keyboard** mode if **Multitap** or **SureType** is not working for you. To do this, turn your BlackBerry horizontally or press the **Menu** key and select **Enable Full Keyboard**.

Press and Hold for Automatic Capitalization

One of the easiest tips is to capitalize letters as your typing them.

To do this, just press and hold the letter to capitalize it.

Automatic Period and Cap at End of Sentence

At the end of a sentence, just press the **space** key twice to see an automatic period (.) and the next letter you type will be automatically capitalized.

Typing Symbols

There are two symbol keys: !?123 and SYM.

There are two types of symbols you can type on your BlackBerry – numbers and most punctuation marks can be found by pressing the key. Parentheses, quotation marks, brackets, and most other symbols not shown on the keyboard are accessed by pressing the (Symbol) key on the keyboard. Both ways allow you to quickly add symbols to your text.

To see images of all the **!?123** and **symbol** keyboards, please see the pages starting on 24 in the **Quick Start Guide.**

Quickly Typing E-mail Addresses

On some smartphones, when you want to put in the @ or the "." in your email, you need a complicated series of commands.

On the Storm, this process is much simpler. While you are typing the email, follow these steps:

1. Type the user name (for instance, **martin**).

2. Press the **space** key once and the Storm will automatically insert the @ martin@

3. Type in the domain name and then press the **space** key again to see the dot "." **martin@madesimplelearning.** No additional keystrokes necessary.

4. Finish the email address with the **com** and you see martin@madesimplelearning.com.

Quickly Changing Drop-Down Lists

There are a few ways to quickly select items in drop-down lists on your Storm. These tips work best if you have set one of your convenience keys to bring up the **Full Virtual Keyboard**. (See the "Changing Convenience Keys" section in Chapter 8 on page 214 to get this done.)

Using the Space Key to Change Drop-Down Lists

Another thing that the **space** key does is to move you down to the next item in a list. Give it a try. Open up any screen with a drop-down list of items.

For example, go to the **Options icon** in the **Screen/Keyboard** section. If you highlight the drop-down list next to Portrait View keyboard and press the **space** key, you will notice that the selection toggles to the next entry in the list. Keep pressing the drop down and you will eventually cycle through all the options (Figure 6-4).

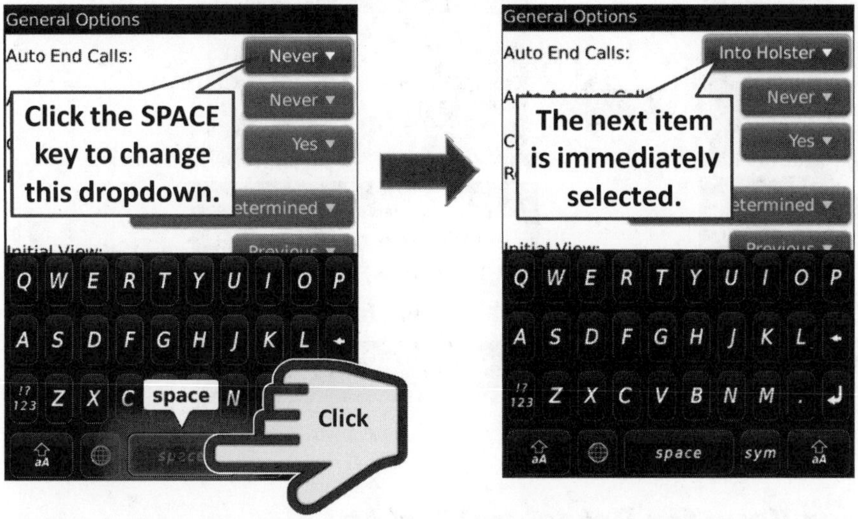

Figure 6-4. *Using the space bar to toggle to the next drop-down list item*

> **TIP:** This **space** key trick can save you time from pressing, dragging up, or down, and then clicking to select an item.

When a time field is highlighted, pressing the **space** key will advance you five minutes at a time. It's a great way to quickly change a time.

> **TIP:** This **space** key also works on non-numeric fields—any drop down list and parts of the date such as day of the week and month.

Using Letter Keys for Drop-Down Lists and More

You can even use the letter keys on your keyboard to instantly jump down to the first item matching either letter on the key (if there are two letters), jumping down to a matching menu item, or jumping down to a matching item in a list (like the long list in the Options icon).

Setting Dates and Times

To set a date or time, you simply click on it to have it pop up in the middle of the screen in a small window. Then you drag your finger up or down to change the highlighted item. To move quickly up or down a list, simply flick your finger up or down and watch the dial really spin (see Figure 6-5).

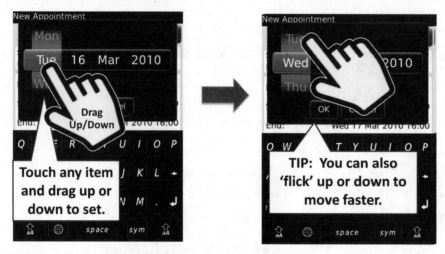

Figure 6-5. *Setting dates and types by sliding your finger or flicking up or down.*

Using Number Keys for Dates and Times

You can use the number keys on your keyboard to instantly type a new date or time or select an entry in a drop down list with that number. Examples include typing "40" in the minute field to set the minutes to 40 or typing 9 in the hour field to get to 9 AM or PM. This also works in the fields where drop down list items start with numbers, like in the Reminder field in calendar or tasks. Typing a number "9" would immediately jump you to the "9 Hours" setting.

Using Your Spell Checker

Your BlackBerry comes with a built-in Spell Checker.

Normally, your Spell Checker is turned on to check everything you type. You can tell if it's on by the little dotted underline that appears while you type. The underlining goes away when the Spell Checker matches your word with one from the dictionary that is spelled correctly. Normally, you will need to turn it on to have it check your outgoing email messages.

Spell Checker

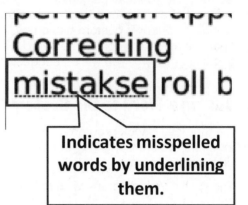

Indicates misspelled words by <u>underlining</u> them.

Another option is to use the AutoText feature (see page 184).

To correct this word, press and click on the word with your finger. You will see a list of suggested changes; just scroll to and press and click on the correct word.

Using the Spelling Custom Dictionary

Sometimes, you may use unique words (such as the names of local places) in your emails that are not found in the standard dictionary. In this case, you may add these words to your own custom dictionary. The advantages of this are (1) that you will never again be asked to replace that word with something suggested and (2) if you misspell this custom word, you will be suggested the correct spelling.

Adding a Word to the Custom Dictionary

Let the Spell Check program notice the word that it believes is misspelled. In this example, we are using Flagler county (a county in Florida) that is not in the standard dictionary.

The spell check program will suggest options for replacing the word.

1. Press the **Menu** key.

2. You may see options to **Ignore** or **Ignore All**.

3. Click the **Add to Dictionary** to add this word to your own custom dictionary.

Next time we spell "Flagler," it will not be shown as misspelled. Even better, the next time we misspell Flagler (e.g. "Flaglr"); the spell checker will find it and give us the correct spelling.

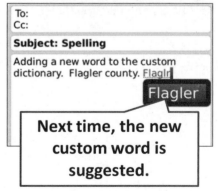

Next time, the new custom word is suggested.

Edit or Delete Words in Custom Dictionary

Mistakes happen. It's fairly easy to press and click the wrong menu item and inadvertently add wrong words to the Custom Dictionary. The authors have done this plenty of times.

1. Return to the **Spell Checker** options screen as shown above. (**Messages icon | Menu key | Options | Spell Check**— or— **Options icon | Spell Check**)

2. Once in the Spell Check screen, press and click on the **Custom Dictionary** button at the bottom.

3. Now you will see a list of every word in your Custom Dictionary.

4. You can either scroll down and find the word(s) that need to be removed, or start typing a few letters to Find the word.

5. Press the **Menu** key once the word you want is highlighted.

6. Select **Edit** or **Delete** from the menu.

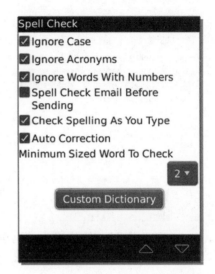

> **WARNING:** Your Spell Checker may not be turned on for every e-mail you send.
>
> By default, many BlackBerry Smartphones will not do a spell check before sending email. You can actually ignore all misspelled (underlined) words and send. Below, we show you how to force the Spell Check to be enabled for outgoing email.

Enabling Spell Check for Outbound Email

One of the great features of your Storm is that you can automatically check the spelling in your emails before you send them out. However, this feature is usually not turned on by default. So you have to enable it.

You can turn on spell checking for email messages in two areas:

1. Start your **Messages** (Email) app.

2. Press the **Menu** key and select **Options.**

3. Then scroll down and press and click on **Spell Check** (Figure 6-6).

4. Check the box next to **Spell Check Email Before Sending**

5. Press the **Menu** key and select **Save.**

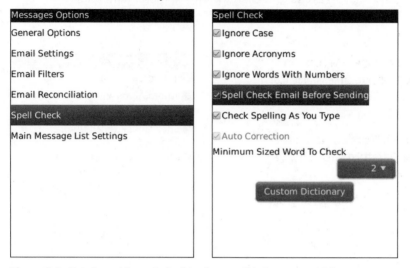

Figure 6-6. *How to enable spell checking for e-mail before you send it.*

Using the Storm's Built-In Help

There might be times when you don't have this book handy and you need to find out how to do something right away on your Storm.

You can get into the **Help** menu from the **Help** icon and almost every application on the BlackBerry has a built-in contextual help menu that can answer some of your basic questions.

Using the Help Menus

The Help menu can be accessed from virtually any application. For our purposes, we will take a look at the **Help** menu built into the **Calendar** app.

1. Once in the Calendar or most any other program on your BlackBerry, press the **Menu** key.

2. Scroll all the way up to the top and click on **Help.** (This will be available in most built-in applications.)

3. You will now see the Calendar-related help topics, as shown in Figure 6-7.

4. Press and click on any item, such as **Calendar Basics** to see more topics or a help screen.

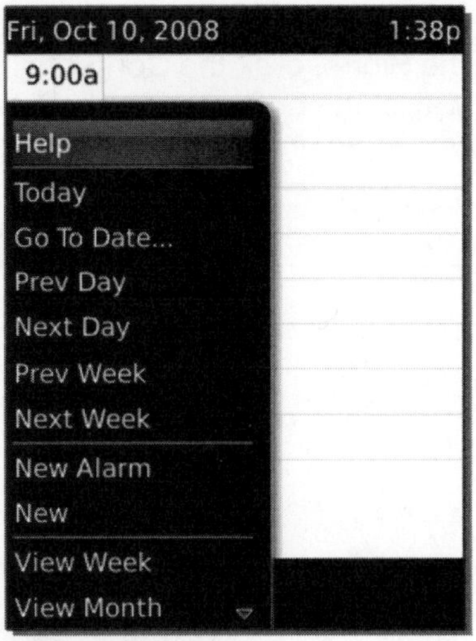

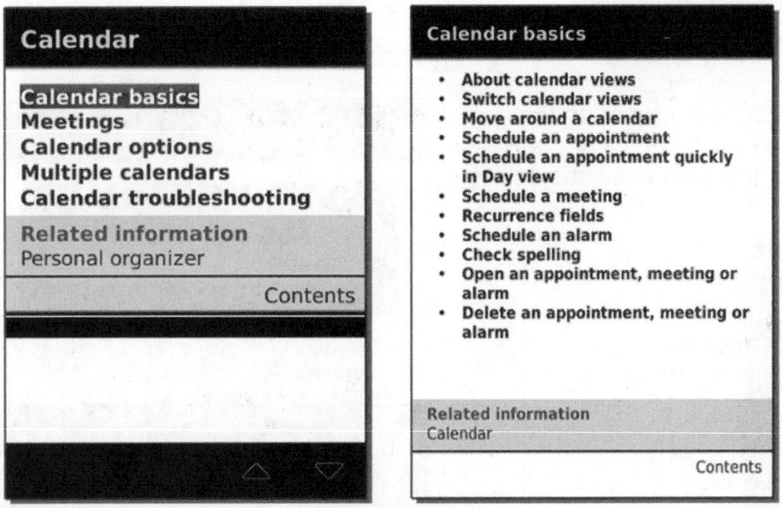

Figure 6-7. *Navigating the Storm's built-in help function.*

5. Continue to click on topics you would like to learn about.

6. Press the **Escape** key to back up one level in the help menus.

7. You can also press the **Calendar** link in the gray **Related Information** bar at the bottom to jump right to the overall calendar help topics.

Overall Help Contents and Finding Help Text

Like pretty much every other feature on the BlackBerry, there are some tips and tricks when using Help.

To see the main Help index of topics for the Storm, click the **Contents** link all the way at the bottom of the help screen under the gray bar of **Related Information**.

Related information
Calendar
Contents

To search for a particular word on the screen (either in a list of topics or the Help text itself), press the **Menu** key and select **Find**.

Save Time with AutoText

In this chapter, we show you some great tips and tricks to save time and increase accuracy for words and phrases that you may have to type many times. For example, you can come up with new AutoText for directions. Or you can create a date and time stamp with a two letter shortcut; this is great if you are taking notes and don't want to bother typing out the current date and time—two letters of AutoText does the trick!

Sometimes, typing on the little BlackBerry keyboard produces less than desirable results. Fortunately, for the more common misspellings, you can create an AutoText entry to solve this problem. The **pre-loaded AutoText** is used to correct common typing mistakes, like leaving out an apostrophe in the word "aren't" or misspelling "the" as shown in Figure 7-1.

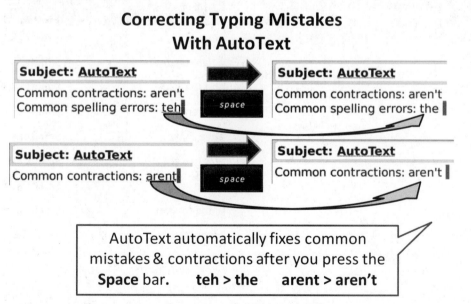

Figure 7-1. *AutoText fixes common spelling mistakes and contractions.*

> **TIP:** Knowing AutoText is there to help you get things right will allow you to type with greater abandon on your BlackBerry.
>
> Take a few minutes to browse the AutoText pre-loaded entries, especially the contractions, so you can learn to type them without ever using the apostrophe.

You can also use AutoText for more advanced things like automatically typing an email signature, driving directions, a canned email, routine text describing your products or services, legal disclaimer text, anything!

Creating a New AutoText Entry

You can get into the AutoText list from the **Edit AutoText** menu item when you are typing an email (by pressing the **Menu** key) or from the main **Options** icon.

To create a new entry from your Home screen, follow these steps:

1. Press and click on your **Options** icon.

2. Click on **AutoText** to see the list of entries.

> **TIP:** Learn the contractions to save time when typing future emails. (Skip typing the apostrophe.)

AutoText	
Find:	
acn (can)	SmartCase
adn (and)	SmartCase
agian (again)	SmartCase
ahd (had)	SmartCase
ahppen (happen)	SmartCase
ahve (have)	SmartCase
alot (a lot)	SmartCase
amde (made)	SmartCase
amke (make)	SmartCase
arent (aren't)	SmartCase

3. Type in the new entry you want to add, in this case **dirh** for **Directions to home** and make sure you see no entries that exactly match.

4. Press the **Menu** key and select **New**.

AutoText

> dirh

> * No Phrases *

> Help
>
> New
>
> Show Keyboard
>
> Switch Application
>
> Close

* No Phrases * shows no matches.

5. Under **With:** type the text you want to appear when you type your new AutoText word **dirh**.

6. Press the **Menu** key and select **Save**.

AutoText: New

Replace:
dirh
With:
1. Take I-95 to exit 268
2. Exit onSR-40 West
3. Follow 3 miles, turn right on Creek Rd.
4. Follow 2.3 Miles, turn left onForest
5. We are the 3rd house on right, #235

Using: SmartCase ▼

Language: All Locales ▼

> **TIP:** Type these directions on your computer and email them to yourself, then copy/paste them into AutoText from the email.

Edit or Delete an AutoText Entry

You may need to edit or remove an AutoText entry. The steps to get this done are very similar to creating a new one:

1. Return to the AutoText list by selecting **Edit AutoText** from the menu while typing an email or from the **Options** icon.

2. Type a few letters to find the AutoText entry. Press the **Menu** key, and select **Edit** or **Delete**.

Advanced AutoText Features — Macros — Time Stamp

With AutoText, you can actually insert macros or shortcuts for other functions such as display the current time and date, your PIN, or owner information. You can even simulate pressing the backspace or delete keys.

Let's create a new entry called **ts** (**time stamp**) that will instantly show the current time and date.

1. Start by creating a new entry as you did above.

2. Type the **ts** under **Replace**.

> **NOTE:** It is easier to type these letters with the **Full Keyboard** showing. But you might have to click next to "ts" after you type it.

3. Move the cursor down to under **With**: by pressing the **Enter** key .

4. Press the **Menu** key and select **Insert Macro**.

5. Now, scroll up or down and select the macro you want. In this case, we want a short date (%d) which is **mm/dd/yy** format.

6. Press **space**, then **!?123**, type a hyphen (-), and then press **space**.

7. Press the **Menu** key and insert the short time (%t) macro. The entry should now look like this image to the right.

> **TIP:** You could also simply type the **%t** to save a few steps. Read below for a list of all the two-character macro shortcuts.

Now, whenever you want to insert the current date and time, just type your new entry **ts** and press **space**.

> **Title: Meeting ts|**

Press the **space** key to see the date/time.

> **Title: Meeting 1/31/2009 - 9:25a |**

Here's a list of the standard **AutoText Macros:**

Here's what they look like:

> **Title: Macros List**
>
> Short Date: 9/22/2008
> Long Date: Mon, Sep 22, 2008
> Short Time: 8:12p
> Long Time: 8:12:29 PM
> Owner Name: Martin Trautschold
> Owner Info: If found, please contact
> Martin Trautschold office: 1-386-506-
> 8224.
> 123 Main Street
> Anytown, STATE 38928

%d	Short Date
%D	Long Date
%t	Short Time
%T	Long Time
%o	Owner Name
%O	Owner Information
%p	Your Phone Number
%P	Your PIN
%b	Backspace
%B	Delete
%%	Percent

Personalize Your Storm

In this chapter, you will learn some great ways to personalize your Storm, like changing your Home screen wallpaper, moving and hiding icons, organizing with folders, setting your convenience keys, changing your theme or look and feel, and adjusting font sizes and types.

Setting Your Home Screen Preferences

The easiest thing to do to personalize your Storm is to change your Home screen preferences which include the background wallpaper, rows of icons, and whether or not you see icons or upcoming calendar events, recent emails, and phone call logs.

Changing Your Wallpaper

You might want to change the background picture on your Storm's Home screen from time to time. To do so, follow these steps:

1. From your Home screen, press the **Menu** key a few times until you see the **Options** menu item. Press and click on **Options**.

2. Click on the **Wallpaper** image, usually at the top (as shown).

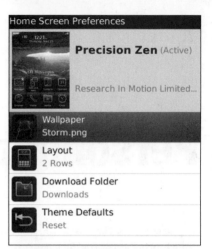

3. To use a picture or pre-loaded wallpaper image, click on the **pictures** folder or roll down and click on an image you see. Skip to step 5.

4. Use your **Camera** to snap a picture. After taking the picture, press the **Menu** key and select **Set As**, then click **Wallpaper**.

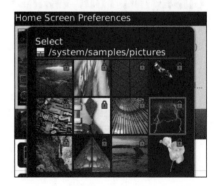

5. Navigate to a folder (there are some good pictures in the **Preloaded Images** folder).

6. Once you get to the image you want to use, press the **Menu** key and select **Set As Wallpaper**.

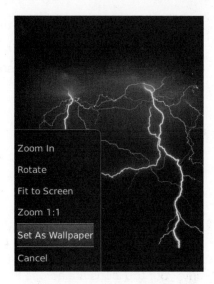

Adding More Rows of Icons or Showing the Today Layout

The default setting on your BlackBerry Storm is to have two rows of four icons on the Home screen. You can easily change this to just one row or to three rows by following these steps:

1. From your Home screen, press the **Menu** key a few times until you see the **Options** menu item. Press and click on **Options**.

2. Press and click on **Layout**.

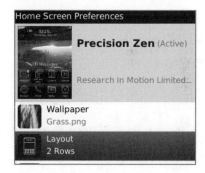

3. Press and click to select the number of rows (1, 2, or 3 rows) or Today.

.4. Select **Save** on the next screen to save your changes.

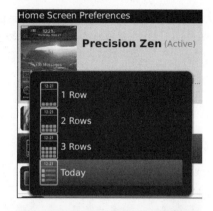

To have your top icons shown on the Zen Home screen, follow the instructions to **Move icons** and **Move icons between folders** in this chapter and make sure your top icons are across the top row or at the top of the list.

> **TIP:** The Today layout shows your most recent messages, phone call logs/missed calls, and upcoming calendar events.

Changing Your Download Folder for New Apps

Also in your Home screen Preferences, you can change where all new downloaded apps are stored. Follow these steps:

1. From your Home screen, press the **Menu** key a few times until you see the **Options** menu item. Press and click on **Options**.

2. Press and click on **Download Folder**.

3. Press and click on the new folder for all your downloaded apps. In this case, the **Applications** folder is chosen.

4. Select **Save** on the next screen to save your changes.

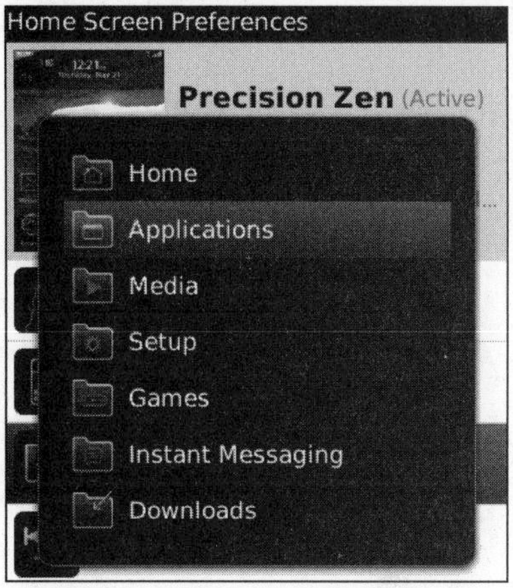

Resetting Your Home Screen Preferences

If you find yourself wishing you had not made so many changes, or you just want to revert your Home screen preferences back to the defaults, follow these steps.

1. From your Home screen, press the **Menu** key a few times until you see the **Options** menu item. Press and click on **Options**.

2. Press and click on **Theme Defaults (Reset)**.

3. Select the items you want to reset by pressing and clicking on them. You can reset any of the following: **Wallpaper, Layout, Download Folder,** or **Icon Arrangement**.

4. Press and click **Apply** when done.

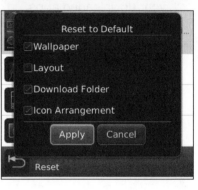

Organizing Your Icons

You may not need to see every single icon on your Home screen, or you may want to move your most popular icons to the top row for easy access. The way you move and hide icons varies a little depending on which Theme you have on your BlackBerry.

Moving Your Icons within a Folder

Press the **Menu** key to see an array of all your icons. If the icon you want to move is inside a particular folder, like Downloads or Applications, scroll to and press and click on that folder.

1. Scroll over and touch the icon you want to move to highlight it. In this case, we are going to move the SMS icon, because it is highlighted.

2. Press the **Menu** key (between your Green phone key and **Escape** key) to bring up the **Move** menu item as shown.

3. Once you select **Move,** you will see arrows around the icon (as shown).

4. Gently touch the screen in the spot where you would like to move the icon.

5. Finally, press and click the screen to set the moved icon at the new location.

Hiding and Showing Icons

Hiding icons is fairly straight forward. Getting them back takes a few more steps.

How to Hide Icons

To hide an icon, follow these steps.

1. Highlight the icon you wish to hide

2. Press the **Menu** key and select **Hide**.

You're done – the icon is hidden.

How to Show Hidden Icons

To show a hidden icon, follow these steps.

1. Press the **Menu** key and select **Show All**.

2. The icons that are hidden appear dimmer or grayed out like the **Maps** icon to the right.

3. Highlight the icon you wish to restore from being hidden. In this case we want to restore the Maps icon.

4. Press the **Menu** key and select **Hide**. Notice that there is a checkmark next to the menu item; this shows the icon is currently hidden. Clicking **Hide** again will un-hide it.

5. Finally, if you want to get rid of all the other hidden icons, you need to turn off the **Show All**. Press the **Menu** key and select **Show All**.

How Do I Know When I'm in a Folder?

When you are in a folder, you see a little tabbed folder icon at the top of your screen and the name of the folder. In the image to the right, you are in the **Applications** folder.

Moving Your Icons between Folders

Sometimes you want to move icons to your Home folder to make them more easily accessible. Conversely, you might want to move some of the icons you seldom use from your Home folder into another folder to clean up your Home screen.

Let's say we wanted to move our **SMS** icon from the Home screen to the Applications folder.

1. Press the **Menu** key to show all your Home screen icons. Then scroll through and tap to highlight the **SMS icon,** as shown.

2. Then, press the **Menu** key and select the **Move to Folder** menu item, as shown.

3. We want to move this icon out of our Home folder into the **Applications** folder, so we press and click on **Applications.**

4. Press the **Escape** key to exit from the Applications folder back to the Home folder to locate our newly moved SMS icon. In this case, it is near the bottom of the list of icons.

Setting Your Home Screen Top Icons

Depending on what theme you have selected on your BlackBerry, you may have noticed that only a limited number of icons (usually 8, but you can change this number; see page 195) show up on your main Home screen. These happen to be the top icons in the list of icons after you press the **Menu** key. So, it's simple to get icons on the limited list—just move them up to the top. Since we use our SMS icon quite a bit on the Storm, let's move it from the Instant Messaging folder to the top.

1. Enter the Instant Messaging folder by clicking on it.

2. Then highlight the icon we want to move, **SMS**, and press the **Menu** key. Select **Move to Folder** and select Home.

3. Next, click on **Home** to get the SMS icon on your main **Home** list of icons and out of the Instant Messaging folder.

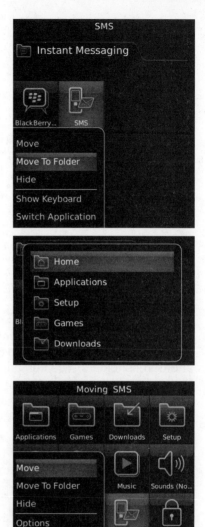

4. Press the **Escape** key to get back to your Home screen of icons to see the SMS icon again.

5. Now, highlight the SMS icon and select **Move** this time.

6. To move the icon, just tap the screen at one of the top spots in the icons list. Press and click to set it into place and complete the move.

Now we see the **SMS** icon on our limited set of icons on the Home screen.

Working with Folders

On your BlackBerry, you can create or delete folders to better organize your icons. There are several folders created by default—typically, the Applications, Settings, Downloads, and Games folders. You can add your own folders and then move icons into your new folders to better organize them.

Creating a New Folder

NOTE: At the time of publication, you could only create folders one level deep. In other words, you can only create new folders when you are in the Home folder, not when you are already inside another folder. This may change with new software versions.

1. To create a new folder, first press the **Menu** key to see all your icons. Then press the **Menu** key again and select **Add Folder**.

> **NOTE:** If you don't see the **Add Folder** menu item, then press the **Escape** key to the right of your **Menu** key once to get back to your home folder.

2. After you select the **Add Folder** menu item, you will see this screen. Type your folder name, then press and click on the folder icon, and scroll left or right to check out all the different possible folder colors and styles.

3. Once you're done selecting the folder icon style, press and click on it, and scroll down to press and click on the **Add** button to finish creating your folder. Now you will see your new folder.

Moving Icons between Folders

Once you create your new folder, you will want to move icons into it. Please see the instructions on page 201 on how to do this.

Editing a Folder

You can edit a folder by highlighting it, pressing the **Menu** key, and selecting **Edit Folder**. Then you can change the name and folder icon, and save your changes.

Deleting a Folder

Whenever you want to get rid of a folder, just highlight it and select **Delete,** as shown.

Setting the Date, Time, and Time Zone

You can adjust the Date, Time, and Time Zone in the Setup Wizard, but there are times when you want to adjust it manually.

1. From your home screen, click on the time at the top to open your clock app.

2. Click anywhere on the clock screen to see a pop-up window.

3. Select **Set Time** to get to the Date/Time setting screen.

4. Click next to **Time Zone** to see a list of all the time zones and select the correct one.

If you leave the **Auto Update Time Zone** to the default **On**, then every time you move between time zones, your BlackBerry will automatically detect the new time zone from the cell towers and update your BlackBerry.

The only way you can manually adjust the date or time is if you change **Use Network Time** to **No**.

Then, click on the time or date field to bring up the setting pop-up window. You can swipe up/down to change a value. Or, in number fields, you can click on the field to bring up the keyboard and type a number like "23." Typing digits can be faster and more accurate than scrolling.

If you prefer **12 hour** format (7:30 AM/ 4:30 PM) to **24 hour** format (07:30/16:30), you set that in **Time Format**. Tap the **space** bar to toggle between the two options.

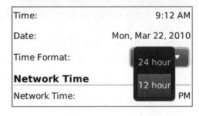

TIP: You can force the BlackBerry to get updates to the time zone by pressing the **Menu** key and select **Get Time Zone Updates**.

Finally, to save your changes, press the **Menu** key and select **Save**.

Date/Time	
Time Zone	
Time Zone:	Eastern Time (-5) ▾
(GMT-05:00) Eastern Time (US & Canada)	
Auto Update Time Zone:	On ▾

Help	No ▾
Copy	9:16 AM
Get Time Zone Updates	n, Mar 22, 2010
Save	12 hour ▾
Show Keyboard	
Switch Application	4:16 PM
Close	n, Mar 22, 2010

Changing Your Font Size and Type

You can fine-tune the font size and type on your Storm to fit your individual preferences.

Do you need to see more on the screen and don't mind small fonts? Then go all the way down to a micro-size 7-point font.

Do you need to see **bigger fonts** for easy readability? Adjust the fonts to a large **14-point font**.

To adjust your font, follow these steps:

1. Press and click on the **Options** icon. Options You may need to press the **Menu** key and scroll up or down to find it.

2. Scroll down to press and click on **Screen/Keyboard** (Figure 8-1).

3. You can change the **Font Family**, **Font Size**, and **Font Style** on this screen. Press and click to change any item. Notice the preview of your currently selected style and size to make sure it will fit your needs.

4. When done, press the **Menu** key and select **Save**.

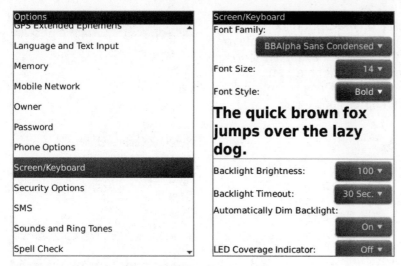

Figure 8-1. *Changing your Storm font family, size, and style*

Changing Your Theme: The Look and Feel

You can customize your Storm to make it look truly unique. One way to do this is to change the Theme of your Storm. Changing Themes usually changes the layout and appearance of your icons by and the font type and size you see inside each icon. There may be only one or a few themes pre-installed on your Storm. The good news is that you can find hundreds of Themes available for download from various web sites.

CARRIER-SPECIFIC THEMES: Depending on your BlackBerry wireless carrier (phone company), you may see various customized Themes that are not shown in this book.

MORE STANDARD/GENERIC BLACKBERRY THEMES: Most of the Standard Themes shown below are on every BlackBerry (or can be downloaded from http://mobile.blackberry.com).

Scroll and press and click on the **Option** icon on your BlackBerry. You may have to press the **Menu** key to see all your icons and then locate the Options icon, or you may have to press and click on a **Settings** folder to locate the Options icon. Once in **Options**, scroll down to **Theme** and press and click.

Inside the Theme screen, just scroll and press and click on the Theme you want to make **Active**. Your currently selected Theme is shown with the word (Active) next to it.

Then press the **Escape** key to get back to the Home screen to check out your new theme.

Downloading New Themes

CAUTION: The authors have downloaded many themes on their BlackBerry smartphones. Some themes can cause problems with your BlackBerry, such as the BlackBerry may stop working or freeze, or you may not be able to see everything on the screen. We recommend only downloading themes from a web site you know and trust.

Download from App World

1. Start BlackBerry App World. See page 467 for help getting App World running.

2. Click on the Categories soft key in the lower left corner.

3. Scroll down and click on the Themes category.

4. Click on the type of theme you would like to download.

5. In this example, we'll choose "Nature"

6. Now you see all the themes in the Nature category.

   Notice that there are FREE and paid themes.

Click on any theme to learn more about it, buy it, or download it.

To learn more about the theme, check out the **Screenshots** and **Reviews**.

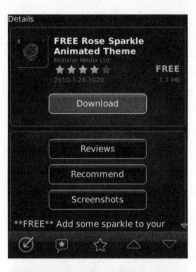

> **WARNING:** Some of the reviews may have explicit language and many have spelling errors.

If you are ready to try the Theme, click the **Buy** button or the **Download** button.

When the theme is downloaded, you will see a message asking if you want to activate it.

Click **Yes** to give the new Theme a try right now.

Here is an example of the new Theme activated.

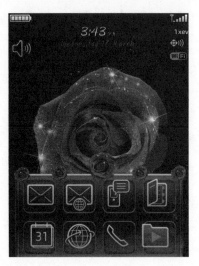

You can't see it in the book, but the rose is animated. It opens and closes slightly, and the sparkles move around.

Download Themes, Wallpaper, and Ringtones from Other Web Sites

You can also find many Themes from BlackBerry-related web sites. To download these themes, follow the steps below:

Press and click your **Browser** icon.

Press and click in the top Address bar to type in one of the BlackBerry community web sites such as:

BlackBerry Mobile Site: http://mobile.blackberry.com

CrackBerry.com : www.crackberry.com

BlackBerry Forums: http://www.blackberryforums.com

Click the **Go** key (where the Enter key usually is located).

Look for a section on the site that says something like personalize, themes, wallpapers or ringtones.

Follow the steps on the site to download the content to your Storm.

CAUTION: Some of the items you find on these web sites may be explicit or offensive. Please view and download with care.

Changing Your Convenience Keys

The two keys on the middle of the sides of your Storm are actually programmable keys called **convenience** keys (named so because each of the two keys can be set to conveniently open any icon on your BlackBerry, even new third party icons that you added to your BlackBerry).

1. Press and click on the **Options** icon (press the **Menu** key if you don't see it listed.)

2. Scroll down to **Screen/Keyboard** and press and click on it.

3. Scroll down the screen until you see Right Side Convenience Key Opens: and Left Side Convenience Key Opens:

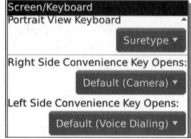

4. To change the application that these keys open, just press and click on the item to see the entire list. Then scroll and press and click on the icon you want.

5. Then press the **Menu** key and select **Save** to save your changes.

> **TIP:** We recommend setting your left convenience key to open the **Virtual keyboard.** It makes it that much easier to just pull up your keyboard when needed.

Now give you newly set convenience keys a try.

> **TIP:** The Convenience keys **work from anywhere**, not just the Home screen.
>
> **TIP:** You can set your Convenience keys to open any icon, even newly installed ones!
>
> After you install new icons, you will notice that they show up in the list of available icons to select in the Screen/Keyboard options screen. So if your newly installed stock quote, news reader, or game is important, just set it as a convenience key.

The Blinking Light - Repeat Notification

One of the features that BlackBerry users love is the little LED that blinks in the upper right hand corner. It is possible to have this light blink different colors:

- Red when you receive an incoming message (MMS, SMS or Email) or calendar alarm rings
- Blue when connected to a Bluetooth device
- Green when you have wireless coverage
- Amber if you need to charge your BlackBerry or it is charging

Red Flashing Message or Alert LED

By default, whenever you receive a new email message or your calendar or other alarm rings, the red LED on the top of your Storm will also flash. The red light can be pretty bright, especially in the dark, so you might want to turn it off. You can disable the red LED feature by following the steps below:

1. Start your Sounds icon.

2. Now you have two options:

3. If you want to fine-tune individual email accounts in your currently selected profile, click on Set Ring Tones/Alerts near the bottom of the list.

4. In order to change the settings for all email accounts at once for the selected profile, click on Edit Profiles.

5. To edit email accounts, click on Messages. You will see each of your email accounts listed as Email [(your email address)], and Level 1, SMS, Text, etc.

6. To edit Calendar and other alerts, click on the Reminders section.

7. Click on any account or app you wish to modify.

8. Set the LED to No to disable the red flashing light.

9. Press the Menu key and select Save.

Ring Tones/Alerts - Normal

Phone

⊖ Messages

Email [Email]

Level 1

PIN

SMS

⊕ Instant Messages

⊕ Reminders

Email [Email] - Normal

Ring Tone: BBPro_Sanguine ▼

Volume: Silent ▼

LED: Off ▼

Blue Flashing Bluetooth LED

In order to disable or enable the blue flashing LED when you are connected to a Bluetooth device, follow these steps:

1. From your Home screen, press and click on the **Options icon** (wrench).

2. Scroll to **Bluetooth** and press and click.

3. Press the **Menu** key and select **Options.**

4. Go down to **LED Connection Indicator** and set to **On** or **Off.**

5. Press the **Menu** key and **Save** your settings.

Green Flashing Coverage LED

To enable or disable the green coverage flashing LED, follow these steps:

1. Click on your **Options** icon.

2. Scroll to **Screen/Keyboard** and press and click.

3. Scroll down to **LED Coverage Indicator** and select either **On** or **Off.**

4. Press the **Menu** key and **Save** your settings.

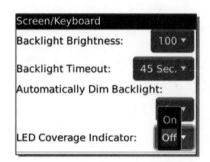

Sounds: Ring and Vibrate

Your Storm is highly customizable—everything from Ringtones to vibrations to LED notifications can be adjusted. Traveling on an airplane but still want to use your calendar or play a game without disturbing others? No problem. In a meeting or at a movie and don't want the phone to ring, but you do want some sort of silent notification when an email comes in? No problem.

Virtually any scenario you can imagine can be dealt with preemptively by adjusting your Sound Profile settings.

Preloaded Sound Profiles

By default, the Storm is set to a **Normal** sound profile, meaning that when a call comes in, the phone rings; when a calendar alarm rings, you will see an alert on the window (without any sound or vibration); and when a message comes in, you hear a sound and the phone may vibrate. The currently selected sound profile has the word "(Active)" next to it. Seven preloaded sound profiles are available on your Storm.

Normal is the default Active profile; in it, the phone rings and messages beep and vibrate.

Loud increases the volume for all notifications.

Medium adjusts all notifications to mid-level volume.

Vibrate Only enables a short vibration for all alerts. (Great for meetings, movies, family dinners, or other places where cell phone rings are discouraged.)

Silent will display notifications on the display and via the LED only.

Phone Calls Only will turn off all notifications except incoming calls.

All Alerts Off will turn off all notifications.

Selecting a Different Preloaded Sound Profile

You can quickly change your sound profile from your Home screen.

1. Press and click the **Speaker** icon in the upper left portion of the Home screen.

2. Press and click to select a new **Sound Profile** (see Figure 10-1).

3. The new profile will be shown by a change in the **Speaker** icon.

Figure 9-1. *Selecting a different preloaded sound profile*

If you don't see the speaker icon on your home screen, then follow the steps below to adjust your **Sound Profile**:

1. Press the **Menu** key or tap the middle of your Home screen to see the entire list of icons.

2. Scroll down then scroll to the **Sounds** (Speaker) icon and press and click on it.

3. As shown in Figure 9-1, press and click on the new sound profile you wish to activate.

Customizing a Sound Profile

There may be some situations where you want a combination of options that one preloaded profile alone cannot satisfy. The Storm is highly customizable, so you can adjust your profile options for virtually any potential situation. The easiest way to accomplish this is to choose a profile that is closest to what you need and edit it as shown below.

1. Press and click on **Sounds** icon (speaker).

2. Select **Edit Profiles** near the bottom of the list by pressing and clicking it.

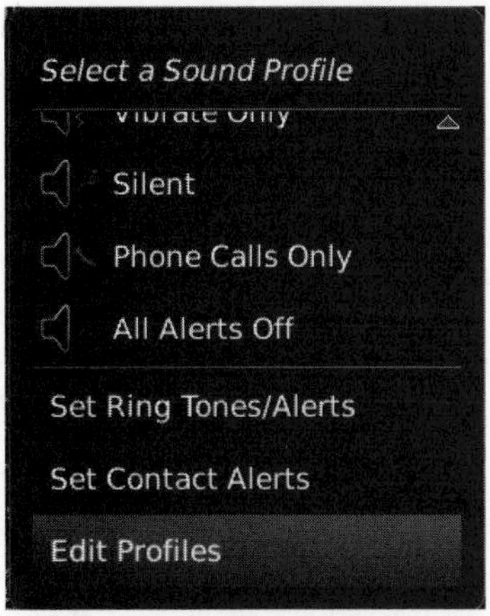

Select a Sound Profile

Vibrate Only

Silent

Phone Calls Only

All Alerts Off

Set Ring Tones/Alerts

Set Contact Alerts

Edit Profiles

3. Now, press and click on a profile that is close to what you want as a custom profile. In this case, we want to tweak the **Normal** profile.

   If you wanted to adjust a different profile, simply press and click on it instead.

Edit Profiles

Add Custom Profile

Normal

Loud

Medium

Vibrate Only

Silent

Phone Calls Only

All Alerts Off

4. Press and click on the category of alert you wish to edit. In this case, we want to edit the Calendar, so we press and click on **Reminders** to see the Calendar listed below.

5. Press and click on **Calendar**.

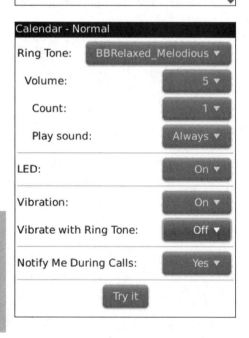

6. The default for the calendar does not vibrate or ring, and we want to change it. You can adjust virtually every aspect of how the Calendar alerts you when a calendar alarm rings. We changed the **Volume** from **Silent** to **5** and set the **Vibration** to **On**.

7. Press the **Menu** key and select **Save**.

TIP: Make sure to leave the Vibrate with Ring Tone to Off. This will give you a few seconds of vibration before the alarm starts ringing, giving you a chance to keep the phone silent if necessary.

8. If you want to adjust your email notifications, click on **Messages** to expand that section, then click on your **Email** account to see the image shown.

9. For example, choose **Email** and notice that you can make adjustments for vibration both "Out of Holster" and "In Holster." (A holster may be supplied with your device or sold separately. This is essentially a carrying case that clips to your belt and uses a magnet to notify your Storm it is "In Holster" and that you should turn off the screen immediately, among other things.)

Email [Email] - Normal	
Ring Tone:	BBPro_Sanguine ▼
Volume:	Silent ▼
LED:	Off ▼
Vibration:	Custom ▼
Length:	Medium ▼
Count:	2 ▼
Vibrate:	In holster
Notify Me During Calls:	Out of holster
Try it	Always

TIP: If you make e-mail sound profile changes **before** you set up individual e-mail accounts, you won't need to adjust each one individually.

Changing Your Phone Ring Tone

Please see page 416 of the Music chapter to learn how to get this done.

Downloading a New Ring Tone

You may find that your stock ringtones just are not loud enough for you to hear, even when you turn the volume up to loud. Sometimes, you just want a fun Ringtone. We have found that you can download a new ringtone from **mobile.blackberry.com** (among other web sites) to help with this problem.

1. Open your **Web Browser**.

2. If can't see a place to type a web address, then **Menu** key and select **Go To...**

3. Type in mobile.blackberry.com and press the **Go** key (where **Enter** was located).

4. Then scroll down and press and click on the link called **Personalize**. Then, just press and click on **Ringtones.**

5. When you press and click, you can **Open** (listen/play it) or **Save** it on your BlackBerry.

6. Go ahead and **Open** a few to test them out. To get back to the list and try more ringtones, press the **Escape** key.

7. If you like the ringtone, then press **Menu** key after you listened to it and select **Save** from the menu.

8. This time, select **Save** and scroll down and check the box at the bottom that says **Set as Ringtone.**

9. You are done. Next time you receive a phone call, the new ringtone should play.

TIP: New Ringtones are available on many BlackBerry user Websites like:

www.crackberry.com

www.blackberryforums.com

www.blackberrycool.com

Some are even free (see Figure 9-2).

Figure 9-2. *Other sources for ringtones for your Storm.*

Setting Different Ring Tones for Contacts

Would you like to know who is calling, emailing, or sending a SMS text message without having to look at the screen?

You can do this by setting what is called a **Contact Alert** on your Storm. You can set these up in two places on your Storm: in the **Sound Profile** app (Speaker icon) and in the **Contacts** app.

Using the Sound Profile App

Since the Sound Profile app is to easy to get to, you might want to use this method:

1. Click on your **Sounds** icon.

2. Scroll down and click on **Set Contact Alerts**.

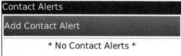

3. Press and click **Add Contact Alert** and select a contact from your Address Book for whom this new profile will apply.

4. Type a name for the Contact alert. In this case, we typed **Gary**.

5. Press the **Menu** key and select **Add Name**.

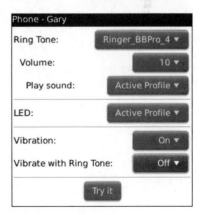

6. Type a few letters of the person's first and last name to find them in your Contact list.

7. Then click on their name to select it.

8. Now, you can adjust the custom alerts for this person for both Messages (e-Mail, SMS, etc.) and the Phone by clicking on **Messages** or **Phone**.

9. Now, make the adjustments for this person. In this case, we want a different ring tone, so we changed it to **Ringer_BBPro_4** and changed the **Volume** to 10.

10. We also adjusted the **Vibration** to **On** and the Vibrate with **Ring Tone** to **Off**.

11. Press the **Menu** key and select **Save**.

Using the Contact List

You can also set up custom ringtones and alerts for contacts directly in your Contacts icon.

1. Start your **Contacts** app.

2. Type a few letters to find a contact to customize.

3. Click on the contact name you wish to edit to see their details.

4. Press the **Edit** soft key  at the bottom of the screen.

5. Scroll down until you see the Custom Ring Tones/Alerts section.

6. Click on **Phone** or **Messages** to adjust either one.

7. Make your changes to Ring Tones, volume, vibration, and more on the next screen.

8. Press the **Menu** key and select **Save** to return to the contact edit screen.

9. Press the **Menu** key and select **Save** again to finish editing the contact.

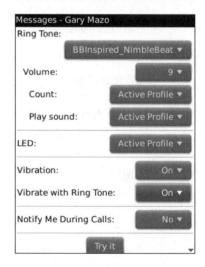

Chapter 10

Phone and Voice Dialing

In this chapter, we dig into the many ways your Storm is a powerful and full-featured phone. You will learn how to quickly make phone calls, use your call logs, and call people from your Contact list. You'll also learn quick ways to dial voice mail, use speed dial, and add new contacts from the phone calls you place or receive. Finally, you will learn how to use voice dialing on your Storm.

Three Main Phone Screens

When you open the phone the first time, you may notice the three soft keys at the top of the phone screen (see Figure 10-1). These soft keys open your Dial Pad (shown by default), Call Logs (middle key), and your Contact List (right key).

Dial Pad
(Default – Dial numbers)

Call Logs
(Calls placed, missed, received)

Contact List
(Find and call your Contacts)

Figure 10-1. *The three phone views on your Storm.*

Working with Your Phone

It helps to get a feel for how the phone works by looking at all the keys, buttons, and on-screen icons shown in Figure 10-2. Your main phone keys are the **Green** and **Red Phone** keys on the bottom of the device. You will also notice that Voice Dialing is triggered by pressing the left side **Convenience** key.

Call Logs
Press to see the phone call logs.

Contact List
Press to bring up the Contact List / Address Book.

Mute key

Your Phone Number

Dial Pad
Press for the regular dial pad (shown)

Volume Up & Down

To dial letters:
Like your old phone, just press the corresponding number key. E.g. to dial "SAM" press "7" "2" "6"

Voice Dial
Button on side

Voice Mail
Press & Hold '1'

Green Key
Start Call

Red Key
End Call

Menu Key
Press & hold to Multi-Task

Escape Key
Jump to Home

Figure 10-2. *Phone keys and buttons on your Storm.*

Placing a Call

Making phone calls is easy. There are many ways to place a call: you can dial a number, use your call logs, or dial by name from your contact list.

Dialing a Phone Number

1. Press the **Green Phone** key at any time to get into the **Phone** application.

2. Your default view should be the **Dial Pad**, as shown.

3. Press the number keys to dial the number.

4. Press the **Green Phone** key to start the call.

TIP: To re-dial the last number you called, simply press the **Green Phone** key when on the Dial Pad. If you are not in the Phone, just press the **Green Phone** key three times to dial the last number.

TIP: Press and hold the * key to enter a two-second pause when the phone is dialed. Press and hold the # key to enter a wait (when the phone waits for you to click a button before it continues). These are both useful tricks if you want to dial an access number, then a password. Learn more on page 266.

Dial from Call Log

You can quickly dial from your Call Logs (calls you have placed, received, or missed).

1. Start the **Phone** by pressing the **Green Phone** key.

2. Click the **Call Log** icon at the top.

3. Once in the call log screen, just scroll to the call log you wish to use and press and click on it to call that number.

TIP: If you want to call a person, but not the number shown on the Call Log (e.g. "Work" is shown, but you want to call "Mobile"), highlight the call log and press the **Menu** key. Then you can select other phone numbers for that contact.

Dialing a Contact by Name

You can quickly dial anyone in your Contact list by following these steps.

1. Start the **Phone** by pressing the **Green Phone** key.

2. Then, click the **Contacts** icon at the top.

> **TIP:** You can skip pressing the Contacts icon by pressing and holding the **Green Phone** key—it will automatically place you in the Contacts screen.

3. Once in the Contacts screen, start typing a few letters of a contact's first, last, or company name to find them.

4. Press and click on the contact's name.

5. If the contact has more than one phone number, you will be prompted to select from the available numbers.

Answering a Call

Answering a call couldn't be easier. When you call comes in, the number will be displayed on the screen. If you have that particular number already in your **Contact** list, the name and/or picture will also be on the screen (if you have entered that information into that particular contact.)

When a call comes in:

Push either the **Green Phone** key or press and click the **Answer** soft key to answer the call.

If you are using a Bluetooth Headset, you can usually press a button on the headset to answer the call (see page **489**).

> **TIP:** Just press the **Volume Down** key to stop the ringing. Press the **Ignore** button to instantly send the caller to voice mail.

Ignoring Phone Calls

Sometimes you can't take a call. In such cases, you need to make a decision to ignore the call or mute the ringing. Both of these options can be achieved quite easily with your Storm.

Ignoring a Call and Immediately Stop the Ringing:

When the phone call comes in, instead of answering by pushing the **Green Phone** key, simply press the **Red Phone** key to ignore. You can also press the **Ignore** virtual button on the screen itself.

 = Ignore call, send to voice mail, and stop the ringing.

TIP: Need to silence the ringer but still want to answer the call?

Just Press and Click the Ringer Off button [Ringer Off] on your screen. If the ringing or vibrating had started while your BlackBerry was still in the holster (carrying case), simply pulling the BlackBerry out of the holster should stop the vibrating and ringing, but still give you time to answer.

Ignoring a call will immediately send the caller to your voice mail.

The **Missed Call** icon will be displayed on your Home screen; it's an icon that shows a phone with a red X next to it. [icon] The number shows the total number of missed calls.

You can immediately call back the missed caller by doing the following:

1. Press the **Green Phone** key.

2. If you are not already viewing the call logs, press the **Call Log** soft key (middle top).

3. Locate and press on the missed call— usually it will be the top entry, as shown in the image.

Using the Mute Button to Turn Off the Ringing Phone

Besides pressing the **Ringer Off** button, you can also mute the call via the mute key on the top of your BlackBerry.

If you would prefer not send the call immediately to voice mail and simply let it ring a few times on the caller's end, but you don't want to hear the ring (perhaps you are in a movie theatre or a meeting), press the **Mute** key on the very top right edge of your Storm.

This will silence the ring. You may still pick up the call or let the caller go to voice mail.

Dialing Numbers, Taking Notes, and Jumping to Other Apps

When you are on a call, you will notice some soft keys at the bottom of the screen that allow you to do a number of useful things. (You may want to press the **Speaker** soft key before pressing any of these keys so you can hold the Storm away from your face.)

Press the **Dial Pad** soft key to bring up the dial pad in case you need to dial numbers; for example, when you have received a company directory that asks you to dial someone's extension, first, or last name. If you have to dial the name, use the number keys, just like on a regular phone.

Press the **Notes** soft key to take notes while on the call. Learn more in the "Taking Notes While On a Call" section on page 237.

Press the **Home** soft key to jump to your Home screen and start any icon you want.

Press the **Calendar** soft key to jump to the Calendar app to check your schedule or book a new event while you are still on your phone.

Press the **Contacts** soft key to jump to your Contacts icon to lookup someone's number, address, or other information.

Taking Notes While On a Call

Have you ever hung up the phone and asked yourself, "What was it that they promised to do?" If so, the **Notes** feature on your Storm is a perfect solution to keep track of exactly what was said or promised during a phone call.

You can take notes, save them, and even email them to yourself or others.

The notes you take while on a call are attached to the call log, also known as **Call History**.

1. In order to take the phone away from your ear so you can type notes, either press the **Speaker** key or use your headset.

2. Press and click the **Notes** soft key at the bottom.

3. Now, you can type your notes using the keyboard.

4. If you need to get back to the phone screen, then press the **Menu** key and select **Hide Notes**.

5. When done, you can simply hang up with the **Red Phone** key.

View, Edit, Delete, or Send Call History and Notes

1. From the Call Log screen, highlight the log entry, then press the **View** soft key.

> **NOTE:** You have to use the View soft key because if you press and click the Call Log entry with your finger, the Storm will start a call to that number.

2. Click on the Call History entry with the small note icon to view it.

3. From this screen, you can also do the following:

   a. Press the **Compose** soft key to write a note for any call history entry. ·

   b. Press the **Open** soft key to view the note (same as clicking on the entry).

c. Press the **Delete** soft key
to remove the Call History item
and related note.

d. Press the **Menu** key and select
Forward to send this note as an
email to anyone.

To: Gary Mazo
To:
Cc:

Subject: Fw: Call Log

Date: 2/6/2010 18:54
Duration: 5:26
Gary Mazo (Work)
386-555-1111

My notes for this call to Gary.
He is interested in the Video Tutorials
from Made Simple Learning for his entire
organization.

Adjusting the Volume on Calls

There may be times when you have trouble hearing a caller. The connection may be
poor or you may be using a headset. Adjusting the volume is easy. While on the phone
call, simply use the two volume keys on the right hand side of the Storm to adjust the
volume up or down.

What's My Phone Number?

You have your new phone, and you want to give your
number to all your friends—you just need to know
where you can get your hands on that important
information.

1. Press the **Green Phone** key to start the
phone.

2. Read your phone number next to **My
Number** at the top of the screen.

3. In the image to the right, the number is
1-519-888-7465. (You may have to
wait a second for it to appear.)

9:57 AM   1xev
My Number: 15198887465

1 ⌒   2 ABC   3 DEF

4 GHI   5 JKL   6 MNO

7 PQRS   8 TUV   9 WXYZ

*   0 +   #

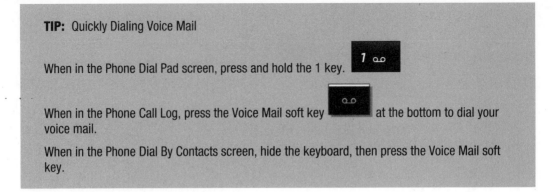

TIP: Quickly Dialing Voice Mail

When in the Phone Dial Pad screen, press and hold the 1 key.

When in the Phone Call Log, press the Voice Mail soft key at the bottom to dial your voice mail.

When in the Phone Dial By Contacts screen, hide the keyboard, then press the Voice Mail soft key.

Changing Your Ring Tone

You can change your main phone ring tone inside the Phone app by following these steps:

1. From any Phone screen, press the **Menu** key (see Figure 10-3).

2. Scroll down and select **Set Ring Tone**.

3. Then click on the button next to **Ring Tone** to select a different tune.

4. You can adjust other properties, such as volume and vibration.

5. Press the **Menu** key and select **Save**.

Figure 10-3. *Changing your ring tone from the Phone app*

You'll find more information in the Media section on page 416.

Calling Voice Mail

 The easiest way to call voice mail is to press and hold the number 1 key from the dial pad. This is the default key for voice mail.

If it is not working correctly, read below for some troubleshooting help or call your phone company technical support for help in correcting it.

To setup voice mail, just call it and follow the prompts to enter your name, greeting, password, and other information.

When Voice Mail Doesn't Work

Sometimes, pressing and holding the **1** key or pressing the voice mail soft key will not dial voice mail. This happens if the voice mail access number is incorrect in your BlackBerry.

You will need to call your phone company (wireless carrier) and ask them for the local voice mail access number. This sometimes happens if you move to a different area or change cell phones, then restore all your data onto your BlackBerry.

Once you have the new phone number from the carrier, you need to enter it into your BlackBerry.

1. Start your Phone by pressing the **Green Phone** key.

2. Scroll down to **Options** item and press and click to select it.

Set Ring Tone	11:49a
Options	
Status	
Switch Application	
Close	

3. Press and click on **Voice Mail.**

Phone Options
General Options
Voice Mail
Call Logging

4. Enter the phone number you received into the Voice Mail **Access Number.**

Voice Mail	123
Access Number:	
5198884369	
Password:	

TIP: You can even enter your voice mail password if you like.

Using Your Call Logs

The Call Log is an especially useful tool if you make and receive many calls. Besides being able to quickly dial them (see page 232), you can use the call log to add contacts to your Contact list, add notes, forward, and view details.

For instance, you can't remember if you added an individual to your Contact list, but you definitely remember that they called yesterday. Here is a perfect situation: use your Call Log to access the call, add the number into your address book, and place a return call.

Checking Your Call Logs

The easiest way to view your call logs is to do the following:

1. Press the **Green Phone** key.

2. Initially, you should see the Dial Pad.

3. Press the **Call Log** soft key in the middle of the top row.

4. The default setting is to show the most recent calls and then move sequentially backwards, showing calls made and received listed by date and time.

You can either touch the screen to highlight a call or press on the call to bring up a more detailed call log.

Why Do I See Names and Numbers in My Call Logs?

You will see both phone numbers and names in your phone call logs.

When you see a name instead of a phone number, you know that the person is already entered in your Storm contact list.

It is easy to add entries to your contacts right from the phone call log screen. We show you how.

Add New Contact Entries from Call Logs

If you see just a phone number in your call log screen, there is a good chance you will want to add that phone number as a new Contact entry.

NOTE: Call log entries are generated whenever you place, receive, miss, or ignore a call from your Storm.

Get into the call log screen by tapping the **Green Phone** key once.

1. Highlight the call log phone number you want to add to your address book.

2. Press the **Menu** key and select **Add to Contacts**.

3. Notice that the phone number is automatically placed in the **Work** phone field but you can also move it.

4. To move the phone number to another phone field, follow these steps:

   a. Tap the beginning and end of the number simultaneously to highlight it.

   b. Click the **Cut** soft key in the lower left.

   c. Press and click in the new phone number field, e.g. Mobile.

   d. Press the **Menu** key and select **Paste**.

5. Fill in as much information as possible, press the **Menu** key, and select **Save.**

Copy and Paste Phone Numbers

For Underlined Phone Numbers:

With underlined phone number like 313-555-1212, or phone numbers in call logs, simply press and click on it to see a **Short Menu** and select **Copy** to copy it.

> **TIP:** This trick works on any underlined email address or PIN as well!

Move to where you want to paste, press the **Menu** key, and select **Paste**.

If you need more tips on entering new addresses, see page 317.

To Show Your Call Logs in the Messages App (Inbox)

It might be useful to show calls made, received, and missed in your message list (inbox) for easy accessibility. This allows you to manage both voice and message communication in a single unified inbox.

1. Press the **Green Phone** key to see your call logs.

2. Press the **Menu** key.

3. Scroll and click on **Options**.

4. Scroll to **Call Logging** and press and click. Under **Show These Call Log Types** in **Message List** select either:

   - **Missed Calls** (see only missed calls)

   - **All Calls** (see all placed, missed, received)

   - **None** (this is the default; don't see any calls)

5. Press **Menu** and select **Save**.

Benefits of Adding People to Your Contact List/Address Book

- Call any number for this person (that is entered into your address book)

- Send them an email (if this person has an email address entered)

- Send them an SMS text message

- Send them an MMS Message (multimedia message with pictures or other media like songs)

- Send them a PIN message

- View the contact information

```
Call History
Gary Mazo
BlackBerry Made Simple

Call Work
Call Mobile
Email Gary Mazo
PIN Gary Mazo              (M)
SMS Text Gary Mazo         (M)
Add Notes                  (M)
Forward
View Contact
Show Keyboard
Switch Application
Close
```

Speed Dial on Your Storm

Speed dialing is a great way to call your frequent contacts quickly. After you setup speed dial, press and hold a number key from the dial pad to have their phone number automatically dialed. There are a couple of ways to set up speed dialing on your Storm.

Set Up Speed Dial from Call Logs

1. Press the **Green Phone** key and then select call logs using the soft key at the top.

2. Highlight the call log entry (either phone number or name) that you want to add to speed dial and press the **Menu** key.

3. Select **Add Speed Dial** and press and click.

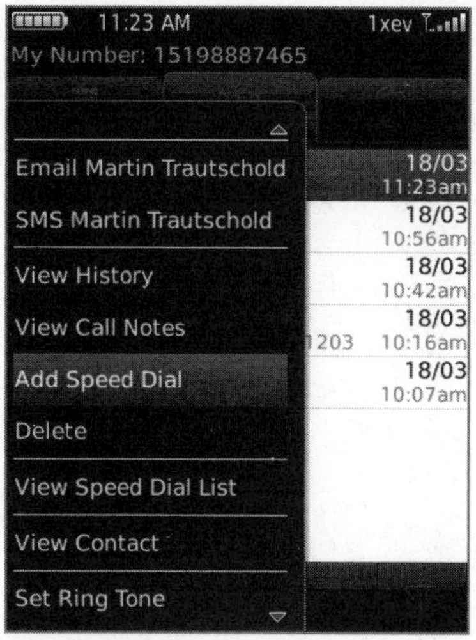

4. You will be asked to confirm that you want to add this speed dial number with a pop-up window looking similar to the right hand screen in Figure 10-4. Click **OK** to continue.

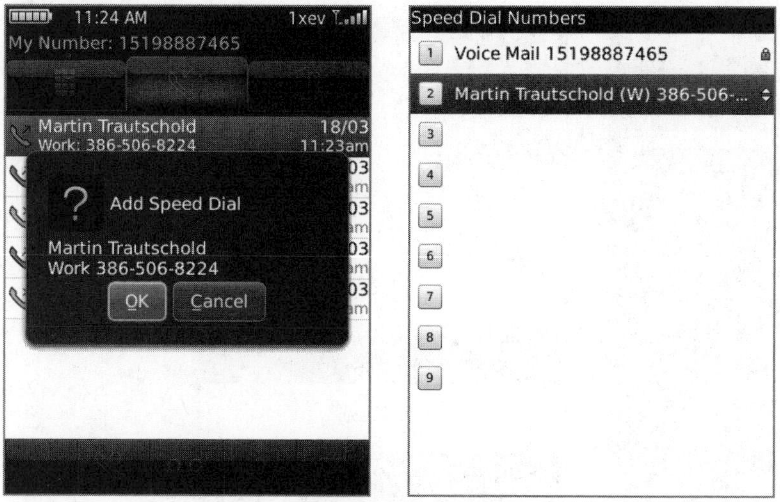

Figure 10-4. *Adding a Speed Dial Number from call logs*

5. In the Speed Dial list, the number defaults to the first unused spot.

6. Press and click on any other number and vacant spot to select that spot instead.

7. Press the **Escape** key to exit the **Speed Dial** list.

Set Up Speed Dial from Dial Pad

If you press and hold **any number key** from the dial pad that has not already been assigned to a speed dial number, you will be asked if you want to assign this key to a speed dial number.

Select **Yes** to assign it.

Then you will be shown your **Contacts** list to select an entry or select "[Use Once]" to type in a new phone number that is not in your Address Book.

Figure 10-5. *Assign Speed Dial by pressing and holding a number on the Dial Pad*

Once you select an entry or **[Use Once]** and type a phone number, you will see the same **Speed Dial Numbers** list. Press the **Escape** key to back out.

Give your speed dial a try by pressing and holding the same key you just assigned.

Set Up Speed Dial from Contacts Icon

Tap the **Green Phone** key, choose the **Contacts** icon, and start entering a contact name or number.

When you see the contact listed, scroll to it and press and click it. You will see whatever contact information you have for that individual displayed. Just highlight the number you want to assign to speed dial.

Press the **Menu** key and select **Add Speed Dial** and follow steps to select the speed dial letter as shown above.

Moving a Speed Dial Number

You can move speed dial numbers.

1. Press the **Green** Phone key to start the phone.

2. Press the **Menu** key and select View Speed Dial List to see the image shown to the right.

3. Highlight the number you want to move.

4. Press the **Menu** key and select Move.

5. Click any other slot to complete the move.

6. Press the **Escape** key to exit the Speed Dial list.

Using Your Speed Dial Numbers

To use any speed dial number, you must be viewing the phone Dial Pad so you can see the speed dial number keys.

1. If you are not already in the phone Dial Pad, press the **Green Phone** key and tap the **Dial Pad** soft key at the top.

2. Press and hold the number key you have setup. Any key from 2-9 is fine. 1 is reserved for voice mail speed dial.

Voice Dialing Basics

One of the powerful features of the BlackBerry is the Voice Dialing program that allows you to voice dial and perform other simple commands. Voice dialing provides a safe way to place calls without having to look at the BlackBerry and navigate through menus. Voice dialing does not need to be trained like on other smartphones—just speak naturally.

Changing Your Voice Dialing Language

If you need to speak in a different language on Voice Dialing, you can change the Voice Dialing language in the Options icon. Start the **Options** icon (usually a wrench), then click on **Language and Text Input** to see the screen in Figure 10-6.

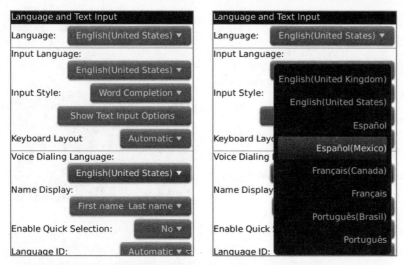

Figure 10-6. *Changing your Voice Dialing language and other options*

NOTE: If you do not see all of these languages displayed, it is likely they were removed during the Setup Wizard process and will need to be re-installed. If you are a Windows PC user, you can use Desktop Manager to add back languages in the Application Loader section. If you are a Mac user, use BlackBerry Desktop Manager for the Mac.

Voice Dialing a Contact

The left-hand convenience key is usually set for Voice dialing. Try pressing that key. If you have set the key for another program, navigate to your **Applications** folder and press and click on **Voice Dialing.**

TIP: We show you how to set or change your convenience keys on page 214.

The first time you use this feature, the BlackBerry will take a few seconds to scan your Contact list.

1. When you hear **Say a Command**, just speak the name of the contact you wish to call using the syntax "Call Martin Trautschold."

2. If this contact has more than one phone number, you will then be prompted with **Which number?** (see Figure 10-7).

3. Again, speak clearly and say **Home**, **Work**, or **Mobile**

4. Say **Yes** to confirm the selection and the BlackBerry will begin to dial the number.

Figure 10-7. *Voice Dialing a contact*

Voice Dialing a Number

Press the left hand convenience key as you did above. (Assuming your convenience key is set to voice dialing; if it's not, you can change it by reading page **214**.)

When you hear "**Say a command**," say "**Call**" and the phone number. Example: "**Call 386-506-8224**."

Depending on your settings, you may be asked to confirm the number you just spoke or it will just start dialing.

Chapter 11

Advanced Phone

Now that you have the basics down for using your Storm as a phone, it is time for some advanced phone topics. For many of us, the basic phone topics covered in the previous chapter will take care of most of our phone needs. Others, however, need to eke out every possible phone feature. This chapter will help you do just that.

In this chapter, we will show you how to set unique caller IDs for contacts, how to use advance voice dialing options, and how to use call forwarding and call waiting.

We will also show you how to set up and manage conference calling on your Storm.

Setting Your Phone Ring Tone

The BlackBerry supports using many types of audio files as Ringtones. You can set one general ringtone for everyone or set up individual tones for your important callers.

Important: Place Ringtones in Ringtone Folders

In some BlackBerry smartphones, when you are attempting to set a ringtone for a specific person in the Contact list or in Profiles, you can only browse to the Ringtone folder, not the Music folder. If this is the case, then you must copy your music ringtones to the Ringtone folder using the methods to transfer media found in this book.

Setting the Ring Tone from Sounds App

You can change your ring tone from the **Sound** app.

1. Click on the **Sounds** icon, either in the top left of the screen or from your Home screen.

2. Then scroll down to **Set Ring Tones/Alerts** at the bottom and press and click (see Figure 11-1).

3. Click on **Phone** in the top line.

Figure 11-1. *Setting the Phone Ring Tone from Sounds App (Speaker Icon)*

4. The top field lists the current **Ring Tone** for the phone (see Figure 11-2).

5. Just press and click the button and you will see all the available ring tones for your phone.

Figure 11-2. *Available Ring Tones*

6. Select the new tone (you can even **Try it** by clicking that button at the bottom).

7. Press the **Menu** key and **Save** your changes.

Setting a Song as a Ring Tone from the Music App

You can set one song (MP3) as your general **Ring Tone**.

1. Navigate to your list of music by pressing the **Music** icon.

2. Highlight the MP3 file you wish to use as the phone **Ring Tone**.

3. Press the **Menu** key and scroll to **Set As Ring Tone** and press and click.

TIP: Unique Ringtones for Callers

Set up unique ringtones for each of your important callers. This way you will know when each of these people is calling without looking at your BlackBerry screen.

Set a Custom Ring Tone for a Caller

We covered how to do this using the **Sound Profile** or **Contacts** app in the Sounds chapter on page 226.

More with Voice Dialing

Last chapter concluded with an overview of voice dialing. Voice dialing is a powerful tool for enabling not only basic phone calls, but also other functions of the BlackBerry— without having to push buttons or input text.

Other Commands

You can use the **Voice Dialing** app to perform other functions on the Storm. These are especially useful if you are in a position where you can't look at the screen (while driving) or in an area where coverage seems to fade in and out.

The most common are:

- **Call Extension** will call a specific extension.
- **Call Martin Home** will call the contact at their home number.

- **Check Battery** will check the battery status.

- **Check Signal** will let you know the strength of your wireless signal and whether you have No Signal, Low Signal, High Signal, or Very High Signal.

- **Turn Off Voice Prompts** will turn off the "Say a command" voice and replace it with a simple beep.

- **Turn On Voice Prompts** turns the friendly voice back on.

Changing Your Voice Dialing Options

You can control various features of Voice Dialing by going into your **Options** icon and selecting **Voice Dialing.**

Options		Voice Dialing	
Memory		Choice Lists	Automatic ▼
Mobile Network		Audio Prompts	Basic Prompts ▼
Owner			Adapt Voice
Password			
Screen/Keyboard			
Security Options			
SMS Text			
Spell Check			
Status			
Theme			
Voice Dialing			

Figure 11-3. *Voice Dialing Options screen*

Change the **Choice Lists** if you do not want to be confronted with lots of choices after you say a command. Your options are **Automatic** (default), **Always On**, or **Always Off**.

Audio Prompts can be set to **No Prompts**, **Basic Prompts** (default), and **Detailed Prompts.** With Detailed Prompts, you will hear more detailed questions and confirmations back from the BlackBerry after you speak. Use Detailed Prompts if you find that you are misdialing a great deal.

Adapt Voice in Voice Dialing

In order to teach the Storm how you speak, you will need to use the **Adapt Voice** function (which used to be called Adapt Digits on earlier BlackBerry software versions).

1. Click on your **Options** icon.

2. Scroll down and click on **Voice Dialing** near the bottom of the list.

3. Click on the **Adapt Voice** button.

4. Click **Start** to begin. It helps to be in a quiet room. See Figure 11-4.

Figure 11-4. *Training your Voice Dialing*

5. After about 15 screens, you will see a message that the device is working to adapt your voice.

6. When it's done, you will be placed back into the Voice Dialing options. Press the **Red Phone** key to jump back to the Home screen.

Now, give your newly trained **Voice Dialing** a try.

Voice Dialing Tips and Tricks

There are a few ways to speed up the voice dialing process. You can also customize the way Voice Dialing works on the BlackBerry.

Make Voice Dialing Calls More Quickly

When using Voice Dialing, give more information when you place the call. For example, if you say "**Call Martin Trautschold, Home**," the Voice Dialing program will only ask you to confirm that you are calling him at home.

The call will then be placed.

Give Your Contacts Nicknames

Make a **Nickname** entry for a contact, especially one with a long name.

In addition to my **Gary Mazo** contact, I might also edit his contact entry to add **GM** as the Nickname.

I would then say: "Call GM."

Call Waiting – Handling a Second Caller

Like most phones these days, the Storm supports call waiting, call forwarding, and conference calling – all useful options in the business world and in your busy life.

If you are on the phone with someone, and a second person calls, you can do any of the following:

- Answer the second caller by pressing the **Green Phone** key. This will put your first caller on hold.

- Ignore the second caller and send them to voice mail by pressing the **Red Phone** key.

Join a Conference Call or Swap

After you have two callers on the phone, you can join them in a conference call or toggle between them (called Swap) see Figure 11-5.

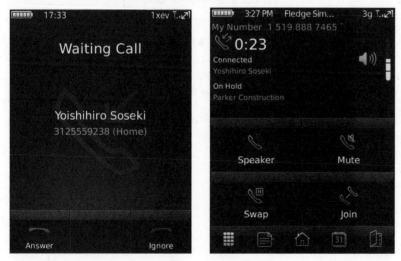

Figure 11-5. *Working with two callers on your Storm*

To swap between the callers (put one on hold and talk to the other), just press the **Swap** soft key.

To join the two callers together in a conference, press the **Join** soft key.

Call Forwarding

Call forwarding is a useful feature when you are traveling or plan on leaving your BlackBerry at home. With call forwarding, you can send your BlackBerry calls to any other phone number you choose.

WARNING: Make sure you know how much your wireless carrier will charge you per call forwarding connection; some can be surprisingly expensive. Also, make sure that your SIM card has been set up by your service provider for this feature.

NOTE: Not all BlackBerry phone companies (service providers) offer this feature.

To Forward Calls Received by Your BlackBerry:

1. Press the **Green Phone** key and then press the **Menu** key.

2. Scroll to **Options** and press and click and then scroll to **Call Forwarding** and press and click.

3. Your screen may look a little different from the one below, but the functionality will be very similar. If your screen just lists **All Calls, Busy, No Answer, Unreachable**, then you need to press and click on these items and select whether or not you want to forward each instance.

4. If your screen looks similar to the one below, then you have two options: **Forward All Calls** or **Forward Unanswered Calls**.

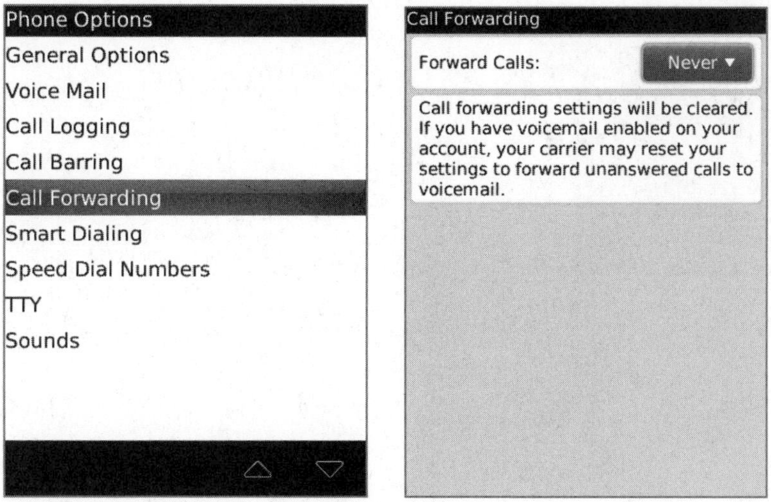

Phone Options

General Options
Voice Mail
Call Logging
Call Barring
Call Forwarding
Smart Dialing
Speed Dial Numbers
TTY
Sounds

Call Forwarding

Forward Calls: Never ▼

Call forwarding settings will be cleared. If you have voicemail enabled on your account, your carrier may reset your settings to forward unanswered calls to voicemail.

Figure 11-6. *Call forwarding options*

5. Click the drop-down next to Forward Calls to select **Never**, **Always**, or **Conditional** (see Figure 11-6). The Conditional setting (Figure 11-7) allows you to specify different phone numbers or actions based on the situation (Busy, No Reply or Not Reachable).

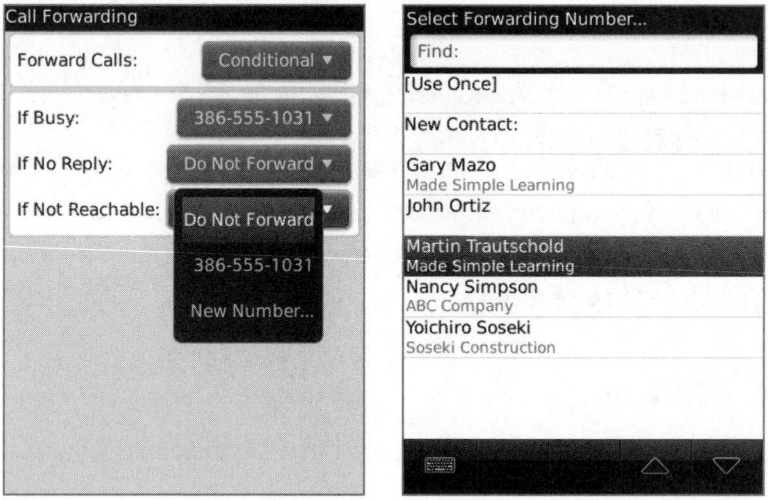

Call Forwarding

Forward Calls: Conditional ▼

If Busy: 386-555-1031 ▼
If No Reply: Do Not Forward ▼
If Not Reachable: Do Not Forward ▼
  386-555-1031
  New Number...

Select Forwarding Number...

Find:
[Use Once]
New Contact:
Gary Mazo
Made Simple Learning
John Ortiz
Martin Trautschold
Made Simple Learning
Nancy Simpson
ABC Company
Yoichiro Soseki
Soseki Construction

Figure 11-7. *The Conditonal option of Call Forwarding*

6. Selecting **Always** will allow you to forward all calls, regardless of the condition to a specific number or contact in your Contact list (see Figure 11-8).

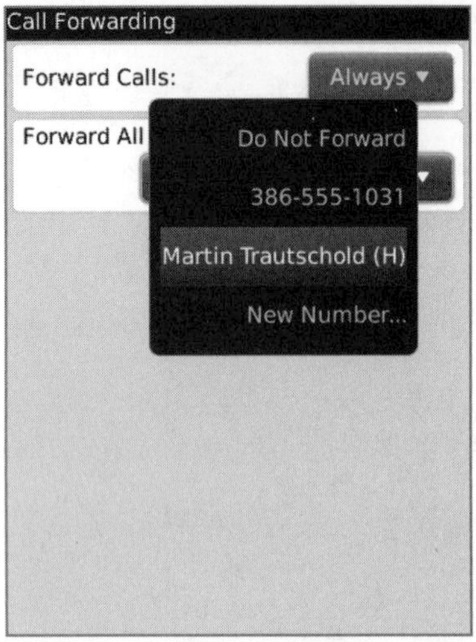

Figure 11-8. *The Always option of Call Forwarding*

> **TIP:** To select a new number (one not in your Contact List), select the [Use Once] item at the top of your Contact List and type the new phone number.

> **NOTE:** The default set up is to send these calls to your voicemail, the phone number that is most likely already in these fields.

7. To delete a Call Forwarding number, repeat steps 1-4 and press and click **Delete** after you have press and clicked **Edit Numbers**.

8. Press the **Menu** key and select **Save**.

Conference Calling

Conference Calling is a very useful option for talking with more than one person at a time.

> **TIP:** In your Calendar, you can pre-load conference call dial-in information so you don't have to dial it every time. This works great if you use the same conference call service regularly. See page 342 for details.

Sometimes conferencing several parties together is the faster (and safer) way to transfer necessary information.

For instance, the author was leasing a new car and the car dealer left a voicemail to call the insurance company to approve the proof of insurance being faxed to the dealer.

The author called the insurance company, expecting they already had received the dealer's fax number.

Unfortunately, the insurance company did not have the fax number.

Instead of hanging up and calling the dealer, asking for the fax number, and calling the insurance company back, the author used the BlackBerry conference call feature.

Over the course of the conference call, the dealer's fax number was relayed, along with any special instructions.

To Set Up a Conference Call:

Place a call as you normally would.

While on the call, press the **Green Phone** key

(press the Conference Call button on the screen) and either choose a contact from your Contact List or type in a phone number.

Choose which number (if the contact had more than one) that you wish to conference.

Figure 11-9. *Conference call setup*

If you add more than two callers to the conference call (Figure 11-9), just repeat the process starting with another **New Call** (press the **Green Phone** key).

Join the calls as you did above. Repeat as needed.

To speak with only one of the callers on a Conference Call:

Press the **Menu** key while on the Conference Call, and select **Split Call**. You will then be able to speak privately with that one caller (Figure 11-10).

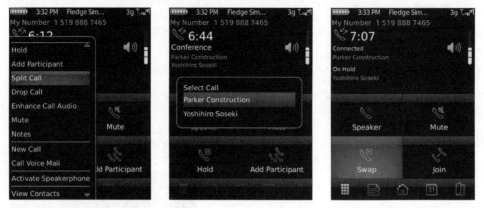

Figure 11-10. *Using the Split Call feature*

To End or Leave a Conference Call

To hang up on everyone and end the conference call for all, press the **Red Phone** key or press the **Menu** key and select **Drop Call**.

Advanced Dialing (Letters, Pauses, and Waits)

You may want to do some advanced dialing whether you are on the phone or entering a phone number in your Contact list. How to dial letters and how to add pauses and waits when a phone number is dialed are all covered in this section.

Dialing Letters on a Phone Call

Sometimes you call a company with a **Dial by Name** directory that will ask you to "Dial a few letters of the person's last name to look them up."

If you have done this in the past with a regular phone or cell phone, you already know how to do it. *(If you are used to dialing letters while holding the ALT key on your old BlackBerry devices, think again!)*

1. To dial a name, you first have to hit the

   Dial Pad button [icon] in the lower left corner to see the dial pad.

2. Then you can dial as you would normally on any other phone. For example, to dial "MAZO" you would press these keys:

   6 (for M)

   2 (for A)

   9 (for Z)

   6 (for O)

Dialing Phone Numbers with Letters in Your Contact List

Typing phone numbers with letters in your Contact list:

If you had to enter **800-CALLABC** into your address book you would follow these steps:

1. Type in **800**

2. Press the **ABC** key  and hold it until it locks. (You see a small lock icon).

3. Then type **CALLABC** using the keyboard normally.

Adding Pauses and Waits in Phone Numbers

Sometimes you want to type a phone number that has preset pauses and waits.

A **Pause** is a 2-second pause, and then dialing continues. If you need more than 2 seconds, just put more than one pause in the phone number.

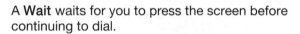

Press and hold the * key.

A **Wait** waits for you to press the screen before continuing to dial.

Press and hold the # key.

If you need a variable amount of time to wait, then you should use a **Wait** instead of a **Pause**.

> **TIP:** This is a great way to enter a voice mail access number to quickly check voice mail on a work or home number.

Here is an example of an address book entry with the VM access number, two waits, a phone number, two waits, then a VM password.

1800-555-1234 ww 386-506-8224 xx 13234.

1. Add a new **Contact** entry with this long phone number.

2. Setup a speed dial number for this new **Contact** entry. See page 246 for help on setting up a Speed Dial entry.

> **TIP:** When you are editing a contact entry in your Contact List, you actually see buttons to add Pauses and Waits. You will see a combined button on the reduced keyboard (SureType or Multitap) and two separate buttons on the Full keyboard layout.

More Phone Tips and Tricks

Like most features on the BlackBerry, there is always more you can do with your Phone. These tips and tricks will make things go even quicker for you.

- To view and dial a name from your **Address Book**, press and hold the **Green Phone** key.

- To insert a **plus** sign when typing a phone number, hold the number zero 0.

- To add an extension to a phone number, press the X key and then type the extension number. It should look like this: **8005551212 x 1234.**

- To check your voice mail, press and hold the number 1.

- To view the last phone number that you dialed, scroll to the top of the Phone screen, and press the **Enter** key. Press the **Send** key to dial the number.

Chapter 12

Social Networking

BlackBerry smartphones aren't just for business executives anymore, but you already know that. Your BlackBerry can keep you in touch in ways beyond the messaging features shown earlier in this book.

Some of the most popular places to connect these days are social networking sites—places that allow you to create your own page and connect with friends and family to see what is going in their lives. Some of the most popular websites for social networking are Facebook, Twitter, and LinkedIn.

In this chapter, we will show you how to access these sites. You will learn how to update your status, "tweet," and keep track of those who are important or simply of interest to you.

Downloading Social Networking Apps

Check in your Applications folder or Social Networking folder for these apps. If you do not already see these apps on your Storm, you can easily download them from **App World**.

1. Start App World by clicking on it.

2. Use the **Search** feature in App World and simply type the name of the app— **Facebook**, **MySpace**, **LinkedIn**, or **Flickr**—to quickly find each of these apps.

3. Download and install any app you want.

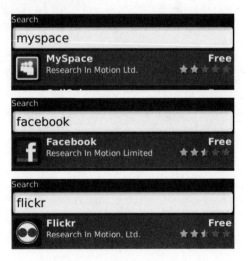

TIP: Follow the steps shown in Chapter 25 "BlackBerry App World" to get each app downloaded and installed.

As of publishing time, BlackBerry had just released its own Twitter client. There are also more than half a dozen pretty good Twitter clients, many of them free. Try out UberTwitter or one of the others.

Logging In to the Apps

In order to connect to your account on Facebook, Flickr, and MySpace, you will need to locate the icon you just installed and click on it. We use the example of Facebook here, but the process is very similar for the rest of the apps.

There is a lot to like about having Facebook and these other social networking apps on your Blackberry. You can always stay in touch. Just log in as you do on your computer and you are ready to go anywhere, anytime from your Storm.

NOTE: You might find your Facebook icon in your Social Networking folder, depending on your carrier.

Once Facebook is successfully downloaded, the icon in your Downloads folder should look something like this.

1. Press and click on the Facebook icon.

2. Enter your login information and click the **Login** link.

3. You are logged in. Usually, you will only have to log in one time to each of these apps.

Facebook

Facebook was founded in February of 2004. Since that time, it has served as the premier site for users to connect, re-connect and share information with friends, co-workers, and family. Today, over 400 million people use Facebook as their primary source of catching up with the people who matter most to them.

If you have the **Facebook** icon on your BlackBerry already, it will look like this:

1. Just press and click on the **Facebook** icon to start it.

2. Login if requested as we showed you above.

There is a lot to like about having Facebook on your Blackberry. All of your messages will be pushed to your device, just like your email, so you can always stay in touch. You also navigate the site in a very similar way to that on your computer.

Facebook Setup Wizard

1. After you login the first time, you will be taken through the Setup Wizard screens.

2. By default, all the boxes are checked. We recommend leaving them checked to have the best integration with your BlackBerry apps.

3. Press and click **Save** at the bottom to continue.

Some of the integration you will get with Facebook includes:

- See Facebook Profile pictures in your **Contacts** list.

- See Facebook calendar events on your BlackBerry **Calendar**.

- Receive a Facebook message in your **Messages** app when you or your friends poke you or do a status update.

- Receive a Facebook messages when anyone comments on photos you have uploaded.

Facebook Intro Messages

Check your **Messages** inbox on your BlackBerry for a few new messages giving you great tips and tricks about Facebook.

Unless they have changed things since we published, you will see one message called **The Next Step** and another called **Getting Started** (Figure 12-1).

Figure 12-1. *Getting started with Facebook*

Status Update and News Feed

Once you log on to **Facebook** for BlackBerry, you can to write you own status update.

1. Click on What's on your mind?

2. Type your status update.

3. You can also see your News Feed from your friends.

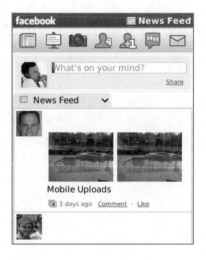

Top Bar Icons

Along the top bar are icons for some of the most use features of Facebook. You will see icons for the News Feed, Notifications, Upload a Photo, Friends, Add a Friend, Write on a Wall, or Send a Message.

Notification/Email in Facebook

Click on the Notifications icon (second from left) to see all your notifications in Facebook. The great thing is that these are fully integrated into your Messages Inbox icon. So every notification you receive in Facebook is also shown in Messages.

This saves you the step of going into Facebook to check for notifications.

Communicating with Facebook Friends

It is easy to communicate with your friends.

1. Click on the **Friends** icon to see a list of friends displayed.

2. If you have contact information or phone numbers in your **Contacts** app, the icons next to your friend's names will show that.

3. Click on the friend you wish to communicate with to see all the options available to you.

4. In this example, we clicked on Martin's name. Now we can poke him, see his profile, write on his wall, or see his BlackBerry contact information.

Uploading Pictures in Facebook

An easy and fun thing to do with Facebook is to upload pictures. You can upload pictures from your Storm to Facebook in using these methods:

- From the **Facebook** app - click on the small **Camera** icon.

- From your **Camera** app – snap a picture and upload it using **Send/Share** menu item or the **Send Picture** icon, then **Send to Facebook**.

- From your **Pictures** app – select a picture, press the **Menu** key, select **Send/Share**, and select **Send to Facebook**.

Once you select a photo to upload, you can specify a caption and a folder. You can also Tag the photo with a Facebook friend's name. We show you the steps from the **Facebook** app, but they are identical when you upload from any of the above options:

1. Click the **Camera** icon at the top of **Facebook**.

2. Navigate through the folders on your Storm to locate the picture you wish to upload.

3. Click on the picture to select it for upload.

4. Now you can write a **Caption**, select an Album for the photo (the default is **Mobile Uploads**), and **Tag This Photo** (left image in Figure 12-2).

5. Click on **Tag This Photo** to identify one or more people from the photo as your Facebook friends. You will be given a small cross-hair to identify the faces of your friends. After the photo is uploaded, your friends will be notified that they have been tagged (right image in Figure 12-2).

6. When you are done tagging, you can click **Upload** to send the picture.

Figure 12-2. *Uploading pictures to Facebook*

TIP: Immediately after you upload the photo from your Storm, you can see it on both on your computer and on your Storm **Facebook** page.

Flickr Uploader

Flickr is a social networking site that is designed to allow you to upload and share your pictures. Similar to **Facebook**, the **Flikr Uploader** app for your Storm allows you to upload photos from a number of different locations.

- From the **Flikr** app.

- From your **Camera** app – snap a picture and upload it using **Send/Share** menu item or the **Send Picture** icon, then **Send to Flickr**.

- From your **Pictures** app – select a picture, press the **Menu** key, select **Send/Share**, then select **Send to Flickr**.

You can also manage your **Flickr** page and upload pictures right from your BlackBerry.

Once installed, you will find a new **Flickr** icon in your **Downloads** folder. Just press and click and log in as you do on the computer to access your Flickr page. You can also press the **Menu** key and upload pictures right away.

TIP: Go to page 436 to see how to enable Geotagging of your pictures. This allows your GPS location to be tagged to each picture you take, so **Flikr** and other software can show you a map of where every picture was snapped.

When uploading from any of the methods listed above, you can specify details for your photo (see Figure 12-7).

1. Type your **Title** for your photo.

2. If GPS is available on your Storm, you can click next to Location and select **Where I am...** to find your location and attach it to the picture.

3. In the **Privacy** field, you can select who you want to see your picture from everyone (**Public**) to limited levels of privacy including **Private, Friends, Family, Friends and Family.**

4. You can select to resize your photo to **Original**, **Medium** or **Small.** Making the picture smaller will allow you to upload it faster. It will also cut down on your mobile data usage.

5. If you want to add more information, click **More Details** at the bottom to enter a **Description** and **Tags**.

6. When you're done, click the **Upload** button at the bottom.

Figure 12-3. *Uploading a photo using the Flickr app*

Twitter

Twitter was started in 2006. Twitter is essentially an SMS (text message)-based social networking site. It is often referred to as a "micro-blogging" site where the famous and not-so-famous share what's on their mind. The catch is that you only have 140 characters to get your point across.

With Twitter, you subscribe to "follow" someone who "Tweets" messages. You might also find that people will start to follow you. If you want to follow us, we are: @garymadesimple on Twitter.

Create a Twitter Account

Making a Twitter account is very easy. We do recommend that you first establish your Twitter account on the Twitter web site.

Full name	Gary Mazo	✔ ok
Username	GaryMadeSimple	✔ ok
	Your URL: http://twitter.com/ GaryMadeSimple	
Password	•••••••••	✔ Weak
Email	adesimplelearning.com	← we'll send you a confirmation

☑ Let others find me by my email address
Note: Email will not be publicly displayed

1. On your computer, go to www.twitter.com.

2. Click on the **Join Today** button.

3. When you establish your account, you will be asked to choose a unique user name— we use **GaryMadeSimple**— and to choose a password.

4. You will then be sent an email confirmation. Click on the link in your email and you will be taken back to the Twitter web site. You can choose people to follow, or post your own Tweets on the web site. You can also read Tweets from your friends.

twitter

Hi, GaryMadeSimple.

Please confirm your Twitter account by clicking this link:
http://twitter.com/account/confirm_email/GaryMadeSimple/8AHA8-A7C69

Once you confirm, you will have full access to Twitter and all future notifications will be sent to this email address.

Using Twitter for BlackBerry

To start using Twitter, follow these steps:

1. Click on the **Twitter** icon (it may be located in your **Downloads** folder).

2. The first time you start the app, you will be asked to log into your Twitter account with your Twitter username and password.

3. Click the checkbox next to **Save my login details** to avoid re-entering your Information.

4. Click **Login**.

5. The initial view in Twitter has a small box at the top of the screen where you can tweet (send messages) to those who are following you.

6. Under that are the tweets from those you are following.

7. Just scroll through the list of tweets to catch up on all the important news of the day!

Sending Out Tweets

1. Press and click in the box that says **What's happening?**

2. Type your Tweet about what is important to you (in 140 characters.)

3. Type your message and then click on the **Update** button to post your Tweet.

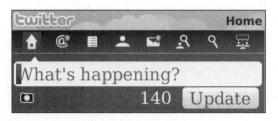

Twitter Icons

Along the top of the Twitter screen are eight icons; these are the quick links to the basic **Twitter** functions.

Figure 12-4. *Twitter icons at top of screen*

Mentions

A "mention" in Twitter speak is a tweet that mentions your @username somewhere in the body of the tweet. These are collected and stored in your Mentions section of your Twitter account.

My Lists

You can create a custom list so that your followers cannot only follow everything you say, they can choose to follow a specific topic (a list) that you create. In this example, I created a list entitle "Made Simple Announcements" so that users can choose to only follow our special announcements if they choose.

My Profile

Just as it sounds, the My Profile icon will take you to your Twitter profile. You can see your followers, your tweets, and your bio. Just click on any field in your profile and a short menu comes up. To edit your information, just choose **Edit Profile** from the menu.

Direct Messages

 Direct Messages are messages between you and another user on Twitter.

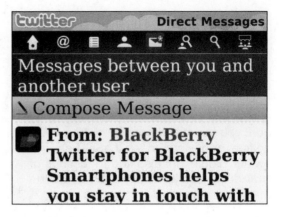

1. Click the **Direct Messages** icon to see your direct messages.

2. To compose a direct message click on the **Compose Message** icon.

3. Fill in the **To** field with the Twitter user name and then type your 140 character message in the box.

4. When you are done, just click on the **Send** button.

Find People

 The **Find People** icon takes you to a search window where you can type in a user name, business name, or last name to search for someone who might be on Twitter.

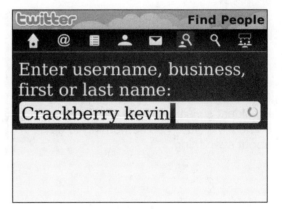

1. Type in the name and your query will be processed.

2. Scroll through the results to see if you find what you are looking for. If so, just click on the entry that matches your search and scroll down.

You will be able to see the statistics of how many followers there are and if they have particular Lists to follow. You can also choose the select **Follow** or **Block** to either follow this contact on Twitter or block all tweets.

Search

 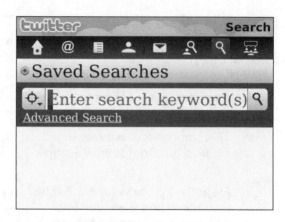 The **Search** icon takes you to another search window. Here you can type in any keyword to find opportunities to follow a topic or individual. For example, if you were to type in the word **golf**, you might find popular golf courses, golfers, or driving ranges that all use Twitter. You might also find thousands of individuals who just want to brag about their golf score.

TIP: Be very specific in your search to help narrow down the search results.

Popular Topics

 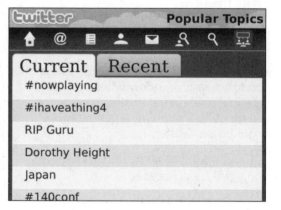 The **Popular Topics** icons will simply list those topics that are currently popular on Twitter. So, if you wanted to scroll through, you might find everything from the current playoff series to the President's visit overseas. On Twitter, someone always has something to say about everything.

Twitter Options

To get to the Twitter options, follow these steps:

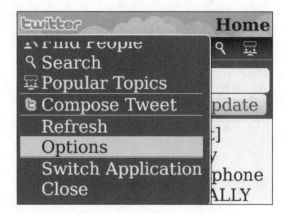

1. From your Twitter home screen, press the **Menu** key.

2. Scroll down to **Options**.

3. You will notice several boxes in which you can click to place or remove a check mark.

The available options are:

- Include Twitter Messages in BlackBerry Messages Application
- Automatic Tweet Refresh
- Notify on new tweets
- Notify on new replies and mentions
- Specify number of tweets per refresh
- Spellcheck before sending
- Show navigation bar
- Show tweet box on home screen

Just put a check box in the corresponding box next to the option you would like to enable.

LinkedIn

LinkedIn has very similar core functionality to **Facebook** but tends to be more business and career focused, whereas **Facebook** is more focused on personal friends and games. With LinkedIn, you can connect and re-connect with past business associates, send messages, see what people are up to, have discussions, and more.

> **NOTE:** The **LinkedIn** app is available as a free download from the BlackBerry App World, but not currently for the BlackBerry Storm or Storm 2. Therefore, Storm users must use the LinkedIn mobile web site which we describe below.

Login to LinkedIn

1. Click on your **Web Browser** icon.

2. Type www.linkedin.com at the top of the address bar in the browser and press the **Go** key.

3. Logon using your BlackBerry browser to m.linkedin.com. **Enter** your login information.

4. Zoom in by tapping the screen, locate and click on the **Sign In** link near the top of the page

Navigating around LinkedIn

LinkedIn has a familiar web based feel to it. When you first logon, you are given a basic page with a **Search** box and a drop down menu.

Under the **Search** box are links to the various page options available.

Press and click any of the links to get to the various pages of LinkedIn which we describe below.

The Update Page

The **Update** page is where you go to post your **LinkedIn** status update and see the updates of your **LinkedIn** contacts.

1. Click on the **Update** link.

2. Type in your message.

3. Click the **Save** button.

NOTE: LinkedIn uses a network system. Someone who is a direct contact is considered a first degree connection in your network. Someone who is connected to one of your contacts (but not you) is considered a second degree contact, and so on.

The Contacts Page

The next page to click on is the **Contacts** page. This will show you the listing of all your **LinkedIn** contacts.

You will see that the email addresses of your contacts are clickable and will launch your email program.

You can also click on the name of your contact to access their profile page.

The Profile Page

Click on the **Profile** page to see your own **LinkedIn** profile.

You can't edit your profile from the **LinkedIn** Mobile web page; you will need to edit your profile from your computer.

The Invite Page

The **Invite** page is where you go to invite others to become a part of your LinkedIn network.

Fill in the recipient's email address and edit the invitation message to invite them to become a part of your network.

When you are ready, just click the **Send Invitation** button to send your request.

NOTE: Unlike the LinkedIn desktop application, you don't have to say how you know the individual with whom you would like to connect. This makes it much easier to send an invitation from the mobile application.

YouTube

A very fun site, **YouTube** lets you view short video clips on just about everything. Your new Storm is able to view most of the **YouTube** videos without doing anything special.

1. Click on your **Browser** icon.

2. Click on the top address bar and type in www.youtube.com.

3. Press the **Go** button on the keyboard.

4. You should now see a list of the most popular videos (Figure 12-8).

5. Press and click on the video image itself to start playing the video.

6. Press and click on the title of the video to learn more about it.

TIP: Set a web bookmark in your Browser for YouTube by hitting the **Menu** key and selecting **Add Bookmark**. Go to page 507 to learn how to set bookmarks

7. Once the video starts playing, tap the screen to show the controls. See the Chapter 23 "Fun with Videos" for more help about how to enjoy videos on your Storm.

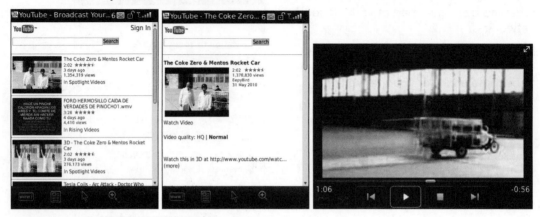

Figure 12-8. *YouTube Mobile on the Storm*

Chapter 13

Email Like a Pro

The Storm, even though small and stylish, is a BlackBerry to the core—a powerful email tool. This chapter will get your up and running with your email. In minutes, you will be an emailing pro.

Composing Email

The Storm, like all BlackBerry smartphones, gives you the freedom to email on the go. With the cellular network, you are no longer tied to a Wi-Fi hotspot or your desktop or notebook; email is available to you at all times almost anywhere in the world.

Send Email from Your Messages App

This first option is perhaps easiest for learning how to initially send an email.

1. Press and click on the **Messages** icon.

2. You have a few ways to start composing a new message.

a. Press the **Compose** soft key in the bottom right corner of your **Messages** list screen, then select the type of message you want to compose.

> **NOTE: Facebook** will only be an option after you have installed the app on your BlackBerry. See page 113 of the "Social Networking" chapter for help.

b. Press and click on a date row separator gray bar and select **Email** or other message type from the pop-up window (see image to right).

c. Press the **Menu** key and scroll down to select **Compose Email**.

3. Type in the recipient's name or email address in the **To** field. If the Storm finds a match between what you are typing and any **Contacts** entries, they are shown in a selectable drop-down list.

4. Select the correct name by pressing and clicking on it.

> **TIP:** Press the **space** key for the @ and "." in the email address. EXAMPLE: To type susan@company.com, you would type "susan" **space** "company" **space** "com"

5. Repeat to add additional **To:** and **Cc:** addressees.

6. If you need to add a Blind Carbon Copy (Bcc:), then press the **Menu** key and select **Add Bcc:** (Figure 13-1)

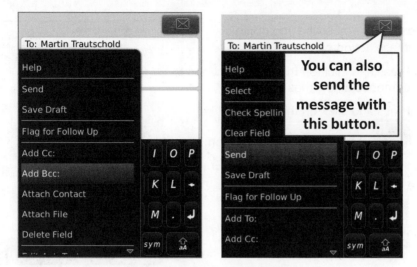

Figure 13-1. *Adding a BCC to your message and sending it*

7.   Then type the **Subject** and **Body** of your email message.

8.   When you are done, press the **Send** button in the upper right corner or press the **Menu** key and select **Send**. That's all there is to it.

Send Email from Your Contacts App

After you have entered or synced your names and addresses to your BlackBerry, you may send emails directly from your Address Book. (See page 88 for help on sync setup for Windows PC users or page 143 for Apple Mac users.)

1.   Click on your **Contacts** icon.

2.   Begin to type a few letters from your person's first and last name to Find them.

3.   Press and click on the person's name to see their contact details.

4. To compose a new message you could
    do any of these actions:

    a. Press and click on the **email address** to
        compose a new message.

    b. Press and click on the email soft key

         at the bottom of the screen.

    c. Press the **Menu** key and select **Email
        (the person's name)**.

Selecting a Different Email Address to Send From

If you have several email addresses integrated with your BlackBerry, you can select
which one to send your email from.

1. Press and click on the field which shows your **email address** or
    [Default] at the top of email compose screen under **Sent From** or **Send
    Using** (Figure 13-2).

2. Scroll up or down to press and click on another **Email Account** to use.

Figure 13-2. *Selecting a different Send From e-mail address*

See the Email Address

When you receive email on your BlackBerry, you will often see the person's name (e.g. Margaret Johnson) and not their email address in the **From** field.

You can see the email address by doing either of the following actions:

- Hover your finger over the person's name (without pressing and clicking) to see their email address in a little pop-up window, as shown.

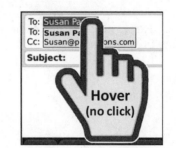

- If your keyboard is visible, then highlight the email address or name and press the Q or QW key.

Replying to Messages

Once you get the hang of emailing on your Storm, you will quickly find yourself checking your email and wanting to respond quickly to your emails. Replying to messages is very easy on the Storm.

1. Press and click on the **Messages** icon.

2. Press and click on the message you wish to reply to.

3. Click on the **Reply** soft key  in the bottom row of soft keys.

4. The recipient is now shown in the **To** field.

5. Type in your message.

6. Click the **Send** button in the top right corner to send your email.

Navigating Around Messages and Other Tidbits

There are a few useful things to know when you are working with your **Messages** inbox. You can get around by using the soft keys at the bottom or the swipe gesture. You may also notice some blank spots in email messages you receive where pictures should be located. In this section, we show you how to retrieve those images. There are times you want to change the importance level from **Normal** to **Low** or **High** depending on the situation. Also, you will want to know how to turn on **Spell Checking** for every email you compose and send from your Storm.

Email Soft Keys

There are a series of soft keys that you can use while in the Email program.

To use a soft key, just hover and you will see the function of the key. Simply press and click to activate that function.

The soft keys are:

Reply – press and click to reply to an e-mail

Forward – press and click to forward e-mail to another contact

Delete – press and click to delete the message

**Scroll Up/Down** – press the Up/Down arrow to scroll up and down in the inbox. You can also swipe your finger up or down to scroll up and down.

> **TIP:** Press and hold the Scroll Up button to jump to the top of your Messages inbox.

> **TIP:** Press and hold the Scroll Down button to jump to the bottom.

Swipe to Navigate Your Inbox

You can use the swipe motion to move around in your email inbox.

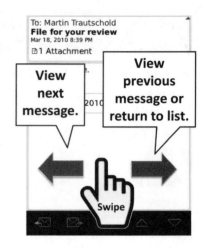

- To move to the next message, swipe from right to left.

- To move to the previous message, swipe from left to right.

- Once you get back to the first message, swiping from left to right will bring you back to the message list.

Getting Rid of Blank Spots in Emails You Receive

On some email messages, you may see blank spaces where images should be. If you see this, follow these steps to see all your images:

1. Press the **Menu** key.

2. Select **Get Image** to retrieve just one image or **Get Images** to retrieve them all.

3. You may see a warning message about exposing your email address; you need to press and click **Ok** or **Yes** in order to get the image.

Setting the Importance Level of the Email

Sometimes you need your email to be noticed and responded to immediately. The BlackBerry lets you set the importance level so that your recipient can better respond.

Begin composing a new email message, then press the **Menu** key.

Select the **Options** menu item.

> **TIP:** Pressing the letter key that matches the first letter of the menu item a couple of times will jump you down to that item.

In the **Options** screen, you will see a line that says **Importance** and the default **Normal** at the end of the line. Press and click on the word **Normal** and you see the options **High** or **Low**.

Just press and click on the appropriate option. Press the **Menu** key and **Save** your choice to return to the email message. Then press the **Menu** key and **Send** the message.

Finally, you will see high importance and low importance messages marked with special icons in your messages list (Inbox):

 High = Exclamation point

 Normal = Nothing

 Low = Arrow pointing down

Spell Checking Your Email Messages

Please see page **180** to learn how to enable spell checking on email messages you type and send. The spell checker may not be turned on when you take your BlackBerry out of the box the first time.

Flag for Follow Up

After receiving and email message, have you ever found yourself thinking:

"This is important, but I can deal with it now."

"I need to spend more time on this email and get back to them later."

"I need to give them a call about this message on Wednesday."

If so, then the **Flag for Follow Up** can be a great feature for you.

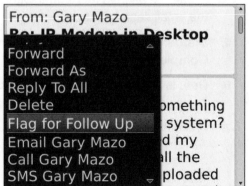

You can set flags of many types and colors with or without due dates from the main email inbox or while you are reading a particular message.

Setting a New Flag

To set a flag, follow these steps:

1. Press the **Menu** key and select **Flag for Follow Up**.

2. You can set various Flag Properties on this screen. As you set these properties, keep in mind that you can use the messages **Search** command to find flags or specific colors of flags.

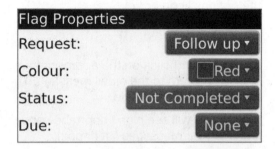

3. **Request type**: There are quite a few types of follow-ups that you can select. Click on the Request field to see them all. In some cases, you might even want to select **No response necessary**.

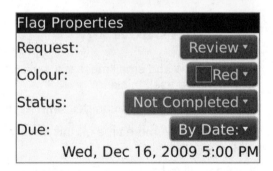

4. **Color/Colour**: You can change the color of the flag, which can help you locate the flagged items later with the email search feature.

5. **Status**: Is either **Not Completed** or **Completed**

6. **Due**: Is either **None** or **By Date** and it lets you specify a due date.

7. Press the **Menu** key and select **Save**.

Changing or Editing a Flag

Once you set the flag, you will see it in the top of the message under the addresses and subject information.

1. Press and click on the flag itself in an email or press the **Menu** key and select Flag Properties.

2. This will allow you to change all the properties.

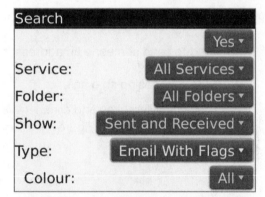

Finding Flagged Items

1. In your email inbox (Messages), press the **Menu** key and select **Search**

2. Scroll down to the bottom where it says **Type** and select **Email With Flags**.

3. Notice you can also select a specific **Color** or **All colors**.

TIP: Set a Hotkey for your Search

Before you execute your Search, press the **Menu** key and select **Save**. This allows you to name your search and set a hotkey combination ALT + some letter.

Try **ALT + Q**

Now, in your email inbox, you can quickly find all flagged items by pressing ALT + Q.

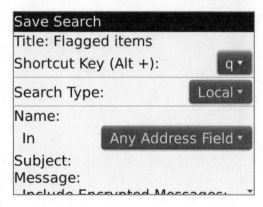

Flag Alarms

When a flagged item alarm rings, you will see a pop-up screen similar to the one shown.

You will also notice a flag on your top status bar with a number next to it showing how many flag due dates have passed.

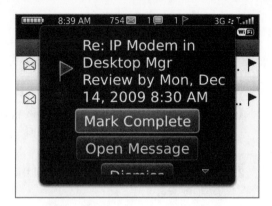

Attaching Contacts, Files, and Pictures

There may be times you want to send a Contact entry to someone who asked for your colleague's mailing address or phone number. There are other times you want to share a picture, a word processing file, or a spreadsheet file. For this, you would attach a file to a message. In this section we show you how to do these things.

Attaching a Contact Entry

If you need to send someone an address that is contained in your **Contacts** list:

1. Start composing an email.

2. Press the **Menu** key and click on **Attach Contact**. (Figure 13-2)

3. Either scroll to the contact you want to add or use the keyboard to type in the first few letters of the desired contact and then press and click the highlighted name.

4. You will now see the attached contact shown as a little address book icon at the bottom the main body field of the email.

Attaching a File or Picture

There may be times you want to send a spreadsheet, document, or picture from your Storm via email. For this, you will need to attach a file (much like you would do on your computer) to the email you send from your Storm.

> **NOTE:** Depending on the version of your BlackBerry software, this **Attach File** menu option may not be available for you.

1. Start composing an email message and press the **Menu** key.

2. Select **Attach file** from the menu.

3. Next, locate the directory in which the file is stored. Your two initial options are **Device Memory** or **Media Card** (see Figure 13-3).

4. Navigate to the folder where the file is stored. Once you find the file, simply press and click on it and it will appear in the body of the email.

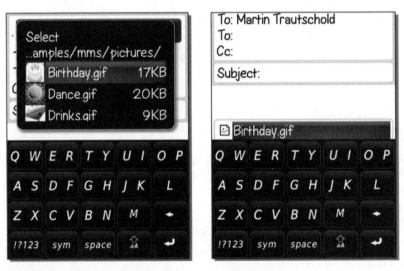

Figure 13-3. *Attaching a file or picture to an e-mail message*

Working with Email Attachments

One of the things that makes your Storm more than just another pretty Smartphone is its serious business capabilities. Often, emails arrive with attachments of important documents: Microsoft Word files, Excel spreadsheets or PowerPoint presentations. Fortunately, the Storm lets you open and view these attachments and other common formats wherever you might be.

Your Storm also comes with the **Documents to Go** program from DataViz. This is an incredibly comprehensive program that allows you to not only view but also edit Word, PowerPoint and Excel documents and it preserves the native formatting. This means that the documents can open on your BlackBerry and look just like they do on your computer.

Supported Email Attachment Formats

Your Storm can open and view the following document and image formats:

- Microsoft Word (DOC)
- Microsoft Excel (XLS)
- Microsoft PowerPoint (PPT)
- Corel WordPerfect (WPD)
- Adobe Acrobat PDF (PDF)
- ASCII text (TXT)
- Rich Text Format files (RTF)
- HTML
- Zip archive (ZIP)
- (Password protected ZIP files are not supported)
- MP3 – Voice Mail Playback (up to 500Kb file size)
- Image Files of the following types: JPG, BMP, GIF, PNG, TIFF

NOTE: Multi-page TIFF files are not supported.

NOTE: Additional file types may be supported in newer versions of the system software running on your BlackBerry.

Features available in attachment viewing:

- Images: Pan, Zoom, or Rotate.
- Save images to view later on your BlackBerry.
- Show or hide tracked changes (e.g. in Microsoft Word).
- Jump to another part of the file instead of paging through it.
- Show images as thumbnails at the bottom of the email message.

Knowing When You Have an Attachment

How do you know if you have an email attachment?

You will see an envelope with a paperclip, as shown.

= Has Attachment

= No Attachment (or it has an attachment that cannot be opened by the BlackBerry)

Opening Attachments

Navigate to your message with the attachment icon showing (paperclip on envelope) and press and click on it.

At the very top of the email, in parenthesis, you will see [1 **Attachment.**] or [2 **Attachments**], depending on number of attachments.

1.   Press and click on the Attachment shown and select **Open Attachment** (Figure 13-4).

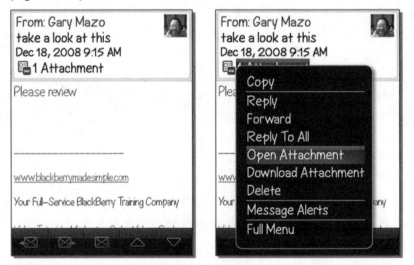

Figure 13-4. *Press and click an attachment to open it.*

2. If the document is a Microsoft Office document format, it will then be presented with the option of **View** or **Edit with Documents to Go.**

    a. For a quick view without true Word formatting, select **View.**

    b. To really see the document the way it was meant to be seen, we suggest you select **Edit with Documents to Go.**

> From: Gary Mazo
> take a look at this
> Dec 18, 2008 9:15 AM
> 1 Attachment
>
> ? Options:
>
> View
>
> Edit with Documents...
>
> Your Full-Service BlackBerry Training Company

3. If you get an error message such as **Document Conversion Failed**, it is very likely that the attachment is not a format that is viewable by the BlackBerry Attachment Viewer. Check out the list of supported attachment types on page 303.

Editing Attachments with Documents to Go

Once you select **Edit with Documents to Go** the document will open on your screen.

1. You can scroll through just like you were reading a Word Document on your computer.

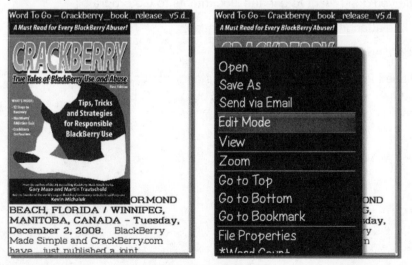

Figure 13-5. *Editing a document with Documents to Go*

2. If you want to make changes to the document, just press the **Menu** key and select **Edit Mode** from the menu (Figure 13-5).

3. If you want to adjust the Formatting of the document, just press the **Menu** key and select **Format** (left image of Figure 13-6).

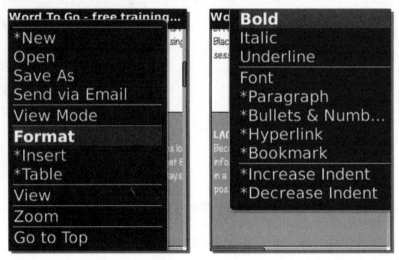

Figure 13-6. *Formatting options in Edit Mode*

4. You will then see the formatting options available to you (right image of Figure 13-6).

Using the Standard Document Viewer

You may decide you don't want to use the Documents to Go program.

1. Click on the attachment in the email message.

2. Select the **View** option (Figure 13-7).

3. You will see the document open with the standard document viewer. The document won't have the same look, but you will be able to navigate through it quickly.

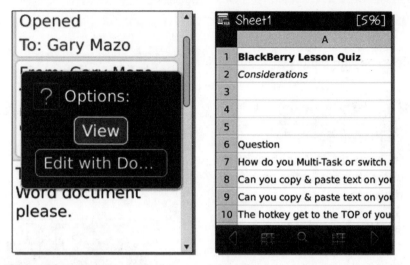

Figure 13-7. *Using the standard document viewer to view a spreadsheet document*

Using Sheet to Go or Slideshow to Go

Following the same steps you did earlier when you opened the word processing document you can edit a spreadsheet with **Edit with Sheet to Go** and a presentation file with **Edit with Slideshow to Go.**

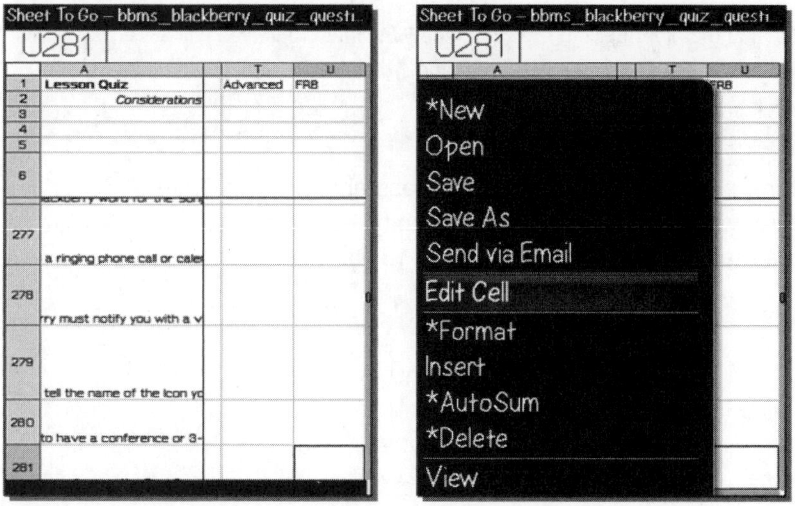

Figure 13-8. *Viewing and editing a spreadsheet with Sheet to Go*

To Open a Picture

1. Open a message with pictures attached.

2. Press and click on the **[1 Attachment]** or **[2 Attachments]**, etc. at the top of the email message.

3. Select **Open Attachment** or **Download Attachment** (to save it on your BlackBerry).

4. Then press and click on the image file names to open them.

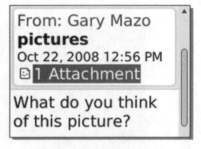

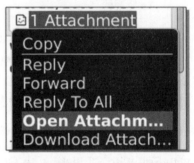

TIP: Once you have opened the pictures, the next time you view that email, you will see the thumbnails of all the pictures at the bottom of the message. You can then just scroll down to them and press and click on them to open them.

5. To save the picture, press the **Menu** key and press and click on **Save Image**. The picture will be saved where you specify, either on your Media Card or the main Device Memory (Figure 13-9).

Figure 13-9. *Viewing and saving an image on your Storm*

6. Other menu options include the following:

    a. **Zoom** - to expand the image

    b. **Rotate** - to rotate the image

    c. **Send as Email** - email as an attachment

    d. **Send as MMS** - a multimedia embedded image as part of email message

7. To save the image as a Caller ID picture, follow these steps:

    a. Press the **Menu** key and select **Set as Caller ID**.

    b. Begin to type in the contact name to find the contact.

    c. Navigate to the correct contact and save as prompted.

Searching for Messages (Email, SMS, MMS)

You might find that you use your messaging so often, since it is so easy and fun, that they really start to collect on your BlackBerry.

Sometimes you need to find a message quickly, rather than scroll through all the messages in your in box. There are three primary ways to search through your messages; searching the entire message through any field, searching the sender, and searching the subject (see Figure 13-10).

Figure 13-10. *Various ways to search your Messages Inbox*

The General Messages Search Command

This is the easiest way to search for a message if you are not sure of the subject or date:

1. Press and click on your **Messages icon** and press the **Menu** key.

2. Scroll down to **Search** and press and click (Figure 13-11).

3. Enter in information in any of the fields available to you. When you are done, press and click the screen.

The messages that match the search criteria are then displayed on the screen.

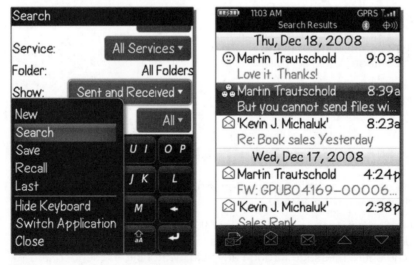

Figure 13-11. *Using the general Search command in messages*

Using the Hover Technique to Search

You can hover over an email message to search for sender or subject on your Storm.

Search Sender or Search Recipient

One of the coolest ways to Search for all messages and call logs (Activity Log) to or from a particular person is to use the hover technique.

1. Simply hover (just gently touch the person's name) on a particular message (Figure 13-12).

Search Sender / Search Recipient

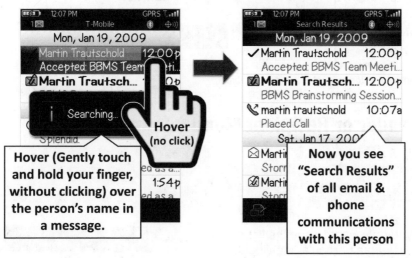

Figure 13-12. *Hover over an e-mail address or name to search sender or search recipient.*

2. Your BlackBerry will display a Searching indicator and then will show you all communication with that particular Contact.

Search Subject

You can also search by subject to quickly find all messages with the same subject by hovering your finger over the subject of a message (Figure 13-13).

Search Subject

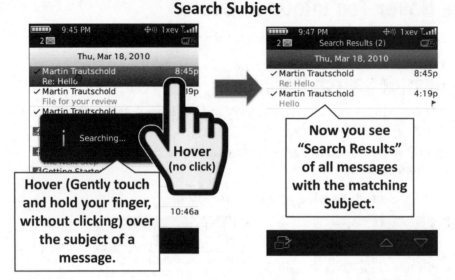

Figure 13-13. *Hover over the subject to search by subject.*

Search Sender or Recipient Menu Command

TIP: The Search, Search Sender, Search Recipient, and Search Subject work on SMS messages, e-mail, MMS —anything in your Messages Inbox!

Sometimes, you only want to see the list of your communication with a particular individual.

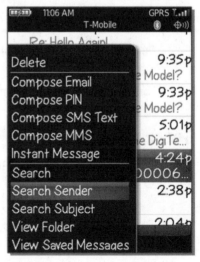

From the messages list, scroll to any message from the person you wish to search and press the **Menu** key. (Say that you want to find a specific message from Martin and you have 50 messages from Martin on your device. Just highlight one of the messages and then press the **Menu** key.)

Only the list of messages sent by that particular person (in this case, Martin) is now displayed. Just scroll and find the particular message you are looking for.

Search Subject Menu Command

You might be having an SMS conversation with several people about a particular subject and now you want to see all the messages about that subject.

1. Navigate to any message which has the subject that you are searching for displayed. The subject is displayed right under or next to the sender's name.

2. Press the **Menu** key and scroll to Search Subject and press and click.

3. All the corresponding messages are now displayed. Just navigate to the one you wish to read.

Chapter 14

Your Contact List

Your BlackBerry excels as a contact manager. You will most likely turn to your **Contacts** app more than any other app on the device. From a contact, you can email, send a text message, call, fax, or even "poke" on Facebook.

One rule of thumb you will hear from us often is to add anything and everything to your contacts. Whenever someone calls, add them to your contacts. Add contacts from emails and messages—you can always go back to them.

The Heart of Your BlackBerry

Your address book is really the heart of your BlackBerry. Once you have your names and addresses in it, you can instantly call, email, send text (SMS) messages, PIN-to-PIN BlackBerry messages, or even pictures or Multimedia Messages (MMS). Since your BlackBerry came with a camera, you may even add pictures to anyone in your address book, so that when they call, their pictures show up as Picture Caller ID.

Picture Caller ID

How to Get Contacts from Your SIM card onto Your Contact List

If you are using your SIM (Subscriber Identity Module) card from another phone in your BlackBerry and have stored names and phone numbers on that SIM card, it's easy to transfer your contacts into your contact list.

Start your **Setup Wizard** icon; it may be in the **Setup** folder.

Complete the screens in order to get to the **Import SIM Card Contacts** item as shown.

Then you will see a message that says "Contacts imported" or "No contacts are saved on your SIM card."

> **TIP:** Your SIM card contains only the bare minimum—name and phone number. You should review your imported contacts and add in email addresses, mobile/work phone numbers, and home/work addresses to make your BlackBerry more useful.

Setup Wizard
Date and Time
Navigation and Typing Tutorials
Email Setup
Set up Bluetooth®
Import SIM Card Contacts
Font
Language
Learn about the touch screen
Help

How Do You Get Your Addresses on Your BlackBerry?

You can manually add contact addresses one at a time (see page 317). You can also sync your computer's contacts with your BlackBerry.

If your BlackBerry is tied to a BlackBerry Enterprise Server, the synchronization is wireless and automatic. Otherwise, you will use either a USB cable or Bluetooth wireless to connect your BlackBerry to your computer to keep it up to date. For Windows PC users, see page 81; Apple Mac computer users, see page 143.

If you use Gmail (Google Mail), you can use the Google Sync program to wirelessly update your contacts on your BlackBerry with your address book from Gmail for free! See page 351.

See page 61 to use the BlackBerry Internet Service to sync your Google contacts.

When Is Your Contact List Most Useful?

Your Contacts program is most useful when two things are true:

- You have **many names** and addresses in it.
- You can **easily find** what you need.

Our Recommendations

We recommend keeping two rules in mind to help make your contacts most useful.

Rule 1: Add anything and everything to your contacts.

You never know when you might need that obscure restaurant name/number, or that plumber's number, etc.

Rule 2: As you add entries, make sure you think about ways to easily find them in the future.

We have many tips and tricks in this chapter to help you enter names so that they can be instantly located when you need them.

How to Easily Add New Addresses

On your BlackBerry, since your address book is closely tied to all the other icons (Messages/Email, Phone, and Web Browser) you have many methods to easily add new addresses:

- **Option #1:** Add a new address inside the **Contacts** app.
- **Option #2:** Add an address from an email message in **Messages**.
- **Option #3:** Add an address from a phone call log in the phone.
- **Option #4:** Add a new address from an underlined email address or phone number anywhere (web browser, email, tasks, MemoPad, etc.).

Option #1: Adding an Address into Contacts

The most obvious way of adding a contact is to use New Contact and type in the information. To do this:

1. Click the **Contacts** icon.

Find:
Help
Filter
New Contact

OR

Find:
Add Contact:

David Ortiz
Red Sox

2. Press the **Menu** key and select **New Contact**, or just scroll to the top and click **Add Contact** at the top of the contact list.

3. Add as much information as you can because the more you add, the more useful your BlackBerry will be!

Edit Contact   123
Custom Ring Tones/Alerts
  Phone
  Messages

Email: David@redsox.com
Work: 617-114-6788
Work 2:
Home: 1800CALLABC
Home 2:
Mobile:

1 .@w	2 ABC	3 DEF
4 GHI	5 JKL	6 MNO
7 PQRS	8 TUV	9 WXYZ
* 0	0 space	
ABC	sym	

TIP: Press the **space** key instead of typing @ and "." in the email address.

TIP: If you add someone's work or home address, you can easily map his or her address and get directions right on your BlackBerry.

TIP: Finding Restaurants

Whenever you enter a restaurant into your contact list, make sure to type the word **Restaurant** into the **Company Name** field, even if it's not part of the name. Then when you type the letters **rest**, you should instantly find all your restaurants!

Need to Put in Several Email Addresses for a Person?

While you are adding or editing their contact entry, just press the **Menu** key and select **Add Email Address**.

Be sure to save your changes by pressing the **Menu** key and selecting **Save**.

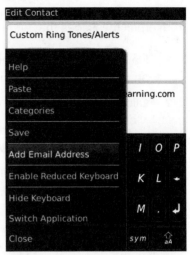

Need to Enter a Phone Number that Has Letters?

Some business phone numbers have letters, like "1 800-REDSOX1." These are easier than you might think to add to your BlackBerry address book (or type while on the phone).

Here are two steps to do this easily:

1. Make sure you have the full keyboard by turning your BlackBerry sideways or selecting **Full Keyboard** from the menu.

2. Press and hold your **ABC** key until you see the little lock sign. Then use the full keyboard to type the letters as you see them.

> **TIP:** Do you need to enter a phone number with pre-set **pauses** or **waits** (like the pause before entering a voice mail password)? See page 266 for more information.

Option #2: Adding an Address from an Email Message

Another easy way to update your address book is to simply add the contact information from email messages that were already sent to you.

1. Navigate to your message list and scroll to an email message in your inbox.

2. Click the email message and press the **Menu** key.

3. Scroll to **Add to Contacts** and click.

4. Add the information in the appropriate fields, press the **Escape** key, and save.

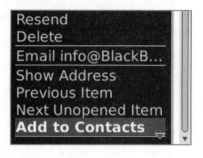

Option #3: Adding an Address from a Phone Call Log

Sometimes you will remember that someone called you a while back, and you want to add his or her information into your address book.

1. Press the **Green Phone** button to bring up your call logs.

2. Scroll to the number you want to add to your address book.

3. Press the **Menu** key and select **Add to Contacts**.

4. Add the address information, press the **Menu** key, and select **Save**.

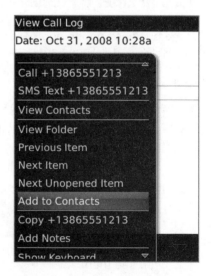

Option #4: Adding an Address from an Underlined Email Address or Phone Number Anywhere (Web Browser, Email, Tasks, MemoPad, Etc.)

One of the very powerful features of the BlackBerry is that you can really add your contacts from just about anywhere. Even though the next steps are shown on the **MemoPad**, they can be applied to tasks, emails (email addresses in the **To, From,** and

CC fields and in the body of an email message), and web pages. Let's say you wrote down a contact's name and phone number in a memo, but never added it to your address book:

1.   Navigate to your **Applications** folder and then click the **MemoPad** icon.

Figure 14-1. *Adding a phone number to contacts from the **Memopad** app*

2.   Scroll to the memo in which the contact information is stored and click.

3.   Click the phone number to bring up the short menu shown.

4.   Click the **Add to contacts** option and follow the previous steps.

Why Can't You See All Your Names and Addresses?

If you are seeing no names, a few names, or if you just added a new name and do not see it on the list, it is very likely your contact list is filtered. This means it is showing you only those names that are assigned to a particular category. The tip-off that it's filtered is the black bar (or other color) at the top with the category name. In the case of the image shown here, the category applied for the filter is Business.

This black bar shows your address book is 'Filtered' to only show contacts in the listed category: "Business"

> **TIP:** See page 330 to learn how to un-filter or see all your names again.

How to Easily Find Names and Addresses

Once you get the hang of adding contact information to the **Contacts** app, you will begin to see how useful it is to have all that information at your fingertips. The tricky part can be actually locating all the information you have input into the BlackBerry.

Option #1: Using the Find Feature in Contacts

Contacts has a great Find feature at the top of the Contacts startup page that will search for entries that match the letters you type into one of these fields:

- First Name
- Last Name
- Nickname
- Company Name

1. Inside Contacts, just type a few letters of a person's first name, last name and/or company name (separated by spaces) to instantly find that person.

2. Press the letter **M** to see only entries where the first name, last name or company name start with the pressed letter:

Martin Trautschold – Match on first name

John Major – Match on last name

Maritz – Match on company name

Find: m
Add Contact:
Martin Trautschold
John Major
Susan Johnston Maritz company

3. Then press the **space** key and type another letter, like T, to further narrow the list to people with an M and a T starting their first, last, or company name.

Find: m t
Add Contact:
Martin Trautschold

4. In this case, there is only one match: "Martin Trautschold."

Option #2: Finding and Calling Someone

Sometimes, you just want to make a phone call to someone in your contacts.

1. Press and hold the **Green Phone** key to start your phone with the Dial from Contacts screen showing.

2. Press the **Contacts** button and you can begin to search your contacts.

Figure 14-2. *Finding a contact from the **Phone** app*

3. Type a few letters of someone's first name (see Figure 14-2), last name, or company name, and the BlackBerry immediately starts searching for matching entries from your contacts.

4. Press the screen on the person's name to view his or her contact details as shown in Figure 14-3. To place a call, just click the number desired (if there is more than one), or press the **Menu** key and select the number to call.

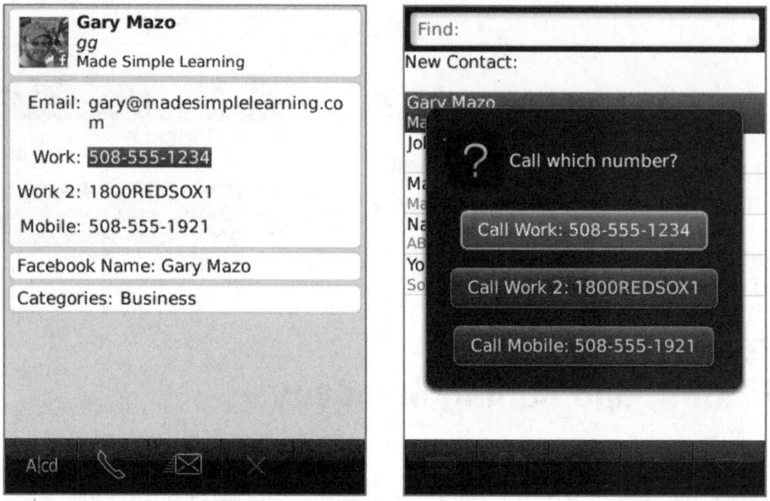

Figure 14-3. *Choosing which number to dial*

Pressing the **Green Phone** key on this contact entry in list view or detail view will also give you the option to immediately call this contact. If this person has more than one phone number, you will be asked "Call which number?"

Managing Your Contacts

Sometimes, your contact information can get a little unwieldy, with multiple entries for the same individual, business contacts mixed in with personal ones, etc. There are some very powerful tools within the **Contacts** application that can easily help you get organized.

Basic Contact Menu Commands

One of the first things to do is to make sure that all the correct information is included in your contacts. To do this, you will follow the steps to select and edit your contact information.

1. Select the **Contacts** icon, and click it.

2. Type a few letters of the first, last, or company name to find the contact, or just scroll through the list.

3. Highlight the contact you want to manage by touching the screen.

4. Press the **Menu** key and choose **Edit** to access the detailed Contact screen and add any information missing in the fields.

For Facebook Users—Cool Things You Can Do from Your Contact List

If you use Facebook, once you load it on your BlackBerry (see page 271) all your Facebook contacts will have their Facebook profile photos loaded, and you can do some cool things right from your contact list to your Facebook friends.

Friend Photos Simply Appear

All your Facebook contacts will automatically have their Facebook profile photos placed in their contact entries. You know it is a Facebook photo because of the little f in the lower right corner.

Martin Trautschold
pp
Made Simple Learning

Martin Trautschold
pp
Made Simple Learning

Email:	martin@madesimplelearning.com
Work:	386-506-8224 Speed Dial: 7
Work 2:	800 CALLABC
Home:	386-555-1103
Mobile:	386-555-1938

Facebook Name: Martin Trautschold

Edit Contact
Title:
First: martin
Last: trautschold
Picture:
Company: BlackBerry Made

Q W E R T Y U I O P
A S D F G H J K L
Z X C V B N M
!?123   sym   space

Poke!, Send a Message, or Write on a Wall

You can also Poke! your Facebook friends, send them a Facebook message, or even write on their walls right from your BlackBerry contact list!

To do this, highlight a Facebook friend in the contact list, press the **Menu** key and select **Facebook...**

Adding a Picture to the Contact for Caller ID

Sometimes it is nice to attach a face with the name. If you have loaded pictures onto your media card or have them stored in memory, you can add them to the appropriate contact in your contacts. Since you have a BlackBerry with a camera, you can simply take the picture and add it as a **Picture Caller ID** right from your camera.

1. Select the contact to edit as you did previously.

2. Scroll down to the **Picture** icon, and click the screen.

3. Choose **Add or Replace Picture** from the short menu.

You have the choice of finding a picture already stored on your BlackBerry or taking a new one with the camera.

If you want to use a stored picture, then navigate to the folder in which your pictures are stored by scrolling the screen up/down and clicking the correct folder.

Once you have located the correct picture, click it, and then click Crop and Save.

You can use the camera instead to take a picture right now. To do this, click the camera, and take the picture. Move the viewing box to the center of the target of the photo, click, and select **Crop and Save**.

The picture will now appear in that contact whenever you speak to him or her on the phone.

Changing the Way Contacts Are Sorted

You can sort your contacts by first name, last name, or company name.

1. Click your contacts—but don't click any particular contact.

2. Press the **Menu** key, scroll down to **Options**, and click (Figure 14-4).

3. Then click **General Options**.

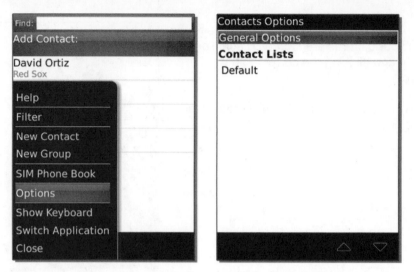

Figure 14-4. *Getting to the general options menu in the* **Contacts** *app*

4. In the **Sort By** field, click the First Name selection (it may say Last Name or Company if you have changed it) and choose the way you wish your contacts to be sorted. You may also select whether to allow duplicate names and whether to confirm the deletion of contacts from this menu.

Using Categories

Sometimes, organizing similar contacts into categories can be a very useful way of finding people. What is even better is that the categories you add, change, or edit on your BlackBerry are kept fully in sync with those on your computer software.

1. Find the contact you want to assign to a category, click to view the contact, click it again, and select **Edit** from the short menu.

2. Click the **Menu** key and select **Categories**.

3. Now you will see the available categories. (The defaults are **Business** and **Personal**.)

4. If you need an additional category, just press the **Menu** key and choose **New**.

5. Type the name of the new category, and it will now be available for all your contacts.

6. Scroll to the category to which you wish to add this contact, and click.

TIP: You can assign a contact to as many categories as you want!

Filtering Your Contacts by Category

Now that you have your contacts assigned to categories, you can filter the names on the screen by their categories. So, let's say that you wanted to quickly find everyone who you have assigned to the business category.

1. Click your contacts.

2. Press the **Menu** key, scroll up, and select **Filter**.

The available categories are listed. Just click (or press the **space** key) on the category you wish to use as your filter. Once you do, only the contacts in that category are available to scroll through.

How Do You Know When Your Contact List Is Filtered?

You will see a black bar at the top of your Contact list with the name of the category. In this case the category is Business.

Un-Filtering Your Contacts by Category

Unlike the Find feature, you cannot just press the **Escape** key to un-filter your categories. You need to reverse the filter procedure.

Inside your contacts, press the **Menu** key. Select **Filter**, scroll down to the checked category, and uncheck it by clicking it or pressing the **space** key when it is highlighted.

Using Groups as Mailing Lists

Sometimes, you need even more organizing power from your BlackBerry. Depending on your needs, grouping contacts into mailing lists might be useful so that you can send mass mailings from your BlackBerry.

Examples

1. Put all of your team members in a group to instantly notify them of project updates.

2. Let's say you're about to have a baby. Put everyone in the notify list into a "New Baby" group. Then you can snap a picture with your BlackBerry and instantly send it from the hospital!

Creating and Using a Group Mailing or SMS List

1. Start the contact list (address book) by clicking the **Contacts** icon.

2. Press the **Menu** key, scroll to **New Group**, and click.

3. Type a name for your new group.

4. Press the **Menu** key again, and click **Add Member**.

TIP: You can make both an SMS text group and an email group. Make sure each email group member has a **valid email address** and each SMS text group member has a **valid mobile phone number**, otherwise you will not be able to contact them from the group.

5. Scroll to the contact you want to add to that group and click. His or her name is now under the name of the group.

6. Continue to add contacts to that group or make lots of groups and fill them using the previous steps.

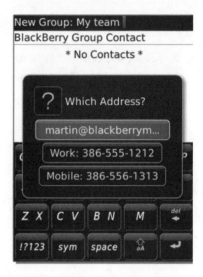

TIP: You can add either mobile phone numbers (for SMS groups) or email addresses for email groups. We recommend keeping the two types of groups separate. In other words, have an SMS-only group and an email-only group. Otherwise, if you mix and match, you will always receive a warning message that some group members cannot receive the message.

Sending an Email to the Group

Just use the group name as you would any other name in your address book. If your group name was "My Team" then you would compose an email and address it to "My Team." Notice that after the email is sent, there is a separate **To** field for each person you have added to the group.

Chapter 15

Manage Your Calendar

The BlackBerry calendar is both intuitive and powerful. In this chapter we will show you how to add events, schedule individual and recurring appointments, accept meeting invitations, and search and utilize all the features of your **Calendar** app.

Organizing Your Life with Your Calendar

For many of us, our calendar is our lifeline. Where do I need to be? With whom am I meeting? When do the kids need to be picked up? When is Martin's birthday? The calendar can tell you all these things and more.

The calendar on the BlackBerry is really simple to use, but it also contains some very sophisticated options for the power user.

How Do You Get Your Calendar from Your Computer to Your BlackBerry?

You can also sync your computer's calendar with your BlackBerry calendar.

If your BlackBerry is tied to a BlackBerry Enterprise Server, the synchronization is wireless and automatic. Otherwise, you will use either a USB cable or Bluetooth wireless to connect your BlackBerry to your computer to keep it up to date. For Windows PC users, see page 81; Apple Mac computer users, see page 143.

 If you use **Google Calendar**, you can receive wireless and automatic updates to your BlackBerry calendar! Learn how on page 351.

Switching Views and Days in the Calendar

The calendar is where you look to see how your life will unfold over the next few hours, days, or weeks (see figures 15-1and 15-2). It is quite easy to change the view if you need to see more or less time in the Calendar screen.

Day View   Week View

Figure 15-1. *Day and week views in the **Calendar** app*

Month View   Agenda View

Figure 15-2. *Month and agenda views in the **Calendar** app*

Swiping to Move Between Days

Navigate to your **Calendar** icon, and click. The default view is the Day view, which lists all appointments for the current calendar day.

Swipe your finger left or right to a previous day or an upcoming day (see Figure 15-3).

Notice the date changes in the upper left-hand corner.

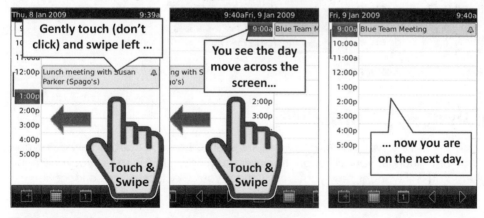

Figure 15-3. *Swiping to move between days on the calendar*

Using the Soft Keys to Change Views, Schedule, or Navigate

Like many programs on the Storm, the calendar has some soft keys at the bottom (or the top) of the screen (Figure 15-4). In the Day View screen, you will see keys for scheduling a new appointment, viewing the month, looking at today, or moving to the previous or next day. Just hover to see the function of the soft key revealed and then click.

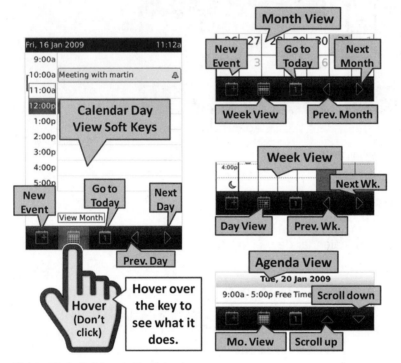

Figure 15-4. *Soft keys in the **Calendar** app*

Scheduling Appointments

Putting your busy life into your BlackBerry is quite easy. Once you start to schedule your appointments or meetings, you will begin to expect reminder alarms to tell you where to go and when. You will wonder how you lived without your BlackBerry for so long!

Quick Scheduling (Use for Simple Meetings)

It is amazingly simple to add basic appointments (or reminders) to your calendar.

1. In Day view, move the cursor to the correct day and time by swiping and gently touching (but don't click).

2. Press the **Menu** key to bring up your keyboard, or use a Convenience key to view the keyboard (see page 214).

3. Start Quick Scheduling by pressing the **Enter** key.

4. Simply type your event in the Day View screen.

5. When you're done, press the **Enter** key

6. to save the new event.

> **TIP:** Quick Scheduling is so fast you can even use your calendar for reminders like:
>
> Pick up the dry cleaning
>
> Pick up Chinese food
>
> Pick up dog food

Detailed Scheduling (Use When You Need Advanced Options)

1. Click the **Calendar** icon.

2. Type the subject and optional location. Click **All Day Event** if it will last all day, like an all-day conference.

3. If you are in Day view you can simply
    click the hour closest to when your
    appointment starts.

```
L 1:00p
  2:00p
  3:00p
```

4. Or, in any view, press the **Menu** key
    and select **New** to get into the New
    Appointment screen.

Figure 15-5. *New Appointment screen*

5. Click the field you need to change, and then just swipe your finger up or
    down to change the field. Click the screen again, and the new value will
    be set.

TIP: Press and hold the **!?123** key to lock the number keyboard. Then you can use your number keys (1, 2, 3…) to enter specific dates, years and times. For example, type **23** to change the minutes to 23.

Alternatively, you can skip changing the end time of the appointment, and instead just change the length of the appointment by scrolling to the **Duration** field and putting in the correct amount of time.

Set a reminder alarm by clicking **Reminder** and setting the reminder time for the alarm from five minutes prior to nine hours prior.

TIP: The default reminder time is usually 15 minutes, but you can change this by going into your Calendar Options screen (see page 342).

If this is a recurring appointment, do the following:

1. Click **Recurrence** and select **Daily**, **Weekly**, **Monthly**, or **Yearly**.

2. Mark your appointment as Private by selecting the **Mark as Private** check box.

3. If you would like to include notes with the appointment, simply input them at the bottom of the screen.

4. Press the **Menu** key and select **Save**.

Customizing Your Calendar with Options

You can change a number of things to make your calendar work exactly the way you need using Calendar Options (see Figure 15-6).

Figure 15-6. *The Calendar options menu*

Before you can make any of the changes, get into your Calendar Options screen. To get there, first open the calendar, press the **Menu** key, and select **Options** from the menu.

Next, click **General Options** at the top of the screen.

Changing Your Initial View (Day, Week, Month, Agenda, or Last)

If you prefer the Agenda view, Week view, or Month view, instead of the default Day view when you open your calendar, you can set that in the Options screen. Click the drop-down list next to the **Initial View** field to set these.

Changing Your Start and End of Day Time on Day View

If you are someone that has early morning or evening appointments, the default 9am–5pm calendar will not work well. You will need to adjust the **Start of Day** and **End of Day** fields in the Options screen. These options are up at the top of the screen, under **Formatting**.

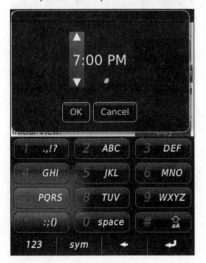

> **TIP:** If you select **Show Keyboard** from the menu, then you may also use the number keys on your keypad to type the correct hours (e.g., type **7** for 7:00 and **10** for 10:00).

Changing the Default Reminder (Alarm) and Snooze Times

If you need a little more advanced warning than the default 15 minutes, or a little more snooze time than the default 5 minutes, you can change those also in the Options screen.

Scheduling Conference Calls on Your BlackBerry

The BlackBerry has some very useful built-in features for scheduling and joining conference calls. You can actually pre-load the conference call participant or moderator dial-in and access code numbers so when the alarm rings as shown, you can simply click the **Join Now** button.

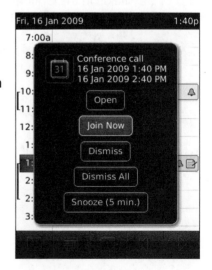

How do you make this happen?

It's easy—in the Appointment Details screen when you schedule a new appointment, select the **Conference Call** check box. Then you can type the access numbers as shown.

> **TIP:** You might want to set the reminder at "**0 Min.**" so you are reminded to dial-in right on time, instead of 15 minutes early (the default reminder).

> **TIP:** If you use the same conference call dial-in service regularly, then you should pre-load the information in your Calendar Options screen.
>
> From the calendar, press the **Menu** key and select **Options**.
>
> Then select **Conference Call Options**.

Calendar Options

General Options

Conference Call Options

Type in the moderator and participant basic information. This is used to pre-load the conference call numbers on all scheduled appointments. If it changes, then you can alter the individual appointment.

Copying and Pasting Information into Your Calendar

The beauty of the Blackberry is how simple it is to use. Let's say that you wanted to copy part of a text in your email message and paste it into your calendar. A few good examples are:

- Conference call information via email
- Driving directions via email
- Travel details (flights, rental cars, hotel) via email

First, scroll to or compose an email message from which you want to copy and open it.

Method #1

1. You can use this method only if you are typing or editing text.

2. Press the **Menu** key and choose **Select**. Then highlight (by touching the screen) the text you wish to copy.

3. Drag the handles that appear to adjust your selection.

4. Once it is highlighted, press the **Menu** key again and choose **Cut** or **Copy**.

Method #2

The multi-touch method allows you to touch the screen at two points and then highlight the text in between. It takes a little practice, but once you master it you will be copying like a pro!

1. Drag the handles that appear to adjust your selection.

2. We recommend placing your thumb at one end of the line you wish to copy and your forefinger at the other.

Notice that when text is highlighted, there are new soft keys at appear the bottom: **Cut** (if you are editing text), **Copy**, and **Cancel**.

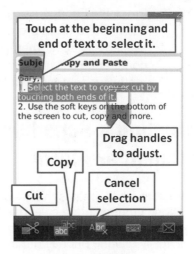

3. Press the **Copy** key to copy the selection.

4. Press the **Red Phone** key to jump back to your Home screen and leave this email message open in the background.

Scroll to and click the **Calendar** icon to open it.

5. Schedule a new appointment by clicking a time slot in the Day view.

6. Move the cursor to the field in which you want to insert the text that is on the clipboard. Then, click the **Paste** icon at the bottom of the screen or press the **Menu** key and select **Paste**. Finally you will see your information pasted into the calendar appointment.

TIP: See page 342 to learn how to enter dial-in information into your calendar for scheduled calls.

7. Press the Escape key (between the Menu key and Red Phone key) and select Save when prompted. Now your text is in your calendar. Now it's available exactly when you need it. Gone are the days of hunting for the conference call numbers or driving directions, or asking yourself "What rental car company did I book?"

Dialing a Scheduled Phone Call from a Ringing Calendar Alarm

What is really great is that if you put a phone number into a calendar item (like shown previously in copy/paste), you can actually dial the phone right from the ringing calendar alarm!

All you need to do is open the event and then click the underlined phone number.

> **TIP:** This is a great way to instantly call someone at a specified time without ever having to hunt around for the phone number!

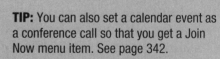

> **TIP:** You can also set a calendar event as a conference call so that you get a Join Now menu item. See page 342.

Alarms and Recurring Appointments

Some appointments occur every week, month, or year. Others are easy to forget, so setting an alarm is helpful to remind us where to be or where to go.

Scheduling an Alarm

1. Navigate to the **Calendar** icon, and click.

2. Begin the process of scheduling an appointment as detailed previously.

3. In the New Appointment screen, scroll down to **Reminder**.

4. The default reminder is 15 minutes— click the highlighted field and change the reminder to any of the options listed.

5. Press the **Escape** key or the **Menu** key, and select **Save**.

Changing the Calendar Alarm to Ring, Vibrate, or Mute

1. Scroll to the upper left-hand corner, click the **Profile** icon, or scroll through your applications, select **Profiles**, and click.

2. If you see only a listing of **Loud**, **Vibrate**, **Quiet**, etc. as shown here, then you need to scroll down to the bottom of the list and click **Set Ring Tones/Alerts**.

Figure 15-7. *Changing calendar alarm/tone/vibration in the* ***Profiles*** *app*

3. Click **Calendar** in the **Reminders** section. You will be able to set a unique ring tone for calendar reminders (and you can use any ring tone or MP3 music track that is on your BlackBerry).

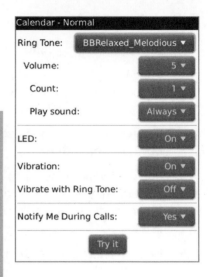

> **TIP:** We highly recommend setting **Vibration** to **On** and **Vibrate with Ring Tone** to **Off** as shown. This allows you to grab your BlackBerry while it's vibrating and (usually) take some action before it starts to make noise.
>
> This can save you some embarrassment if you are in a location where noise would be a problem.
>
> You can adjust the LED to flash or not flash for calendar reminders. In short, virtually every aspect of notification can be customized from this screen.

4. Press the **Escape** key or the **Menu** key, and select **Save**.

Setting a Recurring (Daily, Weekly, Monthly, or Yearly) Appointment

1. Click your **Calendar** icon.

2. Click an empty slot in the Day view to bring up the Appointment Scheduling screen.

3. Scroll down to **Recurrence**, and click in the highlighted field.

4. Select either **None**, **Daily**, **Weekly**, **Monthly**, or **Yearly**.

5. Press the **Escape** key or the **Menu** key, and select **Save**.

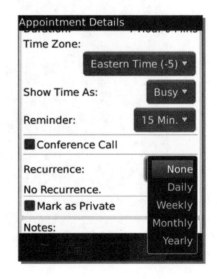

> **TIP:** If your meeting is every two weeks, and ends on 12/31/2008, then your settings should look like this.

Recurrence:	Weekly
Every:	2
Days:	S M T W T **F** S
End:	Date
	Wed, Dec 31, 2008
Occurs every 2 weeks	

Snoozing a Ringing Calendar or Task Alarm

When a calendar or task alarm rings, you can open it, dismiss it or snooze it.

To make sure you have the Snooze option active:

1. Open the **Calendar** application.

2. Press the **Menu** button and scroll down to **Options**.

3. Click **General Options**.

4. Look under the **Actions** sub-heading and click in the **Snooze** field.

Figure 15-8. *Snoozing a Calendar appointment*

If you don't see a **Snooze** option as in Figure 15-8, then you need to change the setting in your Calendar or Task options screen from none to some other value.

Clicking the **Snooze** option does just that—it will snooze five minutes, ten minutes, or whatever you have set in the Calendar or Task options screen.

What If Your Pre-Set Snooze Time Is Not Going to Work for You?

In this case you should select **Open**, scroll down to the scheduled start time, and change that. Click the **Number** field to bring up the keyboard and use the number keys to change the date or time. For example, typing **55** in the **Minutes** field would change the time to ":55."

You can also simply click the number you wish to change, and then just swipe up or down with your finger anywhere on the screen. When you are done, just click the screen to set the change.

Inviting Attendees and Working with Meeting Invitations

Now with your BlackBerry you can invite people to meetings and reply to meeting invitations. If your BlackBerry is connected to a BlackBerry Enterprise Server ("BES"), you may also be able to check your invitees' availability for specific times as well.

Inviting Someone to Attend This Meeting

1. Create a new appointment in your calendar or open an existing meeting by clicking it.

2. Click the **Menu** key.

3. Click **Invite Attendee**, follow the prompts to find a contact, and click that contact to invite them.

4. Follow the same procedure to invite more people to your meeting.

5. Click the **Menu** key and select **Save**.

Respond to a Meeting Invitation

You will see the meeting invitation in your messages (email inbox).

Open the invitation by clicking it, and then press the **Menu** key.

Several options are now available to you. Click either **Accept** or Accept with Comments, or **Tentative** or **Tentative with Comments**, or **Decline** or Decline with Comments.

Changing the List of Participants for a Meeting

1. Click the meeting in your **Calendar** application.

2. Navigate to the **Accepted** or **Declined** field and click the contact you wish to change.

3. The options Invite Attendee, Change Attendee, or Remove Attendee are available. Just click the correct option.

Contacting the Meeting Participants

1. Open the meeting, your meeting invitation, or even one of the responses from the participants.

2. Simply highlight the contact and press the **Menu** key.

3. Scroll through the various ways you can contact that person—email, PIN message, SMS, or call the contact directly.

Sending an Email to Everyone Who Is Attending the Meeting

1. Navigate to the meeting in your calendar and click it to open it.

2. Click **Email all Attendees** and compose your email message.

3. Click the **Menu** key and select **Send**.

Using Google Sync to Sync with BlackBerry Calendar and Contacts

IMPORTANT NOTE: You can sync your Google contacts using the BlackBerry Internet Service when you set up your email (see page 61). We would strongly suggest not trying to sync Google Contacts with Google Sync as well as BlackBerry Internet Service—you are just asking for trouble. Instead, just use Google Sync for your Google Calendar.

The great thing about using Google Sync for BlackBerry is that it provides you a full two-way wireless synchronization of your BlackBerry Calendar and Contacts with your Google Calendar and Address Book. What this means is anything you type in your Google Calendar/Addresses "magically" (wirelessly and automatically) appears on your BlackBerry Calendar/Contacts in minutes! The same thing goes for contacts or calendar events you add or change on your BlackBerry—they are transmitted wirelessly and automatically to show up on your Google Calendar and Address Book.

NOTE: The only exceptions are those calendar events you have added on your BlackBerry prior to installing the Google Sync application—those old events don't get synced. However, contacts on your BlackBerry prior to the install are synced.

This wireless calendar update function has previously been available only with a BlackBerry Enterprise Server (whether in-house or hosted).

Getting Started with Gmail and Google Calendar on Your Computer

First, if you don't already have one, you must sign up for a free Google mail (Gmail) account at www.gmail.com.

Then, follow the great help and instructions on Google to start adding address book entries and creating calendar events on Gmail and Google Calendar on your computer.

Installing the Google Sync Program on Your BlackBerry

1. Click your browser's icon to start it.

2. Type this address in the address bar on the top: http://m.google.com/sync.

3.   Then click the **Install Now** link on this page.

> **NOTE:** This page may look slightly different when you see it.

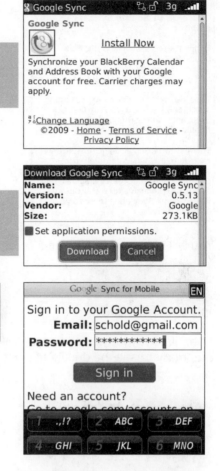

4.   And click the **Download** button here.

> **NOTE:** The version numbers and size will probably be different when you see this page.

After you download and install it, you can run it or just click OK. If you clicked OK and exited the browser, you may need to check in your **Downloads** folder for the new **Google Sync** icon.

After you successfully login, you will see a page similar to this one describing what Google Sync will sync to and from your BlackBerry.

Notice at the bottom of this screen, you will see details on which fields (or pieces of information) from your BlackBerry will be shared or synchronized with your Google address book.

Finally, click **Sync Now** at the bottom of this page.

Google Sync for Mobile

Welcome to Google Sync for mobile.

To get started, click the **Sync Now** button below and Google Sync will start synchronizing your handheld's calendar and contacts with Google automatically.

To access settings or initiate a manual synchronization, click on the **Google Sync** entry in the menu of your handheld's Calendar.

The first time Google Sync runs, it may take quite a while to complete the synchronization. If you have many Contacts, your Blackberry may also feel a little unresponsive for a short period, while Google Sync adds them to your Address Book.

Google Sync can synchronize the following fields with your handheld: Title, First, Last, Job Title, Company, Email, Work, Work 2, Home, Home 2, Mobile, Pager, Fax, Other, Work Address, Home Address, and Notes. Other fields will not be synchronized with your Google Contacts.

Sync Now

You will see some sync status screens.

Then, finally, you will see a screen like this. Click **Summary** to see the details of what was synced.

Google Sync for Mobile

Last Successful Sync

Calendar 20 Jan 2009 20:48:51
New Events   3
Deleted events   0
Updated events   0

Contacts 20 Jan 2009 20:49:25
New contacts   6
Deleted contacts 0
Updated contacts 6

Data Usage

Transfered since 1 Jan **22 KB**

From this point forward, the Google Sync program should run automatically in the background. It will sync every time you make changes on your BlackBerry or at a minimum every two hours. From both the BlackBerry **Calendar** and **Contacts** icons, you will see a new **Google Sync** menu item. Select that to see the status of the most recent sync. You can also press the **Menu** key from the Sync status screen to **Sync Now** or go into **Options** for the sync. If you are having trouble with the sync, check out our "Fixing Problems" section on page 563 or view Google's extensive online help.

Looking at the Results of a Successful Google Sync (Calendar and Contacts)

Here are views of the same calendar items in Google and BlackBerry.

Google Calendar on the computer:

BlackBerry Calendar:

Notice the calendar events from Google Calendar are now on your BlackBerry. Anything you add or change on your BlackBerry or Google calendar will be shared both ways going forward. Automatically!

Google Address Book on your computer:

BlackBerry Contact List:

Notice all contacts from your BlackBerry contact list are now in your Gmail address book. Also, all contacts from your Gmail address book are now in your BlackBerry.

Chapter 16

Get Tasks Done

The Task Icon

Like your contacts, calendar, and MemoPad, your task list becomes more powerful when you share or synchronize it with your computer. Since the BlackBerry is so easy to carry around, you can update, check off, and even create new tasks anytime, anywhere they come to mind. Gone are the days of writing down a task on a sticky note and hoping to find it later when you need it.

How Do You Get Your Tasks from Your Computer to Your BlackBerry?

You can mass load or sync up your computer's task list with your BlackBerry **Task** icon.

If your BlackBerry is tied to a BlackBerry Enterprise Server, the synchronization is wireless and automatic. Otherwise, you will use either a USB cable or Bluetooth wireless to connect your BlackBerry to your computer to keep it up to date. For Windows PC users, see page 81; Apple Mac computer users, see page 143, "Viewing Tasks On Your BlackBerry."

Viewing Tasks on Your BlackBerry

1. To view your tasks, locate and click the **Tasks** icon.

2. Push the **Menu** button to bring up all your applications on the BlackBerry Home screen.

3. You may need to click the **Applications** folder.

4. Then, find the icon that says **Tasks** when you scroll over it. You may need to press the **Menu** key (between the **Green Phone** key and **Escape** key) to see all your icons.

5. The first time you start tasks on your BlackBerry, you may see an empty task list if you have not yet synchronized with your computer.

Adding a New Task

Press the **Menu** key and select **New**. Then you can enter information for your new task in the screen in Figure 16-1.

TIP: Keep in mind the way the Find feature works as you name your task. For example, all tasks for a particular "Project Red" should have "Red" in the name for easy retrieval.

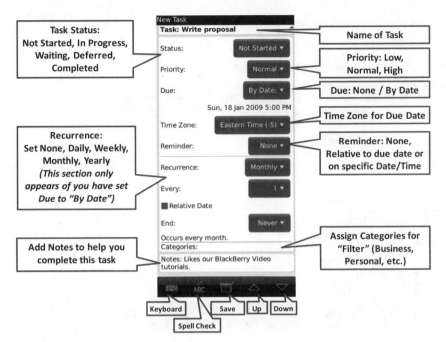

Task Status:
Not Started, In Progress,
Waiting, Deferred,
Completed

Name of Task

Priority: Low,
Normal, High

Due: None / By Date

Time Zone for Due Date

Recurrence:
Set None, Daily, Weekly,
Monthly, Yearly
*(This section only
appears of you have set
Due to "By Date")*

Reminder: None,
Relative to due date or
on specific Date/Time

Add Notes to help you
complete this task

Assign Categories for
"Filter" (Business,
Personal, etc.)

Keyboard Save Up Down

Spell Check

Figure 16-1. *New task options menu*

Categorizing Your Tasks

Like Address Book entries, you can group your tasks into categories. And you can also share or synchronize these categories with your computer.

Assigning a Task to a Category

1. Highlight the task, click the screen, and open it.

Figure 16-2. *Setting New Task status and priority*

2. You can set the status of your task, as well as the priority and the due date, from this screen.

3. To categorize, press the **Menu** key and select **Categories**.

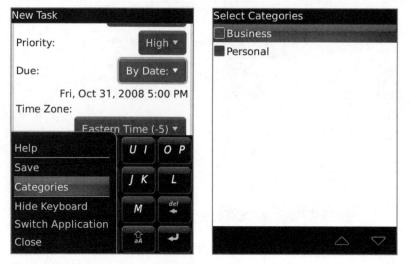

Figure 16-3. *Assigning a task to categories*

4. Select as many categories as you would like by checking them by clicking the screen or pressing the **space** key.

5. You may even add new categories by pressing the **Menu** key and selecting **New**.

6. Once you're done, press the **Menu** key and select **Save** to save your category settings.

7. Press the **Menu** key and select **Save** again to save your task.

Finding Tasks

Once you have a few tasks in your task list, you will want to know how to quickly locate them. One of the fastest ways is with the Find feature. The same Find feature from the address book works in Tasks. Just start typing a few letters to view only those that contain those letters.

In the example here, if we wanted to quickly find all tasks with GO in the name (Figure 16-4, then we type the letter **g** to quickly see them.

Figure 16-4. *Finding exactly the task you are looking for*

Managing or Checking Off Your Tasks

1. Scroll down to a task and touch it to highlight it. (Don't click it, unless you want to open it and make changes.)

2. Once a task is highlighted, you can use the soft keys at the bottom to manage the task.

3. Mark it completed.

4. Mark it in-progress.

5. Or you can delete it.

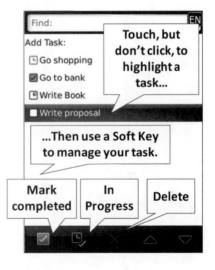

Sorting Your Tasks and Task Options

You may sort your tasks by the following methods in your Task Options screen: **Subject (default)**, **Priority**, **Due Date**, or **Status**.

You may also change the **Confirm Delete** field to **No** (default is **Yes**). You may also change the **Snooze** field from **None** to **30 Min**.

Tasks Options	
Views	
Sort By:	Subject
Actions	Priority
	Due Date
Snooze:	Status
Confirm Delete:	Yes ▼
Number of Entries:	4

Chapter 17

MemoPad: Sticky Notes

One of the simplest and most useful programs on your BlackBerry is MemoPad. Its uses are truly limitless. There is nothing flashy about this program—just type your memo or your notes, and keep them with you at all times.

Using MemoPad is very easy and very intuitive. The following steps guide you through the basic process of inputting a memo and saving it on your BlackBerry. There are two basic ways of setting up memos on the BlackBerry: either compose the note on your computer organizer application and then synchronize (or transfer) that note to the BlackBerry, or compose the memo on the BlackBerry itself.

How Do You Get Your MemoPad Items from Your Computer to Your BlackBerry?

You can also sync your computer's MemoPad notes list with your BlackBerry **MemoPad** app.

If your BlackBerry is tied to a BlackBerry Enterprise Server, the synchronization is wireless and automatic. Otherwise, you will use either a USB cable or Bluetooth wireless to connect your BlackBerry to your computer to keep it up to date. For Windows PC users, see page 81; Apple Mac computer users, see page 143.

The sync works both ways, which extends the power of your desktop computer to your BlackBerry—add or edit notes anywhere and anytime on your BlackBerry—and rest assured they will be back on your computer (and backed up) after the next sync.

1,001 Uses for the MemoPad (Notes) Feature

OK, maybe we won't list 1,001 uses here, but we could. Anything that occupies space on a sticky note on your desk, in your calendar, or on your refrigerator could be written neatly and organized simply using the **MemoPad** app.

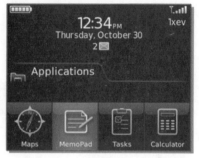

Common Uses for the MemoPad

- Grocery list
- Hardware store list
- Any store list for shopping
- Meeting agenda
- Packing list
- BlackBerry Made Simple videos you want to watch
- Movies you want to rent next time at the video store
- Your parking space at the airport, mall or theme park

Adding or Editing Memos on the BlackBerry

Locate the **MemoPad** icon (your icon may look different, but look for MemoPad to be shown when you highlight it).

> **NOTE:** You may need to first click the **Applications** folder to find it.

To add new memos to the list, simply click **Add Memo** at the top of the list.

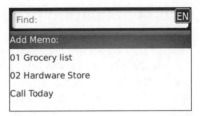

To open an existing memo, just scroll to it and click it.

When typing a new memo, you will want to enter a title that will be easy to find later by typing a few matching letters.

1. Type your memo in the body section.

2. Press the **Enter** key to go down to the next line.

3. When you're done, press the **Menu** key and select **Save**.

Notice, if you have copied something from another icon, like **Email**, you could paste it into the memo. (See page 344 for details on copy and paste.)

Quickly Locating or Finding Memos

MemoPad has a Find feature to help you locate memos quickly by typing the first few letters of words that match the title of your memos. Example, typing **gr** would immediately show you only memos matching those three letters in the first part of any word, like "grocery."

Ordering Frequently Used Memos

For frequently used memos, type numbers (01, 02, 03, etc.) at the beginning of the title to force those memos to be listed in order at the very top of the list. (The reason we started with zero is to keep memos in order after the tenth one.)

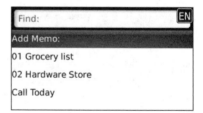

Viewing Your Memos

1. Scroll down by gently touching the screen and scrolling to a memo, or click in the **Find** field at the top to type a few letters to find the memo you want to view.

2. Click the highlighted memo to instantly view its contents.

TIP: Typing **ld** (stands for "Long Date") and pressing the **space** key will insert the date "Tue, 28 Aug 2007," and "**lt**" ("Long Time") will enter the time: "8:51:40 PM" (in the local date/time format you have set on your BlackBerry).

Organizing Your Memos with Categories

Similar to your address book and task list, MemoPad allows you to organize and filter memos using categories.

> **TIP:** Categories are shared between your address book, task list, and MemoPad. They are even synchronized or shared with your desktop computer.

Similar to your address book and task list, MemoPad allows you to organize and filter memos using categories.

First, you must assign your memos to categories before they can be filtered.

One way to be extra organized with MemoPad is to utilize categories so all your memos are filed neatly away.

The two default categories are **Personal** and **Business**, but you can easily change or add to these.

Filing a Memo in a New or Existing Category

1. Start the **MemoPad** icon by clicking it.

2. Locate the memo you want to file to one or more categories by scrolling and clicking it or by typing a few letters and using the Find feature at the top.

3. Press the **Menu** key again and select **Categories**.

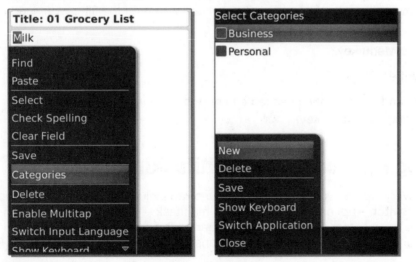

Figure 17-1. *Creating a new category for filing memos*

4. Now you will see a screen similar to the one shown in Figure 17-1. Scroll to a category, and click to check/uncheck it. You can also bring up the keyboard and use the **space** key as well. You can add a new category by pressing the **Menu** key and selecting **New**.

5. Then save your category settings, and save the memo.

To filter memos using categories or to see memos only in a specific category, do the following:

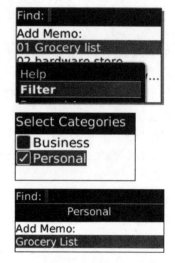

1. Start **MemoPad** by clicking it.

2. Press the **Menu** key and select **Filter**.

3. Now scroll to and click (or press **space**) the category you would like to use to filter the list of memos.

When you see a black bar at the top of your list of memos (just under the **Find**: field,) you know that the list is filtered by that category. In the case of the image to the right – the list is filtered to show only memos that are in the category called Personal..

Un-filtering (Turning Off the Filter) on Your MemoPad

You probably noticed that pressing the **Escape** key (which clears out the characters typed in the **Find** field) will do nothing for the Filter—it just exits the MemoPad. When you re-enter, you still see the filtered list. To un-filter or turn off the filter, you need to do the following:

1. Press the **Menu** key.

2. Select **Filter**.

3. Scroll to and uncheck the checked category by clicking the screen, or by pressing the **space** key.

Switching Applications / Multitasking

From almost every icon on your BlackBerry, MemoPad included, pressing the **Menu** key and selecting **Switch Application** allows you to multitask -- leave your current icon open and jump to any other icon on your BlackBerry. This is especially useful when you want to copy and paste information between icons.

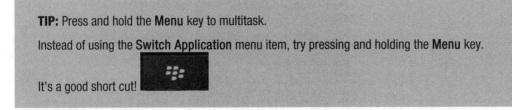

TIP: Press and hold the **Menu** key to multitask.

Instead of using the **Switch Application** menu item, try pressing and holding the **Menu** key.

It's a good short cut!

Here's how you jump or switch applications:

1. Press and hold the **Menu** key until you see a little pop-up window with icons appear in the middle of the screen. This is called the Switch Applications window. You can also get to this window by tapping the **Menu** key and then selecting **Switch Application** from the menu.

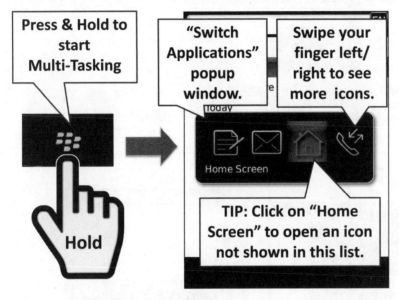

Figure 17-2. *Multitasking on the BlackBerry*

2. You will now see the Switch Applications pop-up window, which shows you every icon that is currently running.

3. If you see the icon you want to switch to, just click it.

4. If you don't see the icon you want, then click the **Home Screen** icon. Then you can locate and click the right icon.

5. You can then jump back to MemoPad or the application you just left by selecting the **Switch Application** menu item from the icon you jumped to.

Press and hold the **Menu** key to jump back.

Forwarding Memos via Email, SMS, or BlackBerry Messenger

You might want to send a memo item via email, BlackBerry PIN message, or SMS text message to others. If so, you can use the **Forward As** command from the menu. Alternatively, if the keyboard is hidden, you will see the **Forward As** soft key on the

bottom of the screen.

1. Highlight the memo you want to send and press the **Menu** key.

2. Select **Forward As**, and then select whether you want **Email**, **PIN**, or **SMS**.

Figure 17-3. *Forwarding a memo*

3. Finally finish composing your message, press the **Menu** key and select **Send**.

Other Memo Menu Commands

There may be a few other things you want to do with your memos. These can be found in the more advanced menu commands.

Start the **MemoPad** icon.

Some of these advanced menu items can be seen only when you are either writing a new memo or editing an existing one.

So you select either **New** and begin working on a new memo, or select **Edit** and edit an existing memo.

From the Editing screen, press the **Menu** key and the following options become available to you:

Find – If you are in a memo item, then this will allow you to find any text inside the memo.

Paste – Suppose you have copied text from another program and want to paste it into a memo. Select and copy the text (from the calendar, address book, or another application) and select **Paste** from this menu. The text is now in your memo.

Select – This allows you to do just the reverse—click here and select text from the memo, press the **Menu** key again, and select **Copy**. Now, use the **Switch Applications** menu item to navigate to another application, press the **Menu** key, and select **Paste** to put the text in that application.

Check Spelling – This will run the BlackBerry spelling checker on the currently open memo item.

Clear field – This clears all contents of the entire memo item—USE WITH CAUTION!

Save – This saves the changes in the memo.

Categories – This allows you to file this memo into either the Business or Personal categories. After selecting **Categories**, you can press the **Menu** key again and select **New** to create yet another category for this memo. (Learn more on page 367.)

Delete – This deletes the current memo.

Enable Multitap – Use this if you want to change from SureType.

Hide Keyboard – Use this to see more of the screen and temporarily hide the keyboard.

Switch Application – This is explained on page 368.

Close – This is similar to pressing the **Escape** key.

Memo Tips and Tricks

There are a couple of tricks you can use to make your filing and locating of memos even easier.

Adding Separate Items for Each Store in Which You Need to Shop

This can help eliminate the forgetting of one particular item you were supposed to get at the hardware or grocery store (and save you time and gas money)!

Putting Numbers at the Beginning of Your Memo Names

This will then order them numerically on your BlackBerry. This is a great way to prioritize your memos and keep the most important ones always at the top of the list.

Chapter 18

SMS Text and MMS

As you may be aware, a key strength of all BlackBerry devices is their messaging abilities. We have covered email extensively and now turn to SMS and MMS messaging. In this chapter, we will show you how to send and view both text messages (SMS) and multimedia messages (MMS.) We will show the various apps from which you can send a message and offer some advice on how to keep your messages organized.

Text and Multimedia Messaging

SMS stands for Short Messaging Service (text messaging) and MMS stands for Multimedia Messaging Service. MMS is a short way to say that you have included pictures, sounds, video, or some other form of media right inside your email message (not to be confused with regular email when media is an attachment to an email message). BlackBerry is beautifully equipped to use both of these services—learning them will make you more productive and make your BlackBerry that much more fun to use.

TIP: SMS and MMS sometimes cost extra! Watch out! Many phone companies charge extra for SMS text messaging and MMS multi-media messaging, even if you have an "unlimited" BlackBerry data plan. Typical charges can be $0.10 to $0.25 per message. This adds up quickly!

The solution is to check with your carrier about bundled SMS/MMS plans. For just $5–10 per month you might receive several hundred or thousand or even unlimited monthly SMS/MMS text messages.

SMS Text Messaging on Your BlackBerry

Text messaging has become one of the most popular services on cell phones today. While it is still used more extensively in Europe and Asia, it is growing in popularity in North America.

The concept is very simple. Instead of placing a phone call, send a short message to someone's handset. It is much less disruptive than a phone call, and you may have friends, colleagues, or co-workers who do not own a BlackBerry—so email is not an option.

One of the authors uses text messaging with his children all the time—this is how their generation communicates. "R u coming home 4 dinner?" "Yup." There you have it—meaningful dialogue with a seventeen-year-old—short, instant, and easy.

Composing SMS Text Messages

Composing an SMS message is much like sending an email. The beauty of an SMS message is that it arrives on virtually any handset and is so easy to respond to.

Option #1: Sending an SMS Message from the Message List

1. Click your **Messages** icon.

2. Press the **Compose** soft key at the bottom right of the screen.

3. Select **SMS**.

4. Begin typing in a contact name or simply type someone's mobile phone number. If you are typing a name, when you see the contact appear, click it.

5. If the contact has multiple phone numbers, the BlackBerry will ask you to choose which number.

6. In the main body (where the cursor is) just type your message like you were sending an email message.

CAUTION: SMS messages are **limited to 160 characters** by most carriers. If you go over that in the BlackBerry, two separate text messages will be sent.

If you want to add some fun to your text message, click the smiley face to bring up a list of potential emoticons.

Tap the emoticon you want to use. Note at the top of the screen there are also the text shortcuts for each emoticon. For example, the shortcut for the "Cool" face is "B)".

When you are done typing, just press the **Enter** key in the lower right corner to send the message. That's all there is to it.

Option #2: Sending an SMS Message from the Contact List

1. Click your **Address Book** icon (it may say Contacts instead).

2. Type a few letters to find the person to whom you want to send your SMS message.

3. With the contact highlighted from the list, press the **Menu** key and you will see one of your menu options is **SMS**, followed by the contact name.

Basic SMS Menu Commands

As with the email feature, there are many options via the menu commands in SMS messaging.

Menu Commands from the Main SMS Screen

The BlackBerry adds an **SMS** icon to the Home screen. One way to initiate SMS messaging is to click the icon.

> **NOTE:** On some models, the icon says **SMS and MMS**.

On the Compose SMS Text screen, when you are typing your text message, press the **Menu** key. The following options shown in Figure 18-1 are available to you:

Help	Gives you contextual help with SMS messaging
Save Draft	Keeps a copy of SMS for later referencing
Add To	Adds a second line for adding another addressee
Choose Address	Allows you to send SMS to a contact in your BlackBerry
Edit AutoText	Allows you to edit your AutoText entries
Options	Brings up the SMS option menus
Switch Input Language	Allows you to type your SMS message in another language
Switch Application	Brings up the Switch Applications pop-up window so you can select another icon for multitasking (see page 368)
Close	This is the same as pressing the **Escape** key. It closes your SMS text window and asks if you want to save changes.

Figure 18-1. *SMS menu commands*

Once you actually start typing your SMS message and press the **Menu** key, a new option appears—**Check Spelling**—giving you the power of the BlackBerry spelling checker in your SMS messages.

Opening and Replying to SMS Messages

Opening your SMS messages couldn't be easier—the BlackBerry makes it simple to quickly keep in touch and respond to your messages.

1. Navigate to your waiting messages from either the **Message** icon on the Home screen or your Messages screen, and click the new SMS message.

2. If you are in the midst of a dialogue with someone, your messages will appear in a threaded message format, which looks like a running discussion.

3. Press the **Menu** key and select **Reply**.

4. The cursor appears in a blank field—type your reply, click the **Menu** key, and select **Send**.

> **TIP:** Need to find an SMS or MMS message? Go to page 309 to learn how to search for messages.

MMS Messaging on Your BlackBerry

MMS stands for multimedia messaging, which includes pictures, video, and audio.

> **NOTE:** *Not all BlackBerry devices or carriers support MMS messaging*, so it is a good idea to make sure that your recipient can receive these messages before you send them.

Sending MMS from the Message List

Perhaps the easiest way to send an MMS message is to start the process just like you started the SMS process earlier:

1.   Click the **Messages** icon, and press the **Menu** key.

2.   Scroll down to **Compose MMS as shown in Figure 18-2**, and click.

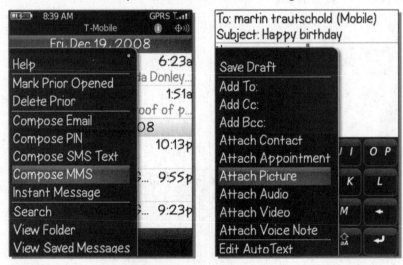

Figure 18-2. *Composing an MMS message*

Depending on the phone company that supplied your BlackBerry, you may be prompted to find the MMS file you desire to send (these are often stored in your templates file).

Some BlackBerry devices have a pre-loaded "Birthday.mms" in this folder.

Click the Birthday MMS, if you have it.

Figure 18-3. *Choosing a contact and phone number for an MMS message*

Then type the recipient in the **To** field, scroll to the appropriate contact, and click.

Figure 18-4. *Choosing an image to send as MMS*

You can add a subject and text in the body of the MMS. When finished, just press the **Menu** key and click **Send**.

There are lots of template MMS files you can download on the web and put into this folder to be selected in the future.

Sending a Media File As an MMS from the Media Icon

This might be the easier and more common way for you to send media files as MMS messages.

1. Scroll to the **Media** icon, and click. You will be brought to the media screen.

2. Click **Pictures**, and find the picture either on your device or media card that you wish to send.

3. Just highlight the picture (no need to click it) and press the **Menu** key.

4. Scroll down to **Send as MMS**, and click. You will then be directed to choose the recipient from your contacts. Find the contact you desire, and click.

> **TIP AND CAUTION:** If you do not have an MMS or SMS text messaging service plan from your phone company, you can usually send an email for no additional cost. The only other thing to be aware of is whether you have an unlimited BlackBerry data plan. If you don't have this unlimited data plan, then you will want to send pictures only very rarely because they can eat up your data much faster than a plain-text email message.

5. Type a subject and any text in the message, press the **Menu** key, and send it.

Basic MMS Menu Commands

You can personalize your MMS message even more through the MMS menu.

When you are composing the MMS message, press the **Menu** key.

Scroll through the menu to see your options; you can easily add more recipients.

You can also attach addresses from your address book. To add an address, just click **Attach Address** and find the appropriate address on the next screen.

If you had scheduled a birthday dinner together, then you might want to add an appointment from your BlackBerry calendar ("Dinner at the Fancy French Restaurant for Two"). Click the **Add Appointment** option.

To add an audio file to accompany the picture, choose **Attach Audio as shown in Figure 18-5** and then navigate to the folder that contains the audio file.

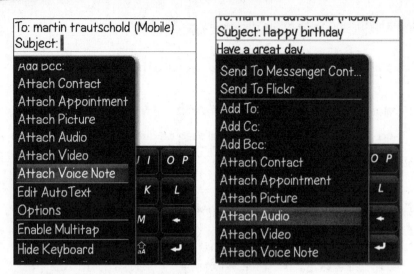

Figure 18-5. *Attaching an audio file to an MMS message*

You can also attach another picture by choosing the appropriate option from the menu.

Advanced MMS Commands

While you are composing your MMS message, press the **Menu** key and scroll down to **Options**.

In the Current Message Options screen you will see the estimated size of the MMS, which is important, because if the file is too big, your recipient may not be able to download it onto his or her device.

You can also set the importance of this MMS as well as set delivery confirmation options.

For additional advanced MMS commands, navigate from the Home screen to Options, and click. Scroll to MMS and click.

From this screen you can set your phone to always receive multimedia files by setting the first line to say **Always**.

You can also set your automatic retrieval to occur **Always** or **Never**.

You can select each check box to set your notification and message filtering options as well.

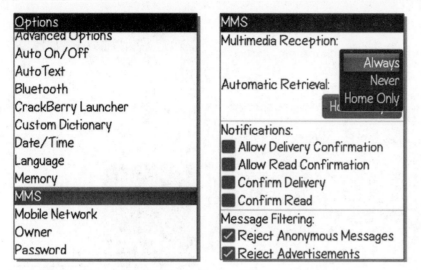

Figure 18-6. *Advanced MMS options*

The Notifications options to the right in Figure 18-6 are as follows:

Allow Delivery Confirmation means to allow you to send delivery confirmation messages when you receive MMS messages from others.

Allow Read Confirmation means to allow your BlackBerry to send a confirmation message when you have opened an MMS message you received.

Confirm Delivery means to request a delivery confirmation from people to whom you send MMS messages.

Confirm Read means to request a read receipt message when your MMS recipient opens the MMS message you sent them.

We recommend leaving the filtering options checked as they are by default.

MMS a nd S MS T ext T roubleshooting—Host Routing Table "Register Now"

These troubleshooting steps will work for MMS, SMS, email, web browsing—anything that requires a wireless radio connection. Please see page 563 for our entire chapter with more detailed steps on troubleshooting your wireless signal.

Host Routing Table—Register Now:

1. From your Home screen, click the **Options** icon.

2. Click **Advanced Options**, and then scroll to **Host Routing Table**.

3. Press the **Menu** key, and then click **Register Now**.

> **NOTE:** This image shows "Verizon." You will see your own wireless carrier name on the screen.

Host Routing Table
Verizon [240]
Verizon [71440]
Verizon [55c40]
Verizon [4d440]
Verizon [1240]
Verizon [80cc40]
Verizon [791940]

View
Register Now
Show Keyboard
Switch Application
Close

4. While the BlackBerry is still on, do a battery pull. Take off the back of the casing, remove the battery, wait 30 seconds, and then re-install it. Once the BlackBerry reboots, you should be all set for SMS text and MMS messaging.

Chapter 19

Even More Messaging

You already know that your BlackBerry is an amazing messaging device. What you may not realize is that there are so many more ways to use "messaging" on the BlackBerry. In this chapter, we will look at PIN messaging (using the unique identifying PIN for each BlackBerry), the famous BlackBerry Messaging (BBM), voice notes, and other instant messaging.

> **TIP:** PIN messages are always free, whereas other SMS text, BlackBerry Messenger, and MMS (multimedia messages) may be charged under an extra service plan by your phone company.

PIN Messaging and Sending Your PIN with the "Mypin" Shortcut

BlackBerry handhelds have a unique feature called PIN-to-PIN, also known as PIN Messaging or Peer-to-Peer Messaging. This allows one BlackBerry user to communicate directly with another BlackBerry user as long as you know that user's BlackBerry PIN number. We'll show you an easy way to find your PIN (Figure 19-1), send an email message to your colleague, and a few good tips and tricks.

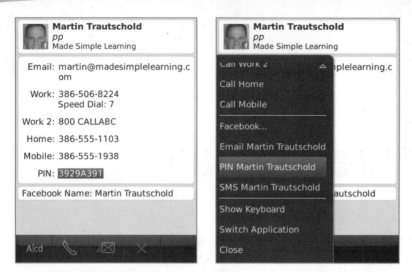

Figure 19-1. *PIN messaging on your BlackBerry*

Compose an email message to your colleague. In the body type of the email message, type the code letters **mypin** and hit the **space** key as shown in Figure 19-2—you will then see your pin number in the following format "pin:2100000A," where the 2100000A is replaced by your actual PIN. Press the **Menu** key and select **Send**.

To: Gary Mazo   EN
To:
Cc:
Subject: PIN Messaging
This is my pin number: mypin

To: Gary Mazo   EN
To:
Cc:
Subject: PIN Messaging
This is my pin number: pin:2100000A

Figure 19-2. *Typing **Mypin** to display your PIN*

Just press the **Menu** key and select **Send** to deliver an email message with your PIN number.

You can also hide the keyboard and use the **Send** soft key at the bottom of the screen.

Replying to a PIN Message

Once you receive your PIN message, you will see that it is highlighted in red text in your inbox.

To reply to a PIN message, simply click the message to open it, click the **Menu** key, and select **Reply**, just like with email and other messaging.

Adding Someone's PIN to Your Address Book

Once you receive an email message containing a PIN number from your colleague or family member, you should put this PIN number into your contact list.

If you don't already have this person in your contact list, then do the following:

1. Click the PIN number to see a short menu.

2. Select **Add to Contacts** from the menu, and then enter the person's information.

3. Be sure to save your new entry.

If you already have this person in your contact list, then you should do the following:

1. Select **Copy** from the menu and paste the PIN into the contact record.

2. Then press and hold the **Menu** key until you see the Switch Application pop-up window.

3. Select **Contacts** if you see it.

4. Select **Home Screen** if you don't see Contacts—then click **Contacts** to start it from the Home screen.

5. Type a few letters of the person's first, last, or company name to find them, press the **Menu** key, and select **Edit**.

6. Scroll down to put the cursor in the **PIN** field, press the **Menu** key, and select **Paste**.

7. Press the **Menu** key and select **Save**.

Now, next time you search through your contacts, you will have the new option of sending a PIN message in addition to the other email, SMS, MMS, and phone options.

BlackBerry Messenger

So far, we have covered email, SMS text, MMS, and BlackBerry PIN-to-PIN messaging. If you still need other ways of communicating with friends, family, and colleagues you can try BlackBerry Messenger, or any one of the most popular instant messaging programs like AIM (AOL Instant Messenger), Yahoo, or GoogleTalk instant messengers. The BlackBerry is really the ultimate communication tool.

TIP: Don't see the BlackBerry **Messenger** icon (Figure 19-3) ?

First, look in your **Messaging** folder or **Applications** folder. If you don't see it, then download and install the BlackBerry **Messenger** icon. Go to mobile.blackberry.com from your BlackBerry web browser and follow the directions.

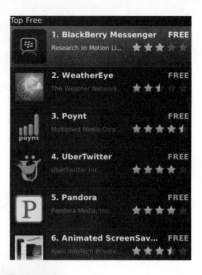

NOTE: You can also go to BlackBerry App World and download the newest version of BlackBerry Messenger for free.

Figure 19-3. *BlackBerry Messenger icon*

Many users have IM programs on their PC, or even their mobile phone. BlackBerry includes a messaging program just for fellow BlackBerry users called BlackBerry Messenger. You will find the **BlackBerry Messenger** icon in your **Applications** menu or your **Instant Messaging** folder.

Setting Up BlackBerry Messenger

BlackBerry Messenger offers you a little more secure way of keeping in touch quickly with fellow BlackBerry users. Setup is very easy.

If you don't see the **Blackberry Messenger** icon, then press the **Menu** key, look for the **Instant Messenger** folder, and click it.

1. Click the **BlackBerry Messenger** icon after accepting the legal agreement.

2. You will be prompted to set your user name.

3. Type your display name (the name that others will see) and click OK.

4. You will then be asked to set a BlackBerry Messenger password. Type your password, confirm, and then click OK.

Adding Contacts to Your BlackBerry Messenger Group

Once your user name is setup, you need to add contacts to your BlackBerry Messenger group. In BlackBerry Messenger, your contacts are fellow BlackBerry users who have the BlackBerry Messenger program installed on their handhelds.

1. Navigate to the main BlackBerry Messenger screen and press the **Menu** key.

2. Scroll to **Add a Contact** and click.

3. Begin typing the name of the desired contact. When the desired contact appears, click the contact. Choose whether to invite the contact by PIN (Figure 19-4) or email.

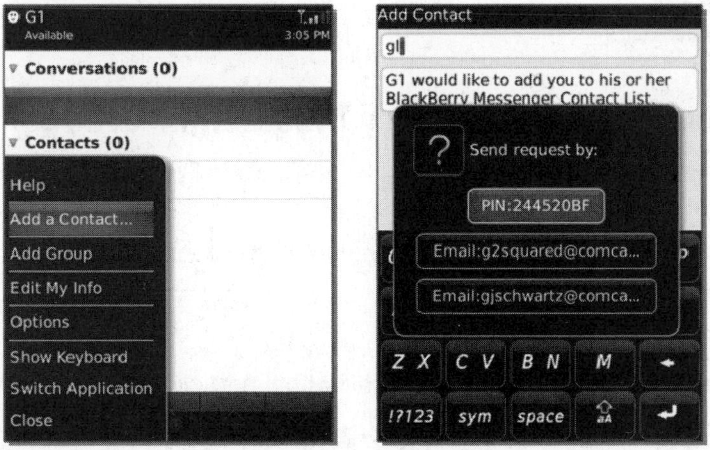

Figure 19-4. *Adding a BlackBerry Messenger contact by PIN number*

4. The BlackBerry generates a message stating: "(Name) would like to add you to his/her BlackBerry Messenger." Click OK and the message is sent to this person.

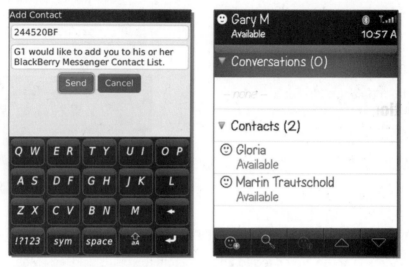

Figure 19-5. *Sending a BlackBerry Messenger invitation*

5. The message request shows up in your Pending group, under Contacts.

6. The contact will be listed under Pending until the recipient responds to your invitation.

If you do not get a response, then click the name and use another communication method (e.g., phone, email, SMS text) to ask your colleague to hurry up.

Joining a Fellow User's BlackBerry Messenger Group

You may be invited to join another BlackBerry user's Messaging group. You can either accept or decline this invitation.

You will receive your invitations via email or you can see them directly in BlackBerry Messenger.

1. Click your **BlackBerry Messenger** icon.

2. Scroll to your Requests group, highlight the invitation, and click.

3. A menu pops up with three options: **Accept**, **Decline**, or **Remove**.

4. Click **Accept** and you will now be part of the Messaging group. Click **Decline** to deny the invitation or **Remove** to no longer show the invitation on your BlackBerry.

BlackBerry Messenger Menu Commands

Open BlackBerry Messenger, go to your main screen, and press the **Menu** key.

Available Options

Add a Contact – Use this to add people to your conversations and groups.

Expand – This simply expands the dialogue screen, if the screen is already open. The menu command reads **Collapse**.

> **TIP:** Clicking the main conversation screen does the same thing.

Collapse All – This hides all group members.

Add Group – Click to add a new messaging group such as Work, Family, or Friends.

Edit Group – Use this to rename your messaging groups.

My Status – Click to make yourself available or unavailable to your messaging buddies.

Edit My Info – Change your name and/or password.

Options – Click to bring up your Options screen.

Switch Application – Press this to multitask or jump to another application while leaving the **Messenger** application running.

Close – Exit the **Messenger** application.

BlackBerry Messenger Options Screen

If you wanted even more control of Messenger, you would press the **Menu** key and select **Options**. On the Messenger Options screen, you can set the following:

1. Whether your BlackBerry will vibrate when someone **PING**s you (the default is **Yes**)

2. Have the BlackBerry force you to enter your password every time you send a "new contact" request, which would be a good security measure if your BlackBerry was lost

3. Whether your requests can be forwarded by other people (the default is **yes**)

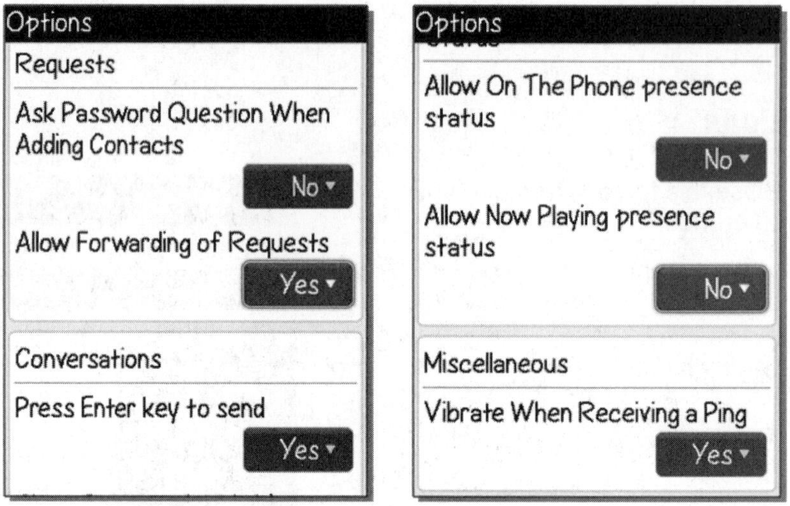

Options	Options
Requests	Allow On The Phone presence status
Ask Password Question When Adding Contacts No ▾	No ▾
Allow Forwarding of Requests Yes ▾	Allow Now Playing presence status No ▾
Conversations	Miscellaneous
Press Enter key to send Yes ▾	Vibrate When Receiving a Ping Yes ▾

Figure 19-6. *BlackBerry Messenger options*

Finally, you may choose to display your Messenger conversations in your messages (email inbox). The default is **Yes**. If you change it to **No** then none of your Messenger conversations will show up in your email inbox.

Starting or Continuing Conversations and Emoticons

While messaging is a lot like text messaging, you actually have more options for personal expression and the ability to see a complete conversation with the Messaging program.

Your conversation list is in your Main screen. Just highlight the individual with whom you are conversing and press and click them. The Conversation screen opens.

Just type the new message, click the **Menu** key, and select **Send**.

To add an emoticon to your message, press the **Emoticon** soft key button ⌂ and swipe your finger to the emoticon you wish to use.

Just click the desired emoticon and it will appear in the message.

> **TIP:** You can also type the characters shown to get the emoticon you want—e.g., ":)" = Smile and "<3<3" = Love Struck, as shown here.

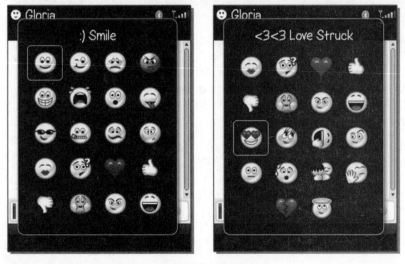

Figure 19-7. *Emoticon options in BlackBerry Messenger*

Sending Files to a Message Buddy

In the midst of your conversation, you can send a file very easily (at the time of publication, you were limited to sending only files that are images, photos, or sound files—ring tones and music).

1. Click the contact in your Conversation screen and open the dialogue with that individual.

2. Press the **Menu** key and select **Send a File**. Choose whether you wish to send an image or an audio file.

3. Using the touch screen, navigate to where the image or audio file is stored on your BlackBerry, and click it.

4. Selecting the file will automatically send it to your message buddy.

> **NOTE:** Some BlackBerry providers (phone companies) may limit the size of file you can send via Bluetooth to a small size, such as 15 kilobytes (kb). Most pictures maybe 300kb or more, and full songs might be 500kb or more.

Pinging a Contact

Let's say that you wanted to reach a BlackBerry Messenger contact quickly. One option available to you is to ping that contact. When you ping a BlackBerry user, their device will vibrate once to let them know that they are wanted/needed immediately.

> **TIP:** You can set your BlackBerry to vibrate or not vibrate when you receive a ping in your BlackBerry Messenger Options screen.

1. Open a conversation with a contact from the Contact screen.

2. Press the **Menu** key and scroll down to **Ping Contact**.

3. The dialogue screen will reflect the ping by showing "PING!!!" in capital red letters.

4. The ping recipient will notice that his or her BlackBerry vibrates and indicates that you have pinged it.

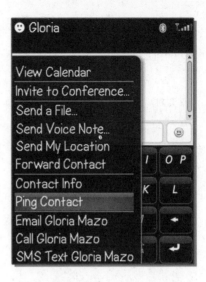

Using the "My Status" Options (Your Availability to Others)

Sometimes, you might not want to be disrupted with instant messages. You can change your status to unavailable, and you won't be disturbed. Conversely, one of your contacts might be offline, and you want to know when he or she becomes available. You can set an alert to notify you.

1. Navigate to your main Messaging screen and press the **Menu** key.

2. Scroll to **Edit My Info** and click.

3. Choose either **Available** or **Unavailable**.

4. To set an alert, just highlight an unavailable contact from your Contact List screen and press the **Menu** key.

5. Scroll to **Set Alert** and you will be notified as soon as he or she becomes available.

Conferencing with BlackBerry Messenger

One very cool new feature on BlackBerry Messenger is the ability to have a conference chat with two or more of your Messenger contacts. Just start up a conversation as you did before. In Figure 19-8 you can see that I am in a conversation with my friend Martin.

Figure 19-8. *BlackBerry Messenger conversation screen*

Now, let's say I wanted to invite my wife Gloria to join the conversation; I would press the **Menu** button and click **Invite to Conference (Figure 19-9)**.

Figure 19-9. *Inviting a third party to a BlackBerry Messenger conference*

I then find the contact from my Messenger list I want to invite—in this case, Gloria.

An invitation is sent for her to join us. When she accepts, it will be noted on the Messenger screen and all three of us can have our conversation (see Figure 19-10).

Figure 19-10. *Three parties in a conference*

Using Groups in BlackBerry Messenger

Another new feature of BlackBerry Messenger is the ability to create and use groups. This is useful when you don't need to send a message to everyone but just want to message a small group of colleagues.

1. From your main Messenger screen, just click the **BlackBerry Groups** tab.

2. If you don't have any groups, you will see only the **Create a New Group** option.

3. Give your group a name and
    description, and even choose a new
    Group icon if you wish.

Create New Group

Description

Team Group

Group Icon

Allow non—admin members to   Yes
invite others

Show on Home Screen   No

4. Click **Create Group** and you will see
    your new group displayed. Click
    Members and begin to choose
    members for your group.

Made Simple Learning
Team Group

● Group Activities

▤ Members   1 Member

▣ Chat   O Active Chats

▣ Pictures   O Pictures

▣ Lists   O Lists

▣ Calendar

5. You can add a member's email
    address, scan his or her barcode, or
    choose an existing BlackBerry
    Messenger contact to be a part of the
    new group.

Add Member

✉ Enter a person's email address,
   PIN, or name

▦ Scan a person's barcode

▣ Select a contact from BlackBerry
   Messenger

                    Group Capacity: 1 / 30

6. In this example, we want to invite
    Martin and Evan to be a part of the
    "Made Simple Learning" team group.
    They are existing Messenger contacts,
    so we choose **Select a contact from
    BlackBerry Messenger** and then
    place check marks next to their
    names.

7. When we are done, we press the
    Menu key and select **Send**.

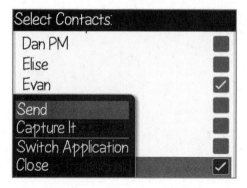

Using Barcodes

Perhaps the most innovative feature of the new BlackBerry Messenger is the use of a unique barcode as a means of connecting to someone as a Messenger contact.

Each BlackBerry can generate its own unique barcode. To find your barcode, just start up the **Messenger** application, press the **Menu** key, and select **My Profile**.

My Profile

Display Name:
Dan

Status: ● Available ▼
☐ Show What I'm Listening To

Status Message:

PIN: 30FE7BD6

☐ Show My Location/Timezone
   Information

My Barcode   What's this?

Display My Barcode

Scroll to **Display My Barcode** and click. The screen will now show your unique barcode. Any other BlackBerry user (with BlackBerry Messenger 5.0 installed *and* a camera on his or her BlackBerry) can snap a picture of the barcode.

What needs to be done is for the other BlackBerry Messenger user to choose **Invite Contact** from their menu and then choose **Scan a person's barcode**. This will activate their camera and they can take a picture of your code.

Invite Contact

✉   Enter a person's email address, PIN, or name

▦   Scan a person's barcode

Using AIM, Yahoo, and Google Talk Messaging

After you get used to BlackBerry Messenger you will begin to see that it is a powerful way of quickly keeping in touch with friends, family, and colleagues. Realizing that many are still not in the BlackBerry world, you can also access and use popular IM programs like AOL Instant Messenger (AIM), Yahoo Messenger, and Google Talk Messenger right out of the box on the BlackBerry. Individual carriers do have some restrictions, however, and you will need to check your carrier web sites to see which services are supported.

Installing More Instant Messenger Applications on the BlackBerry

1. First see if your carrier has placed an **IM** or **Instant Messaging** folder icon in your Applications directory (see Figure 19-11). This may already have the icons installed that you want to use.

2. Navigate to **Applications** and scroll for an icon that simply is called **IM**.

Figure 19-11. *Other instant messaging icons on your BlackBerry*

3. 3. If you have an **IM Folder** icon, click it, and follow the on-screen prompts.

4. 4. If there is no **IM** icon, start your web browser on the BlackBerry.

5. 5. Press the **Menu** key and select **Go To...**. Then type www.mobile.blackberry.com or mobile.blackberry.com to get to the BlackBerry Home page, which may look something like the image in Figure 19-12.

   (Please forgive us if this web page looks very different by the time you see it—web sites can change very frequently!)

Figure 19-12. *Installing other IM apps from mobile.blackberry.com*

6. 6. Locate the Instant Messaging topic under the Communicate group. You need to scroll down a bit, and then click the **Download** link for the instant messenger application you want to install.

> **NOTE:** The group name may be slightly different. Simply look for "Instant Messaging" or "IM."

At publishing time, this was the list of currently available instant messaging applications from mobile.blackberry.com.

Instant Messaging

Windows Live Messenger
AOL Instant Messenger
ICQ
Yahoo! Messenger
Google Talk

Almost certainly this list will be different by the time you are reading this book.

For more information to help you download and install third-party software, please check out our chapter devoted to adding and removing software starting on page 515.

Add Memory and Media

Boosting Your Memory with a Media Card

Your BlackBerry comes with 256 MB (Megabytes) of flash memory and 2 GB of "on-board" memory, but all that won't all be available to you. The operating system and installed software take up some of that room and so will all your personal information. (The image of the SanDisk MicroSD card and the SanDisk logo are copyrights owned by SanDisk Corporation.)

Since your BlackBerry is also a very capable media device, you will probably want more room to store things like music files, videos, ring tones, and pictures.

That's where the MicroSD memory card comes in. Some wireless carriers are pre-installing an 8GB or 16GB memory card in the BlackBerry—if you have a smaller card or no card at all, you can expand the memory to 16GB if you need.

Installing Your Memory Card / Media Card

The BlackBerry actually has the MicroSD card slot inside the back cover, near the battery. Getting to it is simple:

1. Just press the release buttons and take off the back battery cover.

2. Hold the memory card with the metal contacts facing downwards.

3. The small notch on the card should be on the right-hand side.

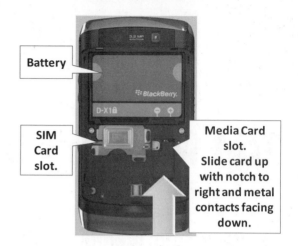

4. Just slide the card into the slot until it stops—don't force it!

To remove the card, we recommend using the eraser tip of a pencil to help move it out of the slot.

You don't even need to power off the BlackBerry; you can insert the card with the BlackBerry on. When the card is correctly inserted you should see "Media Card Inserted" appear on the screen.

Verifying the Media Card Installation and Free Memory

Once installed, it is a good idea to double-check that the card is installed correctly and the amount of free space is available.

1. Press the **Menu** key, scroll to the **Options** icon, and click it.

2. Scroll down, select **Memory**, and click.

3. This image shows, at the bottom, that this BlackBerry does not have a media card (memory card) inserted.

Memory	
Compression:	Enabled ▾
Media Card Support:	On ▾
Mass Storage Mode Support:	
	On ▾
Auto Enable Mass Storage Mode When Connected:	
	Prompt ▾
Application Memory Free Space:	132.2 MB
Device Memory Total Space: Free Space:	859.7 MB 851.2 MB

A media card is not presently inserted in the device.

4. This image shows that a media card has been inserted (see very bottom).

5. Look at the total space figure at the bottom of the screen. An 8.0 GB card will read about 7.3GB (1GB equals about 1,000 MB). If you see that, all is well.

6. This image shows a media card with 5.0 GB of free space.

Memory	
Mass Storage Mode Support:	
	On ▾
Auto Enable Mass Storage Mode When Connected:	
	Prompt ▾
Application Memory Free Space:	22.0MB
Device Memory Total Space: Free Space:	879.2MB 872.9MB
Media Card Total Space: Free Space:	7.3GB 5.0GB

Transferring Content to Your Storm Using Mass Storage Mode (for Mac and Windows)

This works regardless of whether you have a Windows or a Mac computer. We will show images for the Windows computer process, and it will be fairly similar for your Mac. This transfer method assumes you have stored your media on a MicroSD media card in your BlackBerry.

1. To get to this screen, go into your **Options** icon, scroll down, and click **Memory**.

2. Make sure your media card **Mass Storage Mode Support** field is set to **On** and other settings are as shown.

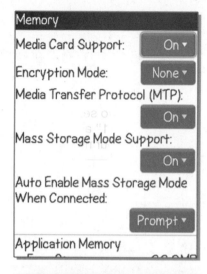

3. Now, connect your BlackBerry to your computer with the USB cable. If you selected **Prompt**, you will see a **"Turn on Mass Storage Mode?"** question.

4. Click **Yes** (you should probably check the box that says "**Don't Ask Me Again**"). When you click **Yes**, then your media card looks just like another hard disk to your computer (similar to a USB flash drive).

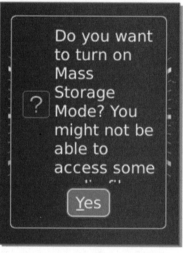

TIP: If you set the **Auto Enable Mass Storage Mode** field to **Yes**, then you won't be asked this question, and the media card on the BlackBerry will automatically look like a mass storage device.

CAUTION: For the newest version of BlackBerry Desktop Manager (v5.0.1 at publishing time) you need to have mass storage mode enabled or turned on, otherwise you cannot see the files on your BlackBerry media card using BlackBerry Desktop Manager's Media Manager. *This was not the case with some previous versions of Desktop Manager.*

5. After your BlackBerry is connected and in mass storage mode, just open your computer's file management software. In Windows, press the **Windows** key + **E** to open Windows Explorer. On your Mac, start your Finder. Look for another hard disk or "BlackBerry (model number)" that has been added.

You may see two separate disks:— "BLACKBERRY1" and "Removable Disk" (this is your media card).

Or, you might see your BlackBerry, and under it, "Device Memory" and "Media Card."

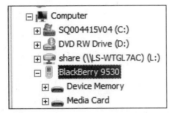

In Figure 20-1 you see Removable Disk (G:), which is the BlackBerry media card. Then navigate to the media type you want (movies, pictures, etc.), and just drag and drop or copy the pictures between your BlackBerry and you computer as you normally do with other files on your computer.

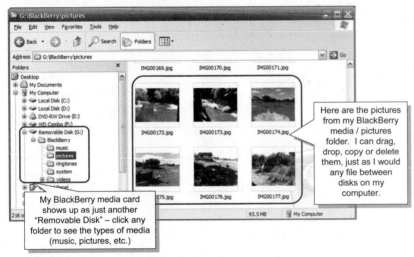

Figure 20-1. *Viewing contents of a media card on your computer*

When you plug your BlackBerry into your Mac, it will identify the main memory and the contents of the Micro SD card as two separate drives and place them right on your desktop for easy navigation.

To copy pictures from your BlackBerry, select the files from the **BlackBerry / pictures** folder. Then draw a box around the pictures, or click one and press **Ctrl+A** or **Command+A** (Mac) to select them all. Or hold the **Ctrl** key (Windows) or **Command** key (Mac) down and click individual pictures to select them. Once selected, right-press and click (Windows) or right-press and click the Mac. Or press **Ctrl** and click (Mac) one of the selected pictures and select **Cut** (to move) or **Copy** (to copy).

Figure 20-2. *Copying a file to a media card using your Mac*

Then click any other disk/folder—like **My Documents**—and navigate to where you want to move / copy the files. Once there, right-press and click again in the right window where all the files are listed and select **Paste**.

On your Mac, click the **Finder** icon in the lower left-hand corner of the Dock.

You will see your Devices (including both BlackBerry drives) on the top and your Places (where you can copy and paste media) on the bottom.

▼ DEVICES

🖥 Macintosh HD

🖴 iDisk

▢ STORM   ⏏

▢ BLACKBER... ⏏

▼ PLACES

🖼 Desktop

🏠 Gary

🅰 Applications

🗒 Documents

You can also delete all the pictures / media / songs from your BlackBerry in a similar manner. Navigate to the BlackBerry / (media type) folder, like **BlackBerry / videos**. Press the key combination shown previously on your computer keyboard to select all the files, and then press the **Delete** key on your keyboard to delete all the files.

You can also copy files from your computer to your BlackBerry using a similar method. Just go to the files you want to copy, and select them (highlight them). Then right-press and click **Copy** and paste them into the correct BlackBerry / (media type) folder.

IMPORTANT: Not all media (videos), pictures (images), or songs will be playable or viewable on your BlackBerry. If you use desktop software such as Desktop Manager (for Windows, see page 88) or PocketMac for BlackBerry (for Mac, see page 143) to transfer the files, most files will be automatically converted for you.

Chapter 21

Your Music Player

Your BlackBerry is more than your personal digital assistant, your email machine, and your address book. Today's BlackBerrys are also very capable media players. With your BlackBerry, it is easy to carry your music, playlists, podcasts, and more. You can transfer playlists from iTunes and other media programs as well.

Listening to Your Music

One of the things that sets your BlackBerry apart from many of the earlier BlackBerry smartphones is the inclusion of multi-media capabilities and the ability to expand memory with the use of a media card. While some of the most popular formats of digital media are supported, you may have to take some steps to get all your music and videos working on the BlackBerry.

With a good sized media card, the media capabilities of the BlackBerry, one might even suggest: **Why do I need an iPhone or iPod? I've got a BlackBerry!**

Getting Your Music and Playlists on Your BlackBerry

The BlackBerry comes with internal memory, but the operating system (OS) and other pre-loaded programs take up some of that space. What's left over is usually not enough to store all your music.

STEP 1: Buy and insert a media card (if you don't already have one) to boost the memory available to store your favorite music—see page 405 for help.

> **NOTE:** Some BlackBerry smartphones come with pre-installed with media cards—see page 440.

STEP 2: Transfer your music from your computer. If you are Windows user, please refer to page 123. If you are an Apple Mac user, please refer to the information found on page 159 and page 407.

Playing Your Music

Once your music is in the right place, you are ready to start enjoying the benefit of having your music with you at all times on your BlackBerry.

The fastest way to get to your music is by clicking the **Music** icon. However, you can also get to the same place by clicking your **Media** icon, and then selecting **Music** from the options.

You are now presented with various preset options to find and play your favorite music.

All Songs: This shows you every song on your BlackBerry.

Artists: This shows you all artists. Then you can click an artist to see all of his or her songs.

Albums: This shows a list of all albums.

Genres: This shows a list of all genres on your BlackBerry (Pop, Rock, Jazz, etc.).

Playlists: This shows all playlists or allows you to create new ones.

Shuffle Songs: Plays all your music in a shuffle mode or random order.

Finding and Playing an Individual Song

1. Bring up the keyboard (either by pressing the **Menu** key and selecting **Show Keyboard** or using your Convenience key if you have mapped it).

2. If you know the name of the song, then just type a few letters of any word in the song's name in the **Find** field at the top to instantly locate all matching songs.

3. In this case, we type **Love** and see all matching songs. To narrow the list, press the **space** key and type a few more letters of another word in the name of the song.

4. Then just click the song to bring up the media player and the song starts playing.

5. Once you click a song, the music player will open and your song will begin to play.

6. Press the **Pause**, **Stop**, **Next Track**, and **Previous Track** keys.

7. Adjust your volume using the volume keys on the side of the BlackBerry.

> **TIP:** Pressing the **Mute** key on the top of your BlackBerry will also pause or resume playback.

The volume keys on the side of the BlackBerry also control the song volume.

Doing Other Things While Listening to Music

You can keep your music playing while you are checking email, browsing the web, or doing just about anything else on your BlackBerry.

Get your music started, as shown previously. Then press the **Red Phone** key to jump out to your Home screen. Start up any icon you want: **Messages**, **Browser**, **Calendar**, **Facebook**, anything. Your music continues playing.

To quickly return to your music player and select another song or playlist, press the **Menu** key and select an item near the top called **Now Playing...** This will instantly jump you right back to the music player.

Figure 21-1. *Jumping from any app to the Now Playing screen*

When a phone call comes in, the music automatically pauses for your call. When you hang up, the music automatically starts up again, picking up where it left off.

The fastest way to pause and silence the music is to tap the **Mute** key on the top edge of your BlackBerry. Tap it again to re-start the music.

Setting a New Song or Ring Tone As Your Phone Ring Tone

1. Navigate to and play the song you want to use as a ring tone, as described previously.

2. Press the **Menu** key and select **Set as Ring Tone**.

3. Now, the next time you receive a call, your favorite song will be played.

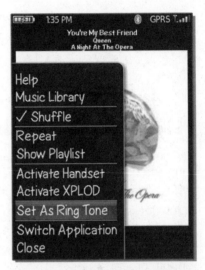

4. If you want to use a pre-loaded ring tone, then instead of going to **Songs** in your **Media** icon, you would select **Ring Tones**.

5. Then select **All Ring Tones**, **My Ringtones**, or **Preloaded Ring Tones**.

6. Then press the **Menu** key and select **Set As Ring Tone**, or press the **Set As**

 button at the bottom 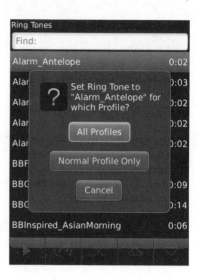 and select to which profile you want to set the ring tone.

Playing All Your Music

Navigate to your music as just shown, and highlight the first song you wish to play. If you have not set up individual playlists, just highlight the first song, and then press the **Menu** key.

Scroll down to either **Play** or **Shuffle**, and the music player will begin to play all the songs listed.

If you select **Shuffle** (see Figure 21-2), then all the songs listed will be played in a random order.

Figure 21-2. *Shuffling all of your music*

Finding Your Music When You Use a Memory Card

Assuming you have followed the previous steps, your music is now on your Micro SD media card. Now, you want to play your music—so what do you do?

From your Home screen of icons, you have two ways to view and listen to music.

Option 1: Click the **Music** icon.

Option 2: Click the **Media** icon, and then click the **Music** icon.

The available music folders are now displayed.

Click the appropriate folder (if your music is on a media card, click that folder) and all of your music will now be displayed.

Click any song to start playing it.

Playing One of Your Playlists

1. To see the playlists on the BlackBerry, just scroll over to the **Media Player** icon, and click it.

2. Find the **Music** icon and click that. Or, just click the **Music** icon from the home page.

3. Then scroll down to click **Playlists**.

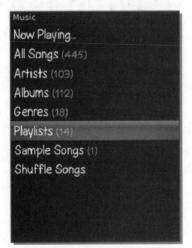

4. You can see that the two playlists synced from iTunes are now listed right on the BlackBerry.

5. Simply click the **Bike Riding** playlist to begin playing the songs.

6. To see the list of songs in a playlist, press the **Menu** key and select **Show Playlist**.

Many MP3 players utilize playlists to organize music and allow for a unique mix of songs.

What types of music are supported on the BlackBerry? See page 423.

Creating Playlists from Your Computer

Use the supported computer software on your computer to create playlists and sync them to your computer.

If you are a Windows user, please refer to page 123. If you are an Apple Mac user, please refer to page 407.

Creating Playlists on Your BlackBerry

1. Click your **Music** icon or your **Media** icon, and then click **Music**.

2.   Click **Playlists** to get into the Playlists section, as shown.

3.   Either click **[New Playlist]** at the top or press the **Menu** key and select **New Playlist** from the menu.

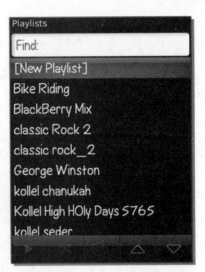

> **TIP:** You can also create playlists from your other views in the **Music** icon such as All Songs, Albums, Artists, and Genres, by clicking the **Playlist** soft key at the bottom.
>
>

4.   Now, you need to select Standard Playlist or Automatic Playlist.

5.   Select **Standard Playlist** to select and add any songs already stored on your BlackBerry.

6.   Then type your playlist name in the **Name** field at the top, press the **Menu** key, and select **Add Songs** to add new songs.

TIP: To find your songs, you can just scroll up or down the list or type a few letters you know are in the title of the song, like "love," and instantly see all matching songs.

7. When you find the song you want, just click it to add it to your playlist.

TIP: You can remove songs from the playlist by selecting the song, pressing the **Menu** key, and selecting **Remove**.

TIP: The Automatic Playlist feature allows you to create some general parameters for your playlists based on artists, songs, or genres. See figure 21-3 below.

Figure 21-3. *Generating automatic playlists on the BlackBerry*

You can also add music to playlists by using the soft keys at the bottom of the screen. This works when you are in the Add Song mode (Figure 21-4), or even when you just have a song playing and decide to add it to one of your existing playlists.

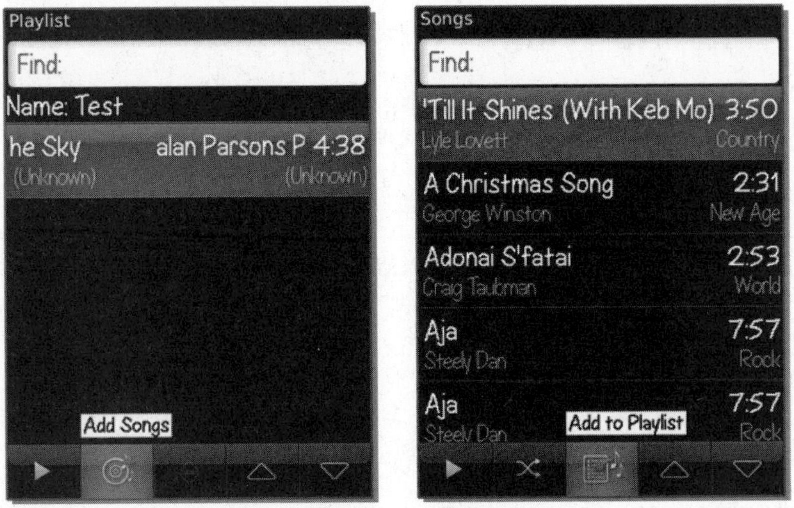

Figure 21-4. *Adding individual songs to your playlist*

Supported Music Types

The BlackBerry will play most types of music files. If you are an iPod user, all music except the music that you purchased on iTunes should be able to play on the BlackBerry. However, if you burn your iTunes tracks to a CD (make a new playlist in iTunes, copy your iTunes tracks, and then burn that playlist), Roxio Media Manager can convert these tracks to play on the BlackBerry.

The most common audio/music formats supported are the following:

- ACC - audio compression formats AAC
- AAC+, and EAAC+ AMR - Adaptive Multi Rate-Narrow Band (AMR-NB) speech coder standard
- MIDI - Polyphonic MIDI
- MP3 - encoded using MPEG
- WAV - supports sample rates of 8 kHz, 16 kHz, 22.05 kHz, 32 kHz, 44.1 kHz, and 48 kHz with 8-bit and 16-bit depths in mono or stereo

NOTE: Some WAV file formats may not be supported by your BlackBerry.

TIP: You can pause (and instantly silence) any song or video playing on your BlackBerry by pressing the **Mute** key on the top of your BlackBerry. Press **Mute** again to resume playback.

Music Player Tips and Tricks

- To pause a song or video, press the **Mute** key.

- To resume playing, press the **Mute** key again.

- To move to the next item, press the **Next** button at the bottom of the screen.

- To move to a previous item (in your playlist or video library,) press the **Previous** button at the bottom left of the screen.

Streaming Internet Radio

If you ever get tired of your music, try free internet radio. You can listen to personalized radio stations that play only the music you like. Select from hundreds of pre-set stations, or make your own new station based on your favorite artist.

There are several applications that allow you to set up and listen to streaming internet radio. There are now several great free applications for the BlackBerry. All work well. The two most popular are Pandora and Slacker Radio, both found in BlackBerry App World. Use the steps in the "BlackBerry App World" section to locate and download these free apps.

After you set up your free account, specify the type of music you like and you should be streaming internet radio in minutes.

> **CAUTION:** All internet radio programs are very data intensive. In other words, you should use them only if you have purchased an unlimited data plan from your wireless carrier. Without an unlimited data plan, you may be surprised with an extremely high wireless data charge on your next bill.

Pandora Internet Radio

Pandora is an outgrowth of the Music Genome project. Essentially, Pandora is streaming internet radio where you control the radio stations. Essentially you build stations based around your favorite artists.

Downloading Pandora

The easiest way to download Pandora is to go to BlackBerry App World (see page 467). If the **Pandora** app is not part of the featured apps, you can find it in the Music section or by doing a search for Pandora.

You can also visit www.pandora.com and download the app from the web site right to your BlackBerry. Just agree to the terms and select **Download** when the Download screen appears.

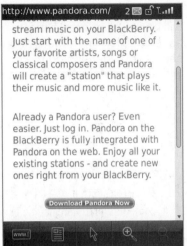

Starting Pandora for the First Time

Once loaded, you will see the **Pandora** icon, usually in your **Downloads** folder.

When Pandora starts for the first time, you will be asked if you already have an existing account or if you would like to create a new account.

Just type your email address and password (for an existing account) or input your email address and password to create a new account. The best thing about Pandora is that it is absolutely free!

If this is your first time using Pandora, you will be asked to create a new station. If you have an existing Pandora account, you will see all your stations on the front page along with the **Create a New Station** option.

Create Station

Enter one of your favorite songs, artists, or classical composers:

foreigner

Foreigner
Johnny Foreigner
Foreigner by DJ Fresh
The Foreigner by The New Lou Reeds

NOTE: Pandora also works on your PC or Mac. You can create your stations, listen on your computer, and then just log in on the BlackBerry. All the stations created on the computer will appear.

Pandora Controls and Options

The interface of Pandora is very clean and intuitive. To play or pause just press the **Play** button or **Pause** button.

To skip to the next song on the station, just click the **Next** button.

Using "Thumbs Up" and "Thumbs Down"

Two buttons that you can click are the **Thumbs Up** and **Thumbs Down** buttons.

If you click the **Thumbs Up** button, a check mark is placed on the song letting Pandora know that you like this song and it can be used again.

Consequently, if you click the **Thumbs Down** button, a very quick check mark appears, and Pandora will skip to the next song and remember to not ever play that song again.

Slacker Radio

Conceptually, Slacker is very similar to Pandora internet radio. You build stations around your favorite artists or choose from hundreds of existing stations for your listening pleasure. Slacker seems to have a few more pre-programmed stations than Pandora and has a cache feature, which allows you to stream music to your computer, and then download the music to your BlackBerry media card. This allows you to listen to music without needing an internet connection—perfect for a long airplane trip or whenever you are out of radio coverage for a while.

Like Pandora, You can listen to Slacker Radio on your PC and Mac, as well as your BlackBerry.

Downloading and Installing Slacker Radio

As you did with Pandora, you have two options for downloading Slacker Radio. You can find Slacker in BlackBerry App World, or you can also go to its website at www.slacker.com and download the latest build for BlackBerry. Follow the on-screen instructions for download and installation. Accept the license agreement and you will be Slacking in no time!

Creating or Logging In to a Slacker Account

As with Pandora, your first screen will ask if you have an existing Slacker account or if you wish to create one. Either log in or create a new account by clicking the button at the bottom of the screen. As with Pandora, you can have Slacker running on your computer also!

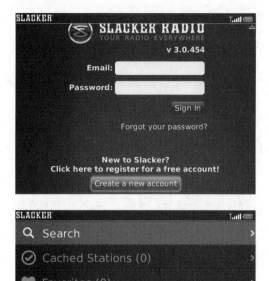

If you have an existing account, you will see a screen with your favorite stations displayed.

If you are signing on for the first time, you have two options:

- Scroll down to check out stations by genre.

- Click **Search** at the top and build a new station with music created from your favorite artist (as you did with Pandora).

In this example, we are creating a new station based on music by Peter Gabriel.

Choosing Your Station

Once you have some created stations, each time you log on to Slacker, you will be able to choose whether to listen to one of your favorite stations or listen to other spotlight stations or genres in the Slacker library of music stations.

Slacker Controls

Slacker offers a few more controls and options than does Pandora. You can access the controls via the dock of buttons at the bottom. The Home button takes you back to the Slacker Home screen, where you can choose your station.

The **Next** button takes you to the next song in the station line-up. Notice that Slacker displays a picture of the next song or artist to the right of the album cover of the current song.

If you like the artist or song, just click the **Heart** button for Slacker to remember that.

If you don't want to hear this particular artist or song again, click the **Do Not Play** or

Ban button.

Slacker Menu Commands and Shortcut Keys

Slacker offers some very cool commands in the menu. Just press the **Menu** button on your BlackBerry and you can see your stations, lyrics to the current song, an artist bio, or an album review, ban the artist, filter explicit content, enable Bluetooth (see page 489 on Stereo Bluetooth), and share Slacker with friends.

One-Key Shortcuts for Slacker

- **N** = Skip to Next Song (with free Slacker you are limited to six skips per hour)

- **space** = Play / Pause Song

- **H** = Heart (you like the song playing, play more songs like it)

- **B** = Ban Song (you don't like the song, don't ever play it again)

Chapter 22

Snapping Pictures

Many BlackBerrys sold today come with a built in camera—perfect for snapping a quick picture. Some BlackBerrys issued by companies might not have a camera for security reasons. Your camera and the photos you take can easily be shared with others via email, MMS messaging, or even uploaded to Facebook and other social media programs.

Using the Camera

Your BlackBerry includes a feature-rich 3.2 mega-pixel camera. This gives you the option to snap a picture anywhere you are. You can then send the picture to friends and family, and share the moment.

Camera Features and Buttons

You can get as involved as you want in your picture-taking with your BlackBerry. Every feature of your photo is configurable. Before we do that, however, let's get familiar with the main buttons and features.

Starting the Camera Application

The camera can be started in one of two ways:

Option #1: The Right Convenience key

Unless you have re-programmed your Convenience key (see page 214 for details), then pressing the **Right Convenience** key will start your camera—the one directly below the volume control buttons.

Push this button once, and the camera should be started.

Start the Camera with this Right Convenience key (unless it has been re-programmed).

Option #2: The Camera Icon

Press the **Menu** key to see all your icons. Scroll to the **Camera** icon, and click.

Icons in the Camera Screen

Usually, when you open the **Camera** application, either the last picture you took is in the window or the camera is active. Underneath the picture window are five icons which are described in Table 21-1.

Table 22-1. *The Five Icons on the Camera Screen*

Icon	Name	Description
	Send / Share	Use this icon to send the picture to others via email, BlackBerry Messenger, or multi-media messaging. You can also use this to upload to Facebook, Flickr, or another site if you have these apps installed (see Chapter 12 "Social Networking").
	Set As - Save as Wallpaper or Caller ID	You can use the picture in the main window as a picture caller ID for one of your people in your address book by selecting the **Set As** button. Then you select **Wallpaper** or **Caller ID**.
	Take-a-Picture	Click this icon to take another picture.
	Save / Folder	With the picture you desire to save on the screen, click the folder to specify a new location or name. We recommend using the media card if you have one installed.
	Delete	Sometimes, the picture you take might not be what you want. Simply scroll to the red X and click. The last picture taken will then be deleted.

You can also set a picture as a background image for your Home screen (like the desktop background image on your computer).

1. Just open a picture from My Pictures.

2. Press the **Menu** key, select **Set as Home Screen Image**, and click.

Sending Pictures with the Email Envelope Icon

Click the **Envelope** icon, which brings up the email dialogue box.

Click one of the six options:

- *Send as MMS* (a multimedia message as the body of an email—learn all about MMS on page 379)

- *Send to Messenger Contact* (this option may not be available if you have not yet set up BlackBerry Messenger—see page **389** for details)

- *Send as Email* (attached to an email message as an image file)

You can also send your picture to your Flickr, MySpace, or Facebook accounts by pressing the appropriate button.

> **NOTE:** These additional options appear only if you have them installed on your device.

Setting the Flash Mode

One of the nice features of the BlackBerry camera is the flash. Just like with most digital cameras, you can adjust the properties of the flash as shown in Figure 22-1.

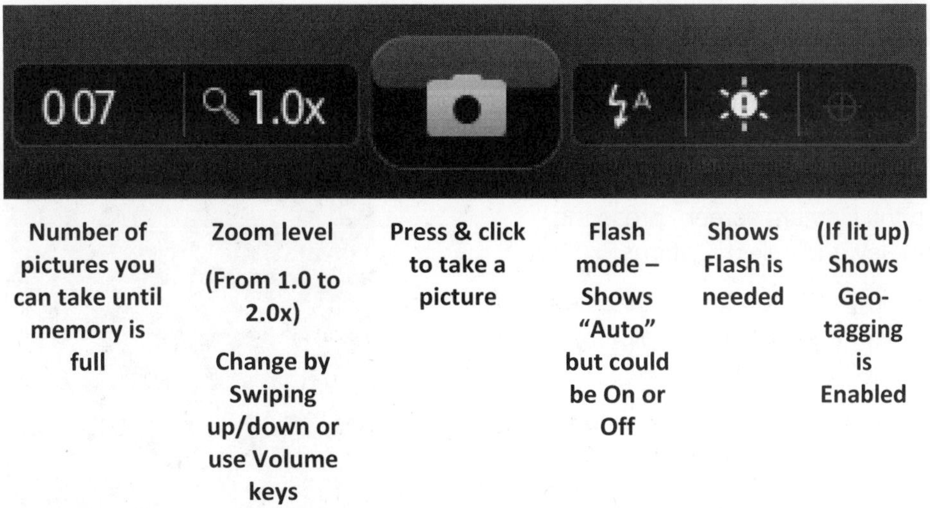

| Number of pictures you can take until memory is full | Zoom level (From 1.0 to 2.0x) Change by Swiping up/down or use Volume keys | Press & click to take a picture | Flash mode – Shows "Auto" but could be On or Off | Shows Flash is needed | (If lit up) Shows Geo-tagging is Enabled |

Figure 22-1: *Changing Flash Mode for the Current Picture*

Your viewfinder gives you lots of information—to the left of the small **Camera** icon is the percentage of zoom currently being used. To the right of the **Camera** icon is the flash mode.

The three available flash modes are:

- **Automatic** (indicated by the Flash symbol with the A next to it)
- **On** (indicated by the Flash symbol (which will use more battery))
- **Off** (indicated by the No Flash symbol)

Changing the Default Flash Mode

1. When in the **Camera** application, press the **Menu** key and select **Options**.

2. Use your finger to click the **Default Flash Settings** field (set to **Automatic** in the image here).

3. Select **Off**, **On**, or **Automatic** (the default).

4. Press the **Menu** key and save your settings.

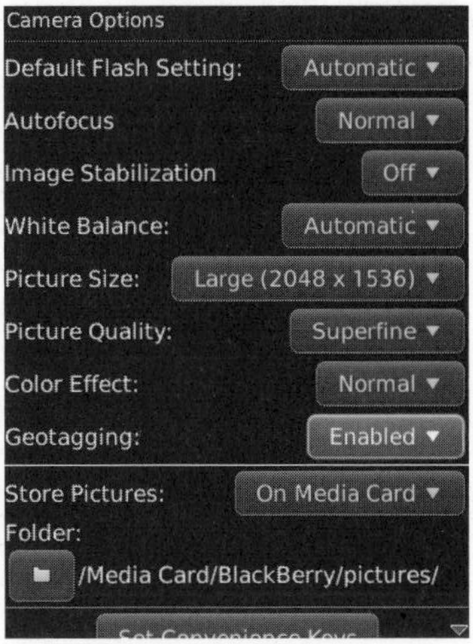

Adjusting the Size of the Picture

The size of your pictures corresponds to the number of pixels or dots used to render the image. If you tend to transfer your BlackBerry pictures to your desktop for printing or emailing, you might want a bigger or smaller picture to work with.

1. From the Camera screen, press the **Menu** key and select **Options**.

2. Scroll down to the **Picture Size** field and select the size of your picture: small, medium, or large.

3. Press the **Menu** key and save your settings.

> **TIP:** If you email your pictures, then you will be able to send them faster if you set the **Picture Size** field to **Small**.

Camera Options

White Balance: Automatic ▾
Picture Size:
Medium (1024 x 768) ▾
Picture Quality: Superfine ▾
Color Effect: Normal ▾
Geotagging: Disabled ▾
Store Pictures:
On Media Card ▾
Folder:
...rd/BlackBerry/pictures/

Geotagging Your Pictures (Adding a GPS Location)

On your blackberry, you can either enable or disable geotagging. Geotagging means to assign of the current GPS (Global Positioning System) longitude and latitude location to each picture taken with your BlackBerry camera.

> **TIP:** You can learn how to get **Flickr** installed on your BlackBerry on page 276.

Why would you want to enable geotagging?

Some online sites such as Flickr (photo sharing) and Google Earth (mapping) can put your geotagged photo on a map to show exactly where you took the picture.

Figure 22-2. *Viewing geotagged photos on Flickr*

This is a map from www.flickr.com showing what geotagging your photos can accomplish. Essentially it will allow you to see exactly where you snapped your photos and help organize them.

Other programs you can purchase for your computer can organize all your photos by showing their location on a map (to find such software, do a web search for "geotag photo software (Mac or Windows)").

To turn geotagging on or off from the Camera screen, do the following:

1. Press the **Menu** key and select **Options**.

2. Roll down to the **Geotagging** field and set it to **Enabled**.

   Make sure your GPS is enabled on your BlackBerry—see page 529.

3.   You will then see this warning
     message. Make sure to select the
     Don't ask this again check box by
     clicking the trackball or pressing the
     space key.

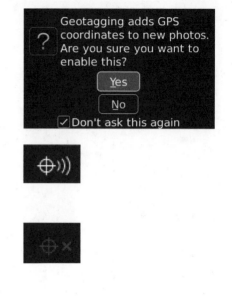

You know that geotagging is turned on if you see
the white plus sign with circle around it and the
three waves to the right of it, in the lower right of
your Camera screen.

When geotagging is turned on, but your
BlackBerry does not have a GPS signal to tag the
pictures, you will see a red plus sign with circle
around it and a red X in the lower right corner.

Adjusting the White Balance

Usually the automatic white balance works fairly well,
however, there may be times when you want to
manually control it.

In this case you would select from the manual options
for the **White Balance** field in the same Camera
Options screen.

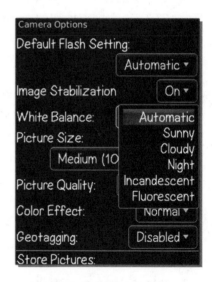

Adjusting the Picture Quality

While the BlackBerry is not meant to replace a 7- or 8-megapixel camera, it is a very
capable photo device. There are times when you might need or desire to change the
picture quality. Perhaps you are using your BlackBerry camera for work and need to
capture an important image. Fortunately, it is quite easy to adjust the quality of your
photos. Realize, however, that **increasing the quality or the size will increase the
memory requirements for that particular picture**.

In one "non-scientific" test, changing the picture quality resulted in the following changes to the file size of the picture at a fixed size setting of "Large (1600×1200)":

- Normal: Approximately 50k
- Fine: Approximately 2X larger than normal
- Superfine: Approximately 3X larger than normal

1. Start the **Camera** application.
2. Press the **Menu** key, select **Options**.
3. Scroll to **Picture Quality**.
4. The choices **Normal**, **Fine**, and **Superfine** will be available. Just click the desired quality, press the **Menu** key, and save your settings.

Using the Zoom

As with many cameras, the BlackBerry gives you the opportunity to zoom in or out of your subject. Zooming on the BlackBerry could not be easier.

Frame your picture and gently scroll up (swipe up) on the screen. The camera will zoom in on the subject.

If your status bar is showing on the bottom, you will see the zoom level displayed to the left of the **Camera** icon, with a **1.0x** up to **2.0x** indicating the power of zoom chosen.

To zoom back out, just scroll down. It takes a little getting used to, but zooming with your finger is very precise and works quite well.

> **TIP:** You can also zoom using your **Volume Up** and **Down** keys.

Managing Picture Storage

Your BlackBerry comes with an 8 GB or 16 GB media card installed. If you find that you need to increase your storage capacity, you can purchase a 16 GB media card. For more information on inserting the media card, please see page 440. See the following for help on storing pictures on the media card.

If you do not have a media card, then you will want to carefully manage the amount of your BlackBerry's main device memory that is used for pictures.

Selecting Where Pictures Are Stored

The default setting is for the BlackBerry to store pictures in the main device memory, but if you have a media card inserted, we recommend selecting that instead.

To confirm the default picture storage location, do the following:

1. Press the **Menu** key from the main Camera screen, scroll to **Options**, and click.

2. Scroll down to the **Store Pictures** field and select **On Media Card** if you have one, or **In Device Memory** if you do not have a media card.

3. Look at the **Folder** field at the bottom and make sure the folder name ends in the word "**/pictures**". This will help keep pictures together with pictures, videos with videos, and music with music, and make it easier when you want to transfer pictures to and from your computer.

Using the Optional Media Card

At publishing time, your BlackBerry can support up to a 16GB Micro SD media card. This is equivalent to **several full-length feature films** and **thousands of songs**. Learn how to install a media card in Chapter 20, on page 405. Verify your card is installed as described on page **406**. Since program files can be stored only in main memory, we recommend putting as many of your media files on the Micro SD card as possible.

Storing Pictures on the Media Card

1. Navigate to the main screen of the **Camera** application, press the **Menu** key, scroll to **Options**, and click.

2. Change the option in the **Store Pictures** field to **On Media Card**.

> **TIP:** You may be prompted to save pictures to your media card the first time you start your camera after you insert a new media card. In case you did not get this choice, read on.

Viewing Pictures Stored in Memory

There are two primary ways to view stored pictures.

Option #1: Viewing from the Camera Program

1. Open the **Camera** application and press the **Menu** key.

2. Scroll down to **View Pictures** and navigate to the appropriate folder to view your pictures (see Figure 22-3).

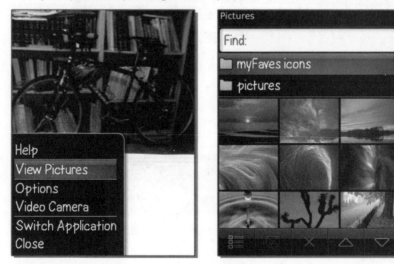

Figure 22-3. *Viewing pictures from the **Camera** app*

Option #2: Viewing from the Media Menu

1. Navigate to the **Media** icon and click.

2. Scroll to **Pictures** and click. Your initial options will be **All Pictures** or **Picture Folders** (Figure 22-4).

3. Click the appropriate folder and navigate to your pictures.

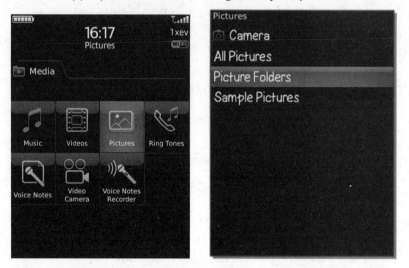

Figure 22-4. *Viewing pictures from the **Pictures** app in picture folders*

Picture Soft Keys

Like many of the other programs we have seen so far, the BlackBerry Storm adds soft keys at the bottom of the picture to put some of the more popular commands right at your finger tips.

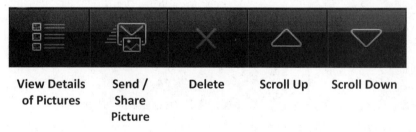

Here are the soft keys shown when viewing an individual picture.

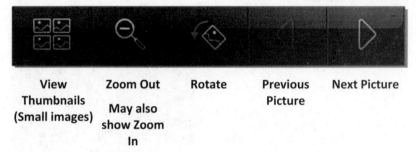

| View Thumbnails (Small images) | Zoom Out May also show Zoom In | Rotate | Previous Picture | Next Picture |

You can view thumbnails of all your pictures, zoom out or in, rotate the picture, or advance through your pictures by clicking the corresponding soft key.

Viewing a Slide Show

1. Follow the previous steps and press the **Menu** key when you are in your picture directory.

2. Scroll to **View Slideshow** and click.

Scrolling through Pictures

One very cool feature of your BlackBerry Storm is that you can scroll through your pictures just by swiping your finger across the screen.

Just click any picture to bring it into the full-screen mode.

Next, just swipe your finger to the left or right to advance through the pictures in that particular folder.

Adding Pictures to Contacts for Caller ID

As discussed previously, you can assign a picture as a caller ID for your contacts. Please check out our detailed explanation, starting on page 325.

TIP: You can set the Convenience keys from the bottom of the Camera Options screen.

This will allow you to set either the left or right key as your camera.

Transferring Pictures to or from Your BlackBerry

There are a few ways to remove pictures you have taken from your BlackBerry and transfer pictures taken elsewhere onto the BlackBerry.

Method 1: Send via email, multimedia messaging, or BlackBerry Messenger. You can email or send pictures immediately after you take them on your camera by clicking the **Envelope** icon, as shown on page 434. You may also send pictures when you are viewing them in your **Media** application. Click the **Menu** key and look for menu items related to sending pictures. See figure 22-5 below. Or, look for a soft key at the bottom of the screen.

Figure 22-5. *Sending options for pictures*

Method 2: Transfer using Bluetooth. If you want to transfer pictures to/from your computer (assuming it has Bluetooth capabilities), you can. We explain exactly how to get this done in the "Bluetooth" chapter, on page **498**.

Method 3: Transfer using your computer with special computer software.

Transferring pictures and other media to your computer is handled using the media section of your desktop software. For a Windows computer, see page 88; for an Apple computer, see page 159.

Method 4: Transfer using mass storage mode. This assumes you have stored your pictures on a media card. (What's a media card? See page 440.)

The first time you connect your BlackBerry to your computer, you will probably see a **"Turn on Mass Storage Mode?"** question. If you answer yes, then your media card looks just like another hard disk to your computer (just like a USB flash drive). Then you can drag and drop pictures to/from your BlackBerry and your computer. For more details, see page 407.

Fun with Videos

We have already taught you how to get the most from music and pictures on your BlackBerry; however, your BlackBerry can handle even more media than what we have discussed so far. For example, your BlackBerry can also handle videos ranging from short videos you shoot on the BlackBerry to full length movies.

Working with Videos on a BlackBerry

In addition to a camera, your BlackBerry also comes with a built-in video recorder that enables you to capture your world in full-motion video and sound when a simple picture will not work. Clicking the **Media** icon lets you play all videos you record or transfer to your BlackBerry from your computer.

Some BlackBerry providers include a free 16.0 GB media card with the devices they sell. All this extra storage and the strong media capabilities of the BlackBerry might make you wonder yet again: *Why do I need an iPhone or iPod? I've got a BlackBerry!*

Adding Videos to Your BlackBerry

Check out page 123 to learn how to transfer videos and other media (e.g., pictures and songs) to your media card. If you are a Windows computer user, then check out the built-in media transfer and sync capabilities of the **BlackBerry Desktop Manger** software detailed on page 422. If you use an Apple Mac, please refer to page 143.

Your Video Recorder

One of the new features of your BlackBerry is the inclusion of a video recorder in addition to the camera. The video recorder is perfect for capturing parts of a business presentation or your child's soccer game. Like pictures, videos can be emailed or stored on your PC for later use.

Starting the Video Recorder

It's a simple matter to start the video recorder; simply follow these steps to do so:

1. Push the **Menu** key, scroll down to the **Media** folder, and then press and click the folder.

2. Scroll to the **Video Camera** icon and press and click it (see Figure 23-1).

Figure 23-1. *The Video Camera icon in the Media folder*

3. The BlackBerry should detect that you have a media card installed and ask you if you want to save your videos to the card. We think it is a good idea to say select **Yes** when presented with this option.

4. Use the screen of the BlackBerry as your viewfinder to frame your picture.

5. When you are ready to record, press the **Record** button. When you're finished recording, press the **Pause** button.

6. You will then see options at the bottom of the screen to **Email**, **Save**, or **Delete** the video.

7. Press the **Menu** button from within the **Video Camera** application and choose one of the following options:

   - Help
   - View Videos
   - Send As Email
   - Options
   - Camera
   - Show Keyboard
   - Switch Application
   - Close

8. Adjust your video options by selecting **Options** from the menu (see Figure 23-2).

9. In this menu, you can adjust the video light. Your choices are to have a constant light from the camera's flash or to set this option to **Off**.

10. You can also adjust the **Color Effect** option:

    - Normal
    - Black and White
    - Sepia (old-fashioned brown tone)

11. You can also adjust the resolution of the camera in the **Video Format** option, selecting either **Normal (320 x 240)** or to send as an **MMS (176 x 144 pixels)**. The latter option delivers a lower quality image and a smaller file size.

12. Finally, the **Store Videos** option lets you store your videos **On Media Card** or **In Device Memory**. You should definitely choose the **On Media Card** option if you have a media card because this will give you more space.

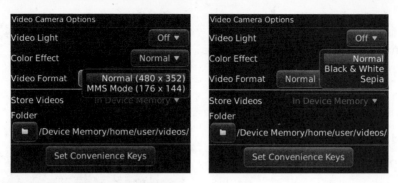

Figure 23-2. *Adjusting video options*

Converting DVDs and Videos to Play on the BlackBerry

One cool thing about your BlackBerry is that you can use it is as a portable media player to help entertain your kids or yourself when you travel. If your car is equipped with Bluetooth, you can use this technology to send audio from your BlackBerry to your car stereo, so everyone can listen to the movie.

To convert a DVD, you need to follow these steps:

1. Copy the DVD onto your computer.

2. Use a video encoder program to transcode the video (convert it so it is viewable on your BlackBerry).

> **CAUTION:** Please respect copyright laws! As people who make our living from intellectual property (e.g., BlackBerry books, videos, and so on), we strongly encourage you to respect the copyrights of any material you are attempting to copy to your BlackBerry.

For security and copyright reasons, some DVDs cannot be copied onto a device like the BlackBerry. Before you buy a video encoder or converter program, make sure that it supports the file formats that will play on your BlackBerry. Many of the user enthusiast forums such as www.pinstack.com, www.crackberry.com, or www.blackberryforums.com offer tutorials for video conversion. (We did not include details here because the process varies, based on which operating system you are running on your BlackBerry.)

Supported Video Formats on the BlackBerry

Video formats are fast-changing, and there are multiple versions of the BlackBerry operating system which support a variety of video formats, so we are not including a list of supported video formats here. However, you can find an up-to-date list in the Knowledge Base on the www.blackberry.com web site. Simply do a search for "supported video formats storm." This link worked at the time of writing:

www.blackberry.com/btsc/articles/216/KB05419_f.SAL_Public.html#7

Viewing Videos on the BlackBerry

The BlackBerry contains a very sharp screen that is perfect for watching short videos. Another nice feature: The video player is as easy to use as the audio player.

Playing a Video

Playing a video is easy enough, require only that you follow a handful of steps:

1. Press and click your **Media** icon.

2. Press and click the **Video** icon and then choose the folder where your video is stored.

3. The **Video Player** screen looks very similar to the **Audio Player** screen – just press and click the screen to pause or play a video, using the volume controls on the side of the BlackBerry.

4. You will see a list of all videos loaded on your BlackBerry (usually on your media card). Locate the video you want to play.

> **TIP:** Tap the **Find:** box at the top of the **Video Player** application to search for a particular title.
>
> For example, we entered the word "basics" in the image to the right, so only videos with the word "basics" in the title appear in the list. You can think of this as a keyword search for videos.

5. Click the video you want to see with your finger to make it start playing (see Figure 23-3).

> **NOTE:** Videos only played in **horizontal** (landscape) mode at the time of writing.

Figure 23-3. *Watching a training video on the BlackBerry*

Showing or Hiding controls

You can tap the screen to show or hide the controls at the bottom of the screen (see Figure 23-4).

Figure 23-4. *Tapping the screen to see video controls*

You can use the slider bar at the top of the controls to move to any other section of the video. Just touch it and drag it left or right (see Figure 23-5).

Figure 23-5. *Dragging the slider to move to another part of the video*

At the top of the controls, you will also see two times. The time on the left is the amount of time already played, while the time on the right, a negative number, counts down how much time remains to be played in the video.

> **NOTE:** The Shuffle and Repeat buttons located between the two times above the top row of controls did not work when playing a video at the time of writing.

This list describes the four buttons along the bottom of the video player, from left to right:

- **Previous Track:** Takes you to the previous video in the list.

- **Play / Pause:** Pauses the video if it's playing and plays the video if it is paused.

- **Stop:** Stops the video and moves you back to the beginning of the video.

- **Next Track:** Takes you to the next video in the list.

The **Video Player** application includes a fairly extensive list of options you can choose from by clicking the Menu button. Specifically, pressing the **Menu** button brings up the following list of menu options for the application:

- **Help:** Displays contextual help with **Video Player** application.
- **Video Library:** Displays the content of your library.
- **Repeat:** Replays the last viewed video.
- **Show Playlist:** Displays all items in the playlist.
- **Activate Handset:** Plays the audio of the video through your headset.
- **Switch Application:** Allows you to go to any other open application.
- **Close:** Closes the application.

Chapter 24

Connect with Wi-Fi

Wi-Fi is a wireless-connection technology that enables you to connect computers, printers, game consoles, mobile devices(like your blackberry) and more to the internet. Today we are fortunate to live in a world where Wi-Fi is increasingly ubiquitous. Indeed, it is difficult to go anywhere and not hear about Wi-Fi.

In this chapter, we will show you how to connect your BlackBerry to available Wi-Fi networks, how to prioritize and organize your networks, and how to diagnose wireless problems.

Understanding Wi-Fi on Your BlackBerry

Like other devices that use Wi-Fi, your BlackBerry can send and receive a wireless signal to and from a wireless router. If your BlackBerry is Wi-Fi equipped, you can take advantage of must faster Web Browsing and file downloading speeds through your home or office wireless network. You can also access millions of Wi-Fi hotspots in all sorts of places, such as coffee shops and hotels, many of which are free!

NOTE: The origin of the term Wi-Fi is disputed. According to some, Wi-Fi stands for Wireless Fidelity (IEEE 802.11 wireless networking), whereas others say that the term refers to a wireless technology brand owned by the Wi-Fi Alliance. Regardless of the term's origins, we're immensely grateful for its increasingly widespread adoption!

The Wi-Fi Advantage

Wi-Fi is a great advantage to BlackBerry users around the globe. The advantages to using a Wi-Fi connection (as opposed to a carrier data connection such as GPRS/EDGE/3G) are many:

- Web browsing speeds are much faster.
- You are not using up data from your data plan,

- Most file downloads will be faster.

- You can get often great Wi-Fi signals when you cannot get any regular cell coverage (1XEV/EDGE/3G), such as in the bottom floors of a thick-walled building.

Setting Up Wi-Fi on Your BlackBerry

Before you can take advantage of the speed and convenience of using Wi-Fi on your BlackBerry, you will need to set up and configure your wireless connection.

You can get to the **Wi-Fi Setup** utility in a couple of ways. Follow these steps to connect using the first approach:

1. Press and click the **Wireless Network** indicators in the upper right corner. This brings up the **Manage Connections** icon window, as shown to the right.

2. Click the **Setup Wi-Fi** option.

> **TIP:** This is the same popup window you see when you click the **Manage Connections** icon.

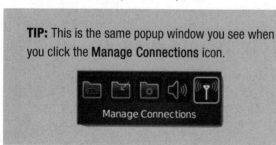

Follow these steps to connect to get to the **Wireless Setup** utility using the second approach:

3. Click the **Set Up Wi-Fi** icon, which is usually found in the **Setup** folder.

4. The **Welcome to Wi-Fi Setup** screen appears. Scroll down to read the introduction to Wi-Fi. When you are done, click **Next** at the bottom of the screen.

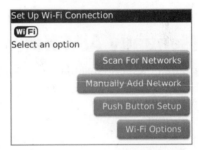

Scan for Networks

In many cases, if you are in a public place with a Wi-Fi network (such as a hotel or coffee shop with free Wi-Fi), then your easiest option for connecting to Wi-Fi is scan for available networks.

1. Press **Scan for Networks**.

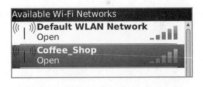

2. Once the scan completes, you will see a list of available networks. Click the one you would like to join.

3. In this case, let's click **Coffee_Shop** to join this network screen.

4. If the selected Wi-Fi Network uses a *pre-shared key* (PSK), follow these steps.

    a. Select **Yes** from this screen.

    b. Type in your PSK at the prompt, and then scroll to **Connect** and click it. You might also be asked if you want to perform a WPS setup.

5. When you have connected, you will see this screen.

6. Adjust the **Profile Name** field so you can easily connect in the future and click **Next**.

Connection Successful!
Save this Wi-Fi Network as a Profile?
Yes ▼
Profile Name:
Coffee_Shop
(Home, Work, etc...)

Back   Next

7. Click **Finish** to complete the process.

Wi-Fi Setup Complete
(WiFi) Success!
Coffee_Shop has been added to your list of Saved Profiles.
Prioritize Wi-Fi Profiles

Finish

Manually Add Network

Sometimes, you will have to manually add the Wi-Fi network, this could be because the network is not broadcasting or it has advanced security settings. Contact the Network Administrator prior to using this option, because you will have to type in detailed information about the Wi-Fi network in order to join it.

1. Click the **Manually Add Network** button.

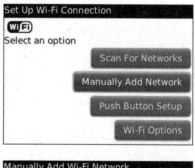

Set Up Wi-Fi Connection
(WiFi)
Select an option
Scan For Networks
Manually Add Network
Push Button Setup
Wi-Fi Options

2. Type in the **Network Name (SSID)**. This is the name that the administrator has assigned to this Wi-Fi network.

3. Click the **Add** button.

Manually Add Wi-Fi Network
Type the Network Name (SSID):
office12365

Back   Add

4. If the network has **No Security** (the default Security Type), then click **Connect** at the bottom.

5. If the Network has security, then follow these steps.

   a. click next to Security Type and select one from the list: , **Pre-Shared Key (PSK), PEAP, LEAP, EAP-TLS, EAP-FAST, EAP-TTLS, or EAP-SIM.**

   b. After selecting the Security Type, more fields will appear. Type in the requested information, such as the WEP key, Pre-Shared Key, or other information.

   c. Click the **Connect** button at the bottom.

6. Now the BlackBerry will try to connect to the specified network.

7. If you are successful you will see a message saying you are now connected to the network. Press the **Finish** button to complete the process.

8. If you have problems connecting, you may need to verify your information and try again.

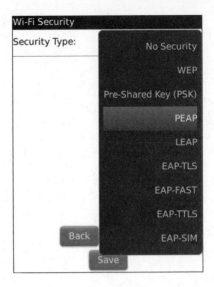

Push Button Setup

If you have a newer Wi-Fi router, it will have a special button to help you quickly connect Wi-Fi devices such as your BlackBerry. You will need to have a button that looks like this on your router to use this method.

1. Press the **Push Button Setup** button.

Set Up Wi-Fi Connection
Wi Fi
Select an option
Scan For Networks
Manually Add Network
Push Button Setup
Wi-Fi Options

2. Press **Next** on this screen.

3. Press the ⟳ button on your Wi-Fi router.

Wi-Fi Protected Setup
To create a secure connection with your Wi-Fi Protected Setup wireless router, click Next. If you do not have a Wi-Fi Protected Setup wireless router, click Back
Back   Next

4. Back on your BlackBerry, click the **Done** button on this screen.

Wi-Fi Protected Setup
On the wireless router, press the Wi-Fi Protected Setup button.
⟳
Back   Done

5. Now you will see a Connecting screen similar to this one.

Connecting...
Time Remaining: 2:25.
Cancel

6. When successfully connected, you will see this screen with the network name in the top row with a checkmark next to it.

7. Click the **Save Profiles** button.

```
Save Profiles
☑ trautschold
  Save Profiles
```

8. Adjust your **Profile Name**, if needed.

9. Click **Next**.

```
Save this Wi-Fi Network as a Profile?
                              Yes ▾
Profile Name:
trautschold
(Home, Work, etc...)



       Back    Next
```

10. Click **Finish** on this screen to complete the process.

```
Wi-Fi Setup Complete
(WiFi) Success!
trautschold has been added to your
list of Saved Profiles.
           Prioritize Wi-Fi Profiles
Many Wi-Fi "hotspots" require
registration (e.g. credit card).
              Wi-Fi Hotspot Login
          Finish
```

Single Profile Scanning

In version 5.0 of the BlackBerry operating system is the ability to have your Wi-Fi-enabled BlackBerry use the **Single Profile to Scan** option, which prompts you for a manual login.

A **Manual Connection** prompt is more secure, and your BlackBerry will never just connect to an available network (which could pose a security risk).

```
Wi-Fi Connections
Active Wi-Fi Connection:              Flint
☑ Enable single profile scanning
☑ Prompt me for manual connection or
  login
Saved Wi-Fi Profiles
◯ Flint                              – ᴀ
```

Putting a check next to the **Enable single profile scanning** option and selecting the radio button with the desired network in the **Saved WiFi Profiles** section will allow your BlackBerry to connect automatically to preferred networks you select.

Connecting to a Wireless Hotspot

Connecting to a wireless hotpot with your BlackBerry is easy. Simply follow these steps:

1. Navigate to your **Wi-Fi Setup** screen as described previously and then press the **Menu** key.

2. You will see a **Wi-Fi Hotspot Login** option (see Figure 24-1); click it.

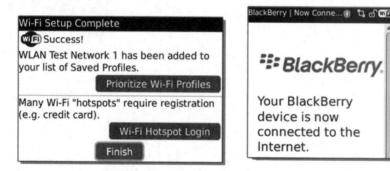

Figure 24-1. *Using the Wi-Fi Hotspot Login option*

3. You should be then taken to the carrier- or store-specific logon screen for that particular hotspot. Enter the required information and you should see this message: "You are Successfully Connected to the Internet."

Sometimes you will already be connected to a wireless network, but will want to change to do a different one. Follow these steps to do so:

4. From the icons on your **Home** screen, click the icon in the upper right corner to bring up your **Manage Connections** popup window, which is shown to the right.

5. Click **Wi-Fi Options** near the bottom of this popup window.

6. You will see the **Active** Wi-Fi connection shown at the top. Press the **Menu** key and select **New** from this menu.

7. Refer back to the "Setting up Your Wi-Fi on Your BlackBerry" section earlier in this chapter and follow those instructions.

Changing/Prioritizing Your Wi-Fi Connection

One of the nice things about Wi-Fi is that you can connect to a wireless network just about anywhere. While you may have saved your home and work networks in the steps above, there may be times you want to prioritize or change networks altogether.

Prioritizing Your Networks

Let's say you connect to your home wireless network 90% of the time. You will want to make sure that your home network is at the top of the list of networks your BlackBerry searches for.

Follow these steps to **Prioritize your Networks**:

1. Access your Wi-Fi settings, as described previously.

2. Scroll down to **Saved Wi-Fi Profiles** at the bottom of the screen and highlight the topmost network.

3. Push the **Menu** key and then select **Move**.

4. The blue highlighted network becomes grey. Simply scroll and **Move** the network into the desired priority.

Using Wi-Fi Diagnostics

There may be times when your Wi-Fi Connection doesn't seem to be working. Thankfully, your BlackBerry has a powerful, built-in diagnostics program to help you in those instances.

Follow these steps to launch the **Wi-Fi Diagnostics** program:

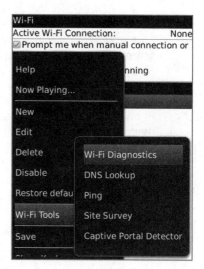

1. Bring up the **Manage Connections** popup window by tapping the upper right corner of your **Home** screen.

2. Press the **Wi-Fi Options** item.

3. Press the **Menu** key, then select **Wi-Fi Options** and click it.

4. Select **Wi-Fi Diagnostics**.

5. The available wireless networks and detailed connection information will now be displayed. If you are an advanced user with experience in wireless networking, click for Access point details.

6. After the reading the diagnosis, press the **Menu** key and select **Email Report**. This will copy the details into an email and send it to your company's Help Desk for assistance.

Wi-Fi Diagnostics (Basic)

Wi-Fi

Now Playing...

Collapse

View Item

Copy All

Copy

Email Report

PIN Report

Options

Show Keyboard

ate:

Wi-Fi radio is not on.

Chapter 25

BlackBerry App World

You can find software applications at BlackBerry's online store, App World. However, App World is a relatively new addition to the BlackBerry environment, so you will also find many applications outside of App World. Check out our chapter on **Adding and Removing Software** starting on page 515 for more information.

The App World Concept

Online application stores are all the rage in the world of smartphones these days. One of the great things about a BlackBerry is that you can find applications for it in lots of places – not just the sanctioned App Store. The BlackBerry App World online store is a new concept for BlackBerry, and it deserves some explanation. Remember that you can always go to the other locations mentioned on Page 515 to find additional applications for your BlackBerry.

Downloading the App World Program

The **BlackBerry App World** program is a free download for all BlackBerry users, and it works particularly well on your new BlackBerry. If the **App World** icon is not already on your BlackBerry, you will need to download and install it (see Figure 25-1). Follow these steps to do so:

1. Start your web browser by clicking the **Browser** icon.

2. In the address bar of the browser, enter this URL: mobile.blackberry.com. It is possible that the **Home** page of your browser is already set to the mobile BlackBerry site.

Figure 25-1. *Downloading BlackBerry App World*

3. At the top (or bottom) of the **Mobile BlackBerry** page, you should see a link to BlackBerry App World. Go to the link and click it.

4. This will take you to the **Download** page for the application. Accept any terms and conditions, and then click the **Download** button (see Figure 25-2).

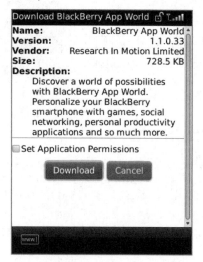

Figure 25-2. *Clicking the Downlaod button installs App World*

Starting App World for the First Time

The **App World** icon may be in your **Downloads** folder. If you want to move it to your **Home** screen, just follow the directions in Chapter 8 on page 195.

Find the **App World** icon and click it. The first time you start the **App World** program, it might take a little while to load – this is normal.

The first time you run the **App World** program, you will have to scroll down a very long license agreement to click the **I Accept** button at the bottom.

Downloading Themes from App World

One of the cool parts about your BlackBerry is that you can find many applications that let you tailor the way it looks and behaves to suit your particular tastes. You can find detailed instructions for doing so in "Personalize Your BlackBerry" in Chapter 8 on page 209.

Featured Programs

The opening screen of the **App World** program shows large icons for its featured items. Many of these items are free; others need to be purchased (you will learn more about this later in this chapter). Flick left or right through the featured programs to find one that interests you. To learn more about a program or to download it, just click it.

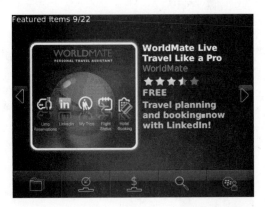

Categories, Top Downloads, and Search

Along the bottom of the opening **App World** screen, you will see five small icons: **Categories**, **Top Free Downloads**, **Top Paid Downloads**, **Search**, and **My World** (see Figure 25-3). Each category gives you a different way to look for, download, or manage apps on your BlackBerry. Simply touch any of these soft keys to go into that area.

Figure 25-3. *The layout of BlackBerry App World*

Categories

As its name suggests, clicking the **Categories** icon shows you all the categories of applications available on the new BlackBerry App World site. At the time of the writing, there were more than a dozen categories, ranging from **Games** to **Sports** to **Finance** to various kinds of references and other items.

Categories

Clicking a category brings up more information about a particular application that may interest you. Once you click a category, the icons for the available programs will show on your screen. Flick up or down to see more apps in the list. You can read reviews or see screen shots for most applications before you decide to download them.

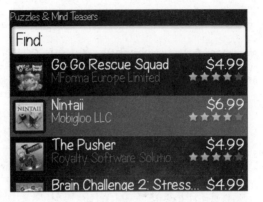

Top Free Downloads

As its name implies, clicking the **Top Free** icon will show you the most downloaded free applications from the App World site. As before, click any program to see screen shots, read reviews, or download the app to your BlackBerry.

Top Free Downloads

Top Paid Downloads

Clicking the **Top Paid** icon will show you the most downloaded applications from purchased from the App World site (prices start at $0.99). As you did previously, click any program to see screen shots, read reviews, or download an app to your BlackBerry.

Top Paid Downloads

Search

Search

The **App World** program has a very good, built-in **Search** tool. If you have an idea of what you might be looking for, but don't know its exact name, just type a word about the general subject into the **Search** bar. In this example, we want to find music applications that are currently available, so we enter *music* into the **Search** bar, which causes all available music-related apps to be displayed (see Figure 25-4).

Figure 25-4. *Searching with the BlackBerry App World program*

TIP: After you see your search results, you can sort the search results by clicking the **Sort** icon in the upper right corner of the screen (see Figure 25-5).

Figure 25-5. *Sort Search results*

After you select a different sort criteria, you can reverse the sort order (e.g., highest to lowest, A to Z, Z to A, and so on) by clicking the **Sort** icon again.

Downloading Apps

As the time of writing, the **BlackBerry App World** program only accepts the PayPal payment type. (This may change in the future.) If you have a PayPal account, all you need to do is input your PayPal user name and password when you purchase an application. If you do not have a PayPal account, go to www.paypal.com from your computer and follow the instructions to setup your account. Setting up a PayPal Personal account is an acceptable requirement for most users.

Downloading and Purchasing an App

Scroll through the applications listed, as you did previously. When you find an app that you want to download, just click the **Download** button from the **Details** screen (see Figure 25-6).

If the application is not a free download, the **Download** button will be replaced by a **Purchase** button. Click the **Purchase** button and input your PayPal information to buy the app (see Figure 25-7).

NOTE: Your PayPal information will be stored to simplify making future purchases easier.

If this is your first time purchasing an app, you will need to log in or set up your free PayPal account. PayPal can be tied to any major credit card or your bank account.

Figure 25-6. *Setting up a PayPal account*

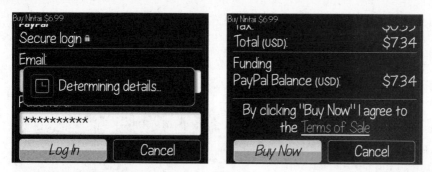

Figure 25-7. *Purchasing an app*

You will see a progress bar showing the progress of your application as it downloads, prepares to install, and then installs on your BlackBerry.

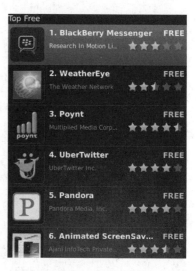

Using the My World Area

My World

All the apps that you purchase or download for free are listed in the **My World** area of the **App World** program.

Glide to and click the **My World** icon (in the lower right-hand corner of the **App World** program) to see a complete list of your downloaded or purchased programs.

NOTE: If you restart your BlackBerry or do a battery pull, you will be logged out of your account, and you will be asked to re-enter your PayPal password.

The My World Menu Commands

The menu associated with the **My World** area of the program has several commands associated with it. Follow these steps to access them:

1. Highlight any app in the **My World** area and press the **Menu** key.

2. From the menu that pops up, you can **Log in** to your account, **Run** the selected program, **Review** the program, **Recommend** the program to someone else, or **Uninstall** the program.

NOTE: If application updates are available, these will also be indicated in the **My World** context menu.

Removing or Uninstalling Programs

After you start to download lots of new apps to your BlackBerry, you may decide that you do not want to use some of them or that you simply want to free up space for new apps.

To delete or uninstall an app, follow these steps from within the **My World** area of the **App World** program.

1. Highlight the app you wish to remove and press the **Menu** key.

2. Select **Uninstall** to remove the highlighted program from your BlackBerry. On the next screen, you will be asked to confirm your selection to remove the program.

3. Most programs will require you to reboot (reset) your BlackBerry to complete the uninstall process.

TIP: If you are removing more than one application, select **Reset Later** or **Reboot Later** until you have selected and uninstalled all the apps. Then, when you're finished uninstalling apps, select **Reset Now** to remove all the apps at once. Following this approach will save you a lot of time waiting for your BlackBerry to reboot!

Connecting As a Tethered Modem

Tethering is the process of connecting your BlackBerry to your computer and using the BlackBerry as a "modem" to access the internet. This is particularly useful if you are in an airport or a hotel with no internet connection on your notebook, and you need capabilities more robust than those provided by your BlackBerry.

Connecting Your Laptop to the Internet with Your BlackBerry

Depending on your wireless carrier (phone company) and what type of software you use, you should be able to use your BlackBerry to connect your laptop (PC or Mac) to the internet. This is variously called a *tethered modem*, *tethering*, or even an *IP modem*. You need a USB cable to connect your BlackBerry to a PC; however, sometimes you can use Bluetooth to connect to a Mac.

NOTE: Not every BlackBerry wireless carrier supports using your BlackBerry as a modem. Please check with your carrier before attempting to use this feature.

Tethering (Usually) Costs Extra

Most (but not all) wireless carriers charge an extra fee to allow you to use your BlackBerry as a tethered modem. You may not be able to connect using your BlackBerry as a modem, however, unless you have specifically signed up for a *BlackBerry as Modem* service or a similar data plan.

TIP: Some carriers allow you to turn this *BlackBerry as Modem* extra service on and off. However, beware that changing or turning this modem service on and off might extend or renew your two-year commitment period. Be sure to check with your particular carrier about its policies before toggling this service on or off. Assuming there are no extra hidden costs or commitments, you could just enable the service for a scheduled trip and then turn it off when you return home.

We have heard of users getting a surprise phone bill in the hundreds of dollars, *even when they had an "unlimited BlackBerry data plan"* (this particular carrier did not include BlackBerry modem data in the unlimited plan).

By the way, you can find some extremely valuable information about tethering at Research in Motion's official BlackBerry site (www.blackberry.com). Specifically, you want to visit the extensive archive at the BlackBerry Technical Solution Center, which is located at this URL: www.blackberry.com/btsc/supportcentral/ supportcentral.do?id=m1. To learn more about tethering, search for *modem how to* when you're at the site.

TIP: When searching the BlackBerry Knowledge Base, do not enter your specific BlackBerry model, but its series name. For example, if you have a Storm2, then enter *storm or 9500 series.* You can also just leave that part out of your search. To locate the modem instructions for your particular BlackBerry, you will need to know the network on which your BlackBerry operates, whether it's EDGE, GPRS, CDMA, or EVDO. Your BlackBerry Storm runs on both the EDGE/GPRS and the CDMA/EVDO networks.

You might be wondering, in the face of all these caveats, why you would want to do use your BlackBerry as a modem. But if you travel frequently, or just need to connect your laptop to the internet when you cannot access a Wi-Fi network, then you might find this feature invaluable.

Unfortunately, the steps and software to use your BlackBerry as a modem have changed often (almost on a monthly basis) and continue to do so. While the information provided in this chapter is accurate at the time of writing; some of the software and information may have changed by the time you're reading this. To ensure, you have the most up-to-date information, please do a web search using terms such as these: *BlackBerry as modem, BlackBerry tethered modem,* or *BlackBerry IP modem.* Also, don't forget that BlackBerry's official site is an excellent resource for up-to-date information about your BlackBerry.

Your Tethering Options

You have several options to choose from if you decide to use your BlackBerry as a tethered modem for your laptop (PC or Mac):

- **Option 1:** Purchase third-party software.

- **Option 2:** Use your wireless carrier's software (contact your carrier to ask whether it has software available).

- **Option 3:** Use the **BlackBerry Desktop Manager** software (this is usually only an option for you if Option 2 is not available.)

Option 1: Purchasing Third-Party Software

Tether is a third-party software program that provides tethering for both Windows and Mac computers (see Figure 26-1). Check out the site for the program at www.tether.com. The software's site asserts that you do not need to pay for a separate modem plan from your carrier, so you may be able to save a lot on monthly connection charges. The cost of this software was about USD $30 at the time of writing. The software's publisher also offers a seven-day free trial, so you can give **Tether** a try before you pay for it.

Figure 26-1. *A third-party tethering app*

Option 2: Using Your Wireless Carrier's Software

As already mentioned, you should contact your wireless carrier's technical support to find out whether it offers software and service plans for this option. Tell your provider that you want to use your BlackBerry as a modem for your laptop. AT&T (USA), Sprint/Nextel (USA) and Verizon (USA) all have simple software (e.g., AT&T's **Communication Manager**, or **Verizon Access Manager**) that you can download and install.

Option 3: Using Desktop Manager to Connect to the Internet

The third option is to use Blackbery's built-in **Desktop Manager** application to enable your computer to access the internet through your BlackBerry. This approach is slightly different, depending on whether you use a Windows PC or a Mac. We'll explain how to connect to the internet using Windows next; if you use a Mac, skip ahead to page 483 to learn how to do this.

Using the Desktop Manager for Windows

If you have confirmed with your carrier that you can use the IP Modem feature in your BlackBerry's **Desktop Manager** program, then follow the steps shown here (see page 84 for information on how to download and install the **Desktop Manager** program):

1. Start **Desktop Manager** by going to Start ➤ BlackBerry ➤ Desktop Manager (see Figure 26-2).

Figure 26-2. *Configuring IP Modem in Desktop Manager for Windows*

2. Click the **IP Modem** icon. If you don't see this icon, then you will need to confirm with your carrier that you can use the program. Sometimes, you can re-enable this program by editing a specific file, as explained on page 482.

3. Configure the **IP Modem** program by clicking the **Configure…** button (see Figure 26-3).

Figure 26-3. *Configuring the IP Modem's connection settings*

4. Now click dropdown list next to the **Connection Profile** option to see whether your carrier is among the carriers listed (see Figure 26-4).

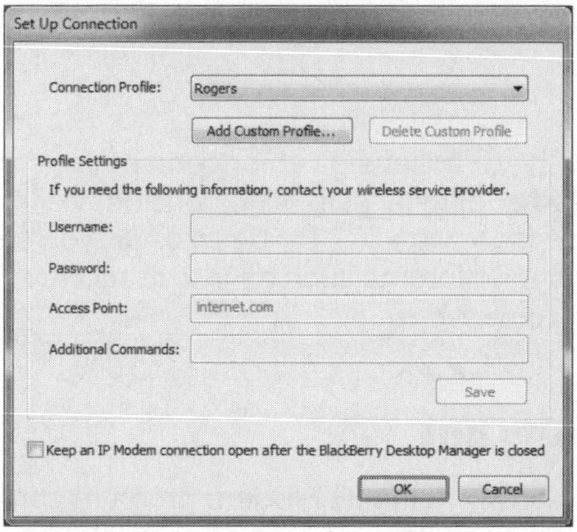

Figure 26-4. *Checking for your carrier*

5. If you don't see your carrier listed, then select **Add Custom Profile** and follow the steps to enter the information. In this case, you will probably need to contact your wireless carrier for the setup information.

6. Make sure you check the box at the bottom of the **Set Up Connection** screen if you want your internet connection to remain active even after you close the **Desktop Manager** program.

7. Click **OK** and then **Save**; this saves your settings.

8. Make sure your BlackBerry is connected to your computer and recognized by the **Desktop Manager** program. You can tell if the **Desktop Manager** program sees your BlackBerry by looking in the lower left corner of the screen.

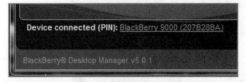

9. Now, you are ready to connect, which you do by clicking the **Connect** button.

10. If you see any error messages, follow the directions given or contact your wireless carrier for setup assistance. If you need additional help, also consider visiting the BlackBerry Technical Knowledge Base (see page 577 for details). Or, you can ask your question at one of the BlackBerry user forums such as www.crackberry.com, www.pinstack.com, or www.blackberryforums.com.

Re-Enabling the IP Modem Program

Under some circumstances, the icon associated with the **IP Modem** program can disappear. *Before* you walk through the steps that follow, be sure to contact your wireless carrier to see whether you can use Desktop Manager's IP Modem feature. If your carrier says you can, then follow these steps to edit the **ip_modem_configuration.xml** file. If your carrier says you can't use this program, then following these steps will likely not work, in which case you should try using the software recommended by your carrier instead.

It is probably best to use the Windows search feature or Google Desktop to find this file, but you may find it in one of these places:

■ Under Vista/Windows 7: `C:\ProgramData\Research In Motion\BlackBerry`

■ Under Windows XP: `C:\Documents and Settings\All Users\Application Data\Research in Motion\BlackBerry`

Once you find the file, follow these steps to make the icon for the **IP Modem** program accessible on your BlackBerry again:

1. Open the **ip_modem_configuration.xml** file using a text editor such as **Windows Notepad** or **Wordpad**.

2. Now locate your wireless carrier's name. Note that carrier names with ampersands (e.g., AT&T) will look like this: *AT&T*.

3. Change the line that reads enabled="false" to enabled="true" (see Figure 26-5).

Figure 26-5. *Using a text editor to edit the Connection string*

Save your changes and restart the Desktop Manager program. The **IP Modem** icon should reappear. If it does not, then restart your computer and try again.

Using the Desktop Manager on the Mac

Next, you will learn how to use the Mac version of the **Desktop Manager** program to enable using your BlackBerry as a modem for your Mac. Follow these steps to do so:

1. Begin by downloading and installing the latest version of the **Desktop Manager** program for Mac from www.blackberry.com (see page 143 for details).

2. Now connect your BlackBerry to your Mac (go to **Settings** ➤ **Network** on your Mac to see this window, as in Figure 26-6).

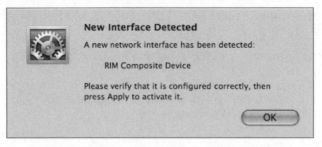

Figure 26-6. *Configuring a BlackBerry as a modem on a Mac*

3. Your Mac now sees your BlackBerry as a new network interface and will attempt to configure it as a dial-up modem for tethering (see Figure 26-7).

4. If you have a tethering or a *BlackBerry as Modem* service plan with your carrier, you can continue with the setup and choose the **Network Preferences...** option.

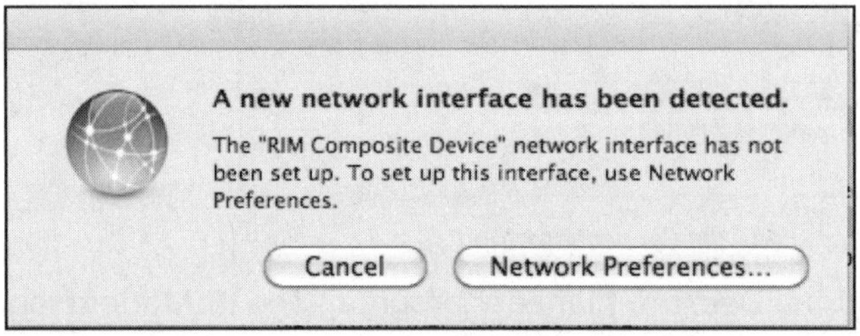

A new network interface has been detected.

The "RIM Composite Device" network interface has not been set up. To set up this interface, use Network Preferences.

Cancel   Network Preferences...

Figure 26-7. *A popup window advising you on how to configure your BlackBerry as a modem*

NOTE: Most (but not all) carriers charge extra for using your BlackBerry as a modem for your Mac to connect to the internet. Contact your carrier for information on pricing. Also, many carriers allow you to toggle this extra service on and off. For example, assume you are taking a trip, and you will need to use the modem feature for three weeks. You can turn this feature on through your carrier, and then turn it off again when you return home.

Network Preferences

The next step is to enter your network preferences. Follow these steps to do so:

1. Click the **Default** option next to the **Configuration:** field and select **New Connection**.

2. Enter a connection name. In Figure 26-8, we chose **BlackBerry 8900** as the connection name; however, you might want to choose **BlackBerry 9700**.

3. Fill in your phone number, account name and password in the appropriate boxes to begin the configuration process.

> **CAUTION:** You should proceed with the steps outlined in this section only if you have all the necessary carrier setup strings provided by your wireless carrier.

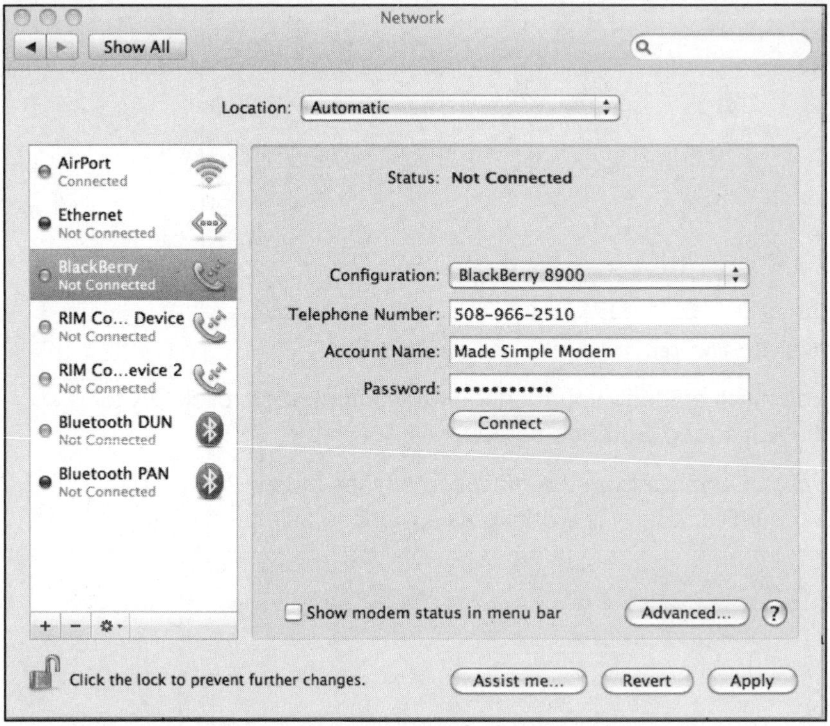

Figure 26-8. *Configuring network settings on a Mac*

4. If you need to access more settings, click the **Advanced...** button in the lower right corner. The **Advanced Settings** screen will have tabs along the top for **Modem**, **DNS**, **WINS**, **Proxies**, and **PPP** settings (see Figure 26-9).

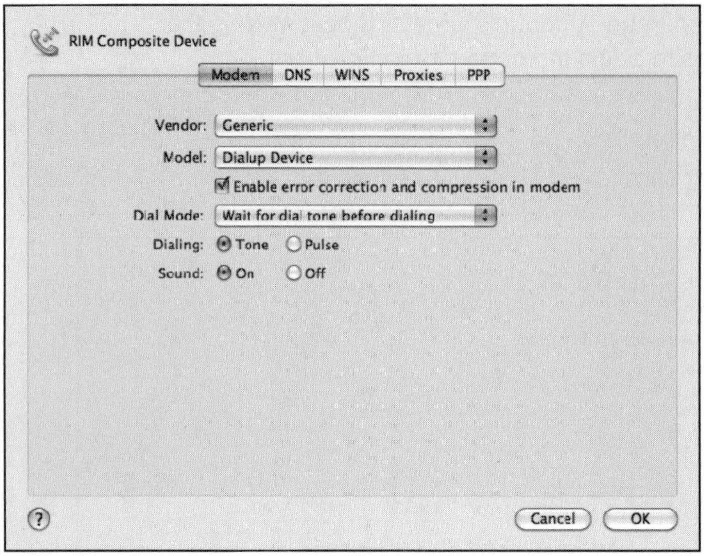

Figure 26-9. *The advanced configuration settings on a Mac*

5. When you finish entering your configuration information, click **OK** to close the **Advanced Settings** screen.

6. Finally, click **Connect** from the main screen (see Figure 26-10) to test whether your BlackBerry is working as a modem, as intended.

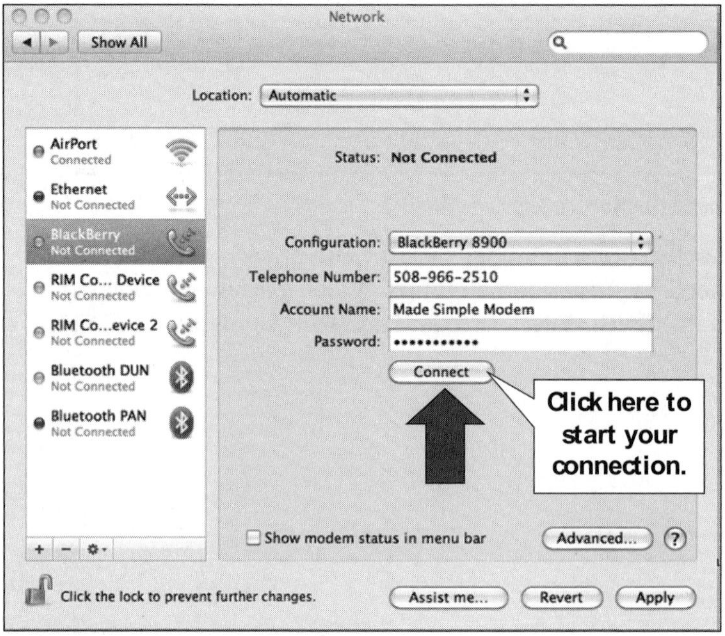

Figure 26-10. *Clicking Connect to go online*

Resolving Issues When Trying to Get Online

If you have any trouble getting connected, please double-check that your BlackBerry is connected to your Mac and that you have entered all your connection information correctly.

If everything looks OK, then contact your wireless carrier for support, check out the BlackBerry Technical Knowledgebase (see page 577), or visit some of the online BlackBerry forums discussed previously (see page 579).

Connecting with Bluetooth

Bluetooth allows your BlackBerry to communicate with devices as varied as headsets, GPS devices, and other hands-free systems with the freedom of wireless. Bluetooth is a small radio that transmits from each device. The BlackBerry gets paired, or connected, to the peripheral. Many Bluetooth devices can be used up to 30 feet away from the BlackBerry.

In this chapter, we will show you how to pair to a Bluetooth headset, how to connect to a Bluetooth stereo device, and how to prioritize your Bluetooth connections.

The History of Bluetooth

The BlackBerry ships with Bluetooth 2.0 Technology. It might help to think of Bluetooth as a short range, wireless technology that allows your BlackBerry to connect to various peripheral devices without wires.

Bluetooth is believed to be named after a Danish Viking and King, Harald Blåtand (which has been translated as *Bluetooth* in English). King Blåtand lived in the 10th century, and he is famous for uniting Denmark and Norway. Similarly, Bluetooth technology unites computers and telecom. According to legend, King Blåtand's name came from his very dark hair, which was unusual for Vikings. Blåtand means *dark complexion*. There also exists a more popular story that states that the King loved to eat blueberries, so much so that his teeth were blue-stained.

You can learn more about King Blåtand at the following sites:

- http://cp.literature.agilent.com/litweb/pdf/5980-3032EN.pdf
- www.cs.utk.edu/~dasgupta/bluetooth/history.htm
- www.britannica.com/eb/topic-254809/Harald-I

Using Bluetooth on Your BlackBerry

We'll kick this chapter off by explaining how to use Bluetooth with your Blackberry. We'll walk you through how to enable Bluetooth, to how to use it to connect to various devices, to troubleshooting some potential issues.

Turning On Bluetooth

Obviously, you can't pair anything to your BlackBerry until you turn Bluetooth on. Follow these steps to do so:

1. You turn on Bluetooth by navigating to the **Settings** folder (see Figure 27-1).

Figure 27-1. *The Set Up Bluetooth icon*

2. Scroll through the application icons and press and click the **Setup** folder. Alternatively, or you may need to find and click the Radio Tower icon (if it's called **Manage Connections**).

3. Next, you should see an icon that called **Setup Bluetooth.** Go ahead and press and click that icon.

4. You should now see a small Bluetooth icon next to the battery meter in the **Home** screen. Click the **Wireless Signal Strength** image in the upper right corner of your device to get to the **Manage Connections** popup window.

5. Finally, press and click the **Set Up Bluetooth** option, so you continue onto the next step: configuring Bluetooth for use on your BlackBerry.

Configuring Bluetooth

Once you have Bluetooth enabled, you will want to follow the steps that follow to take full advantage of the Bluetooth capabilities on your BlackBerry.

Sometimes, there can be two or three ways to get into the **Set Up Bluetooth** and **Bluetooth Options** screens. The way you do this depends a bit on your BlackBerry software version and your BlackBerry carrier (e.g., cell phone) company.

You have three basic approaches for navigating to the **Bluetooth Options** screen, which I'll outline next. Choose the one most appropriate for your device.

Method 1: Navigating to the Setup Folder

To use the first method for navigating to the **Bluetooth Options** screen, you need to navigate to the Setup folder. Once you do so, follow these steps:

1. Press and click the **Setup** folder.

2. Scroll down to the **Setup Bluetooth** option, and then press and click it.

3. If you see a Window asking you whether you want to search or be discovered, press the **Escape** key.

4. Finally, you can press the **Menu** key and scroll down to **Bluetooth Options**.

Method 2: Navigating to the Options Icon

To use the second method for navigating to the **Bluetooth Options** screen, you need to begin by navigating to the **Options** icon on your **Home** screen. Once you do so, follow these steps:

1. Scroll down to the **Bluetooth** choice, then press and click it.

2. Press the **Menu** key to bring up a list of choices from which you can get to the Bluetooth Options screen.

Method 3: Navigating to the Manage Connections Icon

To use the third method for navigating to the **Bluetooth Options** screen, begin by navigating to the **Manage Connections** icon. Once you do so, follow these steps:

1. Scroll to the **Manage Connections** icon, and then press and click it.

2. Scroll to the **Set Up Bluetooth** option at the bottom of the device.

3. Press and click the **Menu** key, and then select **Options**.

If you have already paired your BlackBerry with Bluetooth devices, you will see those devices listed at this point (we will cover how to pair your devices later in this chapter).

Prepping Your BlackBerry for Bluetooth

You need to do a few more things before you'll be ready to pair your BlackBerry with another Bluetooth device. For example, assume you want to share your address book via Bluetooth. Follow these steps to do so:

Begin by changing the **Device Name** property of your Blackberry (other Bluetooth devices use this property to identify your BlackBerry). Do this by pressing and clicking where it says **Device Name** and enter a new name (this step is recommended for security purposes).

1. Next, you need to make your BlackBerry *discoverable* (findable) to other devices. Press and Click next to **Discoverable** and select **Yes** (the default is **No**). As we will explain later, security reasons dictate that you should set this back to **No** after you finish the pairing process.

2. Make sure that it says **Always** or **If Unlocked** after the **Allow Outgoing Calls** option.

3. Set **Address Book Transfer** property to **Enable.** Depending on the software version of your BlackBerry, you may see the options of **All Entries** or **Enable, Hotlist Only,** or **Selected Categories Only**). This option allows your address book data to be transferred to another device or computer using Bluetooth.

4. To see a blue flashing LED when connected to a Bluetooth Device, set the **LED Connection Indicator** property to **On.**

Bluetooth Security Tips

If you're going to use Bluetooth on your Blackberry, you need be cognizant of the security concerns around this technology. For example, here are a few security tips from a recent BlackBerry IT Newsletter. Following these will steps help you prevent hackers from getting access to your BlackBerry through Bluetooth:

■ Never pair your BlackBerry when you are in a crowded public area.

■ Disable the **Discoverable** setting after you're done pairing your BlackBerry with a device.

■ Do not accept any pairing requests with unknown Bluetooth devices, and only accept connections from devices with names you recognize.

■ Change the name of your BlackBerry to something other than the default value (e.g., *BlackBerry 9550*). This will help you keep hackers from easily finding your BlackBerry.

You can find this information and many other useful facts at this URL: www.blackberry.com/newsletters/connection/it/jan-2007/managing-bluetooth-security.shtml?CPID=NLC-41.

Supported Devices

Your BlackBerry should work with most Bluetooth headsets, car kits, hands-free kits, keyboards, and GPS receivers that are compliant with Bluetooth 2.0 and earlier. At the time of writing, Bluetooth 2.1 was just entering the marketplace; you will need to check with the device manufacturer of newer devices to make sure they are compatible with your BlackBerry.

Pairing with a Bluetooth Device

You can think of *pairing* as the act of establishing a wireless connection between your BlackBerry and a peripheral, whether it's a headset, global positioning device, external keyboard, or a Windows-based or Mac computer. Pairing is dependent on entering a required *passkey* that locks your BlackBerry into a secure connection with the peripheral. Similar to getting into the Bluetooth options screens, you have several choices for getting into the **Bluetooth Setup** screen to pair your BlackBerry and establish this connection.

Begin by putting your Bluetooth device in **pairing** mode, as recommended by the manufacturer. Also, have the passkey ready to enter. Next, navigate to the **Bluetooth Setup** screen using one of the following three methods:

- **Method 1:** Press and click the **Options** icon. (This icon may be inside the **Settings** icon). Next, scroll to the **Bluetooth** option, and then press and click it.

- **Method 2:** Scroll to the **Set Up Bluetooth** icon, and then press and click it.

- **Method 3:** Scroll to the **Manage Connections** icon, and then press and click it. Finally, select the **Setup Bluetooth** option.

Once you open the dialog for **Setup Bluetooth**, your BlackBerry will ask you whether you want to *Search for a device* or *Listen for another device to find me* (see Figure 27-2). Choose your preferred option, and then press and click **OK**.

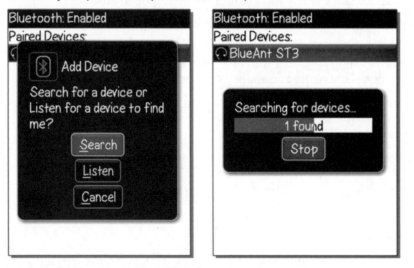

Figure 27-2. *Searching for Bluetooth devices*

> **NOTE:** If you are pairing your BlackBerry with your computer, then you need to make sure that both your BlackBerry and your computer are in **Discoverable** mode. Set this in the **Bluetooth Options** screen by setting the **Discoverable** property to **Yes** or **Ask**. (The default setting is **No**, which will prevent you from pairing your BlackBerry and computer.)

When the device is found, the BlackBerry will display the device's **Device Name** on the screen. You're now ready to configure the device for pairing. Do so by following these steps:

1. Press and click the **Device Name** to select it (see Figure 27-3).

Figure 27-3. *Entering a passkey to paira device*

2. You will then be prompted to enter the four-digit passkey provided by the manufacturer of the Bluetooth peripheral. Enter this passkey, and then press the **Enter** key. (Many default passkeys are just *0000* or *1234*.)

3. You will then be prompted to accept the connection from the new device; do so.

> **TIP:** If you check the box next to **Don't ask this again**, you will only have to do Step 3 once.

Your device should now be connected, paired, and ready to use.

Answering and Making Calls with a Headset

Some Bluetooth headsets support an **Auto Answer** protocol that will, as it sounds, automatically answer incoming calls and send them right to the headset. This is very helpful when driving or in other situations where you should not be looking at your BlackBerry to answer the call. Sometimes, you will need to push a button – usually just one – to answer your call from the headset. You have two options for answering and making calls with a headset, which are covered next.

Option 1: Answering Directly from the Headset

When a call comes into your BlackBerry, you should hear an audible beep in the headset. Just press the **Multi-function** button on your headset to answer the call. Press the **Multi function** button again to disconnect when the call ends.

Option #2: Transferring the Caller to the Headset

When a phone call comes into your BlackBerry, follow these steps to transfer the caller to your headset:

1. Press the **Menu** key.

2. Scroll to **Activate (***your Bluetooth headset's Device Name***)**, and the call will be sent to the selected headset.

In image to the right, the headset's **Device Name** is *Jawbone*.

The Bluetooth Setup Menu Commands

There are several options available to you from the **Bluetooth Setup** menu. Learning these commands can help you to take full advantage of Bluetooth on your BlackBerry.

The Bluetooth Menu Options

Scrolling to the appropriate menu is a simple, three step process. Follow these steps to do so:

1. Navigate to the **Options** icon, and then press and click it.

2. Scroll to the **Bluetooth** option, and then press and click it. You will now see the list of devices paired with your BlackBerry.

3. Highlight one of the devices listed and press the **Menu** key to bring up a robust set of options for interacting with the device.

You can access the following functionality from the **Bluetooth Setup** menu:

- **Disable Bluetooth:** Gives you another way to turn off the Bluetooth radio, which can help you to save battery life if you don't need the Bluetooth active.

- **Connect / Disconnect:** Lets you immediately connect/disconnect you to/from the highlighted Bluetooth device.

- **Add Device:** Lets you connect to a new Bluetooth peripheral.

- **Delete Device:** Removes the highlighted device from the BlackBerry.

- **Device Properties:** Lets you check whether the device is trusted or encrypted. It also lets you see whether the **Echo** control is activated (see Figure 27-4).

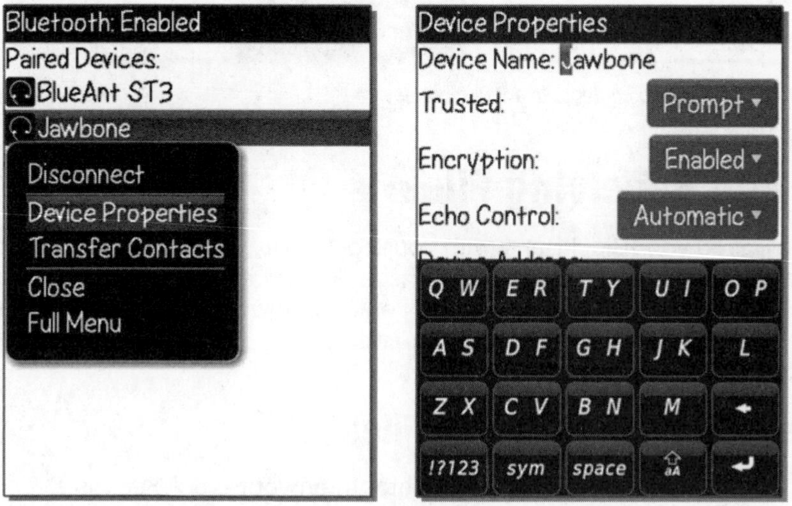

Figure 27-4. *The Bluetooth Device Properties dialog*

- **Transfer Contacts:** Enables you to send your address book through Bluetooth to a PC or another Bluetooth smartphone, assuming you are paired and connected to that device (see Figure 27-5).

- **Options:** Shows the **Options** screen, which we've covered previously.

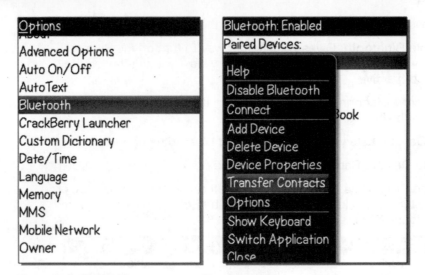

Figure 27-5. *Transferring contacts to a Bluetooth device*

Sending and Receiving Files

Once you have paired your BlackBerry with your computer, you can use Bluetooth to send and receive files. At the time of writing, these files were limited to media files (e.g, videos, music, and pictures) and address book entries; however, we suspect that you will be able to transfer more types of files in the future.

Sending and Receiving Media Files

Sending and receiving media files through Bluetooth on your BlackBerry is a straightforward process. All you need to do is follow these simple steps:

1. Open the **Media** folder by pressing and clicking it.

2. Navigate to the type of file you want to send or receive, whether it's a music, video, ringtone, picture, or something else.

3. Next, navigate to the folder where you want to send the file from or receive the file to. Your choices here are **Device Memory** or a media card.

4. If you are sending a file to your computer, then scroll to and highlight the file you want to send.

5. Now select **Send using Bluetooth**. From here, you will need to follow the prompts on your computer to receive the file.

NOTE: You may need to set up your computer so it can receive files through Bluetooth.

6. If you are receiving a file (or files) on your BlackBerry, then you need to select the **Receive via Bluetooth** option. Go to your computer and select the file or files you want to send, and then follow the commands required to **Send via Bluetooth**. You may be asked on the BlackBerry to confirm the Bluetooth transfer.

NOTE: You can send (transfer) only media files that you have put onto your BlackBerry yourself. You cannot use Bluetooth to transfer the pre-loaded media files.

Troubleshooting Bluetooth

Bluetooth is still an emergent technology, and sometimes it just doesn't work as well as you might hope. If you are having difficulty, perhaps one of these suggestions will help. So in this section, we will cover common problems and possible approaches to solving them.

Problem 1: The Device Refuses Your Passkey

Sometimes a Bluetooth device just won't accept your passkey. In this case, it's possible that you have the incorrect passkey. Most Bluetooth devices use either *0000* or *1234* for the passkey; however, but some have unique passkeys.

If you lost your product manual for the Bluetooth device, you can often find a PDF version of the manual online using a search engine such as Google or Yahoo. Typically, you'd find this PDF at the device manufacturer's site, but it can show up on other sites, too.

Problem 2: The Device Won't Pair Even with the Correct Passkey

Sometimes you have the right passkey, but you still cannot pair the device. In this case, it is possible that the device is not compatible with your BlackBerry. One thing you can try is to turn off encryption. Follow these steps to do so:

1. Press and click the **Options** menu.

2. Choose Bluetooth, highlight **Device Name** of the problem device, and then press and click it.

3. In the **Device Properties** dialog, disable encryption for that device and try to connect again.

Problem 3: You Cannot Share Your Address Book

Sometimes you might encounter problems when trying to share your address book with a Bluetooth device. Follow these steps if you encounter this issue:

1. Inside the **Bluetooth Setup** screen, press the **Menu** key and select **Options**.

2. Double-check that you have enabled the **Contacts Transfer** field. If you haven't, do so.

NOTE: Many Bluetooth headsets and car kits do not fully support address book transfers; be sure to double-check the documentation that came with your Bluetooth device

Web Browser

A requirement for any smartphone today is that you need to be able to get online and browse the Web. While smartphone browsing the Web on your smartphone will never be a substitute for desktop browsing, you might be surprised by all the features that facilitate surfing the Web on your BlackBerry.

In this chapter, we will show you how to get online, how to set your **browser** bookmarks, how to manipulate your browsing history, and how to use some *hotkeys* to maneuver around the **browser** program quickly.

Web Browsing on Your BlackBerry

One of the amazing features of smartphones like the BlackBerry is that you can use them browse the Web with ease and speed right from your handheld. Plus, an ever-increasing number of web sites are now supporting mobile browser formatting. These sites sense you are viewing the site from a small mobile browser, and they automatically reconfigure themselves for your BlackBerry so they can load quickly. The specialized mobile version of some sites load more quickly than when using their desktop browser equivalents!

Using Alternative Web Browsers

The Blackberry's native **Browser** program may seem slow to some people, so many vendors have begun creating alternative, third-party web browser programs for your BlackBerry.

We have seen several alternatives to the BlackBerry's native **Browser** program appear on the market. A couple of the more notable ones recently are **Opera Mini** and **Bolt Browser**. We have not extensively tested them, but these third-party vendors do keep improving the look, feel, and performance of their programs' overall web browsing experience. You can locate these browsers and other alternatives by performing a web search for *BlackBerry Storm web browser* or *BlackBerry web browser*.

This list points you to the current links (at the time of writing) for two alternative web browsers to the native **Browser** program that comes with your BlackBerry:

- **Opera Mini Browser**: www.opera.com/mini or m.opera.com
- **Bolt Web Browser**: www.boltbrowser.com

> **NOTE:** The rest of this chapter assumes you're using the native **Browser** program that ships with every BlackBerry.

Locating the Web Browser from the Home Screen

You can actually start browsing the Web from a few of the icons on your **Home** screen. The easiest way to get started is to find and use the **Browser** icon, which looks like a globe. Follow these steps to do so:

1. Use your finger to navigate to the **Browser** icon, and then and press and click it. The text for the icon might say *BlackBerry Browser*, or *Internet Browser*, or simply *Browser*, as in the figure to the right.

2. You will either be taken to directly the **Home** screen of your particular carrier or to your list of bookmarks. You can set where clicking this icon takes you by navigating to the **Options** screen under your **Browser program** (you can learn more about this on page 510).

Using the Browser Menu

Like most other applications on the BlackBerry, the heart of the **Browser** program lies in the capabilities you access from the program's **Menu** options. One push, one press, and/or one click can mean you are off to specific sites, bookmarked pages, recent pages, your internet history, and much more.

All the fun begins on the **Browser** program's **Start** page. The **Start** page view includes a **Web Address** box; a **Web Search** box (e.g., Google, Yahoo!, and so on); a **Bookmarks...** section that shows your bookmarks; and a **History...** section that shows, just as you'd expect, a list of recently visited pages (see Figure 28-1).

Figure 28-1. *Type in a web address from the browser start page*

To visit a Web site, you can press and click one of the links in **Bookmarks...** or **History...**; alternatively, you can type in a new URL, and then press and click it. (Remember: You use the **space** key for the "." in the address.)

Exploring the Browser Program's Menu Options

What follows is a list and short explanation of the **Menu** options that become visible when viewing a web page with the BlackBerry's native **Browser** program (see Figure 28-2). You can view these options by pressing the **Menu** key as you view a web page:

- **Help:** Shows on-screen text help for the **Browser** program. This is useful when you forget something, and need quick assistance.

- Column View/Page View: Toggles between the Column and Page views. Column view shows a more zoomed-in view; whereas a Page view shows you a view of the entire page, which is more like what you see in a desktop computer's web browser.

- **Zoom In:** Zooms you in on specific part of the page, so you can see that part of the page more clearly. You can zoom in several levels.

- **Zoom Out:** Zooms you out, so you can see more of the page.

- **Find:** Searches for text on a web page.

- **Find Next:** Searches for the next occurrence of the last **Find** search.

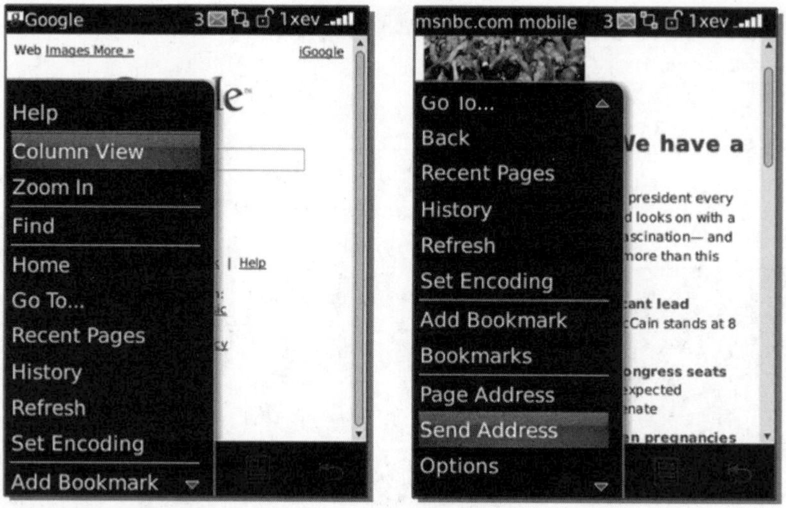

Figure 28-2. *Reviewing menu options in the native Browser program*

- **Home:** Takes you to the **Browser** program's **Home** page. You can set or change the **Home** page from the **Browser program's Options** screen (see page 510 for details).

- **Go To...:** Allows you to type in a specific web address (see page 505 for details).

- **Start BB Connection:** Takes you online if you are viewing an offline, saved Web page.

- **Recent Pages:** Allows you to view the most recent web pages browsed.

- **History:** Shows your entire web browsing history.

- **Refresh:** Updates the current web page.

- **Set Encoding:** Lets you change the character encoding used when web browsing; you probably won't need to change this advanced setting.

- **Add Bookmark:** Sets the current page as a **Favorite** (i.e., a bookmark). For obvious reasons, this feature is extremely useful (see page 507 for additional details).

- **Bookmarks:** Lists all your bookmarks. This is also extremely useful (see page 511 for additional details on using Bookmarks; and see page 510 for details on organizing bookmarks with your folders.

- **Page Address:** Shows you the full web address of the current page (see page 507 for additional details).

- **Send Address:** Sends the current page address to a contact (see page 507 for additional details).

- **Options:** Sets the **Browser** program's **Configuration, Properties,** and **Cache** settings.

- **Save Page:** Saves the page as a file and puts it in your Messages folder (i.e., your email inbox).

- **Switch Application:** Jumps or switches over to other applications, while leaving the current web page open.

- **Close:** Terminates the current instance of the Browser program and exits to the **Home** screen.

Using Your Address Bar

The first thing you will want to know how to do is get to your favorite web sites. In the case of one of this book's authors, that site is www.google.com. On your desktop computer, you simply type the web address or (URL) into your browser's **Address Bar** box. You won't see an **Address Bar** box on the BlackBerry. Instead, you have to use the **Go To...** menu command or the "." (period) shortcut key to type in your web address. Follow these steps to do so:

1. Open the **Browser** program by pressing and clicking the **Browser** icon.

2. Press the **Menu** key and select **Go To...** command (see Figure 28-3).

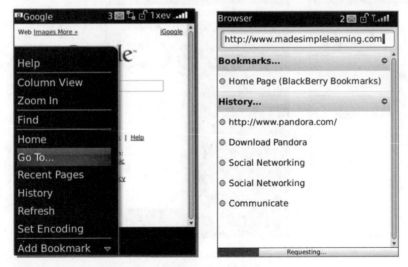

Figure 28-3. *Using the Go To... command from the menu.*

3. The **Address Bar** comes up with the "http://www." part in place, waiting for you to type the rest of the address. Simply type in the web address of the site you wish to visit. Remember: pushing the space key will insert the dot "." automatically

4. Press the **Enter** key when you are done. The **Browser** program will take you to the entered web page.

Once you have type in a few web addresses using the **Go To...** command, you will notice that they appear in a list below the web address bar the next time you select **Go To...** section. You can select any of these sites by scrolling down, and then pressing and clicking one.

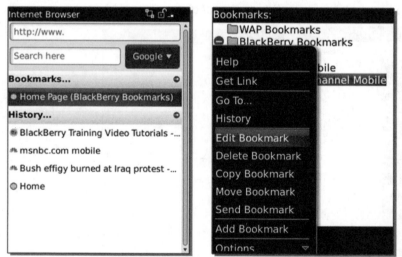

Figure 28-4. *Frequently visited web sites in the Bookmarks... (if set) and History... sections*

TIP: You can save time by editing a bookmark. If you want to enter a web address that is similar to one that you have a bookmark for, you can highlight the previously entered address, press the **Menu** key, and then select the **Edit Bookmark** option.

Copying or Sending a Web Page

The BlackBerry's native **Browser** program makes it easy to copy or send a page you might be viewing to someone else. Follow these steps to do so:

1. Press the **Menu** key while viewing a web page in the **Browser** program.

2. Scroll down to the **Page Address** option, and then press and click it.

3. The web address is now displayed in the window. Scroll down with your finger for more options.

4. Scroll to **Copy Address**, and then press and click it. This will copy the web address to the clipboard; from here, you can easily paste the URL into a contact, email, memo, or even the **Calendar** program.

5. Alternatively, you can scroll to **Send Address**, and then press and click it. This will allow you to send the particular web address information in an email or with MMS, SMS, or PIN messaging. Simply select your preferred communication form and then the contact.

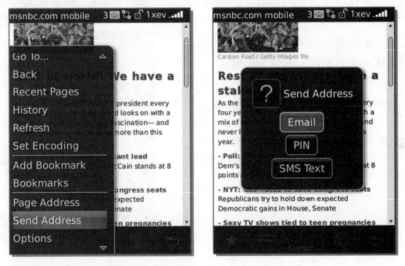

Figure 28-5. *Using the Page Address option*

Setting and Naming Bookmarks

One of the keys to a great web browsing experience on your BlackBerry is the liberal use of the **Bookmarks...** feature. Your BlackBerry comes with a couple of bookmarks already set. It is very easy to customize your bookmarks to include all your favorite sites for easy browsing.

> **TIP:** You can instantly find bookmarks by typing a few letters of a bookmark's name. You do this in exactly the same way you look up contacts in the **Address Book** program. Remembering this tip can save you a considerable amount of time!

Naming Bookmarks for Easy Retrieval

One of the keys to a positive web browsing experience is to name add and name bookmarks in a way that makes them easy to find later. In the next section, we will cover how to set up an example bookmark that lets us look up our local weather instantly.

1. Open the **Browser** program and use the **Go To...** command (or the "." shortcut key) to input a favorite web page. In this example, we will type in www.weather.com.

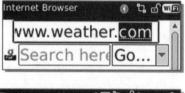

2. Type in your ZIP code or city name to see your current weather (see Figure 28-6).

3. Once the page loads with your local weather, press the **Menu** key and select the **Add Bookmark** option (or use the **A** shortcut key).

4. The full name of the web address is now displayed. In this case, you will probably see *TWC Weather*. You may want to rename the URL (see the upcoming section on naming booksmarks well).

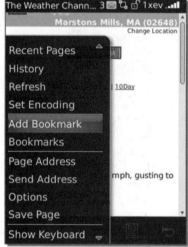

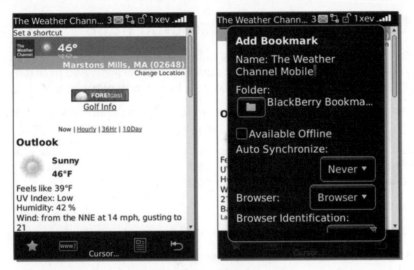

Figure 28-6. *Adding a bookmark for your local weather*

5. In this case – in most cases, really –we recommend changing the bookmark's name to something short and unique.

> **NOTE:** If you were to bookmark four different weather forecasts, the default bookmark names would all show up as *The Weather Channel*. This would be rather useless if your goal were to get straight to the ten-day forecast.

Be sure to keep the following tips and trick in mind as you edit and rename your bookmarks:

- **Keep all bookmark names short:** You will only see about the first 10-15 characters of the name in your list because the screen is small, so any characters beyond that won't be displayed.

- **Make all bookmark names similar, but unique:** If you were to add four bookmarks for the weather in New York or your area, you might adhere to this advice by naming them along these lines:

    - NY – Now
    - NY – 10 day
    - NY – 36 hour
    - NY – Hourly

This approach lets you instantly locate all your forecasts by typing the letters *NY* in your bookmark list. Only those bookmarks with the letters *NY* will be displayed.

Viewing the Bookmark List or Home Page

You might prefer to see your list of bookmarks rather than a **Home** page when you open the **Browser** program. The reason is probably obvious: this will allow you to use the **Find** feature in the bookmark list to instantly locate a bookmark, press it, and click it.

This approach speeds up the time it takes to get to favorite bookmarked web pages, whether you want to see the local weather or fire up your favorite search engine.

It might also be that your BlackBerry automatically opens up to your list of bookmarks, but you would prefer to see a particular **Home** page instead. If so, you can follow these instructions to change a given page your **Home** page:

1. Press and click the **Browser** icon.

2. Press the **Menu** key and select **Options**.

3. Press and click **Browser Configuration** (see Figure 28-7).

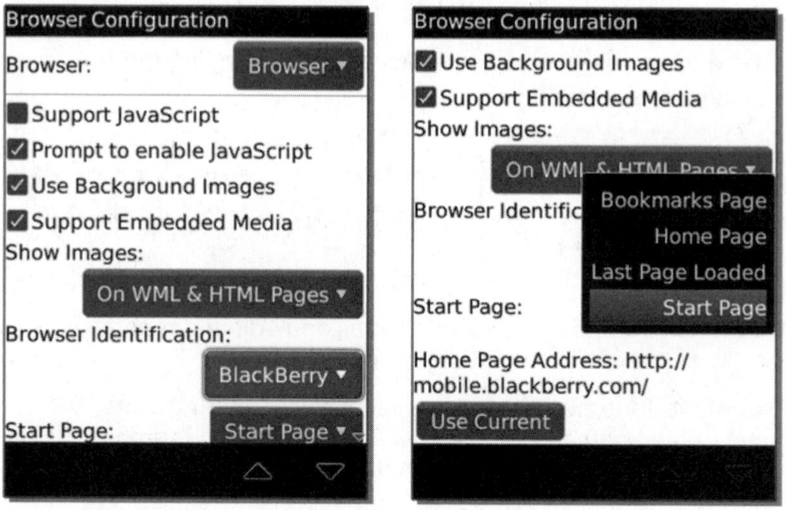

Figure 28-7. *Exploring the Browser Configuration options*

4. Scroll all the way down to the **Start Page** option near the bottom of the dialog, then press and click the button to see its options. You will most likely see three options: **Bookmarks Page** (shows a list of bookmarks); **Home Page** (shows the web site you have listed as your **Home** page, which you do on this screen); and **Last Page Loaded** (shows the last web page in memory and brings it back up when you re-enter your **Browser** program).

5. To select a bookmark from the list, choose the **Bookmarks Page** option and make sure you save your settings.

Using Your Bookmarks to Browse the Web

At this point, you are ready to begin using your bookmarks to simplify the process of browsing to your favorite sites on the Web. Follow these steps to do so:

1. Press and click the **Browser** icon.

2. If you don't see your list of bookmarks automatically when you start the **Browser** program, press the **Menu** key, scroll down to **Bookmarks** option, and press and click it (see Figure 28-8).

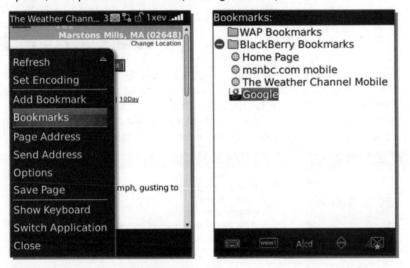

Figure 28-8. *Viewing your list of bookmarks*

3. All of your bookmarks will be listed, including any default bookmarks that were put there automatically by your phone company.

You might want to press and click a particular folder to open all the bookmarks contained within or to see whether the bookmark you need is located within a given folder. To open a folder of bookmarks, press and click that folder to see its contents.

However, if you have a lot of bookmarks, then you should use the **Find:** feature and type a few letters that match the bookmark you want to find. For example, in Figure 28-8, typing the letters *go* will immediately find all bookmarks with *go* in the bookmark name (e.g., *Google*).

Once you get familiar with your bookmark names, you can type a few letters and find exactly what you need quickly and easily.

Searching with Google

Google also has a mobile version of its site that loads quickly and is quite useful on your BlackBerry.

To get there, just go to www.google.com in your BlackBerry's **Browser** program.

The BlackBerry's native Browser program includes a built-in **Search Address** box immediately beneath the regular **Address Bar** box. You can set the **Search Address** box to Google, Yahoo!, or some other built-in search engine (see Figure 28-9). Do so by pressing the **Search Address** box and clicking the **Dropdown Arrow** icon to the right of the **Search Address** box to see a list of availabe search engines.

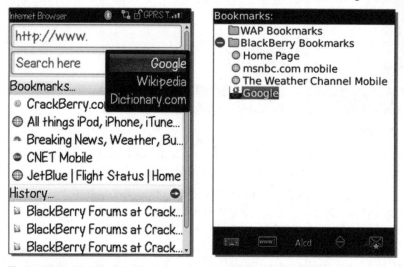

Figure 28-9. *Changing the Browser program's default search engine*

We highly recommend creating an easy-to-use bookmark for this site and all your favorite web sites (see page 507 for more information on this topic).

Just as on your computer, you can type in your search string and hit the **Enter** key. This saves you the time it takes to scroll to, press, and click the **Search** button). If you want to find (and even call) pizza restaurants in a certain ZIP code or city, then you would enter in *pizza* and your ZIP code or city (see Figure 28-10).

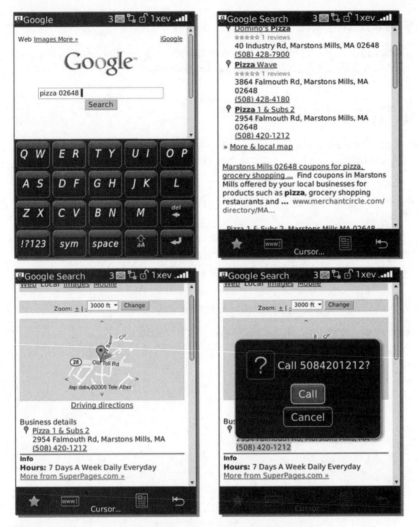

Figure 28-10. *Finding (and calling) a pizza place in a given location*

Viewing a Google Result's Location

It might be that you will want to determine the location of a place you find in a Google search on Google. For example, assume I want to figure out the location of the pizza place I found and called in the preceding example. In this case, I can press and click the name of the restaurant from my search results.

Once I press and click the link to the pizza place, Google will display a map that shows the location of the pizza place.

If I were to press and click the **Driving Directions** option, I could find a quick path from my current location to the restaurant – all from my BlackBerry!

Finding Places with Google Maps

In a later chapter, we will describe in detail how to obtain and use Google Maps on your BlackBerry. Please see page 535 for more information on this topic.

Web Browser Tips and Tricks

You can take a number of steps that help you navigate the Web faster and more easily (see page 505 for more information). Here's a short excerpt from that list to whet your appetite:

- To insert a period (.) into a web address in the **Go To...** dialog box, press the **space** key.

- Go to Browser ➤ Menu Key ➤ Options ➤ Browser Configuration ➤ Browser Identification, and then set this option to either **Firefox** or **Internet Explorer**. Now every website will think you're a PC rather than a phone.

- To stop a web page from loading, press the **Escape** key.

- To close the **Browser** program, press and hold the **Escape** key.

Adding or Removing Apps

Your BlackBerry comes with most of the major apps you will ever need already installed. However, there are literally thousands of third-party apps available in virtually any category you can think of that can help you get the most out of your BlackBerry.

There are apps for productivity, reference, music, and fun – including lots of great games. One nice thing about the BlackBerry platform is that while there is an official **App World**, there are also lots of ways to find and download apps. In this chapter, we will show you how to navigate BlackBerry's App World site and how to download and install apps onto your BlackBerry.

Downloading and Adding New Software

One of the cool things about your BlackBerry is that, just as on your computer, you can go onto the Web and find software to download. You can download everything from ringtones, to games, to content that is pushed out to your BlackBerry on a regular basis (using the same approach that you *probably* see with email on the BlackBerry – each phone company or carrier uses a slightly different approach).

Adding Push Content

Sometimes you need (or simply want) to add special *push* content related to your job or that otherwise strikes your fancy. As mentioned previously, push content is *pushed* from a remote web site down to your BlackBerry device, similar to the way email is delivered to your BlackBerry. Follow these steps to add push content to your device:

1. Start your BlackBerry's **Browser** program.

2. Press the **Menu** key, select the **Go To...** command, and enter this web site: http://mobile.blackberry.com/.

3. Next, press and click the **News and Weather** icon on the BlackBerry's **Home** page.

Figure 29-1. *Adding pushed content from the BlackBerry web site*

CAUTION: Web sites change frequently. All of the web site images you see in this book are accurate at the time of writing. And while it's quite possible that a given page or site shown in this book will look exactly the same on your BlackBerry, it is also possible that the page or site will look completely different on your device. It is even possible that the site or page is no longer available. If a site is missing or looks completely different, we recommend searching for a link with approximately the same name.

Several news sites now allow you to put an icon on your **Home** screen that will automatically launch a given news site. For our purposes, let's say we wanted to put the icon for the *Wall Street Journal* (*WSJ*) on our **Home** screen (see Figure 29-2). Follow these steps to do so:

1. Scroll down to the link for the *Wall Street Journal* and select **Download**.

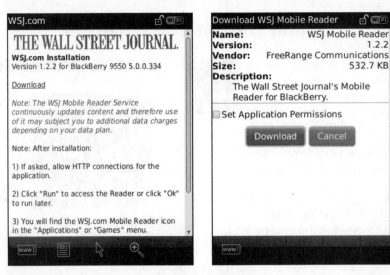

Figure 29-2. *Downloading the Wall Street Journal app*

2. Press and click the **Download** option to place the icon for *WSJ* on your BlackBerry.

3. Once the program has successfully installed, you will see a screen that looks like the image to the right. To find the Wall Street Journal shortcut, just go to your **Applications** screen and then to the **Downloads** folder.

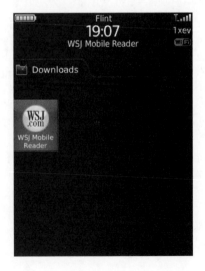

4. Inside this folder, you should see the **WSJ Mobile Reader** icon. Press and click the icon to go directly to the mobile version of the *WSJ* site.

Changing Your Default Downloads Location

By default, your BlackBerry saves the icon of all programs you download to the device's **Downloads** folder. Follow these steps to change the default folder your BlackBerry saves new programs to.

1. Pressing the **Menu** key from your **Home** screen and select **Options**.

2. Next, press and click on the button at the top of the **Set Download Folder** area to change the download default location to a new location.

> **TIP:** Select **Home** if you want your new icons easily accessible!

Downloading and Installing Games

The BlackBerry can truly be a multimedia entertainment device. And sometimes you might want to play a new game on your BlackBerry, a desire the device will happily accommodate. Sure, your BlackBerry comes with a few games; however, there are many places on the Web where you can find still more games that might suit your tastes and interests better.

The best place to start looking for additional games is the Mobile Blackberry web site at http://mobile.blackberry.com (see Figure 29-3).

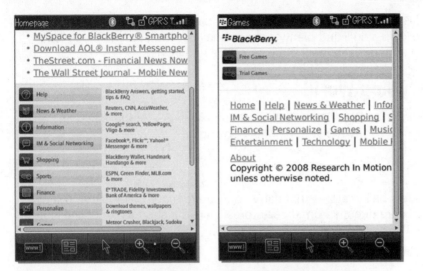

Figure 29-3. *Downloading gamse and more from the Mobile Blackberry site*

Follow these steps to navigate to the games area of the site:

1. Enter the site's address, which is `http://mobile.blackberry.com`.

2. The best place to find games is usually under the **Games and Entertainment** category. So press and click the site's **Games and Entertainment** icon to bring up everything from free games, to classic games, to demos of games that you can try out before you buy. The content changes often, so you would need to visit the site frequently to keep abreast of current games available for your BlackBerry.

3. Locate the desired game, then download and install it exactly as you did when installing the **Web Push** icon. By default, any games you download will go into your **Downloads** folder, as stated previously. You can always move the icon for a game you download into your **Games** folder (look back at page 201 for more information on how to do that).

Finding More Software

There are quite a few additional places where you can find software and services for your BlackBerry. One place we recommend highly is the **Partners** section of `www.madesimplelearning.com`. You can get to this section directly by entering the following URL into your computer's web browser: `www.madesimplelearning.com/partners`.

Of course, the BlackBerry App World site has been discussed throughout this book. But in the section that follows, you'll find plenty of additional links that can help you tailor your BlackBerry with software that best fits your needs and interests.

The BlackBerry App World

Look back at the chapter on BlackBerry App World on page 467. At this site, you can find just about any kind of software you might be looking for.

Web Stores

You can find quite a few online stores that carry software for your Blackberry. You can usually purchase software directly from these stores. Here's a short list of online sites that sell software for the BlackBerry.

- www.crackberry.com
- www.shopcrackbery.com
- www.bberry.com
- www.eaccess.com
- www.handango.com
- www.mobihand.com

Reviews of Software, Services, and More

There are so many programs, services, and other items available for your BlackBerry that it can be difficult to know where to start or what is worth having. Fortunately, you can also find many web sites that provide reviews of all the software, services, ringtones, themes, wallpaper, accessories, and other items and services of interest for your BlackBerry. Some of the sites that provide these reviews include the following:

- www.allblackberry.com
- www.bbhub.com
- www.berryreview.com
- www.blackberrycool.com
- www.blackberryforums.com
- www.boygeniusreport.com
- www.howardforums.com (The RIM-Research In Motion Section)
- www.pinstack.com
- www.RIMarkable.com
- www.blackberryrocks.com

Official BlackBerry Sites

In addition to the many web sites dedicated to providing and reviewing programs and services for the BlackBerry, you might also find it worthwhile to check out the official BlackBerry Solutions Guide, which you can find online at: https://www.blackberry.com/SolutionsGuide/index.do.

The software and services included in the Solutions Guide are tailored more for business users than individuals; however, you might find items of items on the site. Another official site that appeal to you is the "Built for BlackBerry software site, which you can find at: http://na.blackberry.com/eng/builtforblackberry/.

Removing Software from Your BlackBerry

There will be times when you wish to remove a program from you BlackBerry, but you are not connected to your computer at the time. Fortunately, it is an easy and intuitive process to remove programs when using the BlackBerry itself.

You have a couple of ways to remove any software program installed on your BlackBerry, which you'll learn about in the next couple of sections. In addition to removing the software you add to the device, you can also remove some of the pre-installed apps that shipped with your BlackBerry. Finally, users who sync their devices to Windows can use the **Windows Loader** to delete unwanted programs.

Option 1: Deleting Apps from the Home Screen

We'll cover the easiest way to delete an app from your
BlackBerry first. This approach relies on deleting the app
directly from the **Home** screen. Follow these steps to do so:

1. Navigate to the app you want to delete, highlight it,
   and press the **Menu** key.

2. Select **Delete** from the menu.

3. Your BlackBerry will throw up a warning screen at
   this point, asking whether you're sure you want to
   delete the application in question. Press and click the
   Delete button to confirm that you want to delete the
   application.

> **NOTE:** Not every
> program can be
> deleted.

Option 2: Deleting Apps from the Options Icon

You can also delete applications from the **Options**
menu. Follow these steps to do so:

1. Press and click the **Options** icon.

2. Press and click **Advanced Options**.

3. Next, press and click **Applications** to see the
   screen to the right.

4. Now type a few letters of the application you want to delete to find it. Or, you can scroll down the list of applications on your BlackBerry and highlight the desired app.

5. Once you highlight the application you want to delete, you can press and click the **Menu** key and select **Delete**.

6. You will be asked to confirm your choice. Do so by clicking the **Delete** button, as in the figure below.

7. You may be told that the BlackBerry needs to restart or reboot to complete deleting the application. If so, press and click **OK** or **Yes** to finish the process of removing the application from your BlackBerry.

> **TIP:** If you are removing a number of icons, you won't need to reboot until you remove them all.

Deleting Apps with the Windows Application Loader

The preceding examples work for both Mac and Windows-based computers. However, BlackBerry users who sync to Windows have a third, unique approach for deleting programs from their BlackBerry devices. These users can rely use the **Application Loader** program built into the BlackBerry's **Desktop Manager** program to remove unwanted apps from their BlackBerry devices.

> **NOTE:** The Windows-only approach is outside the scope of this particular chapter. However, you can check out the authors' free videos on using the **Desktop Manager** at www.madesimplelearning.com or www.madesimplelearning.com to see exactly how this is this done.

Traveling: Maps & More

Regardless of whether you intend to leave the country with your BlackBerry, there are a few travel-related things you should know how to do. For example, everyone with a BlackBerry can probably benefit from one of the many mapping applications for the BlackBerry that rely the device's built-in GPS (Global Positioning System). Such applications can help you find navigate to your destination with turn-by-turn directions, find nearby stores with services or products you might need, or even mark where you parked your rental car so you can find it when you're ready to leave.

If you to intend to travel to another country, however, there are some definite steps you should take before you , not least so you do not get surprised with a huge data roaming phone bill. We'll cover this topic and many others related to traveling with a BlackBerry in this chapter.

International Travel: Things to Do Before You Go

Some BlackBerry smartphones are well equipped for international travel, while others present more of a challenge if you want to use them during a trip. Networks in the US operated by companies such as Verizon and Sprint use CDMA technology. This technology is widely available in North America, but less so in other countries.

BlackBerry smartphones that use SIM cards – the technology used in phones by AT&T and T-Mobile in the US – are much more common throughout the rest of the world.

In any case, we always recommend that you call your cell provider well in advance of a trip to see whether there is an **international** feature you can turn on in your BlackBerry.

Avoiding a Shockingly Large Bill

One thing you want to avoid when traveling is returning home to a shockingly large bill with high data or voice roaming charges. For example, we have heard of people who returned home after a trip abroad to find a phone bill totaling between $300 and $400 in monthly data and voice roaming charges. You can avoid such a surprise by taking a few easy steps before and during your trip.

Before Your Trip

There are a few simple steps you can take before you leave to ensure that your BlackBerry will always work – no matter where you might be in the world.

Step 1: Make Sure You Have a SIM Card Inserted

If you are traveling to a country where you will need to connect to a GSM network, then you will need to have a SIM card in your BlackBerry. In most cases, your BlackBerry will already have a SIM card pre-inserted by the phone company.

Follow these steps to see whether you already have a SIM card in your BlackBerry:

1. Click the **Options** icon.

2. Select **Advanced Options**.

3. Scroll down to the **SIM** or **SIM Card** option and click it. If you see a screen that says: **SIM Card: No Valid SIM Card**, then you do not have a SIM card, or your SIM card is not inserted correctly.

You can also quickly check whether you have a SIM Card by removing the back cover of your BlackBerry and taking a look inside (see page for a picture that shows where the SIM card slot is located).

Step 2: Call Your Phone Company

You should also contact the provider that supplies your phone service before you leave. When you call, you should check with your wireless carrier about any voice and data roaming charges you might incur when traveling. You can also try searching on your phone company's web site for this information, but usually you will have to call the company's Help Desk and specifically ask what the voice roaming and data roaming charges might apply for the country or countries you plan to visit. If you use email, SMS Text, MMS messaging, web browsing, and any other data services, you will also want to specifically ask about whether any of these services are charged separately when traveling abroad.

Some phone companies offer an **International Rate Plan** that you will need to activate before your trip. In some cases, you must activate such a plan to use your BlackBerry at all; in other cases, activating such a plan will allow you to save some money on the standard data and voice roaming charges. You should check out these plans in advance to see whether they can save you some money while you are on your trip, especially if you need to have access to data while you are away.

Using a Foreign SIM Card:

In some cases, your BlackBerry phone company won't offer special deals on international data roaming plans, or its rates will be unreasonably high. In these cases, you may want to ask your phone company to unlock your BlackBerry, so you can insert a SIM card you purchase in the country you're visiting. In many cases, inserting a local SIM card will eliminate or greatly reduce data and voice roaming charges. However, you should carefully check the cost of placing and receiving international calls on that foreign SIM card. Using a foreign SIM card may save you hundreds of dollars, but it's best to do some web research or try to talk to someone who has recently traveled to the same country for advice before settling on that approach.

Airplane Travel: Getting into Airplane Mode

Some airlines force you to completely power-down your electronic devices during take-off and landing, but then allow the use of "approved electronic devices" (read: you must turn off your BlackBerry's wireless radio) while in flight (see page 565 to learn how to turn off the wireless radio and other connections on your BlackBerry).

International Travel: Things to Do When Abroad

Once you've completed the steps described so far to prepare for your trip, you will need to address some additional issues once you get to your destination. The next sections explain the things you need to keep in mind after you arrive at your destination.

Getting Your BlackBerry Ready

Once you arrive at your destination, you will need to do a couple of thing to make sure your BlackBerry is ready to use while you're traveling.

Step 1: Make Sure the Time Zone Is Correct

When you arrive, you will need to make sure your BlackBerry is displaying the correct time. Usually, your BlackBerry will auto-update your time zone when you arrive at a new destination. However, if it doesn't, you can manually adjust the time zone (see page 206 for help with setting the BlackBerry's time zone).

Step 2: Turn Off Data Roaming If It's Too Expensive

If you were unable to find out about data roaming charges from your local phone company, try to contact the phone company in the country you're traveling to find out about any data roaming or voice roaming charges.

The worst case: If you are worried about the data roaming charges, and you can do without your email and web browser while you're away, then you should disable data services for the duration of your trip. Follow these steps to do so:

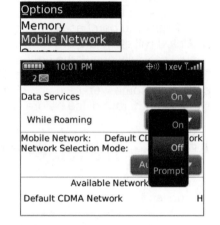

1. Click the **Options** icon or the **Manage Connections** icon.

2. Select **Mobile Network** and click it.

3. Your **Data Services** will most likely say **On**, but there is a secondary tab for **While Roaming.** We recommend setting the switch to **Off** in the **While Roaming** field, so that you can continue to receive data in your **Home** network.

4. Press the **Escape** key; your new settings will be saved automatically.

Setting the **Data Services** value to **Off While Roaming** should help you avoid any potentially exorbitant data roaming charges. (You still need to worry about voice roaming charges, but at least you can control those by watching how much you talk on your phone).

The nice part about using the **Off While Roaming** setting: When you return to your **Home** network, all your data services (e.g., email, web browsing, and so forth) will work automatically.

Step 3: Register with the Local Network

If you are having trouble connecting to the local wireless network, you may need to register your BlackBerry on the local network (see the Host Routing Table's *Register Now* entry on page 566 for more information).

International Travel: Returning Home

As you did when you arrived at your travel destination, you will need to make a few changes to your BlackBerry's settings once you arrive back home before your device will work as expected.

Step 1: Check Your BlackBerry's Time zone

As mentioned in the section on traveling abroad, your BlackBerry usually will auto-update your time zone when you arrive at a particular location. If the device does not auto-adjust after you return home, you can manually adjust your time zone (see page 206 for help with setting your device's time zone).

Step 2: Reset Your Data Services to On

If you have turned the **Data Services** field to **Off**, then you will need to make sure to reset it to **On** or **Off When Roaming**, so you can receive data when you return home.

Step 3: Register Your BlackBerry on the Local Network

Depending on the actions you took while preparing for your trip or while traveling, you might need to re-register your BlackBerry on your local phone network (see the Host Routing Table's *Register Now* entry on page 566 for more information).

Step 4: Turn Off Your Special International Plan

The final step is optional. If you have activated some sort of special international roaming rate plan with your BlackBerry phone company, and you do not need it any more, contact the company to turn it off to save yourself some money.

BlackBerry Maps, Google Maps, and Bluetooth GPS

In addition to the myriad ways your BlackBerry to help you manage your life, the device can also take you places – literally. With the aid of software that is either pre-loaded on the BlackBerry or easily downloaded from the Web, you can use your BlackBerry to find just about any location, business, or point of attraction.

Enabling GPS on Your BlackBerry

You will need to turn on the GPS location on your BlackBerry to enable mapping software to track your precise location. You will also need to turn this feature on if you want to turn on the geotagging (see page 436) feature for your camera. Follow these steps to do so:

1. Start your **Options** icon.

2. Click **Advanced Options**.

3. Click on **GPS** from the list of options.

4. Make sure that the **Location ON** property is selected next to **GPS Services** field, as shown in the figure to the right.

5. Leave **Location Aiding** as **Enabled**.

6. Finally, press the **Menu** key and select **Save**.

Using BlackBerry Maps

Your BlackBerry ships with the **BlackBerry Maps** software, which is a very good application for determining your current location and tracking your progress through your GPS (Bluetooth or built-in) receiver.

Follow these steps to enable GPS use with the **BlackBerry Maps** program:

1. Press and click the **Maps** icon in the application's menu and then press the **Menu** key.

2. Click **Options**.

3. Under **GPS Source**, select either **Internal GPS** or an external GPS unit, if you have one.

4. Press the **Escape** key and **Save** your choices.

NOTE: If you use a Bluetooth GPS or have a GPS unit built in, then you will need to press and click **Options**, and then press and click the first field in the **Options** screen, **GPS Device**. Select the Bluetooth GPS receiver that you just paired with your BlackBerry, and the GPS commands will now be available to you.

Viewing a Contact's Map

Sometimes you may want to look up the location of one of the contacts in your device. For example, perhaps you want to meet near the contact's home, and you will use the address information in the contact's profile to look up where exactly the contact lives. Follow these steps to view a map for the contact (see Figure 30-1):

1. In the **Blackberry Maps** program, press the **Menu** key from the main **Map** screen.

2. Scroll down and select **Find Location**.

Figure 30-1. *Finding your location in the BlackBerry Maps program*

3. You can search for a map based on your current location; you can select the **Enter Address** option; you can search the **From Contacts field**; or you can look at recent searches (see the figure to the right). In this case, you should scroll down to and select **From Contacts** (see Figure 30-2).

4. Scroll down to press and click the name of a contact; a map of that contact's location will appear on your screen.

Figure 30-2. *Finding a map for a contact*

Getting Directions with BlackBerry Maps

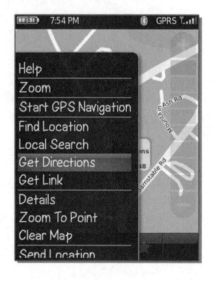

Now assume that you want to get directions to a particular location (see Figure 30-3). Follow these directions to do so:

1. Press the **Menu** key from the **Map** screen and select **Get Directions**.

2. Select a **Start** location by scrolling down to **Where I Am, Enter Address, From Contacts, From Map, Recent**, or **Favorites**.

3. Repeat the same steps to select the **End Location**.

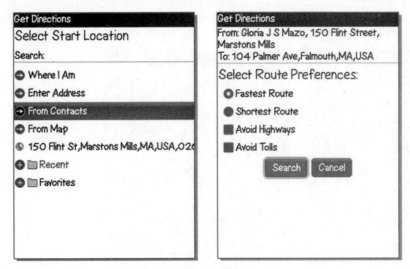

Figure 30-3. *Getting directions from BlackBerry Maps*

4. When you're done, press and click your **Start Location**.

5. You can choose whether you want to take the **Fastest** or **Shortest** route, as well as whether you want to avoid highways or tolls. Then just press and click the **Search** option to have your route displayed for you.

6. If you press and click **View on Map**, you will see a **Map** view of the route (see Figure 30-4).

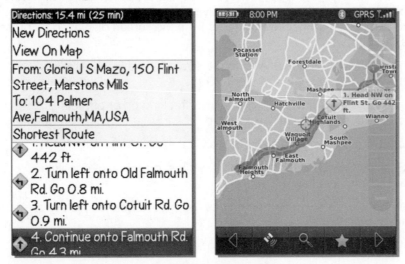

Figure 30-4. *Displaying your route with BlackBerry Maps*

You can start your BlackBerry's GPS by pressing the soft key at the bottom left of the screen. At the time of writing, the GPS will track you along the route, but it will not give you voice prompts or turn-by-turn voice directions.

You can also press the gold star to mark a location as a **Favorite** on your BlackBerry (see Figure 30-5).

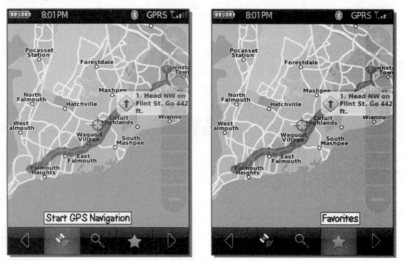

Figure 30-5. *Setting a location as a Favorite*

BlackBerry Maps Menu Commands

You can accomplish a great many tasks with the **BlackBerry Maps** application. You can get a sense of what it lets you do by pressing the **Menu** key, which brings up a screen with a ton of options you can choose from simply by scrolling, pressing, and clicking. Specifically, you can perform the following tasks from the screen displayed by pressing **BlackBerry Maps** program's **Menu** key:

- **Zoom:** Takes you from street level to the stratosphere (keyboard shortcut keys: **L** = Zoom In, **O** = Zoom Out).

- **Start/Stop GPS Navigation:** Toggles GPS tracking on or off; this works only with the GPS feature enabled.

- **Find Location:** Jumps you to an address you enter.

- **Local Search:** Searches for restaurants, stores, or points of interest near your current location.

- **New Directions:** Lets you find directions using your location history or by typing in new addresses.

- **Get Link:** Connects you to a web site so you can find an address.

- **View Directions:** Switches you to **Text** mode if you are in **Map** mode.

- **Zoom to Point:** Shows the map detail around the currently selected point in your directions; this option is available only when viewing directions.

- **Clear Map:** Erases the current map or route on the screen.

- **Send Location:** Forwards your map location via email.

- **Send Directions:** Sends your directions to an email, SMS, MMS or Messenger contact.

- **Copy Location:** Adds your current location to the **Address Book** program or another application.

- **Add to Favorites:** Adds your current location as a Favorite for easy retrieval on the map.

- **Layers:** Shows layers of recent searches, Favorites, or links on the map.

- **Options:** Changes settings on your GPS Bluetooth device. For example, this choice lets you disable the backlight timeout settings, change units from metric (kilometers) to imperial (miles), enable or disable tracking with the GPS device, and show or hide the title bar when starting.

- **About:** Shows information about the current provider of the mapping data and software.

- **Show Keyboard:** Lets you enter text or numbers.

- **Switch Application:** Jumps you to any other application while keeping the current application open.

Google Maps: Downloading & Installing

If you have ever used **Google Earth**, then you have seen the power of satellite technology in mapping and rendering terrain. **Google Maps Mobile** brings that same technology to handheld devices, including the BlackBerry.

With Google Maps, you can view 3-D rendered satellite shots of any address, anywhere in the world. To get started with this amazing application, you need to first download it onto your BlackBerry. Follow these steps to do so:

1. Press and click the **Browser** icon from your **Application** menu.

2. Press the **Menu** key, scroll to the **Go To** command, and press and click it.

> **TIP:** Use the period (.) shortcut hotkey to execute the **Go To** command.

3. Enter this address to perform an *over the air* (OTA) download onto the BlackBerry: www.google.com/gmm.

4.   Press and click **Download Google Maps**, and the installation program
     will begin (see Figure 30-6).

Figure 30-6. *Downloading the Google Maps program*

5.   Press and click the **Download** button on the next screen.

6.   Finally, you will see a screen indicating that the application was
     successfully installed. Select OK to close the window or Run to start
     Google Maps Mobile right away. Or, you can press and click the Google
     Maps icon on the BlackBerry, which should be in the Downloads folder.
     You might get prompted to reboot your device – if so, just press and
     click **Reboot**, and then try to run the program.

The first time you start up **Google Maps Mobile**, you
will need to read the terms and conditions for the
program, and then click **Accept** to continue.

Google Map Menu Commands

Google Maps Mobile is full of great features – most of which you can access right from the program's menu. Press the Menu key to see it.

One cool new feature is Street View, which Google Maps Mobile tells you about at the first screen.

When you first start the program, it will try to determine your location based on the built-in GPS or the cell tower closest to your phone.

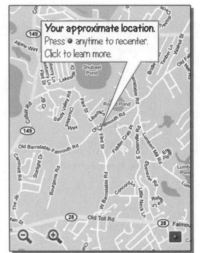

Google Maps Search - Finding an Address or Business

It's easy to find an address or business with Google Maps Mobile. Follow these steps to do so:

1. Press and click the Google Maps icon to start the application.

2. Press the Menu key and choose Search. Next, press and click Enter new search or scroll down to press and click a recent search.

3. You can type just about anything in the search string: an address, type of business and ZIP code, business name and city/state, and so on. For example, if you wanted to find bike stores in Winter Park, Florida, you could enter *bike stores winter park fl* or *bike stores 32789* (assuming you know the ZIP code).

4. Finally, press the Menu button and select OK. Or you can press the Enter key on the keyboard to begin the search.

5. Your search results will show a number of matching entries. Just scroll up/down to locate an entry. Touch that entry to select it, and then press and click the screen to see details for that entry (see Figure 30-7).

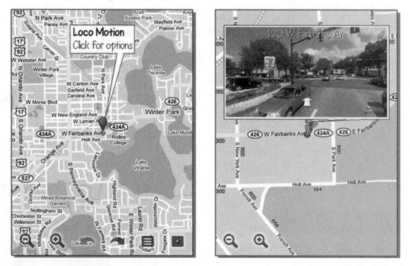

Figure 30-7. *Search results in Google Maps Mobile*

6. Press the **See on Map** button at the bottom to see the search results on the map.

7. To see the new street view, press and click the **Street View** option from the menu (see Figure 30-8).

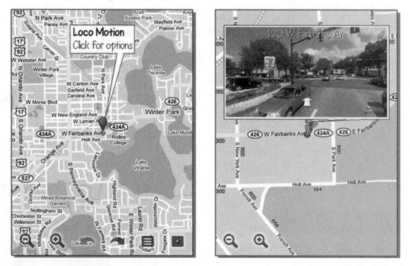

Figure 30-8. *Viewing map results with Street View*

Exploring the Shortcut Keys

Google Maps Mobile includes quite a few shortcut keys that you let you get at the program's core functionality quickly and easily. To use these, you need to press the **Menu** key and select **Show Keyboard**. Next, press and hold the **!?123** button to show the keypad. A list of the available shortcut keys and what they do follows:

4   Shows previous search results.

6   Shows the next set of search results.

Toggles between **Map** view and the **Search Results** list.

2   Toggles between **Satellite** and **Map** views.

1   Zooms out.

3   Zooms in.

*   Shows the **Favorites** list or adds a new **Favorite**.

9   Lists mobile search options.

0   Shows or hides your location (if available).

Getting Directions

Obviously, one of the key reasons you might want to use Google Maps Mobile is because it can provide turn-by-turn directions for your BlackBerry that integrate nicely with the device's built-in GPS feature. Follow these steps to get directions on your BlackBerry:

1. Press the **Menu** key and select **Get Directions**.

2. Set your **Start Point**; the default will be **My Location**. and then

3. Set your **End Point**

4. Choose your **Travel by** (mode of transport).

5. Press and click **Show Directions** to display turn-by-turn directions to your destination.

TIP: With the newly released version of Google Maps, you can actually choose from **Car**, **Public Transit**, **Walking** and **Bicycle** as modes of transport for your directions. The **Bicycle** choice tries to route you on bike paths and bicycle-friendly roads.

Google Latitude

Another new feature in **Google Maps Mobile** is **Google Latitude**, which enables people in your **Google Contacts** to see where you are in real time – you can also see them once you accept their invitations. Follow these steps to enable the **Google Latitude** feature:

1. Press the **Menu** key and select **Latitude** to get started.

2. Once you set this feature up, your location on the map is shared with whomever you choose.

NOTE: In some places, the software cannot find enough information about your location to display it – it will tell you when that's the case.

Layers – Finding More Things Nearby

The newest version of **Google Maps Mobile** (version 4.2.0 at the time of writing) includes a new feature called **Layers**. Essentially, this feature will show you Wikipedia entries for things nearby, including traffic conditions, transit lines, or personal maps. The data will be overlaid on the current map.

In this example, I have used the **Latitude** feature to locate Martin in Florida. I then used the feature to find things nearby (see Figure 30-9).

Figure 30-9. *Using Layers in Google Maps Mobile*

In the Wikipedia entries, I see that the Granada Bridge is near him, so I click it. I can now find more details about the location and even see a picture of the bridge (see Figure 30-10).

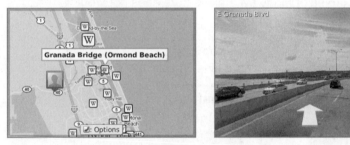

Figure 30-10. *A street view of a Google Map layer*

Layers – Seeing Transit Lines

Have you ever wondered where the closest subway or train station was located? You can follow these steps to find transit locations with the **Layers** feature:

1. Press the **Menu** key and select **Layers**.

2. Select **Transit Lines**. If you don't see this option listed, you will need to click the **+ More Layers** option to see it (see Figure 30-11).

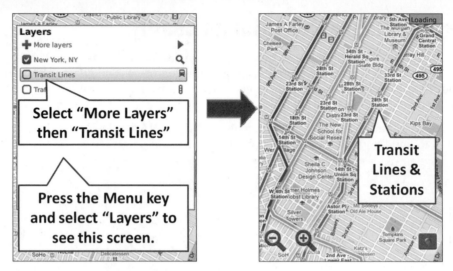

Figure 30-11. *Viewing transit lines in Layers*

Viewing Current Traffic

Google Maps Mobile also includes another cool feature: you can view the current traffic in major metropolitan areas or on major highways (this feature does not work everywhere). Follow these steps to do so:

1. Map the location you want to view traffic for.

2. Press the **Menu** key and select **Show Traffic** (see Figure 30-12).

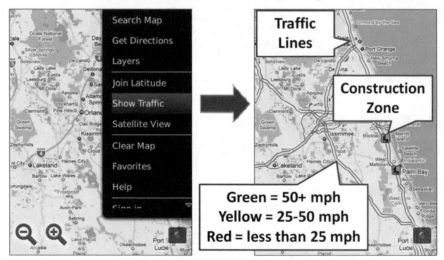

Figure 30-12. *Using the Show Traffic feature of Google Maps Mobile*

Chapter 31

Other Applications

As if your BlackBerry doesn't do enough for you, RIM thoughtfully included even more utilities and programs to help you keep organized and manage your busy life. Most of these additional programs will be found in the **Applications** folder.

In this chapter, we will show you how to use your BlackBerry as a calculator, an alarm clock, a voice-note recorder, and a password keeper.

The Calculator

There are many times when having a calculator nearby is handy. I usually like to have my 15-year old "Math Genius" daughter nearby when I have a math problem to figure out, but sometimes she needs to go to school, and she isn't available to help. In such cases, I rely on the BlackBerry's built-in **Calculator** program:

1. To start the **Calculator** program, go the **Applications** folder, press it, and click it. One of the icons should say **Calculator** (see Figure 31-1).

Figure 31-1. *Using the Calculator app on your BlackBerry*

2. Input your equation as you would in any **Calculator** program.

3. One handy tool in the **Calculator** program is that it can convert imperial values to metric ones. Just press the **Menu** button and scroll to the **Convert to Metric** option.

The Clock

The BlackBerry has long included a **Clock** program. However, it now includes some very cool new features and customization features that prove especially useful when the BlackBerry is on your bedside table (see Figure 31-2).

To start the **Clock** application, you can find and click the **Clock** icon; however, it is easier just to tap the time in the top middle of your **Home** screen.

On some devices, the **Clock** icon might be located only in the menu, not a folder. By default, the **Clock** program displays an analog face – but that be changed.

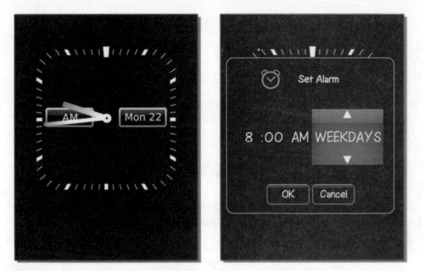

Figure 31-2. *Setting an alarm on the Clock app.*

The first feature to look at is the **Alarm**. Follow these steps to bring up and manipulate the **Clock** program's **Alarm** settings:

1. Press the **Menu** button and click **Set Alarm**. The **Alarm** menu will appear in the center of the screen.

2. Press the desired field and then scroll up or down in that highlighted field to change the option's value.

3. Highlight the right-most field and scroll to select **Off, On,** or **Weekdays** for the alarm setting.

4. Press the **Escape** key to save your changes.

The **Clock** application also includes **Stopwatch** and **Timer** features; you can start either feature by selecting it from the menu. Finally, you give the clock facelift, selecting the following faces from the Options menu: **Digital Clock, Flip Clock,** or **LCD Digital** (see Figure 31-3).

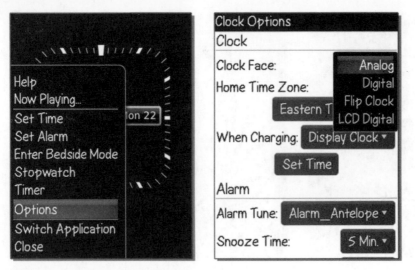

Figure 31-3. *Changing the clock face*

TIP: If you do not want your clock to display every time you plug your BlackBerry to the charger, then change the setting for **When Charging** to **Do Nothing** in the **Clock** program's **Clock Options** screen.

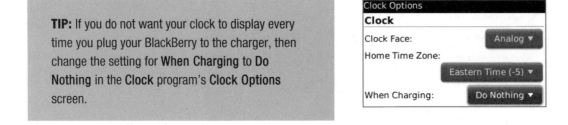

Bedside Mode:

One of the nice new features of the **Clock** application is the **Bedside Mode** setting. Many of us keep our BlackBerry by the side of the bed – we now have the option of telling the BlackBerry not to flash, ring, or buzz in the middle of the night, which is accomplished by following a handful of simple steps:

1. Press the **Menu** key in the **Clock** application.

2. Scrolling down to **Options**, from which you can configure the **Bedside Mode** options.

3. You can find the specific **Bedside Mode** options towards the bottom of the **Options** menu. From here, you can disable the LED, the radio, and dim the screen when **Bedside Mode** is set.

Voice Notes Recorder

Another useful program in your **Applications** folder is the **Voice Notes Recorder**. Say you need to dictate something you need to remember at a later time. Or, assume you would rather speak a note instead of composing an email. Your BlackBerry makes that very easy; simply navigate to the Applications folder and select **Voice Notes Recorder** to launch the program.

This is a very simple program to use:

1. Launch the program, as just described.

2. Press and click the screen when you are ready to record your note.

3. Press and click it again when you finish recording your note.

4. You will then see the following icons along the lower part of the program: **Continue recording**, **Stop**, **Play**, **Resume**, **Delete**, **Save**, and **Email the Voice Note**. Press and click the appropriate icon to perform the desired action (see Figure 31-4).

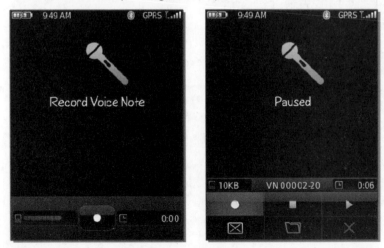

Figure 31-4. *Using the Vocie Notes Recorder app*

The Password Keeper

It can be very hard to manage passwords in today's web-oriented world, where you need to keep track of so many sites with different passwords and different password rules. Fortunately, your BlackBerry has a very effective and safe way for you to manage all your passwords: the **Password Keeper** program (see Figure 31-5).

Figure 31-5. *Using the **Password Keeper** app to set a password*

Using the Password Keeper app to set a password is easy:

1. Go to your **Applications** folder, navigate to the **Password Keeper** icon, and then press and click it. The first thing you will need to do is set a program password for **Password Keeper** – pick something you will remember (see Figure 31-6)!

Figure 31-6. *Using the Password Keeper app to set individual passwords*

2. Once your password is set, you can add new passwords for just about anything or any web site. Press the **Menu** button and select **New** to add passwords, user names and web addresses that you want **Password Keeper** to help you remember.

Searching for Lost Stuff

Your BlackBerry can hold so much information – so much different information – that it can sometimes be difficult to keep track of where everything is on the device. Fortunately, the BlackBerry comes with a comprehensive **Search** program to help you find exactly what you might be looking for.

In this chapter, we will show you how use the **Search** program across applications, messages, and contacts, as well as how to filter your search information to show only what you want.

> **TIP:** You can even use the **Search** program to search through your calendar events and answer questions such as the following:
>
> - When is my next meeting with Sarah?
> - When did I last meet with Sarah?
>
> For this feature to work, you need to type people's names into your calendar events as you enter them. For you example you might enter the following: **Meet with Sarah** or **Lunch with Tom Wallis**.

Understanding How Search Works

As you get used to your BlackBerry, you will begin to rely on it more and more. The more you use it, the more information you will store within it. It is truly amazing how much information you can place in this little device.

At some point, you will want to retrieve something – a name or a word or a phrase – but you won't remember exactly where you stored that particular piece of information. This is where the **Search** program can be invaluable.

You can find icon for the **Search** program in your **Applications** menu.

From your **Home** screen of icons, scroll to find the **Search** icon. It may be located within the **Applications** menu, and it usually looks like a magnifying glass.

Searching across Several Apps

It is possible that the desired text or name you're looking for could be in one or several different places on your BlackBerry. The **Search** tool is quite powerful and flexible. It allows you to narrow down or expand the list of programs you want to search through. If you are sure your information is in the **Calendar** app, then check only that box. However, if you might find this information in any of a wide variety of programs, you can simply check all the boxes using the **Select All** option from the menu. Follow these steps to initiate a search:

1. Press and click the **Search** icon when the main search screen is visible.

2. By default, only the **Messages** field is checked. In this example, you want to search through all the BlackBerry's programs for a name or bit of text. So press the **Menu** key, scroll to **Select All**, and then press and click that option.

Figure 32-1. *Searching through several apps*

3. If you hide the keyboard, you can press the **Select All** or **Deselect All** soft keys at the bottom of the screen.

Searching for Names or Text

In the **Search** program's **Name** field, you can search for a name or email address. The **Text** field enables you to search for any other text that might be found in the body of an email, a calendar event, an address book entry, in a memo or task.

If you decide to search for a name, then you can either type a few letters of a name, such as *Mar* – or press the **Menu** key and **Select Name** (see Figure 32-2).

Figure 32-2. *Searching by name across various apps*

If you are looking for a specific bit of text, such as a word, phrase, or even a phone number that is not in an email address field, then you would type it into the Search program's **Text:** field.

When you are ready to start the search, press the **Menu** key and click **Search**.

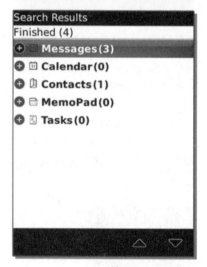

The results of the search are displayed with the number of found entries. The image to the right shows a search that returned four total matches found. Three of the matches occur in the **Messages** folder (email), while one occurs in the **Contacts** folder.

Press and click the corresponding plus sign to show the search results for a particular category.

Improving Your Search Quality

So far we've covered some of the things you might search for, as well as how to go about implementing a search. Next, we will cover some valuable tips and tricks that help you create more effective searches.

The more information you enter on your BlackBerry (or enter on your desktop computer and sync to your BlackBerry), the more useful your device becomes. Combining a great deal of useful information with this **Search** tool means you truly have a very powerful and useful handheld computer. As your BlackBerry fills up, however, the possible places where your information is stored increases. Also, a search might not turn up the exact information you are looking for due to inconsistencies in the way you store the information.

> **TIP:** You can even search notes added to calendar events. For this to work, you need to remember to add notes to your calendar events and the **Notes** field at the bottom of your contacts. You can do this on either your BlackBerry or your computer; just be sure to sync the devices so the information is in both places. Use the **Search** app to find important notes on your BlackBerry when you need them.

Try to be consistent in the way you type someone's name – for example, always use *Martin* instead of *Marty* or *M* or any other variation. This way, the **Search** program will always find what you need.

Occasionally, you should check your address book for contacts with multiple entries. It is easy to wind up with two or three entries for one contact if you add an email one time, a phone number at another time, and an address on still another occasion. Restricting your contacts to one entry each helps you stay organized – and helps you find what information you're looking for more easily.

> **TIP:** It is usually easier to do this cleanup work on your computer, and then sync the changes or deletions back to your BlackBerry.

If you're not sure whether you are looking for *Mark* or *Martin*, just type in *Mar* and then perform your search. This way, you will find both names.

If you want to find an exact name, then scroll to the **Name** field, press the **Menu** key, and choose **Select Name** to select a name from your address book.

Do your best to put consistent information into calendar events. For example, if you want to find the next dentist appointment for Gary, you could search for *Gary Dentist* in your calendar and find it. But this only works if you made sure to enter the full words *Gary* and *dentist* in your calendar entry. In this case, it would be better to search only for the word, *dentist*.

If you want to find a phone number, but you remember only the area code, then you would type that area code into the **Text** field and search the **Address Book** program.

On the other hand, if you want to find when the name *Gary* was in the body of an email, but not in an **Email Address** field (e.g., **To:**, **Cc:**, **From:**, or **Bcc:**), then you would enter the name in the **Text** field, but not the **Name** field on the **Search** screen (see Figure 31-3).

TIP: Assume you're traveling, and you want to find locals from your list of contacts. For example, let's say you're going to visit New York City, and you want to find everyone in your BlackBerry address book with a 212 area code. Type *212* in the **Text** field, and then check the **Address Book** program and click **Search** to immediately find everyone in your lists of contacts who has a 212 area code.

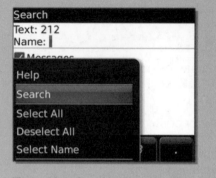

Figure 32-3. *Searching by area code*

Chapter 33

Securing Your Data

You have a lot of valuable and highly personal information on your BlackBerry; obviously, keeping it private and personal is critically important. In this chapter, we will cover general security principles for your BlackBerry, including how to secure your BlackBerry data. For example, we will cover how to prepare for the possibility that you lose your BlackBerry, and the steps you should take to hedge the potential downside from such an unfortunate occurrence.

We will also show you how to enable and use password security and alert you to good email and web security tips and tricks.

Losing Your BlackBerry

Consider what would happen if your BlackBerry were lost or stolen. Would you be uncomfortable if someone found and easily accessed all the information on your device? For most of us the answer would be, "YES!"

On many of our BlackBerry smartphones, we store vital information about our friends and colleagues, including their names, addresses, phone numbers, confidential emails, and notes. Some of our devices may even contain Social Security Numbers (SSNs), passwords, and other important information in your **Contact** notes or your **MemoPad** program.

For this reason, you will want to enable or turn on the **Password Security** feature. When you turn this on, you will need to enter your own password to access and use the BlackBerry. In many larger organizations, you do not have the option to turn off your password security; it is automatically turned on by your BlackBerry Enterprise Server Administrator.

Preparing for the Worst Case Scenario

Fortunately, you can take several steps to make this worst-case scenario less painful, should it ever occur. For example, taking the following steps will help you minimize the potential impact of losing your BlackBerry or having it stolen:

- **Step 1**: Back up your BlackBerry to your computer, a detached hard drive, a USB memory stick, or some other device or service.
- **Step 2**: Turn on (**enable**) the BlackBerry's **Password Security**.
- **Step 3**: Fill out the **Owner Information** field; be sure to include an incentive for returning your BlackBerry.

In the next several sections, we will walk you through how to implement each of these steps.

Step 1: Back Up or Sync Your Data

Windows users can use the **Desktop Manager** software described in Chapter 2, which starts on page 81, to back up the device's basic data. Mac users can follow the steps for synchronizing the device's data with a Mac, as explained in the Chapter 4, which starts on page 143.

> **CAUTION:** If you have important media (e.g., personal pictures, videos, music, and so on) stored on your media card (see page 405 for more information on media cards), then you will either have to check the box to **Include Media Card** in the **Desktop Manager** backup or to copy your media card information manually (and separately) from the sync or backup process described previously. For more information, Windows users can refer to Chapter 3 for more information on syncing or transferring media (see page 123). Mac users can learn more about this in Chapter 5 (see page 159).

Step 2: Turning on Password Security

A critical step in securing your BlackBerry is to make sure you enable **Password Security**. This is really your plan B to safeguard all your data, should the device get lost or stolen. Follow these steps to enable **Password Security**:

1. Click your **Options** icon on your Home screen, hit the letter **P** to jump down to **Password**, and click that option.

Options
Owner
Password
Phone Options

2. Then, select **General Settings** to see this screen.

3. Click the **Disabled** setting next to **Password** and change it to **Enabled.**

4. Click **Set Password** to create your password. You can adjust the other settings unless they are locked out by your BlackBerry administrator.

5. **Save** your settings.

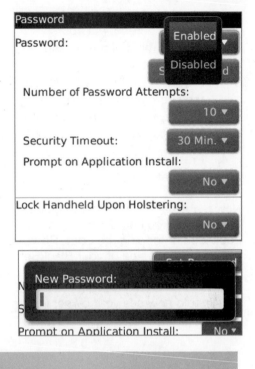

CAUTION: If you cannot remember your password, then you will lose all the data on your BlackBerry, including email, addresses, calendar events, and tasks – everything!. Once you enter more than the set number of password attempts (the default is ten attempts), the BlackBerry will automatically *wipe,* or *erase all data.*

Step 3: Setting Your Owner Information

We recommend including something like this in the **Owner Information** field: *Reward offered for safe return.* This is the text that would show up if someone found your BlackBerry in a **Locked** mode. You may have already set your owner information in the **Setup Wizard**; however, you can also set it by going to the **Options** icon and selecting **Owner Information.** Follow these steps to set this information:

1. Click your **Options** icon on your **Home** screen.

2. Scroll down and click **Owner** in the list.

3. In the **Owner Information** settings screen, put yourself into the mind of the person who might find your BlackBerry and give them both the information needed – as well as an incentive – to return your BlackBerry safely to you.

4. Press the **Menu** key and **Save** your settings.

Now test what you've entered by locking your BlackBerry. You can do this by pressing the **Lock** icon or tapping the **Lock/Power** button in the upper left side of your BlackBerry.

You should now see your owner information, as shown in the figure to the right.

Owner
Name: Martin Trautschold
Information:
Call 1-386-506-8224 to claim a REWARD for returning my BlackBerry.

TIP: Quickly tapping the **Lock/Power** key on the top left of your BlackBerry will lock the device.

Email Security Tips

You should *never* send personal information or credit card information via email. Examples of other information you should never send through email include: credit card numbers, Social Security Numbers, your date of birth, your mother's maiden name, or sensitive passwords / PIN numbers (e.g., a bank account ATM card). If you have to transmit this information, it's best to call the trusted source or, if possible, visit that source in person.

Web Browsing Security Tips

Next, we'll cover some basic safety tips you should keep in mind when browsing the Web. If you are in an organization with a BlackBerry Enterprise Server, then all the browsing you do with the built-in Browser program is secured by the encryption from the Server. Your communications will be secure as long as you are browsing sites within your organization's intranet. Once you go outside the intranet to the internet, and you are not using an HTTPS connection, your web traffic is no longer secure.

Anyone who visits a site with HTTPS (Secure Socket Layer) connection will also have a secure connection from your BlackBerry to the web site, just as when you're using your computer's web browser.

Whenever you are browsing a regular HTTP web site on the internet (not your organization's secure intranet), then you need to always be aware that your connection is not secure, even if are using a BlackBerry Enterprise Server. In this case, please make sure that you do not to type or enter any confidential, financial, or personal information.

Losing Your BlackBerry

If you work at an organization with a BlackBerry Enterprise Server or use a Hosted BlackBerry Enterprise Server and you lose your Blackberry, then you should immediately call your Help Desk and let it know what has happened. Most Help Desks can send an immediate **Wipe** command to erase all data stored on your BlackBerry device. You or the Help Desk should also contact the cell phone company to disable the BlackBerry's phone service.

If you are not at an organization that has a BlackBerry Enterprise Server, then you should immediately contact the cell phone company that supplied your BlackBerry and let it know what happened. Hopefully, a good Samaritan will find your BlackBerry and return it to you.

Turning Off Password Security

It's possible that you might want to turn off your BlackBerry's **Password Security** feature for some reason. Follow these steps to disable **Password Security**:

1. Go into the **Options** icon, as described previously. Click **Password** and change it to **Disabled**.

2. **Save** your settings – you will be required to enter your password one last time to turn it off for security purposes.

> **NOTE:** If you work at an organization with a BlackBerry Enterprise Server, you may not be allowed to turn off your password.

Adjusting the SIM Card Security Options

With any GSM phone such as your BlackBerry, your SIM card could be removed and used to activate another phone if your phone is every lost or stolen. Follow these steps to adjust the device's SIM card **Security** options:

1. Click **Options** and then Advanced Options.

2. Click **SIM card**.

3. Press the Menu key and select **Enable Security**.

4. Enter a PIN code to lock your SIM card to your BlackBerry.

5. Finally, change the PIN2 code for added security.

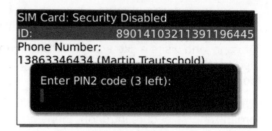

Chapter 34

Fixing Connection Problems

Your BlackBerry is virtually a complete computer in the palm of your hand. However, sometimes it needs a little tweaking to keep it in top running order. This chapter provides some valuable tips and tricks you can use to fix problems and keep your BlackBerry running smoothly. This chapter particularly concentrates on walking you through how to resolve problems with sending emails or connecting to the internet. It describes several possible reasons for these issues, and provides tips for how you might work around the problems described.

Clearing the Event Log

Your BlackBerry tracks absolutely everything it does. You can use this fact to help with debugging and troubleshooting in what is called an **Event Log**. Periodically clearing this log helps your BlackBerry run smoother and faster. Follow these steps to clear the **Event Log**:

1. Bring up the keyboard by pressing the **Menu** key and selecting **Show Keyboard**.

2. Tilt your blackberry sideways to bring up the landscape **QWERTY** mode full keyboard.

3. Press and hold the **!?123** key to see the number keys and basic symbols.

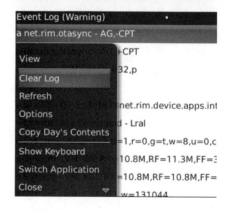

4. Now enter a forward slash (/) to see the Event Log screen, as shown in the figure to the right.

5. Press the **Menu** key and select **Clear Log** to erase all the log entries.

6. Confirm your selection on the next screen. Once the log is cleared, press the **Escape** key to return to your **Home** screen.

Solving Connection Issues

Thanks to the engineers at RIM (Research In Motion) – the company that makes BlackBerry devices – traveling away from a wireless signal for a significant amount of time (a few hours) will prompt your BlackBerry to turn off its wireless radio automatically. This feature is intended to conserve the device's battery strength; the wireless radio that makes your BlackBerry so powerful also consumes a lot of power when it is trying to find a weak or non-existent wireless signal.

The nice thing about this feature: All you need to do to turn your wireless radio back on is to hit the **Menu** key and select the **Manage Connections** icon.

Low Signal Strength

You may have already figured this out, but signal strength is usually stronger above ground and near the windows, if you happen to be inside a building. Signal strength is usually at its best outdoors and away from large buildings. We once worked in an office building that was on the edge of coverage, and we all had to leave our BlackBerry devices on the windowsill to get any coverage at all! We're not sure why, but sometimes turning your radio off and on will recover a stronger signal.

Managing Connections Manually (Airplane Mode)

Sometimes you might transition from a low signal to no signal at all. Many times the simple act of turning your wireless radio off and then back on again will restore your wireless connectivity. Follow these steps to manually turn your device off and then on again:

1. Go to your **Home** screen, and press and click the **Manage Connections** icon.

2. Press and click **Turn all Connections off**.

Figure 34-1. *Managing connections options manually*

3. Now press and click the checkboxes next to Mobile Network and Bluetooth under the Turn All Connections On area.

4. Look for your wireless signal meter and one of the following uppercase phrases: 1XEV, EDGE, or GPRS. Check to see whether your email and internet connection are working (see page 27 for more on how you read the wireless signal meter letters).

Registering with the Host Routing Table

If you try all the steps we've outlined in the chapter so far, but you're still have trouble sending or receiving emails or experiencing other problems related to your wireless connection, you can try one more thing to solve the problem: registering with the Host Routing Table (see Figure 34-2). This technique lets you connect to your network provider's data connection, and it can sometimes help you resolve difficult-to-fix networking issues. Follow these steps to implement this technique:

1. From your **Home** screen, tap the **Menu** key, and then press and click the **Options** icon.

2. Press and click **Advanced Options**

3. Select the **Host Routing Table** option.

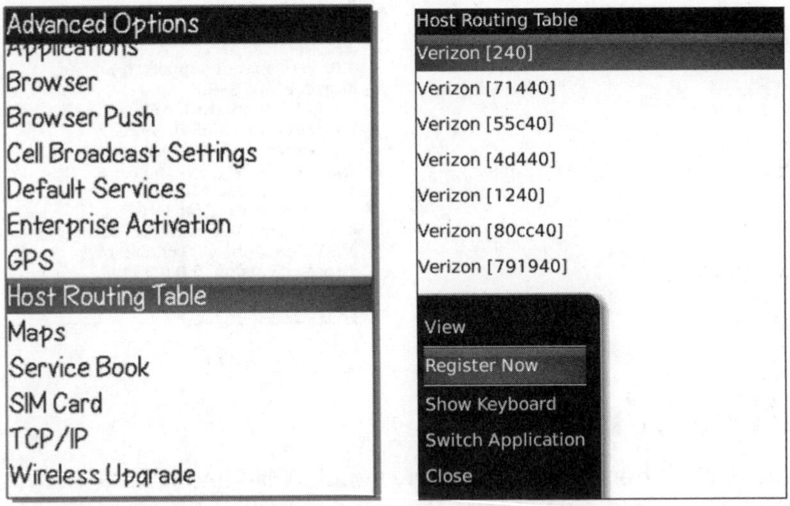

Figure 34-2. *Registering a BlackBerry with the Host Routing Table*

4. On the **Host Routing Table** screen, you will see many entries related to your BlackBerry's carrier. Press the **Menu** key and select **Register Now**.

5. At this point, you might see a message like this one: "Request queued and will be sent when data connection is established." If so, skip to the next section.

Checking the Status or Help Screen

Your BlackBerry's software includes a special **Diagnostic** screen that shows you detailed information about your BlackBerry. You might need this information to talk with a Help Desk or technical support person. Follow these steps to access that screen:

1. Press the **Green Phone** key.

2. Dial: #4357*

3. Press the **Green Phone** key. At this point, you should see a Status screen similar to the one shown in the following screenshots.

```
Status
Phone Number: 15198887465
Device ESNhex: 1f6c0013
Device ESNdec: 03107077907
Device BBPIN: 2100000A
Technology: dual-band CDMA 1x
Language List:

   English

   English(United Kingdom)

   English(United States)

   Español

   Français

   Português

   Português(Brasil)

Device Software Version: 5.0.0.334
Model: 9550
H/W Version: 1
```

```
Status
   Français

   Português

   Português(Brasil)

Device Software Version: 5.0.0.334
Model: 9550
H/W Version: 1
PRL Version: 3
ERI Version: not supported
Current SID: 8930
HomeSID/HomeNID: 8930, 65535
BlackBerry HomeSID: 8930
Network Scan Mode: Automatic
Band Class: 1
CDMA Channel: 1125
IP Address: 192.168.1.102
Device Capabilities: SMS, Packet DATA,
VOICE capable, GPS enabled
Browser Version: 5.0.0.334
BREW: not supported
Battery: 100%
```

Saving Battery Life

Here's a tip that can both extend your BlackBerry's battery life and ensure that you receive the best signal possible. Specifically, you need to make sure your BlackBerry uses the optimal kind of network connection for the carrier you have your BlackBerry service with (see Figure 34-3). For example, if you're in the US, and you're using your BlackBerry on a CDMA Network (such as Verizon), you will want to make sure that your device's Network Technology option is not set to **Global**. The problem here is that if your device is set to **Global** all the time, then your phone will continually search for both types of cell signals, which will drain your battery more quickly. Follow these steps to change your Technology Network to CDMA (i.e., **1XEV**).

1. Press and Click on Mobile Network Options from the Manage Connections screen.

2. Make sure your Data Services are On, and then scroll down to Network Technology.

3. If you are using your BlackBerry on a CDMA network (such as Verizon), then set this value to 1XEV. You will use this network exclusively in the US; however, if you travel outside of the US, you will need to change this value to either Global or GSM/UMTS.

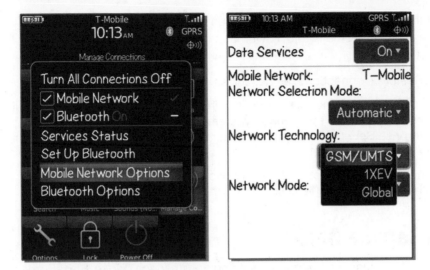

Figure 34-3. *Choose the right network under **Network Technology**.*

Performing a Hard Reset

Occasionally you will need to perform a *hard reset*; that is, you will need to remove and reinsert your BlackBerry's battery.

Follow these steps to perform a hard reset:

1. Power down your device by pressing and holding the power button (the **Red Phone** key).

2. After your BlackBerry is off, remove the battery cover, and turn the device over.

3. Press the two release buttons on the sides of the battery cover and slide them towards the top.

4. Gently pry out and remove the battery —look for the little indent in the upper right corner to stick in your finger tip.

5. Wait about 30 seconds, then replace the battery. Make sure you slide in the bottom of the battery first, then press down from the top.

6. Replace the battery door by aligning the tabs and then sliding the cover until it clicks into place.

7. Power-on your BlackBerry (it may come on automatically), then wait for the hourglass. This part is similar to a soft reset.

8. Wait. If the BlackBerry is not already turned on, tap the **Menu** key, and then press and click the **Radio Tower** icon that says **Manage Connections**.

9. Finally, Restore Connections, as described earlier in this chapter.

Let's assume you've tried all the techniques covered in this chapter so far, and your email and/or browser still aren't working. If you are using your BlackBerry with a BlackBerry Enterprise Server, please contact your organization's Help Desk or your wireless carrier's support number.

If your email and internet connection still aren't working, and you do not use your BlackBerry with a BlackBerry Enterprise Server, then proceed to the next section.

Sending Service Books

At this point in the process, you might try sending your *service books*. BlackBerry service books are configuration files that determine how your BlackBerry will connect with RIM's servers and enables certain features that require a different configuration. Without unique service books your BlackBerry will be limited in its functionality. For example, the web browser and each unique email address you have will have their own unique service book. Note that the step covered in this section is for people who use the BlackBerry Internet Service and personal email users. This step will work for you only if you have set up internet email or personal email on your BlackBerry or you are using your wireless carrier's web site (for more information on email and internet issues, see page 50). Follow these steps to send your service books (see Figure 34-4):

1. Press and click the **Menu** key, and then press and click one of the following icons: **Setup Wizard**, **Manage Personal Email**, or **Set Up Internet Mail**. (Each carrier uses a slightly different approach.)

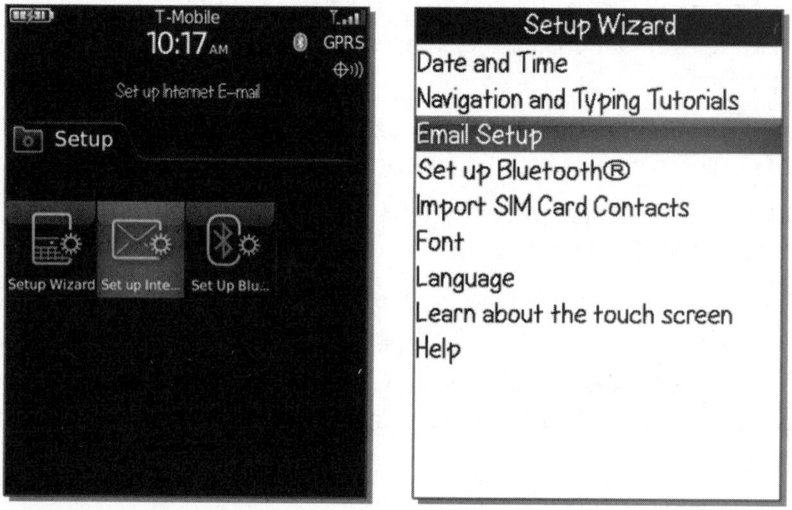

Figure 34-4. *Preparing to send your service books*

NOTE: If you have not yet logged in and created an account for your BlackBerry Internet Service with your carrier, you may now be asked to create such an account to log in for the first time.

2. If you already have an account (or you have just created your new account), you will be automatically logged in, and you will see a screen like the one below. Scroll down to press and click the **Service Books** link (see Figure 34-5).

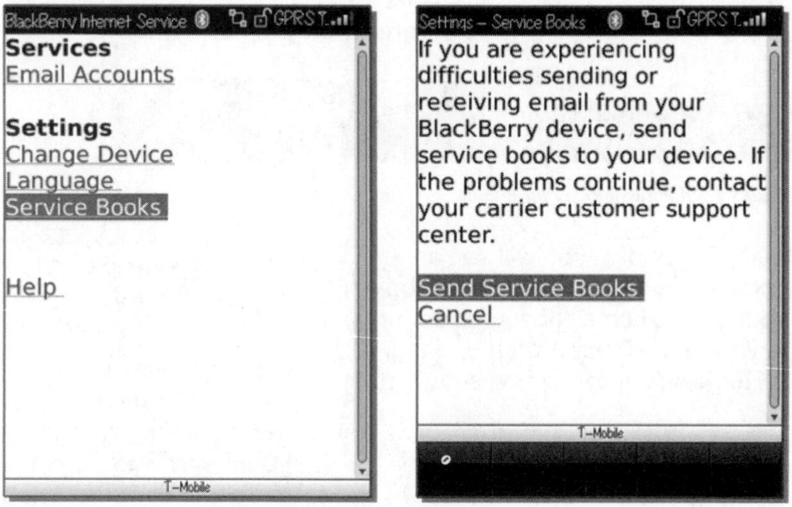

Figure 34-5. *Clicking the Send Service Books link*

3. On the next screen, press and click the **Send All** link.

4. You should now see a **Successfully Sent** message (see Figure 34-6). If you see any other message, such as one that indicates the message was not sent, then you may want to verify that you have good coverage at your current location. You may also want to repeat some of other the troubleshooting steps described previously.

Figure 34-6. *Succesful activation server emails*

After sending the service books, you will see an **Activation Message** in your Messages email inbox for each one of your internet email accounts set up or integrated with your BlackBerry. When opened, each message will look similar to the one shown to the right.

From: Activation Server
Congratulations!
Dec 22, 2008 10:17 AM

Congratulations, you have successfully setup gary@blackberrymadesimple.com with your BlackBerry device. You should begin receiving new messages in approximately 20 minutes.

If the Problem Persists...

If you still cannot send email or connect to the internet, then we recommend visiting the **BlackBerry Technical Knowledge Base** (see page for more information on how to do this). Or, you can post a question at one of the BlackBerry user forums such as www.crackberry.com or www.pinstack.com.

Chapter 35

Boost Your Battery

As everyone knows, your BlackBerry's battery is critical to its smooth operation. But what you may not know is what happens when it gets too low, how often you should charge it, whether there are extended-life batteries available, or even what things can cause it to be drained more quickly. In this chapter, we will give you an overview of battery the issues that relate to using your BlackBerry.

Charging Your BlackBerry

Many users wonder how frequently the BlackBerry's battery should be charged. We recommend charging the battery every night. Using your phone is the fastest way to consume your battery life; so, if you talk a lot on your BlackBerry, you will definitely want to charge it every night. Another big drain on your battery is using its speaker to play music or video sound – especially at higher volumes.

> **TIP:** Plug in your BlackBerry charger cable wherever you set your BlackBerry down every night. Then, before setting the BlackBerry down, plug it into the charging cable.

Low Battery Warnings

Also, your BlackBerry provides displays a series of increasingly critical warnings as your battery power drops below certain percentages of a full charge. The following list describes the various battery-related warnings the BlackBerry displays:

- **Low Battery Warning:** This warning is displayed if the battery drops to only 15% of its full charge. If this happens, you will hear a beep and see a warning dialog. Also, the device's **Battery Indicator** meter will usually change to red. At this point, you will want to start looking for a way to charge your BlackBerry – either by connecting it to your computer with a USB cable or through its regular power charger.

- **Very Low Battery:** When the battery gets down to 5% of its full charge, you are in a **Very Low Battery** condition. At this point, the BlackBerry will automatically turn off your wireless radio to conserve what little remaining power there is. This will prevent you from making any calls, browsing the Web, sending/receiving email or messages of any kind at all. You should try to charge the device immediately or turn it off.

- **(Almost) Dead Battery:** When the BlackBerry senses the battery is just about to run out altogether, then it will automatically shut off the BlackBerry itself. This is a preventative measure, meant to ensure your data remains safe on the device. However, we recommend getting the BlackBerry charged as quickly as possible after you are in this condition.

Places to Recharge Your BlackBerry

You can charge your BlackBerry in many on-the-go other settings, including in your car or from your computer. The next couple sections provide more information on the various places you might be able to recharge your BlackBerry.

Recharging in a Car

Obviously, if you're traveling, you will want to be able to recharge your BlackBerry in a car. The easiest way to do this is to purchase a car charger from a BlackBerry accessory store. To find a car charger online, type *blackberry car charger* in your favorite search engine.

NOTE: If you are coming from an older BlackBerry, the Storm uses the new Micro USB charger; your older chargers will not fit this device.

The other way to charge your BlackBerry is to use what is called a *vehicle power inverter* that converts your vehicle's 12V direct current (DC) into alternating current (AC) that you can plug your BlackBerry charger into. The other option with a power inverter is to plug your laptop into it, and then connect your BlackBerry with the USB cable to the laptop (a true mobile office setup!).

Recharging from Your Computer

As outlined previously in this book, you can also recharge your BlackBerry by connecting the device to your computer with a USB cable. Your device will charge as long as your computer is plugged into a power outlet (or vehicle power inverter) and your BlackBerry is connected to your computer through the aforementioned USB cable.

Extending Your Battery Life

If you are in an area with very poor (or no) wireless coverage, you can extend your battery life by turning off your device's wireless radio through the **Manage Connections** feature. When the wireless radio is searching for the network, it consumes much more battery power.

Here are some additional tips you can follow to extend your BlackBerry's battery life:

- **Use headphones instead of the built-in speaker to listen to music or watch videos:** The built-in speaker consumes much more power than a headset does, so minimizing the use of the speaker will extend your expected battery life.

- **Use your speakerphone sparingly:** The speakerphone uses much more energy than either the regular speaker or your headset.

- **Decrease the backlight brightness or reduce the timeout:** You can control this property through your device's **Screen/Keyboard** options dialog, as shown to the right.

- **If possible, set your profiles (see page 219) to ring and/or vibrate less often:** You might want to turn off the vibration feature for every email you receive. This will not only extend your battery life, but it may help you live a calmer and more peaceful existence. Instead, you can check your BlackBerry for new messages at regular intervals, not as every single message arrives.

- **Use data intensive applications sparingly:** Such applications make a lot of use of the radio transmit/receive feature, which uses up the battery more quickly. For example, mapping programs transmit large amounts of data to show the map moving or related satellite imagery.

- **Send email or text instead of talking on the phone:** The phone is probably the most intensive user of your BlackBerry's battery life. If possible, send an email or SMS text message instead of making a call. Lots of time, this is less intrusive for the recipient, and you may be able to get an answer when a phone call might not be possible. For example, your contact might be in a meeting and able to respond by text, even though he can't talk to you if you were to call instead.

More Resources

One of the great things about owning a BlackBerry is that you immediately can share in the large, worldwide camaraderie of BlackBerry owners.

Many BlackBerry owners can be classified as enthusiasts, and many participate in any number of BlackBerry user groups. These user groups, along with various forums and web sites, serve as great resources for BlackBerry users.

Many of these resources are available right from your BlackBerry, while others are web sites that you might want to visit on your computer.

Sometimes you might just want to connect with other BlackBerry enthusiasts, ask a technical question, or keep up with the latest and greatest rumors, apps, and accessories. This chapter will point you to some great resources for getting the most out of your BlackBerry.

The BlackBerry Technical Solution Center

The BlackBerry Technical Solution Center is often the first place you should consider going to for help for anything to do with your BlackBerry.

To access the site, do a web search for *BlackBerry Technical Knowledge Base*. One of the top links will usually get you to this page, which is located on the larger www.blackberry.com Site. You may also be able to get directly to the Solution Center by typing in this web address: www.blackberry.com/btsc/.

When you reach the site, ask your question in as few words as possible in the Search box in the middle of the screen. The Solution Center may look similar to this image you see in Figure 36-1).

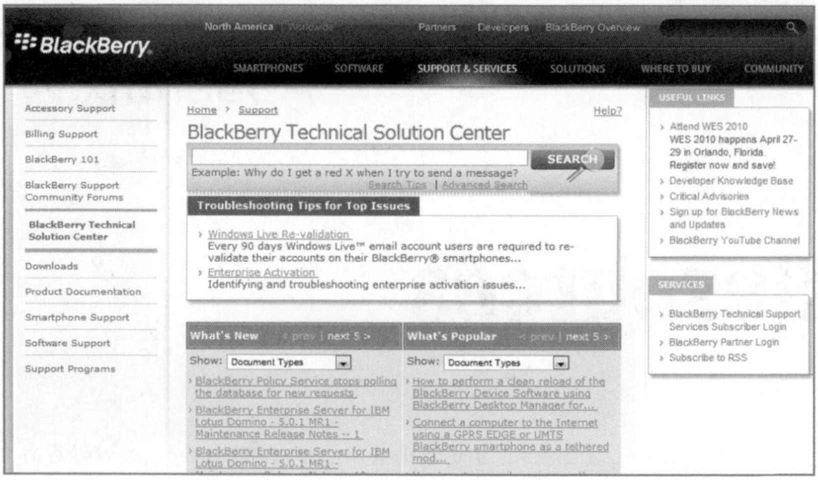

Figure 36-1. *The BlackBerry Technical Solution Center web page*

Accessing Resources from Your BlackBerry

Sometimes you'll be using your BlackBerry and want to access help resources directly from your device. In this case, the best place to start is by clicking the **Help** item found on most of screens' menus. You can learn all about how to use BlackBerry built-in **Help** feature on page.

Some of the resources you'll encounter actually include software that you can install as icons right on your BlackBerry's **Home** screen. For other resources, you will want to create a bookmark in your BlackBerry's **Browser** program (learn about bookmarks in Chapter 28, which starts on page).

You will also want to acquaint yourself with the official BlackBerry mobile website. Follow these steps to visit that site.

1.   Start your BlackBerry's **Browser** program.

2.   Press the **Menu** key and select the **Go To...** option.

3.   Type in http://mobile.blackberry.com.

The page it presents is organized with the following sections, all of which may prove useful at some point:

- Help Directory
- What's Hot
- Fun and Games
- Great Sites
- Messaging
- Maps & GPS
- A **BlackBerry** page

You can click various links on the site to download software or visit a linked web site.

BlackBerry Forums and Discussion Groups

There are many of these discussion groups focused on the BlackBerry, including CrackBerry, BerryReview, BlackBerry Rocks, and the BlackBerry Forums. A forum is an organized discussion about anything and everything BlackBerry. On each of these sites, you can discuss your BlackBerry and find tips and tricks for getting more out of it. You can also post questions and read answers to other user's questions.

Here is a list of the more popular forums at the time of writing:

- www.boygeniusreport.com
- www.blackberrycool.com,
- www.blackberryforums.com
- www.crackberry.com
- www.berryreview.com
- www.blackberryrocks.com

Some sites even provide a way to install an icon in your BlackBerry **Application** menu for one-click access to participating in their respective discussions right from your BlackBerry.

You can navigate through their forums manually or use a search tool to find a particular topic of interest. At least one of the forums will be specific to your particular BlackBerry. Look for forums that match your BlackBerry Model or Series. For example, you might search for one of the following: **BlackBerry Storm 9500**, **BlackBerry Bold 9700**, or **BlackBerry Curve 8500**.

At a site dedicated to a specific model, you will find various discussion threads pertaining explicitly to that model. In other words, the signal to noise ratio should be extremely high for the BlackBerry model covered!

> **TIP:** Try your best to enter your question under the correct forum topic – you are much more likely to find people answering you if you are in the correct topic area – and ask your question nicely. Nothing invites a non-response or hostile response like being rude to people who might otherwise *want* to help you.

There are many, many other web sites to visit for more information and helpful resources. These sites offer everything from news to information to discussion forums.

Made Simple Learning Free BlackBerry Tips

The authors of this book also host a web site at www.madesimplelearning.com. This site provides free BlackBerry tips via email, as well as free sample video tutorials. We also have a **Contact Us** page, so please drop us a line and let us know what is on your mind.

Thanks Again!

Again, we sincerely thank you for purchasing this book, and we hope it has helped you get every last drop of productivity and fun out of your BlackBerry!

Index

■Special Characters and Numbers

■A

groups, 330–332

map of location of, 531

menu commands, 324–325

nicknames for, 258

overview, 154–155, 315

pinging, 396–397

sending messages from, 376

setting ring tones for, 226–227

sorting, 327–328

voice dialing by, 251–252

Contacts application, 291–292. *See also* contacts

Contacts page, LinkedIn, 286

Contacts Transfer field, Options app, 500

Continue recording icon, 547

Convenience keys, 4, 10, 22, 173, 178, 215, 230

Convert to Metric menu option, 544

Copy Address option, Browser program, 507

Copy Down button, Media Manager program, 128–130

Copy key, 345

Copy Location menu item, 535

Copy menu item, 344, 371, 388

copying, 20

corporate data, securely connecting to, 80

corporate emails, 54–55

Create a New Group option, Messenger screen, 399

Create a New Station option, Pandora, 426

Create Group option, Messenger screen, 400

Create New Account button, carrier web site, 72

Crop and Save option, 327

cursors, positioning, 176

custom dictionary, 182–183

Custom Ring Tones/Alerts section, Contacts app, 228

customizing. *See* personalizing

Cut menu item, 344

Cut soft key, 244, 345

D

data

corporate, securely connecting to, 80

moving from Palm or Windows Mobile devices, 87

databases

backing up, 119

erasing or clearing, 119

restoring, 120

DataViz, 303

Date item, Media Manager program, 127

dates

personalizing, 206–208

setting, 180

using number keys for, 180

Date/Time setting screen, 206

Day View screen, Calendar app, 337

DC (direct current), 575

Decline menu item, 351

Decline option, 393

Decline with Comments menu item, 351

Declined field, 351

Default Flash Settings field, Options app, 435

Default option Desktop Manager, 484

Q

R

■ S